# MOMENT
## A DAILY DEVOTIONAL

## GREGG MATTE

### HOUSTON'S FIRST
BAPTIST CHURCH

## LUCIDBOOKS

**Moment**: A Daily Devotional

Copyright © 2020 by Houston's First with Gregg Matte

Published by Lucid Books in Houston, TX

www.LucidBooksPublishing.com

ISBN-10: 1-63296-379-5 | ISBN-13: 978-1-63296-379-6

Printed in Canada.

Special Sales: Most Lucid Books titles are available in special quantity discounts. Custom imprinting or excerpting can also be done to fit special needs. Contact Lucid Books at Info@LucidBooksPublishing.com.

*Every Sunday, hundreds of heroes step up to teach the Bible at our church.*
*They aren't pastors or professional speakers.*
*Even better, they are volunteers, giving their all to teach God's Word.*
*We call them Life Bible Study teachers, and I'm so grateful for them.*
*Truly, we are Sunday teaching teammates!*
*This devotional is dedicated to all those who make*
*Life Bible Study a place of life change.*

# SPECIAL THANKS

We would like to say a very special thanks to our ministry partner, El Centro Network (ECN). For the past several years, El Centro has helped Houston's First Baptist Church transform and translate teaching content from Pastor Gregg Matte and others into daily devotional plans for the YouVersion Bible app.

Each devotional plan they produce consists of three to seven days of devotionals. Each devotional has at least one Bible reference. Users of the Bible app can subscribe to these plans. When a user reads all three to seven days of a devotional plan, the plan is marked "completed." A completed plan represents significant Bible engagement on the part of the users and gives ECN a way to track the fulfillment of its mission through measurable results. Today, the number of completed plans is above the 5 million mark.

Established in 2016, El Centro Network is a non-denominational, nonprofit organization whose primary focus is to provide resources for English and Spanish speakers to engage with the Bible at least four times per week. We are pleased to be arm-in-arm in ministry with this amazing group of people who are producing transportable content in English and Spanish with such a global reach.

If you'd like to know more about the mission and ministry of the El Centro Network, please visit the website at **www.elcentronetwork.com**.

If you are interested in finding reading plans on the YouVersion Bible app, do a search using the keywords "Houston's First" or "Gregg Matte" on the app's home screen.

# INTRODUCTION

*Why, you do not even know what will happen tomorrow. What is your life? You are a mist that appears for a little while and then vanishes.*

—James 4:14 NIV

*Lord, make me aware of my end and the number of my days so that I will know how short-lived I am.*

—Psalm 39:4

On a crisp, October day in Philadelphia in 1839, Robert Cornelius took the first selfie ever recorded on the American continent. Yes, I said selfie. And yes, I said 1839, as in quite a long time ago. Cornelius set up his newly acquired camera gear outside his father's lamp store. This early camera consisted of a small, square light box with a brass assembly on the front that the operator pointed toward the subject. In this case, Cornelius was his own subject, and it would be the world's first selfie.

With his arms crossed and sporting a stylish coat with a high collar, he was about to preserve his likeness for the ages. Google "Robert Cornelius," and you'll see that his expression and style seem remarkably contemporary. He could pass for someone you might see on the street or on a screen today.

Early photography pioneers such as Cornelius were able to accomplish something with their hobbies on a truly existential level. They were able to do what no person in human history had ever done before. They were able to capture **moments in time**.

The Bible speaks about time and the span of a human life in terms of vapor, shadow, and breath (James 4:14, Ps. 39:4–5). The length of life is also described as but the width of a hand. Psalm 90 contains Moses's famous prayer in which he asks the Lord for help to "number our days carefully so that we may develop wisdom in our hearts" (Ps. 90:12). David's plea in Psalm 39 is to be "aware of my end and the number of my days so that I will know how short-lived I am" (Ps. 39:4). In the middle of the storm of life, the prayers and pleas of both Moses and David are asking for God to reshape their perspectives.

What if you asked the Lord to do the same?

Did you know the Centers for Disease Control and Prevention (CDC) puts the average American life span at 78.6 years? That's 28,689 days, to be exact. If the CDC is right, that's how much we are each allotted.

Using that number, we can estimate that a 30-year-old has been alive for 10,950 days so far and has an estimated 17,739 days left. A person at age 40 has an estimated 14,089 days left. Sobering, isn't it?

As I write, according to this math, I have 10,585 days left! Sobering, isn't it? Wow!

Now, I'm thinking two things:

1. Praise the Lord, the CDC is not in charge. If you are more than 78.6 years young today, good news! You're not living in the bonus; you're living out God's plan!
2. God help me be about the business of spending the days I have left doing important things.

My friend Robert J. Morgan, in his book *Mastering Life before It's Too Late*, describes how Jesus constantly models what it means to be about the Father's business. We see in Jesus what it means to prioritize times alone with His heavenly Father. If Jesus went out before it was "still dark…to a deserted place" (Mark 1:35) to pray, how much more should we be about capturing time in the day to develop the *holy habit* of prayer and meditation on His Word. As we see in the life of Jesus, these truly are the important things.

You found this devotional book at a specific moment in time. You are reading these words because somebody either bought it for you as a gift or you picked it up to supplement your times alone with God. Either way, it's not by chance that you picked it up just now and have read it this far. God desires to spend some time with you, His child. That is exactly who you are—His child. He knows the number of your days. He knows when you got up out of bed this morning, and He knows the microsecond you will fall asleep this evening (Ps. 139). He knows everything about you, and *still*, He wants to whisper His thoughts to you (Ps. 25). What a moment!

As we journey together through each part of this daily devotional, I would ask you to do a few things:

1. Let these pages serve as a guide for deeper meditation on Jesus. Let the words I've put together serve only to lift Him up.
2. Open your Bible as well as this book and let His Word satisfy your heart in ways greater than you can imagine. Each day, read and focus on the key passage and a few of the others for further study.
3. Pray for your heart and the hearts of others who are reading so these moments alone with God will drastically affect all the moments of the day and ultimately all the days God has given you to live.

Be encouraged! You are not alone on this journey. I can't wait to see and hear what God does in you. Maybe someday we'll be able to share what God has done and what He will do in the days to come. Maybe it will look like a gigantic photo album of our moments with God and the moments He has spent with all the people in the Bible. For now, let me offer up this prayer for you as we begin:

> *Father, do your work now in me and in the readers. Help our eyes be opened to all the days You have given us here on earth. May we spend them on the good stuff, the important things, otherwise known as a deepening relationship with You. Be glorified today! We love You, and we trust You. In Jesus's name, amen.*

Welcome to this moment!
Pastor Gregg

*In 1839, Robert Cornelius took the first selfie in history. Even today, his image seems somehow contemporary.*

# MOMENT

## A DAILY DEVOTIONAL

# FOLLOWERS OF CHRIST

---

1 Corinthians 11:1

---

Most churches celebrate Jesus's birth during Christmas and then just cruise along until Easter. They celebrate the resurrection and then cruise along again. But I think it's important to look at Christ's life before the cross and use that as an example for our everyday lives. The journey of the Christian life is to be a follower of Christ—to look at His life and follow it.

Everybody wants to be a leader and make a difference, but to do so, you must first be a follower. Our leading is based on our following. Paul told the Corinthians to follow him as he followed Christ. I don't think there is a greater example of a person who led people to be followers of Christ. Paul was someone who led by following—by following the example of Christ.

If you want to be a leader who leads well but also has the characteristics and decision-making skills that Christ had, you have to be His follower. Read God's Word, understand Christ's teachings, and know His heart so you can lead well. Lead professionally. Lead your marriage. Lead your children. Lead a church. Become a Christ-following leader here on earth.

Everyone has the ability to be a person of impact somewhere—in your house, your church, at work. If you're wondering how you can be the best mom, it is by following Christ. How can you be the best husband to your wife? By being a follower of Christ. How can you be the best employee? It is by following Christ's example today. It is not about titles, money, personality, or things.

The word *leader* definitely sounds more powerful than follower. But true leadership is based on following. I encourage you to be a follower of Christ, just like Paul, so you can lead the way Christ desires for you.

*For further study: Ephesians 5:1–2*

# PRAYING

Matthew 6:5–7

One of the greatest aspects of being a follower of Christ is prayer. We want to be going deeply into our lives of prayer, not just thanking God for the day or for our food. We want to be a person who calls out to God in the good and the bad.

Usually, people feel they need to pray more. We all do. Jesus talked about being prayerful people. He tells us not to worry about the number of words we are using. There's no need to stand on street corners praying long, eloquent prayers for everyone to hear. Now, I know you're thinking, *praying on street corners? That would get us arrested in today's society.* But that is what the Pharisees did 2,000 years ago. Jesus is saying that none of that is necessary. How He wants us to pray is privately and individually at a time and in a place where we can connect and be intimate with the Father.

Followers of Christ choose invisible power over visible praise. It's not about how smart or spiritual you look when you pray in front of your friends or pastor. It is about pouring out your heart to God. Even when there's nothing to say, He knows what you're thinking. The prayers you pray today from the privacy of your own space can affect something that happens 10 years from now. Do you know that God is going to answer some prayers you might have prayed a while ago? Before I was married, I was praying for my wife. Before I had kids, I was praying for my kids. I love throwing prayers into the future. There's a power with invisible prayer that has nothing to do with visible praise.

Choose intimacy with God through prayer. It's not about big words but about a big heart. Asking God to do something deep within you gives you clarity. Jesus spent a lot of time in solitude praying with the Father. He spent all night in the Garden of Gethsemane praying to God.

Think about a marriage. A good marriage is not based on how good the couple is with a group of people but how they are when it's just the two of them. We've all had friends whom we thought were a great couple, and then we get the news of their divorce. It's the same with God. It's not about your public life with God but your intimacy with Him.

# THE LORD'S PRAYER

Matthew 6:9–13

In Israel, there's a church in the Mount of Olives called Pater Noster, which is Latin for Our Father. In the church, there are more than 100 plaques of the Lord's Prayer translated into various languages. Try to think of 20 languages, and I bet you'll struggle to get there. I have been to Pater Noster, and I will say that it's pretty amazing to see the Lord's Prayer translated into that many languages. It tells me that this prayer is a worldwide thing.

The Lord's Prayer meets all our needs. Isn't it amazing to think about that? Jesus was showing us through this prayer that this was the form to pray. He didn't need big words or prayers on the street. He was teaching us how to pray.

Now for Jesus to teach the Jews how to pray was a huge deal. The Jews were people who prayed. They would spend all day praying on the Sabbath. They prayed three times a day, they prayed at their festivals, and they even wore prayer shawls. And then Jesus stepped forward and gave them the Lord's Prayer.

The Lord's Prayer is not just something you hang in your home or on a keychain. It's a prayer from the heart of Jesus. It's telling God that He is holy and meets our every need, that we love Him and desire to be a prayerful person. We pray with the desire for God to do something great in and through us.

I encourage you to recite the Lord's Prayer today. Pray it all week, and encourage your household to learn it.

# GOD WANTS INTIMACY

## Matthew 6:14–15

Jesus spoke the Lord's Prayer to teach us how to pray. However, right after, He slipped in a verse that says to forgive others. He enables us to do the hardest thing we can do, and that is to forgive. Isn't that the hardest thing to do on earth—to forgive someone when they have wronged you?

Jesus is saying that when you come from an intimacy with Him and with the Father, you will realize how great He is. It means He is great enough to meet your every need and allow you to usher in forgiveness to others because you know the forgiveness He has given you.

The great thing about prayer is that you can go to the Lord as your companion. Billy Graham put it like this: "Jesus prayed briefly in a crowd, a little longer with His disciples, and all night when He was alone."* Today, many reverse the process. We want to show off our prayers but we don't make time to be alone with the Father.

Prayer with the Lord is for every moment of our lives. It's not just for times of suffering and joy, but prayers of place—a place where you meet God in genuine conversation. Remember, He knows your needs before you ask. You can really say anything you want. Pray with honesty and simplicity.

If you do an Internet search for prayers written by children, you may learn a thing or two from them. "Dear God, I think the stapler is one of your greatest inventions." "Dear God, in Bible times did they really talk that fancy?" "Dear God, I think about you sometimes, even when I'm not praying." Kids know that they can be honest and say anything to God. That is intimacy, my friend.

God wants intimacy. He wants you to walk with Him, to know His heart well enough to trust Him. That happens through prayer, not in a group, but individually, alone with God.

# FASTING

Matthew 6:16–18

Let's take this a step further as followers of Christ. Are you inspired to take another step—one that requires application? It's going from level 101 to 201. This next step is fasting.

Fasting is moving from intimacy with God to being hungry for God. Here is the phrase I use: No Food, Know Prayer. Fasting is not something weird or odd, or something done only in Bible times. It has nothing to do with diet and health. It's about our hearts.

There's something special about pulling back from our norm and our routines to fast, using the time we would normally spend eating to seek God. It's allowing the rumblings in our stomachs to be a hunger for Him. We turn to food for comfort and all sorts of stuff, but we've got to be able to show God we want deeper walks with Him.

Fasting is letting go of a physical need for a spiritual plea. It's hungering for something higher, which is symbolic of the hunger in our stomachs. Fasting is referenced more than 70 times in the Bible. When we fast, our hunger aches become our prayer aches.

Fasting is a sacrifice. It should be a sacrifice! Let me say something that is considered completely incorrect in the Christianity of our day and age. Christianity involves sacrifice. It involves suffering at times. In this small place of sacrifice, we are telling the Lord that our hearts desire something bigger. We are saying that we want more than a hamburger; we want Him to move in our lives. You may think, "Of course we want God more than a burger," but wait until you miss out on that burger and hunger for food. That's the sacrifice.

Fasting is a statement that says, "We're more than physical beings; we are spiritual beings." It elevates heavenly needs over earthly needs. It's not only about removing food; it's about adding prayer. It's using your cravings and mealtime as prayer time. It's dining on true, heavenly bread.

*For further study: Matthew 4:4*

# LIFE AND GODLINESS

### 2 Peter 1:3–4

In 2 Peter 1:3–4, the Apostle Peter tells us that God's divine power has given us everything required for life and godliness. He said that by the precious promises of God, we can share in His nature and stay out of sin.

When we know Christ, we have all we need for life and godliness. It is not through us or what we do. Knowing Jesus is what will rescue us from living a life of sin.

At times we feel like this: "I don't have the resources to do what God has called me to do in life." And yet Jesus is our resource. He has given us everything we need for life and everything we need for godliness (Rom. 8:32).

When I need courage, Jesus is my resource for courage. When I need wisdom, He is my resource for wisdom. When I need help in parenting, He is my resource for help in parenting. When I need help in marriage, He is my resource for life in marriage. For those who are single, He is your resource for life in singlehood. He is your wisdom. He is your heart. He is your strength for life and godliness.

I love that. We often say, "Eh, I hope I can do this." Jesus is saying, "You've got this. You can do it. You can walk in a spiritually mature and godly way because I am your resource."

All of us struggle with sin. There are some, though, who have such sweet, meek, or persuadable personalities that they get mowed down by peer pressure. They say yes to something but know in their hearts that they should be saying no. They say no to something and know they should be saying yes.

I want you to hear from the Apostle Peter and from the Word of God that you have the strength to live for God. You don't have to sin. You don't have to follow that path. You have everything you need for life and godliness. Jesus is your resource. When you need strength to follow Christ—not others—Jesus is your resource. When you need guidance in life, Jesus is your resource. When you need peace in the storm, Jesus is your resource. When you need wisdom in decisions, Jesus is your resource. It is through knowing Him that we are equipped to live a life for Him (Phil. 3:10).

So who do we "trust fall" into? God says, "I'll catch you. I've got you right here."

*For further study: 1 Corinthians 3:21–22*
*Additional references: Romans 8:32, Philippians 3:10*

# OUR OWN RESOURCES: EPIC FAIL

### 2 Peter 1:3–4

Sometimes, life can make us feel like a Swiss Army knife. We think, "Okay, I have these four, five, or six little tools that will help me out. I have a little bit of education. Some smarts. Some wisdom. Some friends. A little bit of money. I have a job. I have this and that. I can saw something when I need to saw something. Cut something when I need to cut something. Whatever my tools are, I have this. With this set of tools, I can figure things out. I can do life, and I can do godliness."

This would be a Swiss Army knife composed of our own strength. But while our Swiss Army knife has these five or six tools, the Swiss Army knife composed of the strength of Jesus has a tool and a resource for whatever we might need in a given situation. This kind of Swiss Army knife wouldn't even fit in your pocket unless you were God. He has something for every circumstance, every problem, every joy, every concern, every moment when you are feeling down, and every moment when you are feeling up. He is the resource.

He says something like this: "You can have this tool that is Me in your heart through the Holy Spirit. It is part of the equal privilege you have as a citizen of the kingdom—just like Paul, just like Peter, just like Billy Graham, just like anybody else. I reside in your heart. If you will abide in me and I abide in you, then you will accomplish much, and you will bear much fruit. But apart from me, you will accomplish nothing" (John 15:1–5).

Throw away your Swiss Army knife with its four or six little tools and grab the greatness of the precious promises of God in your life. It is scary to let go of our tools and take up the resources of Christ. But God says to fear not. The Bible says "fear not" 365 times. There is a "fear not" for every day of the year so you and I can stand—not on cultural myths and assurances but on the promises of God through knowing Christ (Isa. 35:4, 41:10–13, Matt. 14:27).

If you will, please pray with me, *Lord, thank You that I can have equal access to You. Thank You that I can live a life pleasing to You. Thank You, Lord, that You're giving me just what I need for that meeting, just what I need for that presentation, just what I need for that school day, just what I need for that relational issue, that emotional issue. You've given me everything I need, and I am going to stand on Your promises, God, trusting that You have provided for me all I need for life and godliness.*

# GOD IS FAITHFUL

## 2 Peter 1:3–4

Precious promises—don't you love those words? Peter loved talking about the precious things of God. In his two letters, he talked about precious faith, precious promises, the precious blood, the precious stones, the precious rock, the precious Savior. He is declaring that there is a preciousness of God.

We are to stand on the precious promises of God. We have equal faith among us all. We have the tool and the resource—Jesus Christ. To live our lives, we fall back and stand on the precious promises of God.

Do you know that God has never failed one single promise and that He is not going to start with you? Do you ever feel like that's hard to believe? "Lord, I know You have been faithful to everybody in human history, but I am just wondering: Are You going to be faithful to me?"

God has not broken a promise, and He is not going to break a promise, because His perfect faithfulness would then be at risk. How much do promises mean in our culture today? Zilch. Zero. Nothing. Promises are broken all the time. But Jesus is saying, "I'll never break a promise. I have great and precious promises. Your life can fall, and I'll catch you on these promises: I am here with you. I live inside you. I am going to love you. I am going to guide you. I am going to take care of you. I am going to provide for you."

This is the truth of God. Live by the promises of God and stand strong on the promise of who He is. Our promises in today's world may mean nothing, but the promises of God mean everything. God is not like someone who has broken their promises to you. Your Father in heaven is not like your father on earth. Your Father in heaven is not like your boss on earth. Your Father in heaven keeps His promises.

He said that no one can snatch you from His hand (John 10:27–28).

Stand on the promises of God. His promises will take you through your darkest time, your best time, and the times in between. His promises are still strong in every situation. Jesus is strong enough to take you through anything.

*For further study: John 10:27–28*
*Additional references: 1 Corinthians 1:9, 2 Corinthians 1:18–21*

# A VERY IMPORTANT QUESTION

How do we live the Christian life?

The word that pops up four times in the first four verses of 2 Peter is the word *through*.

Do you know how many of us are spelling Christianity? We are spelling it D-O—do. But it should be T-H-R-O-U-G-H—through. Through Jesus. How do we live this kind of life? With Jesus living *through* us. We live it *through* Him.

My greatest desire is to live a life pleasing to God. Time and attention to Christ—listening, watching, seeking, and questing after Him—result in love and honor for Jesus. And when we love and honor Jesus, we live a life that is pleasing to God.

How do we live this type of life? Through Christ. He does it through us (Rom. 8:37). That simply happens when we surrender our time and attention to Him so we can love and honor Him.

If you don't know Jesus Christ as your Savior and you've never laid down your life at the cross, say this out loud: "Jesus, I want to trust in You. Not in my wit, not in my own way of doing life. I want You. I lay down my life at the cross and say, 'Jesus, I want You to be my Savior. I want You to wash me clean. I am trusting in You alone for salvation in heaven when I die.'"

That's what it means to be saved. That's what it means to be born again. That's what it means to know Jesus personally. Through the cross and the resurrection of Christ, place your faith in Him.

Maybe you already know Him as Savior but you're not walking in spiritual maturity. Walk in a pleasing way before the Lord because He loves you, and let Him live His life through you as you live your life through Him.

*For further study: Romans 5:1*
*Additional references: Romans 8:37, 1 Corinthians 15:57, Galatians 4:7,*
*Philippians 1:10–11, Colossians 3:17*

# WHERE YOUR TREASURE IS

## 2 Peter 1:1–4

A certain man received an inheritance from his aunt. While waiting for the reading of the will, he was thinking, "What am I going to get?"

Then he listened to what his aunt said in her will: "To my beloved nephew, I bequeath my family Bible and all that it contains, along with the residue of my estate, after my funeral expenses and all the just and lawful debts are paid."

When everything had been settled, the nephew got a couple hundred dollars and the family Bible. He was really disappointed. He said to himself, "Man, I thought I was going to get more than that."

In a short time, he had spent the $200 and closed up the Bible. He put the Bible in a trunk in the attic and lived a good portion of the rest of his life in poverty.

Finally, he had become an old man himself, and it was time for him to move in with another family member. So he went up to the attic, opened the trunk, and saw that Bible. He pulled it out and thought, "Oh, yeah. I remember getting this as an inheritance."

He opened the Bible for the first time and began to turn through it, only to find that his aunt had put cash throughout all the scriptures in various passages of the Bible. All told, there was $5,000 in cash stashed inside that Bible.

Now, if you open your Bible, most likely there won't be cash inside. But there will be treasures—treasures that will be greater than any amount of money you could ever imagine.

Think about the symbolism this aunt was trying to show her nephew. He would be provided for as he walked through the scriptures.

The greatest treasure we will find when we open our Bible is Jesus. How do we walk in God's ways? Through Jesus. Him through us. That's realizing the treasure of who He is.

Walk with Him. Love Him. Realize you have everything you need and that you are spiritually equal with the apostles of old and today. Stand on His promises. Give Him your time and attention.

Then, as you mature in that relationship, you'll quit looking down at people and begin to look up to heaven on behalf of them. As you trust in this relationship, in His words and promises, you will live a life that is pleasing to Him.

*For further study: Matthew 6:19–21*
*Additional references: Matthew 5:38–48, 1 Corinthians 1:5*

# RESPONDING TO ANXIETY

Psalm 34:4

I've been doing some research on anxiety and also asking people this: How do you respond to anxiety? What goes on with you when you experience anxiety? Here is what I found out. Of all the people I asked, not one person said, "I don't know what you're talking about." If I had asked, "Tell me about fasting in your life," some people would have said, "I don't know what you're talking about, and pass the chips and queso."

But when you talk about anxiety, nearly everyone says, "Yes, I know what that feels like. I feel it in the back of my neck, my lower back, and my shoulders. My stomach gets upset, I feel nervousness, I worry, and I have fear."

I feel all these things, too, when anxiety comes around. We live in an anxious world. In the summer of 2017, Hurricane Harvey hit Houston. Right after that was the Las Vegas shooting. And if you were listening to international news, you would have known there was tension with North Korea, and terrorist events were happening around the world. There were a lot of things to be anxious about.

America is an anxious country. And you might be in an anxious city right now. People are saying about Houston that they don't know if they want to keep living there with all the hurricanes coming through. There are many things to be anxious about. One way to determine if anxiety is present in our society is the level of irritability—anxiety makes us irritable.

We are an irritable society. We're upset with each other all the time. In traffic, we yell at each other. People bicker on TV all the time. We've made an industry out of irritability. We start wondering how we can get help for our irritability. Maybe it's two glasses of wine at night. Maybe it's some sort of medication. How do we get through anxiety and irritability?

Throughout scripture, we read things such as don't fear, don't be anxious, and cast your anxieties upon God. Fear, anxiety, worry—they are all in the same pile of feelings. What you and I are anxious about might be different, but the feelings are all the same. The psalmist said, "I sought the Lord, and he answered me and rescued me from all my fears" (Ps. 34:4). In this series, we're going to explore fear as well as the anchors that are available to us when we are anxious.

# WHAT IS ANXIETY?

## Isaiah 41:10

Here is the clinical definition of anxiety: "Anxiety is a psychological, physiological, and behavioral state induced in animals and humans by a threat to well-being or survival, either actual or potential."*

That's a mouthful! It comes from the National Institutes of Health. It says that anxiety is psychological—that means our minds. It is physiological, so our bodies start getting tight, and we need to go to the chiropractor or massage therapist. The mind is thinking that something is a threat. If it's a low-level threat, it's anxiety. If it's a medium-level threat, it's fear. A high-level threat, or something that is perceived to be so, is panic.

When I was in business school, I remember studying for a final exam. I also remember sitting down in class as my friend walked in and said, "What's the big deal?" I said, "What's the big deal!? Today is the final exam!" To which he replied, "Today is the test?!" I nodded. He literally grabbed his desk and said, "This is not happening, this is not happening, this is not happening!" In a very Christian manner I said, "Oh, yes it is happening." The tests were passed out, and we both took the test. It was spring semester, and my friend was supposed to graduate and get married that summer. Now he was about to fail this test, which meant he would have to retake the class. Panic set in.

Anxiety is not only psychological and physiological, it is also spiritual. Anxiety is rooted in unbelief and the unknown. It's a place where we believe God will *not* be able to take us through. So we have to be able to say, "Lord, I'm anxious about this, but I want to give it to you spiritually."

When we're able to think things through spiritually with a renewed mind in Christ, our bodies can follow. But we have to be led by the Holy Spirit in order to be able to say, "Lord, I'm going to believe you. Even the flowers of the field don't worry about how they are clothed. So I'm not going to worry about how I'm clothed. Even the birds don't worry about how they're fed, so I shouldn't worry about what I will eat. Paul was in a jail cell by himself, but he said, 'The Lord stood with me' (2 Tim. 4:17). I don't have to worry socially because God is with me, no matter what comes my way."

*For further study: 1 Peter 5:7*
*Additional references: Matthew 6:26–29*

# THREE TYPES OF ANXIETY

Let's take a look at three types of anxiety.

*Chemical Anxiety:* Chemical anxiety means there is a chemical imbalance in the neurotransmitters in your brain—the way your body is wired. There is help for that. Your body could be going through a stage of puberty, and your chemicals could be firing in various places. But things will settle down eventually. Or maybe you're later on in life, and you might require medication.

*Reactive Anxiety:* If a person has been in a state of constant stress for an extended period of time, the brain may not be able to shut off the anxious responses on its own. That's called reactive anxiety. In our society, anxiety has become the new normal. Maybe you have been in a constant state of stress, and your mind is now unable to shut it off. Let me just be the chief of sinners here—this is the one I struggle with. I don't have time to rest and recover from the event I just went to because I have to prepare for the next event. I've been in a constant state of anxiety and stress, and now when it's time to shut it off, I can't.

When you're going to become a parent, you worry about this child for nine months and then continue worrying year after year. That's part of being a parent, but worry is not the lead story in parenting. We have to trust that God loves our kids more than we love them. The Lord can deliver us from the fear of what is going to happen and fear for the safety of our loved ones.

*Traumatic Anxiety:* If the stimulus is sufficient to overwhelm an individual's coping mechanisms, then that person can experience psychological trauma. That's basically an extreme form of arousal. It's what happened in Houston after Hurricane Harvey, whether your house was flooded or not. Trauma happened in people's lives in Houston, and they were so overwhelmed. They saw the water rising, they saw all their belongings on the curb, and their coping mechanisms were overwhelmed.

We look at all the things happening in our city, our society, or our world and say, "What do we do now?" People end up looking for places to cope. And that leads perfectly to the message of the gospel because God wants your overwhelming feelings to draw you to Him. Jesus Christ was never overwhelmed, even by the grave. He rose from the dead! When you place your faith and your trust in Jesus to live your life, you put your faith in the strongest One there ever was and ever will be. It's the good news that Jesus loves you even in the traumatic experiences.

# ANXIETY CAN BRING EXCELLENCE

## 1 Timothy 1:15–17

Did you know there can be a positive side to anxiety? I am a hard worker, a go-getter. I like the adrenaline rush. But what was a blessing for me in my 30s is turning on me now in my 40s. I can only assume that it will get worse later in life, and now I realize I have to go to the chiropractor who can help me relax my back. Anxiety turns on you!

There is a difference between anxiety and ambition, and if you are operating from adrenaline rush and anxiety, you are going to crash. But if you are operating from an ambition standpoint where you say, "God, I want you to do something great through the gifts you have given me," that's different. I have vacillated between the two of them. Am I doing this because I am nervous about something and want to perform at a high level and do a great job? Or am I being ambitious and saying, "Lord, you do what you want to do."

You have to pay attention because those two are hard to distinguish. If it is anxiety, then you'll end up in this reactionary track where you will be stressed out for a long time, and it will become your new norm. The day will come when you won't have anything to do, and you'll say, "Wait a minute! Why do I keep trying to find something to do?"

Men and women, you'll feel more comfortable at work because you're in control. Outside of work, you may be out of control. You'll end up being a workaholic. Your vacation will end up looking like a spreadsheet of all the things you have to accomplish instead of having a real vacation to actually rest. We break the commandment of honoring the Sabbath. That is one reason we are like this; we don't "sabbath."

Sure, anxiety can bring excellence, but it's not what should be pushing you forward. You want the power and will of God—not fear—to be the wind in your sails. So be careful of ambition and anxiety. Be careful of being reactive. Be mindful of the chemical aspects of anxiety, and see a doctor about it, if necessary. And for those who have experienced any tragedy such as Hurricane Harvey, God wants you to turn to Him with all of it.

*For further study: Colossians 3:23–24*

# SEEKING THE LORD

— Psalm 34:4 —

What are we seeking in our state of anxiety? Are we seeking a drink or drugs to take the edge off? Are we seeking ambition, trying to make enough money so we think we're safe? Where do we find help? We find help by seeking the Lord. He delivers us from *all* our fears.

We seek Him in a variety of ways. One way is through our own perspective. What is your perspective of this thing called life? Are you tired? Are you sad? Maybe you're saying, "I'm so tired. I've been going for so long." Or maybe, "I'm just sad. I see all this, and I'm just sad."

Or is it depression? Is your perspective fear, is it hopelessness? Where are you coming from? The world is after us in a lot of ways. It's molding our perspective. We might be afraid because we're taking in too much bad news over and over and over.

Newsrooms fill us with news—not so much information but entertainment. Do you remember the days when TV went off the air at 11:00 p.m. or midnight? It would be awesome if that would happen again. It would be great if there wasn't 24-hour news shows since we wouldn't always think we were missing something.

Someone from a news station called a friend of mine and informed him that so and so made some comment. The producer asked him, "Are you outraged about that comment?" My friend said, "Well, I don't like the comment, but I'm not outraged about it." The reporter then asked, "Can you be outraged by tomorrow morning?" My friend said, "I don't think I can." The reporter turned to someone else for the interview.

News stations use hyperbole and try to get people excited with statements such as "It's an outrage" or "It's a bombshell statement." Then we have to ask ourselves if the phrase they used was an accurate description of what really happened. Most of the time, it is not.

When I was in college, one of my professors told the class, "If you find what people are afraid of, you can make a million dollars. You play to people's fears, and people will respond with the need for protection." That is exactly what happens all the time in our society. But God will deliver you from all your fears. The answer is not turning off the TV, although that may help. The answer, of course, is turning on Jesus.

*For further study: Proverbs 4:23*

# THE GOOD NEWS

### John 3:16

It's the gospel! Jesus meets my anxieties. Jesus meets my worries and my fears. I can come through any news report because I'm not going to die until Jesus decides it's time for me to go home. I'm going to trust Him with every trial because every trial is going to give me an opportunity to talk about eternity.

I'm going to believe there is an upper story in heaven, not just the lower story of what's happening on earth. As society disconnects from God, we get nothing but the lower story. The lower story is the earth aching with pains to declare that we need God in heaven through Christ to meet our needs.

If you only got a lower story, you would be hopeless, and you would be anxious. Those are the only possible responses. But if you get an upper story that God is at work in some way, you can rest. You can say, "I don't like what is going on, but I am saying this: 'On earth as it is in heaven.'" Let's bring some heaven down to earth, and let's let God do His work. He is the fixer. We're not the ones in control. We're not the ones with all the answers all the time. God is the fixer of all things.

Let me share with you a quote from Corrie Ten Boom: "Worry is a cycle of inefficient thoughts whirling around a center of fear."*

I call that sideways energy—in other words, energy that is just leaking out. When I start getting worried, I have to ask these questions: "Why am I like this? What is going on inside?" Get the right perspective; God is in control.

How do we seek God during anxiety? Never underestimate the power of obedience to Christ. When you followed Jesus Christ, you trusted that His death on the cross was for you and that His grace and forgiveness reached you. Now you are able to walk the rest of your life in obedience to the Lord.

Our disobedience, on the other hand, will actually increase our fears. If I'm nervous about something I'm going to do, this is the first thing I say, "Lord, is this what You want me to do?" We shouldn't say, "This is what I want to do. Lord, please bless it." His power always accompanies His ideas. His power doesn't always accompany your ideas.

*For further study: Psalm 42:5*
*Additional references: Romans 8:21*

# CONFESS YOUR GUILT

## Psalm 38:18

Are you anxious about your marriage? Are you being obedient to Christ in your marriage by honoring your wife or your husband? If you are obedient to the Lord and trust God with your marriage, you will have a lot less anxiety. It will be a blessing instead of a burden.

Are you worried about finances? Are you faithful to God with your finances? If you're not obedient on your finance path, you're going to be anxious about it. It's up to you. The best way to stop being anxious about finances is to say, "God, it's all yours, not just 10 percent but 100 percent. And I'm trusting you with it. I want to be faithful and able to give." It's not about giving to the church or to a ministry or because God is broke and needs your money. It's about not being anxious. If you're disobedient in your spending and you always buy the biggest and the best, then of course you're going to be anxious because you're enslaved to Visa instead of being Jesus's servant.

How do we seek God during anxiety?

If our passion is not Jesus, then we're asking for anxiety. We have to be passionate about the things of God. Seek first the kingdom of God. Do not worry about tomorrow, and here's how. Seek first His kingdom and His righteousness. And then, as you're seeking them, you're letting God take care of tomorrow.

I seek the Lord, I trust the Lord, I love the Lord, but I still wake up at 2:00 in the morning. I've got the right perspective, I'm walking the right path, I have passion for Jesus more than anything else, but I'm still waking up at 2:00 in the morning. At times, I'm still anxious. What do I do with that? Here is what I do in those moments. I get out of my bed, go down to the study, and kneel down next to the couch that I use as my altar. I just call out to the Lord in prayer, "What am I worried about, Lord? What is going on here? What do I need to give to you?" And that sofa—that altar—becomes an altar where I lay things down.

That is what the gospel is. I've laid down my life before Jesus, and I've taken up His life in me. And now I have the security of Christ in my heart.

*For further study: 1 John 1:9*
*Additional references: Matthew 6:33–34*

# CHURCH HISTORY

Galatians 2:16

On October 31, 1517, Martin Luther, who struggled with depression and anxiety, nailed 95 theses to the door of a church in Wittenberg. All he was trying to do was get an academic discussion going at the university where he was teaching. He wasn't trying to start a worldwide movement. He was speaking against indulgences. Leo X, the pope at the time, was a big-time spender. He spent one-seventh of the Vatican's money on his coronation when he became pope. He also wanted to raise money to build St. Peter's Basilica in Rome.

Pope Leo X asked his people to sell indulgences to raise money. Indulgences were pieces of paper with the pope's seal on them. They were said to forgive sins or get someone out of purgatory. His friar Johann Tetzel went from town to town selling indulgences and proclaiming, "As soon as the coin in the coffer rings, the soul from Purgatory springs."* Martin Luther spoke out against indulgences, and the pope said he would have to recant his statements. The pope sent Luther a message, but he burned it.

When Leo X died, the church was bankrupt and even had to borrow candles for his funeral from another funeral. Luther also spoke out against that, and in doing so, he brought about what came to be called the Protestant Reformation. Because of his protests, a lot of things changed. Ministers could marry (praise God for that!). Church services were in the native tongue, not Latin. The Bible was translated into different languages. People—not just priests—could own Bibles. The services were centered on preaching, and people could read what priests were teaching from the Bible. There was also congregational singing. Luther was able to do all this because the emperor was away at war. The Protestant Reformation ended up with the Five Solas.

The solas are five anchor points we can hold onto in times of anxiety.

*Sola Scriptura:* Scripture alone. The Bible alone is our highest authority. I can trust that the scripture has a word for my soul.

*Sola Fide:* Faith alone. We are saved through faith alone.

*Sola Gratia:* Grace alone. We are saved by the grace of God alone. I don't have to work to get to heaven.

*Solus Christus:* Christ alone. Jesus Christ alone is our Lord, Savior, and King. Don't look at humans; look to Jesus.

*Soli Deo Gloria:* To the glory of God alone. We live for the glory of God alone.

# FIVE ANCHORS

## 2 Corinthians 10:5

Martin Luther had this advice when he was in the lowest of lows:

- Avoid being alone for long periods of time.
- Seek out people or situations that bring you joy.
- Sing and make music.
- Deliberately dismiss heavy thoughts.
- Make a list of all the things for which you can give praise.
- Exercise patience with yourself.
- Believe that depression can have a positive and fruitful side.

Luther took the weight of being excommunicated from the church and came up with the Five Solas. These five anchor points—the Bible, faith, grace, Christ, and His glory—are the anchors we can grab onto in times of need.

Are you giving your anxieties to Jesus, or are you just trying to stuff them down? Where is the place of unbelief in your life? You need to tell God that you have a place of unbelief. You need to believe that you are stronger than you think in that area of your life.

Where is the hope in your life? Are you just taking the negativity from the news intravenously? Or are you letting the IV of Jesus and his blood be your blood? Yes, the world is terrible. It is always going to be terrible. But Jesus Christ is Lord. He is always going to be Lord. He is always going to be above all the things that are happening. Praise the Lord! Jesus Christ has overcome the world!

The Welland River turns into the Niagara River, which turns into Niagara Falls. When the two rivers meet, there is a sign that says, "Do you have an anchor? Do you know how to use it?" I have given you an anchor. Do you know how to use it? If so, when the rapids come, throw the anchor out and let it dig in. Take that anxiety to the Lord and say, "God, I'm trusting you with this. Show me how to believe deeper. Increase my faith."

Give your anxieties to God right now, and trust in the gospel of Jesus Christ. He lives inside of you, and He has overcome the world.

*For further study: Ephesians 5:19*
*Additional references: Romans 8:28, Psalm 40:8, John 16:33*

# GOD FIGHTS FOR US!

**Joshua 10:7–15**

All of us go through seasons in life when we cannot see the light. Each day seems darker than the day before. Sometimes, it is so dark that we may even wonder if the sun is there. Likewise, in the midst of trials and problems, we doubt if God is there for us. Today and all through the next seven devotionals, we are going to be inspired by an amazing story. The Creator of the sun and every other star you can see in the sky (as well as those you cannot) is going to stop the sun and extend the day to fight for His people.

Yes, what you have just read is right! One day in history, God listened to a man named Joshua who trusted in Him so strongly that he bluntly prayed for God to stop the sun so he could finish a battle. Five—not one, but five—kings of the Amorites were so afraid of Joshua that they came together to go against him and God's people.

In Joshua's time, the people of Israel were conquering the Promised Land. The Gibeonites, a people who lived in that land, sent word to Joshua asking him to help them because five Amorite kings were threatening to take one of the Gibeonite cities. Joshua had made a treaty with the Gibeonites, so the Israelites were forced to honor that promise. The Lord told Joshua, "Do not be afraid of them, for I have handed them over to you. Not one of them will be able to stand against you" (Josh. 10:8). Joshua marched all night with his entire army, took the five Amorite kings by surprise, and won the battle.

In our Christian journey, we, too, find ourselves in battles. We may feel surrounded by many enemies, just as Joshua did. But I have good news for you. No one will be able to stand against you! It does not matter how many enemies you are facing today. Do not be afraid because you are not alone. God is with you and not against you. God will journey with you through these battles so you can grow in your trust in Him. He knows that you are not perfect, but He does not turn His face away from you. God wants to show Himself to you in these moments. Do not be discouraged. The Lord will be with you, and He will give you the victory!

Whatever battle you are facing, know that the Lord's face is toward you.

*For further study: Deuteronomy 1:30, 3:22, 20:4*
*Additional references: 2 Chronicles 20:15, 17*

# THREE TYPES OF STRUGGLES

Joshua 10:7–15

Have you found yourself going through periods when it seems that everything and everybody are against you? Undoubtedly you have. We all do. Can you remember a time when you desperately asked for help, and a friend or parent showed up and fought for you? I am sure you can.

In our spiritual walk, we encounter different types of difficulties. They can be inconveniences, challenges, or battles. First, let's consider what an inconvenience is. That's when our luxuries and comfort get pushed away. For example, "This line is so long. Why can't they open another register?" Or "Why can't the plumber come on Tuesday? I'll have to cancel my nail appointment." Do you see yourself here? These are not battles or challenges. They are mere inconveniences.

Challenges are different. They have to do with difficulties in marriage or parenting. Challenges are when we encounter incompetent people at work who do nothing and we end up doing all their work. It's when expensive bills arrive and you are facing difficult months ahead. These are challenges. You need time to find the answer to the problem, and the solution may require effort, discipline, and work. But still, you can find a solution to a challenge and solve it yourself.

Battles are completely different. When you face grief, depression, anxiety, financial debt, cancer, or a relationship crisis, you are in a battle. You cannot solve the problem on your own. You may not have the necessary skills to do that. You are either going to move forward or backward. You win or you lose. You need God's power. You need His intervention to go ahead. You cannot do it by yourself.

Joshua found himself in a battle. To win the battle, he needed God. He could not face five enemies and their armies with just one army of his own. He needed a miracle. God did three things for Joshua and the Israelites: He confused the enemy, He threw hailstones from the sky, and He made the sun stand still in the sky until the Israelites could defeat their enemies. Joshua 10:14 closes this way: "The Lord fought for Israel."

I wonder what your battle is. What is your impossible? It may look like you are surrounded and there is no humanly possible way to address the matter. Expect a miracle! Jesus fought our battles on the cross. We can cast our cares on Him. He cares for us!

# TRUST IN HIS PROMISES

## Joshua 10:8

I can honestly say that one of the hardest things to learn in life is to trust. I would even dare to say that the more we know people, the more we tend not to trust. However, if we were to analyze the core of the problem, it does not have to do with the act of trusting. The real issue is the one in whom we place our confidence. When we trust, we rely on the character, ability, strength, or truth.

Trusting requires only one action: to stand still and do nothing but wait for the one in whom we have placed our confidence to act. It is so simple and yet so difficult! The only thing we have to do is wait and allow the person we trust to do what they have said they will do. But our instinct is to try to take the matter into our own hands. Nevertheless, when we are facing battles, we know we do not have the power to do what is needed. The only thing we can do is trust and wait for the One who has the necessary strength to step in and win the battle.

The amazing story of Joshua that we have been focusing on teaches us a crucial lesson. God told Joshua not to be afraid because no enemies would be able to withstand him (Joshua). God made a promise, and Joshua believed and trusted in God's word. The result: The Lord fought for Israel! Joshua did not have the ability or the strength to win this battle. The first and only thing Joshua could do was trust God, who does not forsake those who seek Him.

The Bible has thousands of promises we can grasp. When the enemy surrounds your life and threatens to destroy you, when you cannot act, the first thing to do is set your mind on God's promises. Trust in God's power to deliver you from evil. It is your choice whether to focus on your ability or on God's. All of life is a chance to learn to trust Him more, to get to know Him, to really know Him.

All of life is a chance to trust Him more. Trust in His promises, in His ability, strength, power, and character. God does not forsake those who seek Him.

*For further study: Proverbs 3:5–6*
*Additional references: Psalm 9:10, Philippians 4:6–8*

# PREPARE TO ADVANCE

## Joshua 10:9

Imagine stepping into an NFL game unprepared—without the proper equipment or training—and having J.J. Watt run toward you. How is that going to work out for you? Some of us trust so much in our personalities, abilities, and experiences that we think we can go into battle unprepared. Fortunately, life teaches us that it takes preparation to succeed. That is a lesson we all learn, sometimes by listening to other people's stories and other times by our own experiences.

The second truth we can learn from Joshua's story is to show up to battle prepared to advance. God promised Joshua that He would fight for the Israelites. After receiving this promise, after believing and trusting in God, Joshua and his army took the time to prepare for battle. They caught the enemy by surprise. They walked 25 miles and had to ascend 4,000 feet, from Gilgal to Gibeon. It took them the whole night to get ready for battle.

It makes you wonder how many times we show up for battle unprepared. How many times do we try to take matters into our own hands before spending time alone with God, before praying, or before studying the Word of God and meditating? It takes time to prepare for battle. It takes effort. You cannot face the enemy without preparation or you will fail and go backward. Remember that in combat, you either win or lose. There is just no other option. Furthermore, the Bible strongly warns us regarding the matter of showing up to battle unprepared.

The most significant spiritual battle that ever took place on earth occurred at Gethsemane. It was the night before Jesus's crucifixion, and Jesus knew He was going to face the enemy at the cross. He did not show up to battle unprepared. His disciples, on the other hand, did not prepare; they did not bother to pray. And when they were tempted later in the battle, they sinned. Jesus prayed all night long. He did it so earnestly that His sweat was like drops of blood falling to the ground. This was the Son of God! If the Son of God Himself took time to pray before going to battle for you and for me, how much more do we need to pray before every battle. Allow this truth to sink in. Let us be humble enough to seek the Lord's face before facing our enemies.

*Lord, help us to be humble and wise enough to realize that we need to prepare before stepping into battle. First we trust, and then we prepare to advance.*

# TRUST HIS TIME FRAME

## Joshua 10:12

How many of us get impatient very easily? Do I hear a resounding "I do"? In our fast-paced generation, we want everything done five minutes ago. However, in the spiritual realm, it is definitely not like that. Everything takes the perfect amount of time. Who determines this? An eternal God. Someone who is not restrained by time and space. In the book of Ecclesiastes, we read that there is a time for everything and a season for every activity under the heavens (Eccles. 3:1). We need spiritual wisdom to understand that God's timing it is not our timing.

Another truth we can learn from Joshua's story is about spiritual wisdom when it comes to time. When we learn to trust God and believe in His promises, we can go through the valley of the shadow of death, knowing that He will fight for us. We also know that we need to prepare before stepping into battle. Joshua and his army marched all night long to prepare for battle and take the enemy by surprise. When the battle began, Joshua prayed and asked God to hold the sun still so they could finish the battle that day.

Clearly, when it comes to us, we would like to get the job on the first interview. We would love it if our kids would take in, through a 20-minute sermon, what took us 20 years to learn. If you were to battle cancer, you would likely pray for it to be beaten on the first round of chemotherapy. It is as simple as that. Not one of us desires to spend time in the valley of the shadow of death. We want to get out of there as soon as possible.

Nevertheless, in order for God to fight our battles, we have to trust His time frame. It is natural that we want victory in our battles as soon as possible. But we must give time for God to move. Allow Him to decide when to act. But remember, that doesn't give us a license for spiritual procrastination. There is a time to move. Joshua and his army did what they had to do, but they trusted God and allowed Him to do His part at just the right time.

For God to fight your battles, you have to trust His time frame.

*For further study: Psalm 28:7*
*Additional references: Ecclesiastes 3:1–8*

# REALIZE HIS GRACE

## Joshua 9:13–15

Our perspective of things causes us to make decisions based on what we can see and understand at any given moment. We are finite beings, so our understanding of situations is based on what we can analyze from what surrounds us, as well as our past experiences. Sadly, we often make decisions in a rush. We do not ask for counsel, and sometimes, the people we love end up paying the price for our bad choices. Or they might help us solve a problem that wasn't theirs to solve. They do it because they love us. They decide to fight for us even though it is not their responsibility.

I want to share the background of the story we have been studying. We know that God fulfilled His promise and fought for His people, but why did they get into battle in the first place? It all started in Joshua 9:3. The Gibeonites were neighbors of the Israelites. When they heard about the victories the Israelites were having, they decided to trick God's people into a peace treaty, pretending to come from very distant lands. They did this because they were afraid of them. The battle that came later happened because Joshua made a treaty with these people before consulting God. Can you believe that? He was tricked into the treaty, so the Israelites had to keep their word and protect the Gibeonites.

This story is surrounded and covered in God's amazing grace. Joshua made a bad decision, and God, in His grace, fought the battle for Joshua anyway. Joshua didn't pray about that initial decision; He did not consult God or include God in his decision. But God, in His grace, decided to fight for His people. Every single battle the Lord fights for you and me will take place because of His grace. We surely do not deserve it, but that is what the cross is all about—love.

Someone who did not deserve to pay for our mistakes decided to take our place, to pay for our faults. That is how amazing God's love and grace are for us. May the realization of how much this cost Jesus teach us to make decisions and plans according to God's heart.

Realize His grace. Move by His plan, not your own perspective.

*For further study: Proverbs 3:5–6*
*Additional references: Ephesians 2:8–9, Ephesians 4:7*

# SURRENDER YOUR BATTLE

## 2 Corinthians 12:9–11

Have you ever seen people speaking to themselves and having entire conversations in their heads? It is so funny (and sometimes scary) to see people so involved in their minds that they forget about the rest of the world. They act as if nobody is watching them. In difficult times, we tend to focus so hard on our thoughts and limitations that the rest of the world seems to vanish. We cannot get our minds to think about anything else. We do not even care if we look like crazy people to those around us.

It is so hard to cast our cares on God and stop thinking about them! Yes, real surrender and trust are based on doing exactly that. It is not our problem anymore. It has become God's problem. That is what allowing God to fight for us means. All of life is a chance to trust Him more. Saint Augustine prayed like this: "You have made us for yourself, and our hearts are restless, until they find rest in you."* Find the rest you need in God. Let us pray together and surrender our cares to the Lord.

Here's a prayer you may want to pray:

*I trust You, Jesus, with my battles. There is nothing in this world that can separate me from Your love. As I trust You, I know You will step in and save me. You will fight my battle for me. I need Your ability, strength, power, and character to intervene.*

*I recognize that I do not have what it takes to win this battle, but Your grace is sufficient for me. Your power is made perfect in weakness. What I do know is that when I am weak, I am strong in You.*

*Thank You, Jesus, because in spite of my bad decisions, You still fight my battles. You already won the victory over sin and death. Thank You for Your saving grace. I surrender my battles to You. Give me Your peace.*

*In Jesus's name. Amen.*

God keeps in perfect peace those whose minds are steadfast because they trust in Him (Isaiah 26:3).

*For further study: John 14:27*
*Additional references: John 16:33, Romans 5:1, Isaiah 26:3–4*

# GOD IS THE CENTER

## Psalm 84:10–12

Can you think of a better visual aid to get your attention than the sun? You cannot escape its grandiosity and power for about 12 hours of every day. It does not matter where you are or what you are doing. The sun is there, reigning sovereignly in the mighty sky.

Undoubtedly, when the psalmist was writing Psalm 84, he had a very clear and simple idea in mind. His purpose was to show us how important God is. He was affirming that the heavens declare God's glory and that God is like the sun. Mighty, overpowering, sublime God is above everything else we can see or touch. God is the creator of the sun, and if God's creation is so powerful, just think about how strong and magnificent God is. Consider this, and let this image become the focus of your day and life.

God is so much more than the sun. He is the creator of everything and should therefore be the center of our focus and attention. Our most profound satisfaction should not be found in what we do or in the things we own. Our deepest satisfaction should be found in the companionship of God. If God is not the center of our lives, then sooner or later we will start looking for satisfaction in other places. The problem is not that we may love our jobs, family, friends, or hobbies too much, but that we may love God too little. In John Calvin's words, "Man's nature, so to speak, is a perpetual factory of idols."* We tend to make idols out of good things and forget that we should love God first. He must be the center of our attention.

I wonder if this is true for us today. Is God the center of our lives? The focus of our attention? Usually, when this is not the case, we will feel empty, unsatisfied, and alone. If this is how you are feeling today, or if you know in your heart that God and His kingdom are not the number-one priority in your life, I urge you to meditate on the fact that the creator of the sun sent His Son, Jesus Christ, to earth to die on the cross for you and for me. That is how important you are to Him.

Just as the Earth revolves around the Sun, so our lives are to revolve around the Son. Jesus is the only One who truly deserves to be the center of your attention.

*For further study: Colossians 1:16*
*Additional references: Matthew 6:33*

# THE PATH OF DISCOVERY

**Psalm 84:10–12**

Maybe you know where you are going. Perhaps your direction and objectives are clear. The only problem you may encounter is choosing which path to take to arrive at that destination without wasting time. As Christians, we know that God, the creator of the sun, sent His Son to earth to become our destination—the center of our attention.

In our Christian walk, we sometimes find ourselves asking difficult but honest questions. What happens when we do not feel satisfied in Christ? Why is it that we still have anxiety, pain, hurt, or fear? What does that mean? Does it mean that God is not satisfying? Does it mean I am walking in sin? We certainly would like to have the answers in as much detail as possible, but would that really help? We tend to remember and learn from what we experience, not from what someone clearly explains to us.

If you are a believer in Christ and you know that God is your number-one satisfaction, you are on the right path to discovering this profound truth. We will never have the complete and ultimate picture or answer to everything until we reach heaven. The Apostle Paul put it like this: "For now we see only a reflection as in a mirror, but then face to face. Now I know in part, but then I will know fully, as I am fully known" (1 Cor. 13:12). Paul was writing to Christians. He was saying that in our Christian path, there will always be things we do not understand completely.

On the path of discovery, we may not have everything figured out, but that is why it is a path of discovery! Paul also gave this piece of advice to another church:

*Not that I have already reached the goal or am already fully perfect, but I make every effort to take hold of it because I also have been taken hold of by Christ Jesus. Brothers and sisters, I do not consider myself to have taken hold of it. But one thing I do: Forgetting what is behind and reaching forward to what is ahead, I pursue as my goal the prize promised by God's heavenly call in Christ Jesus.*

—Philippians 3:12–14

The most important word in these verses is *in*. Jesus is the center of attention, and *in* Him you have the answer to everything.

Stay on the path of discovery. Satisfaction is discovered in Christ.

*For further study: 1 Corinthians 13:12*
*Additional references: Philippians 3:12–14*

# THE PATH OF EXPERIMENTATION

Psalm 84:10–12

When considering what truly gives meaning to our lives, we may find ourselves either on the path of discovery or the path of experimentation with satisfaction. When you know that true satisfaction in life is found in Jesus Christ, then you are on the path of discovery. You may not have everything figured out, but you understand that Jesus is the reason for living and that ultimate satisfaction is found in Him. What happens when that is not where you are? Then you are walking down the path of experimentation.

When you take the path of experimentation, you are still looking for something. It can be spiritual or not. As teenagers, we usually look for approval or excitement. Single adults often crave accomplishment and companionship. If we already have that, we tend to look for stability and the blossoming of our loved ones. In adulthood, satisfaction and top priorities may come from comfort, consistency, and convenience.

Remember, these are all good things. However, they do not satisfy us completely. You may think that you would be truly satisfied if you could teach the Bible like your brother or sister in Christ, sing and worship like the worship leader, or have some gift or another. When we think like that, we are walking down the path of experimentation. We believe that once we check off the points on our list, we will finally be satisfied. Unfortunately, we later realize that emptiness is still there and that satisfaction does not come from the outside. It is a matter of the inside.

When you worship the wrong things, nothing else in life comes out quite right. But when you worship the only One who is truly capable of giving you real satisfaction, you will have a new sense of what really matters, and you will prioritize your life accordingly. I can promise you this: If you get off the path of experimentation, you will find yourself saying the same words written by the psalmist: "Better a day in Your courts than a thousand anywhere else. I would rather be at the threshold of the house of my God than live in the tents of wicked people" (Ps. 84:10).

When you stay on the path of discovery in Christ, true worship will flow out of your lips, and God's kingdom will be your number-one priority.

*For further study: John 14:6*

# THE LORD IS LIKE THE SUN

---
## Psalm 84:11–12
---

Creation is a symbolic representation of a real and personal God. It's God's poem. It is not that God is a tree, a flower, a hummingbird, or the sun—that would be pantheism. God is the Creator, the artist. Creation is His work of art, a living poem.

Some people confuse the creation with the Creator and end up worshiping created things instead of the Creator. When the psalmist wrote, "For the Lord God is a sun and shield" (Ps. 84:11), he was portraying God's grandeur. The Creator's supremacy and power are over everything.

Imagine if we were to buy all the energy the sun produces in 24 hours. We would have to cover the entire surface of the United States four miles deep with silver dollars. The amount of energy the sun produces could last 30 billion years. Can you imagine that? It is such a powerful image! God is portrayed as the source of unlimited power.

On the path of discovery in Christ, you may face anxiety, pain, hurt, or fear. Yes, that does happen to Christians. We may feel like we are living on the edge, but we have the power to overcome every situation. When Paul wrote his letter to the Philippians, he said this:

> *I know both how to make do with little, and I know how to make do with a lot. In any and all circumstances I have learned the secret of being content— whether well fed or hungry, whether in abundance or in need. I am able to do all things through him who strengthens me.*
>
> —Philippians 4:12–13

We all face different circumstances and trials. However, we can make it through things like depression through Christ who strengthens us. You can and will make it through hurts through Jesus who gives you strength. You will overcome financial need, infirmity, and every type of problem you can think of. Jesus is your source of unlimited power!

We can overcome the world because we have believed that Jesus is the Son of God. He will give us the strength we need and the power to be content in any and every situation. I encourage you to keep this thought in your mind and heart today. Meditate on it and make it yours.

The Lord is a sun. That source of unlimited power will give you all the strength you need in any given situation.

*For further study: Philippians 4:12–13*
*Additional references: 1 John 5:5*

---
## JANUARY 30
---

# THE LORD IS OUR LIGHT

### Psalm 84:11-12

Psalm 84 was written for people on a pilgrimage. The people of Israel would travel from their homes to the Temple in order to worship and be together in the presence of God. The journey was, indeed, long and took many days. As soon as the sun went down, travelers had to stop and camp. It got cold, and they could not see the way, so they had to wait for the rising of the sun to follow the road. The sun was essential for them to know where to go and to keep them warm in the desert where the temperature dropped significantly at night, and a fire was needed to keep warm. You could not continue your journey until dawn.

As Christians, we, too, are on a journey. We are journeying through teenage years, singlehood, marriage, and adulthood. Sometimes, we face dark moments, and the world becomes a very dark place for us. We desperately need light; we need guidance. In Psalm 23, one of the most famous and most quoted psalms of the Bible, King David speaks of those feelings like being in the darkest valley—the valley of the shadow of death, a place where there is no light. The road is not clear. So what does the psalmist do in this situation?

First, the psalmist realizes that he is not alone—God is with him. Then he holds onto what he is certain of. For example, Psalm 119:105 says, "Your word is a lamp for my feet and a light on my path." God's Word is the most certain, the safest, and the clearest ally when we face difficult times. Do you find yourself in a dark place today? Is your path unclear? God's Word is the right place to go. God's Word has the correct answer to every situation.

As pilgrims, we encounter dark places and valleys filled with shadows, but we are not alone. We also have this reassurance: 2,000 years ago, the Light of the world came to earth and took our place on the cross. That day, at noon, darkness came over the whole land until 3:00 in the afternoon, for the sun stopped shining. Jesus paid the price so we could be reunited with the Father. The source of unlimited power shined His light to show us the way.

The Lord is a sun, our needed light. He is living and shining inside of you.

*For further study: Psalm 23:4*
*Additional references: Psalm 119:105, Isaiah 9:2*

# THE LORD IS OUR SHIELD

— Psalm 84:11–12 —

I wonder what your relationship with the sun is like. In my case, it is twofold: warmth and warning. On the one hand, I love the sensation of warmth covering every inch of my skin. On the other hand, once I start feeling that this warmth is going beyond a pleasant sensation, I take it as a warning and thank God for sunscreen. It is interesting that the psalmist used this powerful image—the Lord as a sun and a shield.

The psalmists use several images to describe God's protection around us. They describe it as a shield and even as wings that cover us with feathers (Ps. 91). When we are in God's presence, we feel protected. These are moments we all cherish and long for. His arms are around us, so nothing and nobody can harm us.

The Lord is a shield. He certainly protects us, and we feel safe and warm. However, this warmth is also a warning for us; it can become protective heat. In God's presence, we encounter His holiness, and the Holy Spirit is in our hearts guiding us to all truth. Have you ever felt the Holy Spirit telling you, "Stop! Go away from this place!" The psalmist indeed knew this when he wrote, "For the Lord God is a sun and shield. The Lord grants favor and honor; He does not withhold the good from those who live with integrity" (Ps. 84:11). When you walk in integrity, you understand that not only does God protect, but He also warns us regarding those things that are not convenient. That is why His Word is a lamp to light our way. We have the freedom to do anything, but not everything is beneficial or constructive.

God does not withhold His blessings from those whose walk is blameless. It is our decision whether we want to live in God's presence or in the tents of the wicked. When we know that it is better to be one day in God's presence than a thousand elsewhere, we not only enjoy the warmth of His presence but also understand that we cannot play around with God. He is holy, and He will not withhold His blessings when we decide to live with integrity.

The Lord is a sun and shield; He does not withhold His blessings from those who walk in integrity. Happy are those who trust in His protection!

*For further study: Psalm 91:1–4*
*Additional references: John 16:13, 1 Corinthians 10:23*

# WORTHY OF PRAISE

---

## Psalm 84:10–12

God's grandeur is portrayed throughout the Bible. Creation is God's poem. God the Creator made the sun, and the psalmist accurately used the image of the sun to remind us of God's magnificence and unlimited power. Allow this image to become the focus of your day and your life. The Father blessed and made the seventh day holy, because on it He rested from all His work of creation. Let us pray together and remind ourselves of our journey.

Prayer:

*As I seek You, Lord, and make You the center of my life, I want to trust in Your unlimited power—even in the midst of difficulties and struggles. I know I have unlimited energy that comes from You, so I can do all things through Christ who strengthens me.*

*In the valley of the shadow of death, tears, and sorrow, You will hold me and guide me with Your light. I need Your light. When my path becomes dark and uncertain, Your Word is a lamp unto my feet and a light unto my path. I need You to guide me as I walk because I am not perfect.*

*I need Your protective shield and heat, that warmth that comes and helps me understand that sin is never the path to satisfaction. I choose to pursue You above all else.*

*Thank You for sending Your Son Jesus to earth to give His life for me. Thank You, Jesus, for taking my place and loving me. You truly are the light, the way, the truth, and the life. Thank You for not withholding Your blessings as I choose to follow You and live my life for You.*

*Lord, I trust You as I walk and continue on the path of discovery of who You are and who I am in You. I can say that it is better to spend one day in your courts than a thousand elsewhere.*

*In Jesus's name. Amen.*

*For further study: Genesis 2:2–3*
*Additional references: Psalm 145:3*

---

# ANXIETY EVERYWHERE

## Psalm 34:4

People deal with anxiety every day. Think about the different stages in your life. Whether you are a student, single, married, a parent, an empty nester, or retired, each age brings some sort of stress. When you were a high school student, you stressed about getting good grades so you could go to the university of your choice.

Once you got into college, you worried about graduating and getting a job. After landing a job, you had enough of the single life, so you stressed about finding "the one." You found Mr. or Miss Right, and then you felt like it was time to tie the knot. You got married, tried to make it work, and realized that doing life with your soul mate wasn't easy at all. And all that produced anxiety. Then you thought, "Let's have kids; that will smooth everything out." But you found out it doesn't, because you were stressed about your kids and parenting. Finally, you got closer to retirement worried if you would have enough money or if the money would outlive you.

The Word of God is full of verses that speak about anxiety and fears. The Apostle Paul tells us in the book of Philippians to not be anxious about anything. All we have to do is present our worries and fears to God; He is our counselor who gives us peace and consoles our hearts. He is our anchor of hope, a God who carries our burdens and gives us rest.

God wants to teach us to grow in our faith through anxiety, to learn to trust and walk in strength with Him.

*For further study: Philippians 4:6*
*Additional references: John 14:27*

# THE THRILLS AND THREATS

Psalm 56:3

I asked our counseling department to give me a definition of anxiety. Anxiety is a psychological and physiological state of arousal caused by the brain's interpretation of a stimulus as a threat.

Life is a combination of thrills and threats. How many times are we thrilled about something, and it immediately turns into a threat? Women, you get invited to a fancy, schmancy party, and what do you think about next? What am I going to wear? Men, your favorite baseball team makes it to the World Series, and your next thought is this: "Will they win the World Series?" A thrill turns into anxiety.

Anxiety is psychological, which can mean constant stressful and fearful thoughts, but it's also physiological, which affects your body. A stiff neck, extreme fatigue, even acid reflux can be due to anxiety. However, it's not only of the mind and body; it is spiritual as well. Anxiety is rooted in unbelief.

There are three forms of anxiety. The first is chemical. Chemical anxiety means the neurons are out of balance. It could be puberty or menopause. It's an anxiety out of our control.

The second is reactive. Reactive anxiety is when you have had constant stress, and now your brain does not know when to stop or turn off. You have been going and going for so long that it no longer turns off. You have a hard time sleeping, and you wake up at 2:00 a.m., stressed about a current situation. Even if you're on vacation, you are stressed about something because your mind is always on the go. The pedal is all the way down, always in gear. Anxiety is your norm.

The last form of anxiety is traumatic. It is when a tragic event has occurred in your life, and anxiety has become your coping mechanism. Everyone will experience this form of anxiety at some point.

As crazy as it sounds, being anxious is also an opportunity for spiritual growth. Your mind, body, and soul feel threatened, yet God is telling you to trust in Him. That is your opportunity. Trusting in God should happen not only in the good times. Why are we not believing God? How can we trust Him more deeply in this moment?

*For further study: Psalm 27:1*
*Additional references: Psalm 9:10*

# GOD LISTENS

Psalm 34:4–8

There's a psalm that King David wrote about searching for God and God answering him. This is such an important factor when dealing with any form of stress or anxiety. David often wrote these psalms because he was anxious. We need to trust that God listens to us when we pray or cry out to Him.

My wife and I were having a discussion on the couch one day. You could call it a tiff. It's when one says, "What I meant," and the other one says, "Well, what I thought," enunciating each word so we get our points across. Finally, I said, "I feel like you never listen to me." It's embarrassing to admit that it is my code for "I'm losing the fight and need to pull an emotional string." I know it's wrong, but it's simply me, gasping for one last breath. Well, my sweet wife then responded, "Not listen to you? All I do is listen to you. For decades I've listened to you. I listen to you at home. I've traveled around the world listening to you. I listen to you multiple times every Sunday. People quote you to me." So yeah, I still lost the discussion because she was right. And that is what God says to us. He tells us that when we pray to Him, He is listening. He listens to our prayers all day, every day. When we are anxious, worried, fearful, or stressed, He is ready to listen and answer our prayers.

Not only does He listen, but He already knows what we are going through. Have you ever heard someone say that their thoughts and prayers are with you? The truth is that their thoughts don't get much done. Sure, it's a kind thing to say, but it's prayers that are seeking and speaking to God.

The silence of God is true in our feelings but not in fact. You will go through a time—numerous times—when you will feel God is silent. I have had those times and can guarantee you I will have them again. It is part of the Christian experience. But you don't give up, because the fact is that He does listen.

Today, through your anxiety, trust more deeply in your faith, realizing that God does listen. Are you stuffing your fears and anxiety, or are you truly giving them to the Lord?

*For further study: 1 John 5:14*
*Additional references: Psalm 17:6, Jeremiah 29:12*

# DEEP QUESTIONS

### Psalm 62:6

Do you want to be a deep person? We have a very shallow society that is imploding. We are self-destructing before our eyes. We don't need any more rich or smart people. We don't need any more singers, preachers, or whatever talent you want to throw out there. This world needs more deep people—people who walk deep roads, ask deep questions, and answer profoundly. No more superficiality. Deep questions develop deep people.

We have the opportunity for growth. The author of the book of Hebrews says we have an anchor of the soul that is firm and secure. Anchors go deep into places we don't see. Do you have an anchor of depth in your life?

The answer is Jesus Christ. He came from heaven to die for our sins. It's not your willpower, money, talent, or knowledge. It is the good news of the gospel. Jesus lives inside of you and can save your soul. You can place your sin on Him, and in return, He gives you righteousness and forgiveness. You can walk and live in greater depth through Him.

A lot of believers have Jesus as their anchor but do not know how to use it. Let's learn to see anxiety and fear as a place for deep, spiritual growth.

There are three things in this deep place:

*Pour out your heart to Him.* There's a psalm David wrote that says to pour out your heart and trust Him at all times. Be honest with God. His Word says He is our refuge. Morning will come.

*Feel the feelings.* The book of Psalms is all about feelings. In times of fear, David would write down his feelings. You don't have to think others are worse than you are in order to be grateful for the food on the table or the roof over your head. It's okay to feel the emotions you're feeling.

*Process forward.* Don't worry about something over and over again. Take a step with it. Ask yourself what is stressing you and how you can move forward. Journal your thoughts. Journaling can help process forward. It's a lot like David crying out to God in his psalms. Write down your prayers. Tell God you need Him. There are songs that have the exact lyrics you need to process forward. There are problems that will require total surrender to God in order to move forward.

*For further study: Psalm 56:3–4*
*Additional references: Galatians 2:20*

# USING THE ANCHOR

David wrote a psalm that says he searched for God, and God delivered him from all his fears. That's incredible! Jesus rescues minds and renews lives. That's the type of business Jesus is in. It seems that some people believe God is in the business of receiving perfect people, but that's completely incorrect. God sent Jesus to rescue you in salvation and grow you in your faith. Anxiety is an opportunity for spiritual growth. We grow when we trust Jesus, who is our anchor.

Do you know how to use the anchor? There are a few things you can do with your anchor to help alleviate the stress you are carrying. First, develop new habits. Make lifestyle changes. Anxiety is physiological and psychological, but it also comes from a spiritual root. That being said, it affects your body. Ask yourself if your lifestyle is conducive for life. Is your schedule packed all the time? Do you constantly eat food that is unhealthy? Are you exercising? Do you sleep enough, or are you surviving on caffeine? Make lifestyle changes that will help you grow in your faith, not in your fears.

Then find some good counseling and friendships. There's a proverb that says, "Anxiety weighs down the heart, but a kind word cheers it up." Ask your church for counseling. Get involved in a Bible study. Connect with people who will encourage you. There is nothing wrong with needing counseling. Anyone at a high level of leadership will have to talk to someone at some point. Anyone may need therapy.

Finally, process the season with your heart. Heart work is soul work. Allow God to work in your heart. The truth is that if you do not allow Him to work in your heart, you will stuff it with anxiety. Eventually, all that stress will leak and affect the relationships around you.

Have you ever been so anxious that you got home and took it out on your kids? They were just being kids, but you were leaking anger and negativity. You've got to do the heart work. I searched for verses that talk about anxiety, and I've been reading them phrase by phrase. I'm not doing that because I'm in a horrible place. I'm actually in a better place because of this. Reading and meditating on the Word is great for the soul and the heart.

Let's take anxiety as an opportunity to grow our faith so we can rise up, minister to others, and walk in strength with Him. The strength is not your willpower, but God's power through you.

# GOD LOVES CITIES

1 Peter 4:7–11

I'm a native Houstonian. I love our city. You don't get any more Houston than I am. I was born in Hermann Hospital and raised in Houston. I've been there my whole life except for going away a little bit for college. A while back, somebody gave me a 1941 edition of a street guide to Houston. What's amazing about this guide is that the phone numbers in the advertisements are four digits. At that time, you only had to dial four numbers to get someone on the phone. There was also a map to help you find the businesses listed in the street guide. It looks like an old pirate's map.

I went to a couple of stores to see if I could find another one of these guides, and I couldn't find one, but I did find one from 2007. The city had grown tremendously, and it has grown even more since 2007. For each of these periods, though, downtown was the heartbeat of what was going on in the City of Houston. From 1841 to 1941 to 2007 to 2018, there was something happening in the city.

In 1900, 10 percent of the world's population lived in cities. In 2005, 50 percent lived in cities. Now, 55 percent of the world lives in cities. Cities are where people are going. On a planet filled with vast amounts of space, we congregate in cities. Cities are the heartbeat of the world, and you have been placed there. So it is crucial for you to reach out to your city. And reach out to the suburbs as well. In the heart of your city, be willing to say, "I want to be part of what God is doing in the smack-dab middle of my city—the epicenter."

It is part of your heart and part of history to reach your city. Go to those difficult places and reach out in a great way. Peter encouraged the people of the city to go out and make an impact.

# PRAY, GIVE, AND GO

## 1 Peter 4:7–10

Peter makes a declaration in the city of Rome. He starts off by saying, "The end of all things is near; therefore, be alert and sober-minded for prayer. Above all, maintain constant love for one another, since love covers a multitude of sins" (1 Pet. 4:7–8). What he wants you to understand is that because Jesus Christ is returning, you need to be focused. He desires for you to understand the importance of ministry and what God can do through you.

Praying, giving, and going bring focus. Peter is saying that if you understand that the end of things is near, you will be disciplined in prayer. This earth will have a completion moment. There will be a time when ministry will be done on earth, and those who have trusted Christ will step into eternity with God.

Ministry is so important for you in this very moment. You can say, "Lord, I'm going for it because I know You're coming back." Do you know that for every prophecy in scripture about Jesus's first coming, there are eight prophecies about His second coming? For every time one of them is mentioned—Christmas, Bethlehem, the birth of the Savior, the Messiah—there are eight prophecies about the return of Christ, the Messiah coming, and the end of time.

By looking at the world today—not just at your city, but everywhere—your heart should say, "I have to be even more about praying, giving, and going because I am in the final days." Now, by no means am I trying to declare to you when the final day is. I do not know. But I know that it's closer today than it was yesterday. I can tell you that. And Peter is saying that, with this in mind, you need to be focused.

What should we focus on? Peter gives us three things. He begins by talking about loving one another. Next, he says, "Be hospitable to one another without complaining. Just as each one has received a gift, use it to serve others, as good stewards of the varied grace of God" (1 Pet. 4:9–10). Peter is saying that you are to love well, be hospitable, and walk in your giftedness.

# LOVE WELL

---

1 Peter 4:8

---

Your life should be marked by loving well, being hospitable, and walking in your giftedness. Peter wants us to love "since love covers a multitude of sins" (1 Pet. 4:8). This doesn't mean that loving somebody gets their sins forgiven. That's not what he is saying. You're not Jesus. You can't forgive sins. It does mean that because of Jesus Christ in your life, because of the understanding that He's coming back, you are going to love well.

Our church loves well. I love how our church loves. If you go through a difficult time, our church will come around and love you well. If you go through grief, they will love you. I hear people say it all the time that they don't know how they would get through difficult times without their church family. The church is a family that loves.

There was a man named Darren at our downtown campus. He had struggled with homelessness and addiction. He went to Open Door Mission, an organization our church has partnered with, and they began to tell him about our Bible study. So he said he needed all the help he could get and agreed to attend. Billy, one of our volunteers at the downtown campus, is an active member and a volunteer at Open Door Mission. She was connected and helped Darren. She told him, "You need to get involved in a church." So Darren showed up at our downtown campus. Even though he was struggling with addiction and homelessness, he showed up. Darren was eventually baptized at our downtown campus, and the church has definitely loved him. We love what God is doing in his life.

That's a testimony of loving well, isn't it? God wants you to be out among the people of the city, being used by Him in a variety of ways. That is a form of loving well. Peter was referring to *agape* love—a love that covers over, that endures, that's tough. When you don't know whether you can go any further, this *agape* love takes you further.

# HOSPITALITY AND GIFTS

1 Peter 4:9–10

Peter asks you to be hospitable. What does hospitality mean? Hospitality is defined as the friendly, generous reception and entertainment of guests, visitors, or strangers. Hospitality in a city shines with the love of Jesus Christ. Even if you're struggling, Jesus wants you to have a welcoming, hospitable heart. How can God use you to reach out to your friends and neighbors? How can He help you love others well and be hospitable?

Last summer, a couple at our downtown campus moved from the suburbs to the downtown area—the east downtown area called EaDo. They built a house from scratch, from the ground up. They built that house so they could be hospitable. And now, they're having married and young adult life Bible studies at their house. They're hospitable by opening their home to men's and women's ministries and Bible studies. They're also planning to reach out to the poor and refugees. That's hospitality. Many of you have rooms in your homes that need to be redeemed, spaces where you need to say, "Lord, I want You to use this. I bought this house so I could have people over. Let's redeem it and give it to You." Be loving. Be hospitable. Be welcoming.

Peter also asks you to walk in your giftedness. God has put a spiritual gift in you, and He wants you to put it to use. If you don't know what your spiritual gift is, you're missing out on the biggest joy of your life. Find out what it is. My gifts are leadership, teaching, and evangelism. So if I wasn't teaching, I'd be withering. If I wasn't leading, I'd be withering. If I wasn't sharing my faith, I'd be withering. If you can find your giftedness and put your service—even your vocation—around it, your life will be very different.

Peter says that some of us have the gift of speaking. If that is your gift, you should speak as if you are speaking God's words. There are also gifts of encouragement, leadership, and teaching. Some have service gifts such as hospitality, mercy, and more. Go and serve in the ways you are gifted. But let God put it together for you. Allow the Spirit to guide you in your talents and gifts.

# LOVING YOUR CITY

Jeremiah 29:7

If you walk in love, in hospitality, and in your giftedness, you'd better look out for what God's going to do in your life.

If your desire is to reach your city, be about loving others, being hospitable, and walking in your giftedness. I am a native Houstonian, as I said. I love my city. I want to see God do amazing things there. The church is a key place for evangelizing the city. It says in the book of Genesis that the first city was founded by a man named Enoch. It says he was the builder of the city.

Right before the famous verse of Jeremiah 29:11, the scripture says, "Pursue the well-being of the city I have deported you to. Pray to the Lord on its behalf, for when it thrives, you will thrive" (Jer. 29:7).

Do you know that Jesus Christ wept only two times—when Lazarus died and when He prayed over the city of Jerusalem. The city is important to God.

If you love your city, you will want to see people come to Jesus Christ and will sacrifice and step forward to make that difference in somebody else's life. Peter says, "If anyone speaks, let it be as one who speaks God's words; if anyone serves, let it be from the strength God provides, so that God may be glorified through Jesus Christ in everything. To Him be the glory and the power forever and ever. Amen" (1 Pet. 4:11). The key points are (1) God's glory and (2) His power.

Loving your city and others is about God's glory and power. That's what it's about. It's not about loving your city because it has the best sports team or the best food. It's not about your ideas and service to the city. It's about God. It's about God wanting to use you so His love is known to the world. You have this moment before you. It is time you step out into the epicenter of your city and say, "I want to be about what Jesus wept over, and that's the city. Because the city is important to God, it is important to me."

*For further study: Genesis 4:17*
*Additional references: 1 Peter 4:11*

# CONNECT WITH YOUR CITY

Sociologist Rodney Stark said, "Early Christianity was primarily an urban movement."* That is very interesting, and I did not know that until I studied it this week. The original meaning of the word *pagan* was rural person. Another way of saying that would be country hick. The term came to have religious meaning because, after Christianity had triumphed in the cities, most rural people remained unconverted.

Isn't that remarkable that *pagan*, meaning nonbeliever, was a word used for someone in a rural community because Christianity had so much to do with the city? And have you seen a shift in modern times where cities have gone away from Christ and country towns have stayed with Christ? Both are important, but we've lost the culture for Christ because we've lost the cities. From its earliest days, Christianity was mainly associated with the cities. Look at the book of Acts and the thrust of missions to the cities.

If your heart is desiring to get involved in your city, to volunteer and love others well, start by saying, "Lord, for Your glory, Your power, Your heart, I will reach my city." The fact is that Jesus is going to return. You've got to be somebody who loves well, is hospitable, and is using your giftedness. Why? So your life can be about His glory and His power, about an impact that can outlast your life. You are a difference-maker. You have a history-changing, Spirit-empowered, life-giving legacy to leave.

You can step out from simply attending church to being the church. So step forward at this moment and go for it. This is about growing in your faith in Jesus Christ. This is about understanding that there is something bigger than your life and your plans. This is about being part of all the great things God is doing in your city. That is powerful. I invite you to pray, give, and go.

# FIRST STEP OF THE JOURNEY

## 2 Peter 1:1–2

If you have been to any camp in the last 20 years, you have probably participated in a ropes course. And there is always what is called a *trust fall*. In a trust fall, you stand on a platform, cross your arms over your chest, fall backward, and then your team catches you. If they don't catch you, you hit the ground. If you bend in half instead of falling straight back, then your bottom goes right through their arms, and you hit the ground. So you have to trust the ones who are catching you—trust them enough to hold your arms tightly and fall straight back into theirs.

In the Apostle Peter's second letter, he wants us to trust the Lord enough so we are willing to fall backward and know that God is going to catch us.

The letter is three chapters long, and Peter asks us a question in each chapter. Here is the first question: How do I live purely? The second is this: How do I discern truth? And here is the third one: How does this all end? The letter is like an arrow shot from a bow. There is the tip that will hit the target, the center of the arrow that holds it steady, and finally, the three feathers at the end that guide it and allow it to fly straight.

The tip is hope—what Peter is trying to use to pierce our lives. The center part that holds it all together is diligent application. And then Peter gives us three feathers, one in each chapter—warnings, reminders, and promises.

Look again at the three main topics in 2 Peter:

> How do I walk purely?
> How do I discern truth?
> Where is this whole thing going?

Now you can impress all your friends in three minutes with what you know about 2 Peter.

Can we fall into the arms of God and really trust Him? Will He catch us? Peter tells us that He will. Is that enough for us to put our trust in the Lord?

The message in 2 Peter is a very important one, particularly for the younger generations, because this is a worldview message. There is a huge fight raging between two paths. Peter is asking us, "Which path will you take for your life?"

# EQUAL PRIVILEGE

## 2 Peter 1:1–2

The Apostle Peter starts his second letter this way: *Simeon Peter.* Isn't it interesting? He uses his Hebrew name, Simeon, and his Greek name, Peter. So he has a past, and he has a present. *Simeon Peter, a servant and an apostle of Jesus Christ: To those who have received a faith equal to ours.*

It may say in your Bible, "A faith of a same kind."

*...through...*

We are going to see this word *through* about four times. How do we obtain this faith? It's *through.*

*...the righteousness of our God and Savior Jesus Christ.*

Now notice what he calls Jesus: "God and Savior." Jesus's deity is emphasized here. Jesus is God in the flesh—our God and Savior Jesus Christ.

*May grace and peace be multiplied to you through...*

Again—*through.*

*...the knowledge of God and of Jesus our Lord.*

So here we have this kickoff. Here is something that everybody is looking for. We are trying to figure this whole thing out, and the scripture gives us the answer. Peter says, "To those who have <u>received</u> a faith equal to ours."

Same kind of faith! Now get that in your mind. Peter is saying that your Christianity and his Christianity are exactly the same. You have the same privileges that Peter had. Now, that blows my mind. Peter was the leader of the early church (Gal. 2:7–8). Peter walked on water (Matt. 14:29). Peter was with Jesus in the garden (Mark 14:32–33). Peter made lots of mistakes, but he was right there at the transfiguration (Mark 9:2). And now Peter is saying that his faith and my faith are exactly the same.

I don't know about you, but every once in a while, I feel like, "Surely Billy Graham had a little more Holy Spirit than I have." "I know we are all equal, but surely some people are more equal than others." "Certainly, Peter had more faith than I have."

But here Peter is saying no, you are equal before the Lord. That is what we are all looking for in our organizations and societies. That is what we are all looking for in a world where people are always seeking equal rights and treatment. But that privilege only comes through God.

We are all trying to figure out how to get everybody to stop being prejudiced. And here is how: Let them realize that God has created them.

# CREATED THE SAME

## 2 Peter 1:1–2

When you're a believer in Christ, there is no room for prejudice because God has created every one of us the same. In His eyes, we are all equal—we all have equal access. It doesn't matter if you're rich. It doesn't matter if you have a bunch of education or not. Every one of us steps forward with just as much Holy Spirit as Billy Graham, Peter, or anybody else.

There are no JV or varsity teams in Christianity. There is just the team of Christians, united in faith. But we often separate ourselves anyway—by what church we go to, by what our giftedness is, by whether we are good in public or not, by the way we declare things, by whether we're shy or bold, by whether we are this or whether we are that.

In God's kingdom, it's all one team (Col. 3:11). We are all equal. The word translated *equal* is used in the Greek language for immigrants who became citizens. That meant they would have all the rights of natural-born citizens. Scripture is saying that God has created all folks equal in His eyes.

We have moved from darkness to light. We have moved from children of wrath to children of God. We have moved from outside the family of God to inside the family of God. We have moved from citizenship in the world to citizenship in heaven. We all now have the same rights and privileges and the same access to God (Eph. 4:7).

Every believer has the same value. That is an amazing thought. That is a blow-your-mind-away thought. That answers so many questions related to what we are trying to do and how we are trying to act as a culture and as a society.

Let's look at this thought that all people are loved by God. There is no question about it. God has created all men and women equal in His eyes. I don't look down upon you because you are a woman. You don't look down upon me because I am a man. We don't look down upon each other because of race or age (Gal. 3:27–29). We say that God has created us all and loves every single one of us. So we should also honor Him together instead of trying to jockey for position (Rom. 8:16–17).

*For further study: Colossians 3:11*
*Additional references: Ephesians 4:7, Galatians 3:27–29,*
*Romans 8:16–17*

# CIVICS 101

Are you familiar with the Declaration of Independence? The second paragraph starts like this: "We hold these truths..."* Truths? But we live in a society based on opinions, right? The second paragraph goes on: "...to be self-evident, that all men [humankind] are created equal..." Created? Oh, my goodness! Don't teach this in public schools (Ps. 100:3).

Divinity and equality are connected—right there in the Declaration of Independence: "...that they are endowed...." That means graciously given by God. They didn't earn it. They were given it "...by their Creator."

Shouldn't that read, "From the primordial swamp that turned into an amoeba, that turned into a tadpole, that turned into a frog, that turned into a fish, that turned into a fish with legs, that turned into a fish with legs that could walk, a fish with legs that could walk that could breathe, that then became a monkey? Then, when it became a monkey, it became a man who was bent over. Then, finally, man just got straighter up"?

If that's the thought, then why should we all get along? Evolution is based on survival of the fittest. So not only should I look down upon your weakness, I should utilize your weakness for my gain. There is no equality. There is just this: I am going to get, and I am going to win.

On the other hand, equality comes from realizing there is a Creator. Why do we have so many problems with prejudice and equality? Because we have erased the Creator and made our own Declaration of Independence instead of recognizing that equality has been bestowed and endowed by God (Prov. 22:2).

If we think through the perspective of evolution, what's next?

Well, there is nothing next. We're it.

Well, isn't that a pretty self-absorbed way to think about it? There is something that has to be next. We have to take another macro jump to become some other species. So why treat each other equally at all if we have to get what we can get in order to keep the process going?

"...endowed by their Creator with certain unalienable Rights, that among these are Life, Liberty and the pursuit of Happiness."

So we have 2 Peter 1:1 right here in the Declaration of Independence. We are all equal, and this equality comes because of the truth of divinity. God has created us (Matt. 19:4), and He loves every single one of us.

# EQUAL SPIRITUAL MATURITY

## 2 Peter 1:1-2

An amazing, godly, and generous friend of mine who passed away some years ago once told me that he was a member of a restaurant and club that required him to be a member in order to use it. People couldn't just walk in uninvited but had to be part of a group. He said, "Gregg, I want you to go there and put the bill for everything you eat in my name."

So we went there, ate together, and had a great time. I was very grateful. For one night I was equal, if you will, to every member in that club, even though I was not a member. My friend's name is what made me equal. Everything was paid for under his name.

We all are endowed by our Creator, Jesus Christ, and because of His name, we are spiritually equal with Peter, Paul, and anybody else. It's on His account, by what He did on the cross, that He provides that spiritual equality for us on the authority of His name.

We all have the same spiritual privilege. But we do not have equal spiritual maturity. God loves every person on earth. But that does not mean that everything people do is pleasing to Him.

Spiritual maturity comes when we begin to live a life that is pleasing to Him (Matt. 16:24, Mark 8:34, Luke 9:23).

We are all equal spiritually, and we can all go to God. But I don't think I have the spiritual maturity of Billy Graham or Peter the apostle. We have the same spiritual privilege and access, and we are citizens of the same kingdom. But I need to grow in my spiritual maturity. We move from just spiritually bumping around to spiritual maturity when we say, "My number-one quest is to live a life that is pleasing to the Lord" (Col. 1:9–11).

Where is your place of spiritual growth? Is it the Bible? Do you need to be reading the scriptures more? Is it church? Do you need to commit your heart more to serving, being part of the fellowship, and attending services? Is it praise? Is there deeper praise than just singing songs? What about obedience? Trust? Giving? Loving others?

Where is your place of spiritual growth? Let that be a place where God uses you as you grow in your spiritual maturity.

We all are equally loved. But we want to grow in our maturity (2 Pet. 3:18). That starts with our life being pleasing to the Lord.

*For further study: Matthew 16:24*
*Additional references: Mark 8:34, Luke 9:23*

# WHAT WILL BE YOUR LEGACY?

2 Peter 1:12

I want to ask you a question. What will be the legacy of your life? Have you ever thought about that? What will you leave behind? Before you start thinking, "Oh, yeah. I'm going to leave my watch to so and so and my sofa to such and such," that's not what I'm trying to say. I'm talking about looking back on your life. What will be the legacy that you leave? Will you leave a statement that says "I was here"?

The most popular form of graffiti in the United States is "I was here." We want a statement that says, "I was here. I made a difference. There's my mark." But instead of doing it with a Sharpie on a bathroom wall, let's do it with our lives. Let's say, "God, You did something in me."

In the 1700s, there was a man named Jonathan Edwards. His wife was Sarah Edwards. Jonathan was an incredible preacher and part of the Great Awakening. You may have heard of his sermon "Sinners in the Hands of an Angry God." In the 1900s, a man named A.E. Winship researched 1,400 of Jonathan and Sarah's descendants. Here is what he found. They had 11 children. Among their descendants were 100 lawyers, 80 holders of public office, 66 physicians, a dean of a medical school, 65 professors, 30 judges, 13 college presidents, three mayors, three governors, three United States senators, one controller of the United States Treasury, and one vice president of the United States.

It's amazing! Their descendants affected even my own personal life. My pastor during college was a descendant of Jonathan Edwards. He baptized my wife. He is an amazing man of God who declared the Word of God over our lives. What will be your legacy?

# REPETITION BRINGS REMEMBRANCE

## Matthew 18:19

When we leave a legacy, it doesn't necessarily mean we leave behind large collections of all sorts of famous people with important positions. You want to leave a difference-making legacy. That's what Peter is telling us. He says, "I will always remind you about these things." I'm interested in leaving a legacy, and I know you are as well.

Repetition results in remembrance. How many times do you think I could get you to read this before you would remember it? Repetition results in remembrance. That means you remember things when you repeat them over and over.

Have you ever gone to a website you don't go to that much, and when it asks for your password, you simply can't remember it? You don't remember it because you don't visit the website or use the password often enough. However, if you pull out your phone and it's time to put in your password to unlock it, you don't even think about it. It doesn't even give you a moment of pause. You just put in the code because you have repeated that action so many times. Repetition brings remembrance.

Peter is saying that there's no harm in reminding you about what this whole thing with truth is about. Do you know that throughout scripture, we see references to remembrance? It's in many places in the Bible.

Paul says, "I give thanks to my God for every remembrance of you" (Phil. 1:3).

"Jesus said again, 'Truly I tell you.'" (John 10:7).

Matthew said, "Again I tell you" (Matthew 19:24).

Paul said, "As we have said before" (Gal. 1:9).

If you're at church and think, "I've heard this before," that's awesome! It's great to have heard it before. The reason you know your phone number is because of repetition. Have you ever driven home from a place and you don't remember how to get home? All of these things happen because repetition brings remembrance. That can also have a negative effect, can't it? If somebody is continually saying negative things to you, it is easy to store that away in your memory. You need to rewire your mind to focus on what God is saying to you. "Rejoice….I will say it again: Rejoice!" (Phil. 4:4). I want you to declare those words. Repeat and declare the words that God is saying to you in His Word.

*For further study: Matthew 19*
*Additional references: Philippians 1:3*

# GODLY PURPOSE

What words are you repeating to others? Nobody has ever gone to marriage counseling and said, "You know what? My husband tells me he loves me all the time, and I'm sick of it." It doesn't happen like that. If anything, we don't say it enough, right?

Do you know what parenting is? It isn't found in some psychological journal, but parenting is basically being a parrot with a right heart. It's repeating the same things over and over but with the right heart. But what happens in parenting? We say the same things over and over and get ticked off about it, don't we? "I think I said pick up your shoes. Do I have to say this every day for the rest of your life?" Yes, you do.

Parenting is a continual repetition. But it's not just saying, "Pick up your shoes." It's also saying, "God has a purpose for you. God has a plan for you. God has a love for you. God can see you through this. The Bible is real. Yes, we're going to church when we're busy. Yes, we're going to be a worshiping family. Yes, we're going to declare the truths of the Lord. Yes, we're going to be generous. Yes, we're going to treat each other well even when it's not convenient."

As parents, we often have two goals: basic morality and earthly success. But these two are not enough. Of course, these goals are important, but God wants to do something deeper in your life. He wants you to have morals and earthly success, but He calls you first to set goals such as spiritual depth and seeking God's purpose.

"For what will it benefit someone if he gains the whole world yet loses his life?" (Matt. 16:26). It's about having spiritual success in this realm as well as the next. That doesn't mean your children have to be missionaries or pastors. What I'm saying is to be cautious that you are only satisfied with basic morality and earthly success. Why? Because your goals will become what you repeat. What will be the result for your children? They will believe this: "I need to be successful. I need to make a lot of money."

What if your desire is to repeat spiritual depth into your children's lives? I want godly purpose to be a goal in their lives. These profound goals keep your marriage together, keep your hearts together, and give you purpose in whatever you do. You could be absolutely miserable and tremendously moral. You don't have to be a believer in Christ to be successful. You want to go deeper than earthly success.

# A TENT

2 Peter 1:13–14

David Livingston, a missionary to Africa, said, "I will go anywhere, provided it be forward."* He is saying that he wants to continue to grow in spiritual depth and godly purpose. Why? Because that is where legacy comes from. Maybe you're thinking, "Well, I'm not spiritually deep. I don't even know what godly purpose is." If you just keep on walking, the cumulative effect of walking with God, being in church, reading the Bible, and praying will give you spiritual depth and purpose.

Peter says, "I think it is right, as long as I am in this bodily tent, to wake you up with a reminder, since I know that I will soon lay aside my tent" (2 Pet. 1:13–14). Peter is saying that life is short, but our legacy is long. Even if you live for 90 years, that's a short life. All those years in light of eternity are short. Paul said, "For we know that if our earthly tent we live in is destroyed, we have a building from God, an eternal dwelling in the heavens, not made with hands" (2 Cor. 5:1).

What you have here is temporary. It's an earthly tent. That's how Paul and Peter speak about it, because 2,000 years ago, they lived in a mostly nomadic culture. They had buildings, but they had lots of tents. It was a normal part of life for them to put up a tent and take it back down, and that's the image they are using to help us picture the short and temporary nature of our earthly lives. Then Peter describes his legacy as a remembrance for generations to come.

Your life, no matter your age, is a tent. It's a window that opens for a moment and through which you get to declare the truths of God. It's the door of Jesus that you get to go through. It's the opening in the heavens that you get to pray through. It is a short-term thing. Peter is saying that although your life is temporary, you can leave a legacy for years to come. What a powerful oxymoron—a tent can leave a lasting legacy. When does that become true? When the things of truth are remembrances in your life and regurgitated through words and actions. When your goals are no longer just morality and earthly success but spiritual depth and godly purpose.

Your days as an earthly tent will eventually be over. The time goes quickly. God sets us up for that moment in time. You are born, the tent is up, and it stays up. It's wobbly at times, there's no question about it, and yet there it is. You can have an impact on eternity. You have an opportunity to leave a legacy that will impact generations.

*For further study: 2 Corinthians 5:1*

# DIFFERENCE-MAKERS

## 2 Peter 1:15

Here is a difference-maker's declaration. I want you to read it, declare it, and repeat it daily. Here it is:

*I was made for more than watching. I have a history-changing, difference-making, life-giving, Spirit-empowered legacy to leave. Jesus, I ask You to work deeply in me and clearly through me as I pray, give, and go in Your love. I am a difference-maker. In Jesus's name, amen.*

You are a difference-maker. God has put something in you. You were born an original. Don't die a copy. Walk with God and let Him use you where you are because you are a tent, a tent that meets with God. You're a tent that declares the praises of God. Live for what lasts as you live in what doesn't. This is confusing, isn't it? I've got to do my taxes, and I've got to go to the grocery store. I've got to go to the dry cleaners, and I've got to put gas in the car. All this stuff that's constantly around can overwhelm me.

I don't believe you purposely are so busy that you do not make time to impact others. Life happens. We have e-mails, text messages, this, and that. That's how life is, right? But instead, I encourage you to live for what lasts in the midst of everything that doesn't. Be in the world but not of the world. Live for a legacy.

What's the legacy? You may leave a legacy of treasure. That's what we think about sometimes, but most importantly, let's leave a legacy of truth. Peter says, "And I will also make every effort so that you are able to recall these things at any time after my departure" (2 Pet. 1:15). This scripture tells us that Peter's mind was set on a legacy. It's not bad to leave a legacy of treasure. It's great to have a will and a testament, but leave a legacy of truth as well.

John Maxwell said, "If you are successful, it becomes possible for you to leave an inheritance *for* others. But if you desire to do more, to create a legacy, then you need to leave that *in* others."*

*For further study: Romans 12:2*
*Additional references: 1 Peter 2:9*

# TESTAMENT OF TRUTH

---

**Psalm 78:4**

---

When you think of the things you are leaving to your generation, you tend to think about money and heirlooms. Who's going to get the china? Who's going to get that pretty vase? Whatever it is, we all think about that. When you show up at your great-grandmother's house, you usually leave with stuff, right?

My wife and I have two children. Once everything has been taken care of with our kids and they're out of the house making their own money, we plan to leave an inheritance to a "third child" when we die. Our two children will each get one-third, and the "third child"—the kingdom of God—will get one-third. We've written that in our wills because we want to have an eternal significance. We'll take care of our children, but we want to give to the Lord as well. We communicated that to our kids, and they said, "That's awesome!"

Allow me to share our family's will:

I Gregory John Matte living in Houston, Texas declare this to be my will and testament. I want all who read this to know that Jesus Christ is my Savior and there is no doubt in my mind that upon death I will enter into heaven. I will do so not on my own worthiness but through the merits of Jesus Christ our Savior and His death on the cross and resurrection from the dead. I ask that my children and grandchildren share God's Word with everyone and to always remember how much you're loved, knowing that God will provide for you. I encourage you to place your faith in Christ alone and never trust the world for your comfort. I look forward to seeing you again in the life hereafter where we will all live together with our Lord and Savior. May God grant you peace and love and strength as He guides you through this life. And then, at the end of time, we will be reunited in heaven as a happy family seeing Jesus face to face.

That's my testament I want to declare to generation after generation. Not just "here's my stuff." This is the truth of my life. The stuff—who cares? The truth of God can change a legacy and a lineage.

*For further study: 3 John 4*

# PETER'S LEGACY

### John 21:18-19

Where is your heart in your legacy? What's the last thing that's going to be spoken about you? I don't care if you redo your will. That's not the goal of this devotional. My goal is to remind you of the legacy you have as a believer. It doesn't have a thing to do with earthly success or basic morality. My goal has everything to do with the heart of hearts.

Peter said he knew he was going to die. He was getting older, and Jesus had already told him that when he got old, someone was going to tie him up and take him someplace he didn't want to go. That meant he was going to be martyred.

He knew his time was coming. He could see Nero's persecution and power on the rise. Peter knew he was going to be martyred and said, "I will also make every effort so that you are able to recall these things at any time after my departure" (2 Pet. 1:15). We're still recalling these things after his departure, more than 2,000 years later. It's absolutely amazing. Peter was killed right after Nero set Rome on fire and blamed the Christians for it.

What is modeled is most remembered. It's not just about what you say. It's what you do. It's how you live. The legacy has to be more than show up early, stay late, build a great business, and be basically moral. It has to be about more. God has a purpose and a spiritual depth for us, and we want to honor Him.

This is what happened to Peter. He was crucified, and tradition tells us that he asked to be crucified upside down because he didn't feel worthy of dying the same death as Jesus Christ. So he was crucified upside down in St. Peter's Square in Vatican City. That's why they call it St. Peter's Square. And that's where he died as a martyr. His bones were buried under St. Peter's Basilica, a huge church right there in Vatican Square. In 1960, they excavated underneath the church and found the bones of a man they believe to be Peter.

Here's what Peter did. Peter lived a life as a fisherman and a leader of the church. He was crucified upside down, and his tent was gone. His legacy, however, is his testament to being a witness to who Christ is, and that legacy is still alive today and part of the seeds that are going to change your life. That's a life worth living. That's what I'm calling you to do, to fall into the arms of Jesus and trust Him to do something through you. It doesn't matter if you ever become famous. The question is this: Will you be faithful?

*For further study: 2 Peter 1:15*

# LOVE FIRST

Have you heard of the Civil War wives? Julia Grant and Varina Davis are the Civil War wives. Varina was married to Jefferson Davis, head of the Confederacy. Julia was married to Ulysses Grant, head of the Union. These two fought against each other in the Civil War. Yet when both men died, these widows ended up moving closer to each other. Not only did they become friends, but so did their children. We are living in times when people are divided. We are seeing racism again and again in our nation. Yet what our nation truly needs in times of hate and division is love.

When we choose to love instead of choosing negativity, hate, and division, powerful things can happen in our personal lives and in the lives of others.

The Apostle John teaches us that very thing. He takes us back to his journey with Jesus and lays a foundation for the church—a foundation of truth and love.

Loving God first and foremost is the first step toward loving. God equals love. He sent His Son to die for us. The love God has for us does not compare to any other love you will experience. It's a love that impacts and transforms. When we choose to love God first, we are able to love others even when it may seem hard to do. God changes our hearts with love. He has the power to change hearts and draw others together, just as the Civil War wives did. God can do great things.

We are a reflection of God's love when we choose to love our friends. Often we want to preach to them or change them. But what about if we just showed love to them? A friend would be more receptive to advice or building trust if we loved first. Showing love is a great start to sharing Christ with others. That is our greatest commandment—to love our neighbors.

And if you partake in a church every Sunday and leave full and blessed, that allows you to bless your home and family. It is important for your heart to begin to love your church, not only through attendance but also by serving. Serve, bless, and love your church the same way it blesses your life.

*For further study: 1 John 1:3*

# JESUS WAS A MAN

### 1 John 1:1-2

Jesus was a man—a real man who walked the dusty roads, a man who ate food just like you and I. He was human! Believing that Jesus was a man is a crucial factor of our faith. The Apostle John tells us so in 1 John. He lays that foundation to prepare us for what is next. He testified, "The infinite Life of God himself took shape before us" (1 John 1:2 MSG).

John wanted us to know that he saw, heard, and touched Jesus. Why did he find that so crucial for Christians to know? Because if Jesus did not exist, He could not die the death He died. He could not bleed the blood that paid for our sins and rise from the grave to then take us to heaven when we die. We need for Jesus to be a man.

But John does not stop there. He wants us to know that Jesus was also the word of life, which means He can give us direction from heaven. He can breathe words of encouragement when we need them and in the direction we need. John said, "In the beginning was the Word, and the Word was with God, and the Word was God" (John 1:1).

Jesus is also eternal life. He wasn't just a man or a teacher. He is our Savior. As God, He came in the form of man. When we understand that Jesus was God and man, it means we are putting our trust and faith in God as our eternal life. He is our eternity. I'm going to break it down. Jesus was a man who was the Son of God, who is our Savior, who is the bridge by which we can connect with God. Jesus existed as a man to die for our sins. He is our word of life who takes us to God to be our eternal life.

*For further study: John 1:1*

# CONNECTION

Psalm 55:14

People yearn for connection. The majority of us—no matter our age, race, or socioeconomic class—desire to connect with people. We live in a society that is hungry for connections. Today, we share playlists. If you have a playlist with your music app and want to share it, you can! Students do it all the time. Or you can stay connected with old friends on social media. You can make new friends on Instagram.

Back in the day, hardly anyone took a taxi unless it was absolutely necessary. Now we have Uber. We Uber everywhere, even to grab a bite to eat. We stay connected with people because our natural being yearns for it. Nevertheless, the connections we make with people have to be more than a hobby. They have to be deeper than a Facebook comment or Snapchat. They have to be better than sharing our favorite sports team. They have to be from the heart.

Connecting from the heart requires vulnerability. It's sharing with a friend when you're hurting or healing. We live parallel lives, yet we are not connecting in the aspects of the heart. We want people to believe we have it all together and put up a wall that keeps us from having true connections with other people. Husbands and wives should not just be roommates but soulmates. They should not only share a house but their hearts. Families should be connecting. Put away your phones and connect with your children. Here are three points that can help you build a true connection from the heart.

1. *Time:* Give your time, whether it's to your children or a friend. Connection requires your time.
2. *Attention:* Be attentive when you're connecting with someone. We all know that you could be home and yet not present. Make sure your mind and ears are present so you can have true connection from the heart.
3. *Resources:* We give our resources with true connection, sharing the resources of our hearts with vulnerability. We let others know our needs and thoughts. We also share our material resources when we connect. Whether it's using a car to give someone a ride or blessing a friend who's in need with food or a gift card, we can have connections from the heart with our resources.

Challenge your hearts to have a true connection with others.

*For further study: Psalm 133:1*

# AQUIFER OF JOY AND PURPOSE

Psalm 94:14

Have you heard of an aquifer? An aquifer is an underground water source. In Texas, Harris County's aquifer is the Gulf Coast. That's why people who live in Houston don't pour paint down their drains because it would end up in the water source. Aquifers require deep digging to get to the water source. Even if it hasn't rained, we have water thanks to aquifers.

Jesus is our aquifer of joy and purpose. Here's what that means. The connection and fellowship you make with Jesus Christ when you accept Him as your Savior goes deep down. It does not matter if you're going through a difficult time in your life. He is the provider of joy and purpose. In the midst of trials, He can be your joy.

John testifies, "We proclaim to you what we have seen and heard, so that you also may have fellowship with us. And our fellowship is with the Father and with his Son, Jesus Christ. We write this to make our joy complete" (1 John 1:3–4 NIV). By sharing this, John says his joy was complete. It was not through receiving but through sharing. Obedience brings greater joy, not sin. Sharing with others, not taking from them, brings greater joy. Loving, not hating, brings greater joy.

It comes through Jesus Christ, the Son of God—who was 100 percent man and 100 percent God—coming into our hearts. And because of that, we can now have communion with Him and communion with others. We can love and connect from the heart with others through the aquifer of joy and purpose. He digs deep down into our hearts, transforms us, and gives us joy, even in the midst of our circumstances and purpose here on earth.

*For further study: Hebrews 12:2*
*Additional references: John 1:12*

# ETERNAL TRUTHS

2 Peter 1:16

Are you acquainted with anyone who says, "I want to live my life according to a cleverly contrived myth"? Most of us would answer no. However, in his Second Epistle, the Apostle Peter wrote, "We did not follow cleverly contrived myths when we made known to you the power and coming of our Lord Jesus Christ" (2 Pet. 1:16).

With just a couple of lines, Peter gives us a challenge, a significant question we have to ask ourselves: Do we live by cleverly contrived myths or by eternal truths?

What is Peter talking about? Why would anyone guide his own life according to a cleverly contrived myth? I don't think we choose to live by myths. Instead, we succumb to them because they are strong and convincing. Their influence is so pervasive that it is just a matter of time before we begin to live by them instead of by the eternal truths of God's Word.

Here's one way that can happen. In America, we watch a screen an average of seven hours per day, and very few of us read the Bible. Daily, we consume seven hours of cleverly contrived myths and very little eternal truths.

We are certainly not talking here about Greek mythology, the Norse gods, or anything like that. We are talking about cleverly defined myths that have been in circulation in our culture for years. They have come to shape our perspective, our pleasure, and our purpose.

Have you felt it? After years of getting seven hours of myths and little or nothing of the Word, we can feel the shift in our minds and hearts. And we can see it in the culture, too. Now it's the time to challenge ourselves: Are we following cleverly devised myths or eternal truths?

*For further study: Romans 12:2*
*Additional references: 1 Peter 1:14*

# MYTHS DEBUNKED

We need to challenge every cleverly contrived myth our culture sends our way. In the scriptures, we find the eternal wisdom of God that defuses the enemy's lies. Here are some examples of cleverly contrived myths our culture swears by, each with its corresponding countertruth rooted in God's Word.

*Myth*: Our worth is external. Women must look beautiful and dress sexy in order to get the attention they feel they need. Men get their significance from money or accomplishments.

*Truth*: You have an eternal identity in Christ. Your worth is eternal, not external. It doesn't matter what you look like or how you act. It doesn't matter how much you have earned or lost or what you have accomplished. What matters is that your identity is in Christ.

*Myth*: Happiness is our ultimate goal, and it justifies anything. If I am not happy in my marriage, I will get a divorce. I am not happy with the way I was created, so I am going to get surgery. I am going to do whatever it takes to make me happy.

*Truth*: God wants your holiness more than your happiness (Rom. 6:11, 8:1, Heb. 12:10). We can have true joy in the midst of suffering. Some of the most significant challenges in our lives mold us to be the people God wants us to be. We grow in the hard times. Can we be happy? Sure. But is happiness our ultimate goal?

*Myth*: There is no longer right or wrong. Nothing is moral or immoral; it's just a personal decision. When there are no absolutes anymore, everything is just a social construct, everything is up to you, and everybody wants everybody else out of their business and separate from each other lest someone get offended.

*Truth*: God puts limits, rules, and other people in our lives for our good and our joy. We will reap what we sow.

Have you spotted any cleverly contrived myth that has gotten in the way of how you think and live? Let's not follow cleverly contrived myths (2 Pet. 1:16). No matter how good the presentation is or how many people are doing it, let's follow eternal truths.

*For further study: Romans 8:1*
*Additional references: Hebrews 12:10, Galatians 6:7–8,*
*Jeremiah 6:16, Matthew 28:19–20, John 16:33, John 15:5*

# EYEWITNESS NEWS

### Mark 9:2–7

In his second epistle, Peter said the reason we come to know the truth is because of what we witness. He uses the transfiguration experience to say that we shouldn't follow cleverly contrived myths. We should follow the eyewitness account.

Peter heard the audible voice of God. He saw the brilliance of Christ. He saw Moses and Elijah. His testimony validated that Jesus is God's Son.

And this is why I believe—because of the eyewitness account.

Do you know your testimony? Can you share it? If you don't have one, you can get one. A testimony is what you were before Jesus and who you are now that you have met Jesus personally.

Sharing mine takes me only 45 seconds, and I have done it thousands of times. I don't have it memorized; I just say it.

Eyewitness is crucial. In the Bible, it says more than 3,000 times, "We saw it." Marvin Zindler from Channel 13 in Houston often said after his news reports, "Marvin Zindler: Eyewitness News." When he said that, he meant "I saw it." It is as if Peter were saying, "Eyewitness news! I saw it, and it changed me from a fisherman to a man used by God."

Eyewitness testimony is the most convincing thing in court. Consider how things are now in our culture. Every crime or incident is somehow on video. You will see more videos of accused acts in the next 10 to 20 years than ever before. We have cameras in buildings. Everybody pulls out their cell phones when something happens. People film things when they see them happening because they can say, "Here is the eyewitness testimony that this happened."

Peter is saying, "I saw it. I was there. It wasn't just me. It is true." Now, Peter is going to say even more than his testimony.

He says that the prophetic word in the Bible was strongly confirmed to us and that we will do well to pay attention to it. It's like a lamp shining in a dark corner until the day Jesus comes and He rises in our hearts. And then he adds, "Above all, you know this: No prophecy of Scripture comes from the prophet's own interpretation" (2 Pet. 1:20). They were not making it up. Prophecy never came simply because a prophet wanted it to. Instead, the Holy Spirit guided the prophets as they spoke.

Peter began by saying he saw it, and Jesus is real. But then he doubled down on it and said the Bible is true.

*For further study: 2 Peter 1:17–20*

# THE BIBLE IS TIME-WORTHY

1 Peter 1:19–21

It has been said that Mark Twain once remarked, "The Bible is a book that everyone praises but few people read." If you say, "I haven't got enough time to read the Bible," then you are way too busy.

Lifeway Research took a look at Bible engagement within the church and found that 34 percent of churchgoers rarely or never read the Bible, 27 percent read it at least once a month, 27 percent read it at least once a week, and only 11 percent read the Bible every day.

For studying the Bible—which means you look at it a little more deeply—these numbers get worse: 3 percent study the Bible every day, 21 percent study it once a week (which is likely counting sermons at church), 22 percent study it at least once a month, and 52 percent rarely or never study it!

Which of these percentages represents you personally?

On average, Americans take in seven hours of talk radio, TV, media, and the Internet every day. Despite all those hours, 89 percent of us don't read the Bible every day. It's not a surprise that we follow cleverly devised and contrived myths.

What does your Bible look like? If you have had your Bible for more than a couple of years and it doesn't have some wear and tear on it, you are not reading it enough. If you die and your family finds your fifth-grade Bible that looks the same as it did in fifth grade, that is a testimony to your family about the lack of scripture in your life. What does your Bible look like? Is it worn out? Many say they don't have enough time to read the Bible. Do you take your Bible with you on vacation, or does it stay at home?

Let me really get in your business. Do you take your Bible to church? You know the pastor is going to preach out of it. Do you take notes at church? Do you want to learn, or are you just waiting for lunch?

If you don't have your Bible with you right now, do you even know where it is in your house? You have many versions of the Bible at your fingertips on apps or the Internet. Think about this: We cannot follow eternal truths unless we read and study the scriptures.

*For further study: 2 Timothy 3:16–17*
*Additional references: Hebrews 4:12*

# THE BIBLE IS TRUSTWORTHY

## Psalm 19:7

Maybe you have heard someone say, "You know what? I don't believe the Bible is trustworthy." Let me just give you a couple of facts. First, more than 3,000 times in the Bible, the authors who were eyewitnesses to events said, "It is true, I saw it." Second, Christ fulfilled 300 Biblical prophecies with His first coming alone.

Other people say, "Well, the New Testament has had all these changes and errors." That's not true. The New Testament is 99.9 percent pure. The other 0.1 percent that may have shifted are little words that make no difference to the meaning.

If we talk about ancient literature, it stands out that there have been 24,000 partial or full copies of the New Testament discovered—24,000! In a distant second place is Homer's *Iliad* with 643 partial or full copies in existence. That's 24,000 versus 643. If a college student asks his or her English professor, "Do you think Homer wrote the *Iliad?*" the professor would certainly say yes. But if another student asks, "Do you think the New Testament is true?" the professor's answer would not be so positive. Yet remember: 24,000 versus 643.

Archaeological digs have proved the Bible over and over and over. Dr. Nelson Glueck, one of the great modern authorities on Israeli archaeology, said this:

No archeological discovery has ever controverted a Biblical reference. Scores of archeological finds have been made which confirm in clear outline or exact detail historical statements in the Bible. And, by the same token, the proper evaluation of Biblical descriptions has often led to amazing discoveries.*

A good archeologist in Israel would go with an Old Testament in one hand and a shovel in the other. That's because if the Bible says it's there, you just keep digging.

The Bible has stood true and unchanged throughout the ages, but scientists constantly make discoveries that debunk previous scientific claims and theories without ever apologizing.

We can be sure of one thing: The Bible is true. It is real. It makes a difference.

*For further study: Psalm 25:10*
*Additional references: Psalm 119:89, Psalm 119:168,*
*Matthew 5:18*

# A FULLY PRODUCTIVE LIFE

Hebrews 10:14

Do you have a vision for your life? Are you purposeful? Are you productively working toward things of eternity?

Once we have trusted Jesus as our Savior and asked the Lord into our lives, we are given everything we need for life and godliness, and the Holy Spirit lives inside of us (2 Pet. 1:3). That doesn't mean that instantaneously we are perfect in the sense that we never make mistakes. It means that we are saved instantaneously. We are washed clean. We are forgiven. Now it is time to let that grow—in our sanctification and in our purity.

Peter tells us that in order to grow and build our new lives in Christ, we should make every effort to add to our faith six building attributes: goodness, knowledge, self-control, endurance, brotherly affection, and love (2 Pet. 1:5–8).

Christian character is intentionally pursued, not passively received. We have to intentionally pursue what we are wanting our Christian character to be (Rom. 6:19). You don't just show up at church, sit down, and all of a sudden become more Christian. The process of growing is participating in worship. It is participating in the message. It is listening. It is trusting. It is knowing. It is letting God do His work in you and through you that makes the difference. You don't just become a car because you are standing in a garage. You don't just say, "Well, I am a believer because I went to church."

When you trust in Christ for salvation, you start a new relationship with Him. Then you begin to grow in this relationship. That is why Peter says that in order to grow, he wants us to add to our faith in these other six ways.

Don't think about building with these six attributes as a serial effort. You don't need to wait to achieve one and then, once you get past 101, move to 201 and then to 301 and on and on. This is more like putting them all together in the blender and hitting blend. This is more like a stew. This is a recipe. All of them are happening in our lives in different ways and at different points in time. We are growing in all these ways, sometimes simultaneously. It is a mix. While we grow, we put all these things together.

*For further study: 2 Peter 1:5–8*
*Additional references: Romans 6:19*

# GOODNESS AND KNOWLEDGE

### 2 Peter 1:5

Growing in our character is like building a house. The first thing you need when you build a house is a foundation. The foundation is key. You can't just go out and build. It says in Matthew that we shouldn't build on an unstable foundation of shifting sand. We are to build on a strong foundation of rock so our lives will make it through the storms (Matt. 7:24–27).

So what is our foundation? Peter says the foundation of our lives is faith. Many people have not made faith the foundation but instead have made it just one of the parts of their lives. Faith in Jesus Christ is a foundational aspect that will take you all the way through eternity.

The first pillar we are going to add to the foundation of our faith is goodness. Goodness is what we call moral excellence. When we hear moral excellence, many of us freak out and think, "Oh, no. Wait a minute. That means perfection." But that is not what Peter means. Moral excellence means we are going to walk in a way that shines with Jesus.

As we have the foundation of faith and the pillar of goodness, the second thing we need to add is knowledge. The knowledge spoken of here is not just about being book-smart. It is not only about knowing things in our heads. There was a group of people written about in scripture called Gnostics. They believed in knowing things, but they were not Christians and were not walking with God. It is a false teaching that all you have to do is know stuff. In today's American churches, we know a ton, don't we?

We are not talking about just knowledge in our heads; this is about knowledge in our feet. It is practical knowledge being lived out (Hos. 4:6). So we want to know things, but we also have to apply things. James says that faith without works is dead (James 2:14–26).

Mark Twain put it like this: "It ain't the parts of the Bible that I can't understand that bother me, it's the parts that I do understand."* We know plenty in order to start moving and put our knowledge into action.

*God, thank you for communicating so clearly with me. Please give me all the wisdom and willingness to diligently add these things to my faith.*

*For further study: Matthew 7:24–27*
*Additional references: Hosea 4:6, James 2:14–26*

# SELF-CONTROL AND ENDURANCE

2 Peter 1:5–6

In the first chapter of his second letter, Peter gave us several characteristics that we are to add to our faith in Jesus Christ. The first two were goodness—our moral excellence—and knowledge—living out what we know (2 Pet. 1:5).

The next attribute Peter gives us to add to our faith is self-control, which can be defined as not giving in (2 Pet. 1:6).

Sometimes, that applies to sin. We have a choice between sin and holiness, and we say, "I am not going to give in to that sin." Sometimes, it doesn't involve righteousness and sinfulness.

We don't need to have queso or dessert at every meal. Maybe it's about accepting the fact that the alarm clock goes off and we have to get up, or that we have to go to bed on time.

You and I were made for much more than just feeding our natural cravings. So don't give in to "I am just going to eat like a crazy person; I am just going to sleep." A lack of self-control is going to get you in the end.

The next thing Peter mentions is endurance (2 Pet. 1:6). Watch how these two tie together. Self-control is not giving in, and endurance is not giving up. Those who spend their lives giving in will ultimately be those who give up. The more you give in when it comes to small things, the easier it is to give up when things get hard (Heb. 12:1).

We are going to encounter many problems in our lives—sickness, mean people, a bad investment, a wrong decision. That's just how life goes. We don't know how God is going to work us through it, but we should not give up (1 Cor. 10:13).

We want to be people who are walking with God in such a way that we are saying, "Lord, we want You to refine our desires. Instead of those worldly, fleshly things my neurons say I need right now, what is my heart saying? What do I really need in my soul? What am I really looking for?" An anonymous quote goes like this: "When a man knocks on the door of a brothel, he is knocking for God." It means that what he is really looking for is not illicit sex but a soulful touch from God.

So if we don't give in, we are going to have a better chance of not giving up. Don't give up. Hang in there. You never know what God has for you.

*For further study: Hebrews 12:1*
*Additional references: 1 Corinthians 10:13*

# GODLINESS

As we each go along our paths to build character, there is something God wants to develop in all of us. That is godliness. Godliness means to worship well. This doesn't mean that you are perfect all the time; it means you worship well.

I'll never sing well. My friends and family will give testimony to that. But I can worship well. I'll never be able to write songs. But I can worship well.

Godliness is not found in being a pastor, a missionary, or a minister. You can be a plumber and worship well. You can be a CPA and worship well. You can be a student and worship well. You can worship God well through your hardest time, your easiest time, and every time in between. Be a person who worships well (1 Tim. 4:8).

The next attribute that Peter gives us is brotherly kindness (some versions say brotherly love). The Greek word is *phileo*. That's why Philadelphia is called the City of Brotherly Love. This kind of love means to show kindness to those around you in your workplace, in your home, on your street—to the person in the apartment next door or the condo above or below you. God wants you to have brotherly kindness.

Finally, Peter ends with love. So why would he say brotherly love and then love? In the Greek, these are two different words. One is *phileo*, which means brotherly love (1 Thess. 2:8), and the other is *agape*, which means God's love (1 Cor. 13).

What Peter is doing here is spiking the ball and saying, "I want you to have these aspects in your life in a growing degree."

You don't need to wait until you have one love to have the other. All these things are happening and growing together. Which ones do you need to really concentrate on right now in your Christian life? Are you about to give in? Are you about to give up? What is it?

When you look at a little baby, do you ever say, "Did you see that baby the other day? He had a 10-year-old hand but five-year-old foot." That wouldn't make sense. Similarly, you would never look at a child and say, "Hey, you are a five-year-old. Why don't you look like a 10-year-old?" Growth happens simultaneously in all areas of your life at its own pace. Will you let God grow you in His perfect wisdom at the rhythm that's best for you and everyone around you?

*For further study: 1 Timothy 4:8*

# UNFINISHED

Here is the truth: God is not finished with you.

I heard a song by Mandisa the other day about trusting in God and letting growth happen in your life. The song is called "Unfinished."* Look it up when you get a chance.

God is not finished with you yet. He who has begun a good work in you will be faithful to complete it. So we continue on the journey, not expecting to ever be perfect but saying, "Lord, on the foundation of my faith, I want to build these six pillars in my life: goodness, knowledge, self-control, endurance, godliness, brotherly love, and love" (2 Pet. 1:5–7).

And here is what is great. Jesus said in John 15:5 that if we abide in the Lord and He in us, we will bear much fruit. But it also says that apart from Him—apart from faith in Him—we can do nothing.

Hebrews 11:6 says that without faith, it is impossible to please God, but that He is a rich rewarder of those who place their trust in Him.

Faith is the foundation from which all these attributes spring. Do you know what these attributes really are? A lot of them are simply fruit of the Spirit. The branches of the vine aren't wishing, "Oh, make grapes. Make grapes. Make grapes." The branches just trust in the vine and its nourishment. Likewise, when you walk with God, just trust in His Spirit and yield to Him. The fruit will come, and you will grow up and mature. Everything will work as it is supposed to (Gal. 5:22–23).

We have all the things we need for life and godliness. From the foundation of our faith up, God will make more out of us than what He originally started with. If we let that happen, your life and my life are going to be something incredible.

*For further study: Philippians 1:6*
*Additional references: John 15:5, Hebrews 11:6,*
*Galatians 5:22–23*

# BUSY BUT UNPRODUCTIVE

## 2 Peter 1:8–11

In his second epistle, Peter tells us to add goodness, knowledge, self-control, endurance, godliness, brotherly love, and God's love to our faith. And these continue to grow in our lives. Peter also says these attributes will keep us from being useless or unfruitful in the knowledge of our Lord Jesus Christ.

Isn't that interesting? It's almost suggesting that if you don't increase in these qualities, if you don't make a concerted and intentional effort to add these things to your life, the moving sidewalk you're on is headed toward unproductiveness.

Peter is saying that if we add these things, we are going to reflect what we are supposed to reflect. We are going to be believers who look like believers.

Being purposeless doesn't mean you won't be busy. You will actually be very busy trying to keep the noise going so you never have to listen to the quietness of your heart as it calls out to God. But if we are going to be truly purposeful and truly productive, it has to come from a place of faith.

If I stand on the foundation of faith and just let the fruit of the Spirit and these intentional aspects come out in my life, I will be purposeful and productive. God will use my life for His purposes. It will be like the description in 1 Corinthians 3: When the day of judgment and the fire come and everything is burned up, the only things that remain will be whatever is built on the foundation of Jesus Christ. We will be able to say, "Our Lord and God, You are worthy to receive glory and honor and power" (1 Cor. 3:11–15, Rev. 4:9–11).

*For further study: 1 Corinthians 3:11–15*
*Additional references: Revelation 4:9–11*

# VISION

2 Peter 1:9

Look out the window, not just into the mirror. Here's what will happen if you change your perspective this way. You will walk with a grander vision for your life.

We often see this perspective in athletes. The quarterback throws five touchdown passes. The reporter asks him, "How was it throwing five touchdown passes?" And he answers, "Our offensive line is incredible." He deflects the attention from himself and says, "The offensive line is the one who got it done."

Peter says that whoever lacks these things we have been talking about "is blind and shortsighted and has forgotten the cleansing from his past sins" (2 Pet. 1:9).

It is really easy to say, "What is God doing in my life? What is going on with me?" However, when we get our line of vision up and look out and beyond ourselves, we can say, "Wow! Look at what God is doing. God is at work. God is moving in a great way."

When somebody asked Phillip Brooks, an old pastor, "What would you do to revive a dead church?" he said, "I would preach a missionary sermon and take up a collection." Think about that. The revival here is not about money but about saying, "There is more, and you are part of it."

If I take off my glasses, I can't see clearly past a couple of feet. Things become fuzzy far away, but I can actually see the things that are near even better. Sometimes I read underneath my glasses because I am nearsighted and can see as clear as a bell at that distance. But those things that are further away are blurry. What happened? I took off the glasses—the lenses—that enabled me to see far and focused only on what was near me. When you take off the lenses of who Christ is and what the purpose and productivity of your life really is, you are only going to see what is close.

Peter is saying something like this: Don't become blind. Don't become shortsighted. I want you to see far. That will show the world that you are God's children, that you are headed to heaven, and that you are already beginning heaven here on earth and trying to share it with everybody else.

Put the lenses back on of who Jesus is and the purpose of what He wants to do in you. Now you can see clearly again.

*For further study: Genesis 13:14–15*

# AN UPSIDE-DOWN TREE

**2 Peter 1:5–11**

We build our lives by first putting the foundation of faith in place. Don't let faith just become a pillar. If faith is not the foundation, what will replace it is what we perceive as happiness. We can then justify anything by saying, "This makes me happy." If the foundation is faith in Jesus Christ, happiness and joy will be all around you. But if you get the foundation wrong, you will not make it through the storm (Luke 6:46–49).

Peter gives us these building blocks—goodness, knowledge, self-control, endurance, godliness, brotherly love, and God's love—so we have purpose and true productivity in our lives. We can then see that this world isn't all there is, and we can also see who Christ is and who He wants us to be. So now our home, our church, and our lives are solid.

Warren Wiersbe, a former pastor of Moody Church in Chicago, said:

> Some of the most effective Christians I have known are people without dramatic talents and special abilities, or even exciting personalities, yet God has used them in marvelous ways. Why? Because they are becoming more and more like Jesus Christ. They have the kind of character and conduct that God can trust with blessing. They are fruitful because they are faithful; they are effective because they are growing in their Christian experience.*

Many of us are trying to grow down, and God is telling us to grow up. We are trying to start on the leaves and then push down to the roots. But is that the way a tree grows?

You may be asking: What is the vision of my life? What college should I go to? Where should I be? What should my job be? Whom should I marry? What should I do?

If you will trust God to handle who you are, all of those other things will take care of themselves. Faith doesn't grow by your efforts; it grows by trusting in Jesus and saying, "You are the One. I want You to work in me and through me."

So just keep walking in faith. Keep focusing on all these things. Be intentional about them. Be patient with yourself. And then all this other stuff will take care of itself. As a mom, as a dad, as a single or married or everything in between person, God is able to do His work.

*For further study: Luke 6:46–49*

# BE ANGRY BUT DO NOT SIN

Ephesians 4:26–27, 30–32

As human beings, we can all relate to struggling with anger. It does not matter how patient, kind, or lovable we are. At any given moment, we can get angry. The Bible recognizes that this is a common reaction and warns us about its consequences.

A survey shows that 70 percent of new American referees quit their jobs within the first three years. Based on the study carried out by the National Association of Sports officials, all those referees agreed on their reason for quitting: pervasive abuse from parents and coaches. Here are the questions that arise from this survey: *Why* do we get angry at what is supposed to be a fun time? How is it possible that something that should be a pleasant and enjoyable time becomes a sort of war zone?

Our culture is filled with movies that show people getting mad and expressing their fury for various reasons and in various ways. Think about *Mad Max*, *Falling Down*, and *Anger Management*. The characters in these movies react with increasing violence as they face their frustrations. It is very common; it is human. A well known Latin saying states, *Errare humanum est, perseverare autem diabolicum*—to err is human, to persist is diabolical.

If anger is so common among human beings, what is the problem? The Bible warns us, "In your anger do not sin: Do not let the sun go down while you are still angry, and do not give the devil a foothold" (Eph. 4:26–27 NIV).

It is crystal clear that the reaction of anger is normal, but the problem is that it can become sinful. The results of anger can hurt us and our relationships. In this series, let's analyze the *why* behind our anger. Let's get to the root of it, expose it, and get rid of all the hindrances that stop us from walking in righteousness.

It is okay to get angry; it is not okay to sin in your anger.

*For further study: James 4:1–10*

# WHY ARE YOU ANGRY?

## Ephesians 4:26–27, 30–32

When we think about anger, we could certainly conclude that it is a secondary emotion. It is the result of another feeling. Anger is at the surface, but the emotion that triggers anger is the root of the problem. That is the answer to *why* we are angry. It is precisely the difference between legitimate anger (not sinful) and illegitimate anger (sinful). Here is the question we should ask ourselves: *Why* am I angry? Is it because of my preferences, or is it because of God's purposes? There is a vast difference between the two.

When you get angry because your desires are not met, the reason behind your *why* is your preferences. There is something you want, but you are not getting it. It might be respect, love, the fastest lane on the highway, a parking space, the best table at a restaurant, and so on. Your selfishness is being confronted, and you want to fight back. You feel you deserve something you are not getting. You get frustrated because of unmet expectations.

The second reason behind your *why* is utterly different. You get angry because God's purposes are challenged. Something illegitimate takes place, and that makes you angry. Some people call this holy anger. For 20 years, William Wilberforce headed the Parliamentary campaign against the British slave trade, and then the Slave Trade Act of 1807 was passed. He and other evangelicals were horrified by what they perceived as a depraved and non-Christian trade and by the greed and avarice of the slave owners and slave traders. God created people in His image and likeness. To see these truths challenged raised holy anger in these Christians who put God's purposes first.

Jesus is always the ultimate example of legitimate anger. In today's Bible passages are some examples of legitimate anger expressions and the reasons behind them. The question we should all ask when anger arises is this: *Why* am I angry? The answer will allow you to realize its legitimacy.

When I get angry, I need to ask myself, *Why* am I angry? Is it because of my preferences or because God's purposes are being challenged?

*For further study: James 4:1–10*
*Additional references: Mark 1:43, 3:5, 10:13–16, 11:15–17,*
*John 11:33–38*

# RESULTS OF ANGER

We have seen that getting angry is a common human reaction. We have considered that the Bible warns us regarding the root of the problem, the reason behind anger that triggers this emotion. Today, we are going to reflect on the second question we should ask ourselves when considering whether our anger is sin. *What* has resulted from our anger? Hurt or help?

When anger is the result of God's purposes being challenged, the result will be to help. When William Wilberforce saw how slaves were being treated, his anger resulted in the abolishment of slave trade in the United Kingdom. Jesus got angry when He saw that the Pharisees lacked compassion for someone in need. His anger resulted in a leper being healed. He flipped the tables in the Temple because His house had become a market instead of a house of prayer. God's intent (purpose) was being challenged, and Jesus's anger resulted in the reestablishment of God's original purpose by helping those in need.

But when anger is the result of our preferences or the expression of hurt and pain, we will end up making matters worse. Either our health or our relationships will be hurt. Long-term anger has been linked to high blood pressure, heart conditions, skin disorders, and digestive problems.

Behind the reason (the *why*) and the result (the *what*) of our anger, there is always a *who* (the recipient of our fury), and most of the time, they are disconnected. For example, let's say you are mad at your boss, and you unjustly reprimand your kids when you arrive home. When we do not address the root of the problem and deal with it as soon as possible, the result is two issues instead of just one. One problem is because of the wrong *why* (the cause), and another problem is with the *who* (the recipient of our anger, our health, or our relationships).

The Bible clearly states that "human anger does not produce the righteousness that God desires" (James 1:20 NIV). We must pay attention to the fruit of our anger. If it does not result in helping others, then we must address it before the sun goes down. Our God is more than willing to forgive us and purify us from all unrighteousness (1 John 1:9).

When I get angry, I need to ask myself this: "*What* is the result of my anger? Hurt or help?"

*For further study: Proverbs 29:11*
*Additional references: James 1:19–21, 1 John 1:9*

# THE DEVIL'S OPPORTUNITY

## John 10:10

Have you ever had revenge conversations going on in your mind? Do you go back to discussions and rewrite the scene according to what you should have said instead of what you did say? That is an unsettled moment. When we do not deal with anger before the sun goes down and when we carry it into the following day, the Bible says we are giving the devil a foothold, an opportunity to make things worse. Satan gets hold of us when we do not deal with anger as soon as possible.

When we give the devil an opportunity, he can expand small things and make them big. Remember, he is the father of lies, and he came to steal, kill, and destroy (John 10:10). When we choose to carry our anger into the following day, we allow Satan to hurt our relationship with God, others, and ourselves.

What is God's advice on the matter? First, make it right daily. Do not let the sun go down while you are still angry. Get over it as soon as possible. Small bricks build big walls. That separates us from God and others. Second, choose to forgive. In Ephesians 4:31–32, we read, "Get rid of all bitterness, rage and anger, brawling and slander, along with every form of malice. Be kind and compassionate to one another, *forgiving each other, just as in Christ God forgave you*" (emphasis added) (NIV). We can forgive because we have been forgiven.

Choose to forgive daily! Do not give the devil an opportunity to separate you from God and others.

*For further study: Ephesians 4:30–32*
*Additional references: Luke 22:39-46, Ephesians 6:10-18*

# DIVE DEEP INTO YOUR HEART

—————————— Psalm 139:23–24 ——————————

One of the hardest things to do in life is examine yourself. In my experience, it is not easy. In the Psalms, we often read that the psalmist asked God to examine his heart: "Search me, God, and know my heart; test me and know my anxious thoughts. See if there is any offensive way in me, and lead me in the way everlasting" (Ps. 139:23–24 NIV).

Knowing that God's compassions are new every morning and that we can approach the throne of grace with confidence and find grace erases any doubt that God loves us. Having the assurance of God's forgiveness gives us the strength to forgive others.

Let me encourage you to dive deep into your heart. If you are or have been angry, ask yourself today, "Why is it that I am angry? What has been the result of my anger? Who has been hurt because of it? Have I been giving the devil a foothold in my life?" Ask God to search your heart and lead you in the everlasting way.

Prayer:

*Heavenly Father, today I lay down my hurts and fears. Help me understand why I am really angry. Help me see the result of my sin, if it has been helping or hurting others.*

*If I have hurt others, I ask for Your forgiveness. I confess my sin against You. Help me forgive those who have hurt me.*

*I do not want to give the devil an opportunity to hurt my relationship with You, Lord, or with others. Help me forgive. I choose forgiveness.*

*Jesus, teach me to understand Your purposes. Show me when Your original intents are being challenged, and give me the strength to address the problem righteously.*

*Holy Spirit, please remind me not to let the sun set on my anger. Search me, and if there is any offensive way in me, lead me in the everlasting way.*

*In Jesus's name, amen.*

I can forgive others because I have been forgiven.

*For further study: Lamentations 3:22–23*
*Additional references: Hebrews 4:16*

—————————— **MARCH 19** ——————————

# THE SUN STOPPED SHINING

### Luke 23:44-49

It was April 1994, and former President Ronald Reagan was flying to China to meet China's government officials when Air Force One lost communication with land. Around that time, there had been a series of sunspot explosions, and they had released so much gas into the atmosphere that it shut down communication between Air Force One and earth. The airplane that never loses connection with land lost communication. For hours, they were in the dark.

Every one of us at some point in our lives has gone through a dark moment. We have felt that communication was shut off. It doesn't matter if you are the most important and powerful person on earth or the poorest and most helpless soul on the planet. You can be rich or poor, old or young. Sooner or later, you will face an obscure moment. We will feel alone, helpless, and overwhelmed by a burden that seems to crash your soul.

In those valley-of-the-shadow-of-death moments, you may find yourself saying, "God, I know You are there, but I can't feel Your presence. I believe You can help me, but please, can You do it faster?" It is precisely in those moments that most of us cry out, "Lord, where are You? Why have You forsaken me?"

Even Jesus endured a dark moment. Yes, Jesus the Son of God experienced a moment so dark that even the ambiance around Him changed. Darkness came over the whole world from noon until 3:00 in the afternoon. The earth became dark because the sun stopped shining. Can you imagine the most challenging moment of your life surrounded by darkness on the inside and the outside?

It was such an obscure and difficult time that Jesus cried out in a loud voice, "My God, my God, why have you forsaken me?" (Matt. 27:46 NIV). Are you in a valley of loneliness? Rejection? Failure? Addiction? Financial ruin? If today you find yourself crying out as Jesus did, I want you to know that *you are not alone.* God is with you. Take this dark moment and turn it into an enlightening one. Embrace it as an opportunity to discover greater intimacy. Allow God to guide you through the storm and find rest under the shadow of the Almighty.

Remember that even in your darkest hour, God is with you!

*For further study: Matthew 27:45–56*
*Additional references: Psalm 23:4, 91:1*

# THE CROSS

## 2 Corinthians 5:21

Nobody wants a trial in their life. Suffering is just not part of our nature. Very deep inside of us, something is telling us that this is not the way things are supposed to be. But Christianity is full of paradoxes. One of them is found in the book of Romans where it says that God will use everything that happens to us for good (Rom. 8:28). Consider trials, temptation, struggles, and difficulties as opportunities for God to show Himself to you.

The greatest paradox of all is found at the cross. In 2 Corinthians 5:21, we read, "God made him [Jesus] who had no sin to be sin for us, so that in him we might become the righteousness of God" (NIV). On the one hand, we find our sin—the sin of the whole world. On the other hand, we find an innocent man who had never sinned. A righteous person (Jesus) took our place at the cross, and all the punishment we deserved fell on Him.

Can you imagine yourself carrying all the vile deeds, moral turpitudes, and lowness of the world? It was so dark and painful that even creation responded to the death of the Creator. There was an earthquake, and the whole land became dark for three hours.

The Bible even tells us that the whole scene became a spectacle for everyone to see. It was as if God were setting the scene for the entire world to see the most crucial moment in history. Darkness covered the earth, and the Light of the world committed His spirit into the hands of the Father. Jesus canceled the charge of our legal indebtedness and nailed it to the cross. How amazing is that! The cross is, indeed, the centerpiece of Christianity. Jesus took His darkest moment and turned it into light!

Nobody wants a trial in their life, but God will bring what we *need* from what we do not *want*. Jesus asked the Father to let the cup (His suffering on the cross) pass from Him. He knew that the cross was not going to be easy. Nevertheless, He considered that the outcome of it all was worth it. In the New Testament, we are called to rejoice and exult in the midst of tribulations.

We do not know what we need, but God does. Therefore, He will allow trials and tribulations to come our way to produce in us the fruit of our faith. We will never realize that we need more perseverance, hope, proven character, or love for others. But God knows better than we do; He knows what we really *need*.

Do not waste the trials of your life. God will bring what you *need* from what you do not *want*! Make the cross the centerpiece of your trial, and let the Lord lead you through it.

# THE VEIL

Luke 23:45

The verses we have been focusing on cover a series of miracles that took place while Jesus was being crucified. One of those miracles was that the Temple veil was torn apart. In the Old Testament, before Solomon built the Temple, people worshipped God in the tabernacle. That was a tent divided into three sections: the outer court, the holy place, and the most holy place.

Between the holy place and the most holy place, there was a veil. Nobody had access to the most holy place—where the presence of God was—except the high priest who could enter only once a year after fulfilling a long list of ceremonial procedures. He represented the Israelites before God.

The veil was a symbol of the separation that existed between God (the Holy One) and humankind. We did not have access to God's presence because of our sin. There was nothing we could do to gain God's favor and enter His presence.

The most striking fact regarding the tearing of the veil is that God wanted to make sure that event was recorded so everybody could rejoice and celebrate the fact that the separation between Him and us was, and is, over. It also demonstrated that only God could restore our relationship—the veil was torn in two, from top to bottom. Jesus was the only One who could fulfill all the requirements of the law, which was a shadow of the things to come (Heb. 10:1).

Humankind could not reach God. It was God's initiative to restore our relationship with Him. At the cross, God pierced into our darkness, and the Light of the world established a new covenant. Greater intimacy with God was then and is now open wide. Moreover, Jesus now lives *in* us; our bodies are the temple of God.

So when difficult times come your way, remember that nothing can separate you from the love of God that is *in* Christ Jesus our Lord. You will make it through. Trust in Jesus and allow Him to teach you what you need to learn from it. Do not waste the trial. Draw closer to the light of Jesus where everything is exposed. He will show you the way through the storm by the power of the Holy Spirit.

Greater intimacy is found and available in the midst of trials. Pull closer to Him! He understands what you are going through and is willing to help you.

*For further study: Hebrews 4:15; 8:5–6, 15; 10:1*
*Additional references: Colossians 2:17, Romans 8:38–39*

# SOFTENING OUR HEARTS

## Luke 23:47–48

When trials come our way, we have two *choices*: to soften or to harden our hearts. We can choose to learn from the trial and draw closer to God, or we can try to get out of the storm as soon as possible, learn nothing from it, and waste the opportunity. We all know that when we do not learn from our experiences, we tend to repeat the same mistakes over and over.

The events that took place during Jesus's crucifixion caused a series of various reactions among the people who belonged to very different social backgrounds and statuses. One of them was a centurion. The officers were respected and admired; they were the higher members of the Roman Empire Army. They were chosen by merit, remarkable for their deliberation, constancy, and strength of mind. The centurion who was by the cross said, after seeing what had happened before his eyes, "Surely this was a righteous man" (Luke 23:47 NIV).

At the same time, two criminals were being crucified beside Jesus. They had been thrown into prison for insurrection and murder. One of them, after seeing that Jesus was innocent and being unjustly punished, said to Jesus, "Remember me when you come into your kingdom" (Luke 23:42 NIV).

Two completely different people from two utterly distinctive backgrounds both softened their hearts and recognized that Jesus was the Son of God. It doesn't matter who you are, where you are from, or how important your status is in society. When it comes to the most critical decision you will ever face, you can choose when you stand before the cross to either soften your heart and recognize that Jesus is Lord of Lords or refuse to do so and harden your heart even more (as the other criminal chose to do). The cross gives all human beings equal footing.

When we go through difficult times, we are confronted with a choice. This choice is not to suffer but to choose God's will—whether it means suffering or not. Let us say as Jesus did, "Father, if you are willing, take this cup [suffering] from me; yet not my will, but yours be done" (Luke 22:42 NIV).

When facing trials, choose to soften your heart and pray that God's will be done in your life.

*For further study: Matthew 27:45–56*
*Additional references: Luke 22:42*

# THE SUPPORT GROUP

## Luke 23:49, 55; 24:1-10

Difficult times give us an opportunity for growth. In Japanese, the word *crisis* actually means *opportunity*. When you face a problem or when you are in the middle of a crisis, it becomes easier to realize who your real, loyal, and I-got-your-back friends are. The night before Jesus's crucifixion, Jesus was abandoned by all His disciples. Peter even denied knowing Jesus. Imagine how difficult that must have been for Jesus.

Nevertheless, at the darkest of hours, Jesus had a support group—a group of women who had followed Him from Galilee and stood at a distance watching what took place. As Christians, we are called to be a group of people who are willing to rejoice with those who rejoice and mourn with those who mourn. Sometimes, it is difficult for us to find who those people are in our lives. You may even be asking God, "Lord, please show me who my support group is. I need help. Who are the people You have placed in my life to help me go through difficult times?"

We all need to be humble enough to say, "I need help, I need wisdom! Brother, sister, pastor, I need your guidance, your prayers." Faith, hope, and love are the greatest anchoring forces that you can experience when facing suffering and uncertainty. Jesus's support group was there for Him, and they were also there for each other. In the darkest moment, they had to endure—the death of Jesus—they were *together*. A couple of days after, they went back to the tomb and found that it was empty and that Jesus had risen! They had mourned together, and now they rejoiced together!

The New Testament promises us that everything that happens is for our good. When facing trials, struggles, temptation, or difficulties, we have the assurance that God will make all things work out for our good. If God was able to turn the greatest evil ever committed (the killing of His own Son) and use it for the greatest good (the salvation of humankind), imagine how capable He is to turn your crisis into an opportunity.

Trust *the cross*—Jesus's sacrifice was and is enough. Know that greater intimacy is open wide; *the veil* was torn. *Soften your heart.* Pray that God's will be done in your life, and *ask for help*! Gather with the community of believers who will mourn and rejoice with you!

*For further study: Romans 12:16*
*Additional references: 1 Corinthians 13:13*

# IMAGINE

Revelation 1:16, 21:22–27

It comes as no surprise that the concept of heaven permeates our culture. Phrases such as "I'm in seventh heaven" or "she moved heaven and earth to get something done" are part of our daily language. Music, films, and TV series also reflect our enthusiasm for such a place. Think about Frank Sinatra's "Pennies from Heaven" and Led Zeppelin's "Stairway to Heaven." And what about Netflix's well known *The Good Place*? The imaginary landscape of yesterday's and today's society presents a hunger for a place where everything is as it is supposed to be: perfect—just perfect.

Heaven is a place where there is no hunger, violence, war, poverty, suffering, tears, or illness. Can you imagine? It sounds too good to be true, and yet it *is* true. This place we all long for and dream of does exist. The Bible is very clear regarding the place Jesus is preparing for us. In the days before His death and resurrection, Jesus referred to it as "my Father's house" (John 14:2). It is also called paradise (Luke 23:43, 2 Cor. 12:4, Rev. 2:7), the better country, (Heb. 11:14, 16), the kingdom of heaven (Matt. 25:1, James 2:5), the eternal kingdom (2 Pet. 1:11), the eternal inheritance (1 Pet. 1:4, Heb. 9:15), the Jerusalem above, the heavenly Jerusalem, and the new Jerusalem (Gal. 4:26, Heb. 12:22, Rev. 3:12).

In the next few days, we will take a closer look at this amazing place. Our faith tank will be entirely refueled by the wonderful promises God has left for us in His Word. Get ready to take a virtual tour and direct your attention to a city where there is no need for the sun or the moon to shine on it, for the glory of God illuminates it. There will be no more death and no mourning, crying, or pain. No more visits to the doctor, no more medical bills to pay. No more decay! Are you suffering from physical pain these days? In heaven, you will never have pain. That is so thrilling! It is hard to contain the excitement that comes from imagining this.

The understanding and profoundness of the verses we are going to examine are a treasure for our souls. It is like receiving a shot that contains all the vitamins we are in desperate need of. It will change the perspective of your life forever. Furthermore, this perspective will transform your attitude toward your plans, goals, and life itself.

You will be forever in the presence of your Creator—your loving God. Everything will be as He promised: perfect.

Jesus is preparing a place for me in heaven. May this eternal perspective of life be the driving force of my attitudes, plans, and goals.

# FACE-TO-FACE

Hebrews 9:1–3, 6–15; 10:19–23

In any relationship we have in life, we go through stages and develop different levels of intimacy. Thousands of books have been written about how to deal with relationships and relationship problems. The most published and read book of all time, the Bible, tells us the story of the Creator's relationship with us, human beings. From beginning to end, from Genesis to Revelation, this story presents the levels of intimacy we used to have, lost, and regained with our loving Father.

In the Garden of Eden, God and human beings walked, talked, and spent time together face-to-face. In fact, the level of intimacy was so profound that, shockingly for us, Adam and Eve were naked and not ashamed (Gen. 2:25). Shame came after sin (Gen. 3:7). Besides being ashamed of their nakedness, they were afraid of God for the first time and hid from Him (Gen. 3:8, 10, 11). God, in His mercy, provided garments for them but banished them from the Garden of Eden (Gen. 3:21, 23). The purest and highest level of intimacy God intended to have with us was ruined because of sin.

In the Old Testament, we read that the closest people could get to God was through worship in special places that God intended for this purpose. And that usually happened only on special occasions. In the desert, the people of God had the tabernacle, and later, Solomon built the Temple. But no one could see God face-to-face (Exod. 33:18–20, Isa. 6:5), not even after fulfilling all the requirements the Law of God explained in such detail (Heb. 9, 10).

In the New Testament, the book of Hebrews masterfully explains to us how all the requirements of the Law were fulfilled—through Jesus's death and resurrection. Jesus's perfect sacrifice has allowed us to have a new level of intimacy with God. Now, we worship in spirit and truth, and God lives in us through the Holy Spirit (John 4:23–24, 1 John 3:24). Nevertheless, we cannot see God face-to-face as in the Garden of Eden.

The Bible tells us that a day is coming when all things will be restored as God promised (Acts 3:21, John 5:28–29, Rev. 21:5). We will again be able to worship God face-to-face (1 Cor. 13:12). No more fogginess, no more shadows. We will have a glorified body, and we will be able to see Him, talk to Him, and walk with Him (Phil. 3:21). There will be no need for the Temple or a special occasion to be with God. He will dwell with us (Rev. 21:3).

One day, we will see Him face-to-face! Take a moment and let that truth sink in. Rejoice!

# GOD'S GLORY IN HEAVEN

## Revelation 21:23

Do you know the sun radiates more energy in one second than all the energy humans have used since the beginning of civilization? That is a powerful thought to ponder, isn't it? In light of this, let's consider the second truth about heaven.

Revelation 21:23 says, "The city [heaven, the new Jerusalem] does not need the sun or the moon to shine on it, for the glory of God gives it light, and the Lamb [Jesus] is its lamp" (NIV). In heaven there will be no need for light; God's glory will take care of that. You may be asking, "What does that mean? What is the glory of God?"

We certainly use the word *glory* a lot, but do we really grasp the whole sense of it? In the context of the verse we have just read, glory means God's essence. It is the sum of all of God's attributes (mercy, grace, truth, goodness, justice, knowledge, power, eternity). All of them together are His glory; they represent the essence of who He is. God's glory radiates, enlightens, and spreads throughout all of heaven. It cannot be contained. It is like an explosion of beauty—all His attributes, His essence. Imagine a place where mercy, grace, goodness, justice, knowledge, power, and eternity are spread all over!

The second aspect of God's glory is that it is intrinsic to Him. What does that mean? Think about this: What makes water wet? Wetness is intrinsic to water; it is part of its essence. You see, a person's glory is not intrinsic to his or her nature; it is granted to him or her. Take any king or queen from the past to the present. Take away their crown, rope, scepter, and ring (or whatever symbolizes his or her power), and do not let this person bathe, shave, or practice personal hygiene for a month. Put that person next to any homeless person in the world, and you will not be able to tell the difference. That is how weak our "glory" is. Our glory (beauty, fame, etc.) is granted to us. It is not part of our essence. How humbling is that?

It doesn't matter what race we are, what school we attended, how much money we make or have. In the light of God's glory, our perspective of the things we value on earth changes completely. There is no snobbery, prejudice, or racism in heaven. We all have the same value before God's eyes. The price Jesus paid at the cross was the same for all of humankind.

I want you to take a minute and reflect on this today. What are you giving importance or prioritizing in your life that does not reflect the perspective of God's eternal glory?

# NO MORE NIGHT—TRUE SAFETY!

Revelation 21:10, 24–27

Studies show that when people are going through difficult times (depression, grief, stress, abuse, any type of trouble you can think of), night is the hardest part of the day. When everything gets quiet and there is no more activity, work, or errands to distract you, it is very hard. Your body relaxes, you are in bed, but your mind becomes an unstoppable force. It is like a fire alarm that just will not stop. You think, and think, and think. Your emotions awake, and rest is over.

For some people, sleep deprivation has to do with the sensation of not feeling safe. All of your fears arise like a sandstorm, and you think you cannot escape its voracity. We wish we could live in a closed-gated city with high walls and guards 24/7. Millions of dollars are spent on security every year, but we still do not feel safe physically, mentally, or emotionally.

The third truth we will focus on today is the revelation of true safety. "On no day will its gates ever be shut, for there will be no night there" (Rev. 21:25 NIV). The image of the holy city that comes down from heaven (Rev. 21:10) describes a city that never closes its gates. In ancient times, cities used to close their gates and have watchmen on the walls to guarantee security. In heaven, the gates will never be shut, for there will be no night there. True safety is guaranteed!

You may be asking, "How is that possible?" Revelation 21:27 says that "nothing impure will ever enter it, nor will anyone who does what is shameful or deceitful" (NIV). God guarantees true security because nothing and nobody that does not belong there will ever enter heaven. Oh, how I long for my true citizenship in heaven!

You may be saying, "Wow! That is very beautiful, but how do I deal with the difficulties I am facing right now?" In Romans 8:18, Paul says, "I consider that our present sufferings are not worth comparing with the glory that will be revealed in us" (NIV). That is the right perspective to have in the midst of suffering—an eternal perspective. The suffering we endure here on earth does not compare with the glory that awaits us in heaven because "we know that in all things God works for the good of those who love him" (Rom. 8:28 NIV). Take comfort in God's promises and hold onto them.

I can lay down my burdens and trust that the suffering I may endure here on earth does not compare to the glory and true safety that awaits me in heaven.

*For further study: Romans 8:18, 28*

# THE BOOK OF LIFE

### Revelation 21:27

When I was in high school, my history teacher organized a school outing to the cinema. We were all very excited about skipping another regular day at school. But once we got there, my excitement lasted about 10 minutes. I was confronted with World War II and found myself crying, not only for the rest of the film but for a couple hours after it was over.

The film was *Schindler's List*. Oskar Schindler was a German industrialist and a member of the Nazi Party. He is credited with saving the lives of 1,200 Jews during the Holocaust by employing them in his enamelware and ammunitions factories. The names of those 1,200 mortal Jewish souls were saved because they were on his list.

Can you imagine being spared from death for being on someone's list? There is another list, and it does not contain the names of those who belong to a VIP club, an exclusive university, or a certain church or denomination. It is more than a list; it is a book with the names of those who will enter heaven. It is the book of life. In Revelation 21:27, the Apostle John writes, "Nothing impure will ever enter it [heaven], nor will anyone who does what is shameful or deceitful, but only those whose names are written in the Lamb's book of life" (NIV).

The book is not called "the good works book" or "the I-am-a-nice-person book—I have never killed anybody." It is called the Lamb's book of life because the merit of being included in it only belongs to Jesus. When John the Baptist (a prophet) saw Jesus walking toward him, he said, "Look, the Lamb of God, who takes away the sin of the world!" (John 1:29 NIV). The only reason we will have total access to eternal life is because of Jesus's love for us (Rom. 5:8).

His sacrifice at the cross was made once and took away the sins of many (Heb. 9:28). You cannot write your own name in the book of the Lamb, and, your name will not be written because of your good behavior, works, or intentions (Eph. 2:8–9). We have eternal life because Jesus's blood paid the full price of our redemption from eternal death. We have been saved from eternal doom because of God's grace and love. It is a gift. You cannot earn it; you can only receive it.

I pray that you will have an eternal perspective of life so your goals, plans, and purpose will be aligned with God's eternal plans and promises.

Rejoice that your name is written in heaven!

*For further study: Hebrews 9:24–28, 12:23*

**MARCH 29**

# COMMITTING TO WISDOM

## Proverbs 1:20

Why is wisdom referred to as a woman in the book of Proverbs? Is it because women are wiser than men? Of course not! We all can be wise. It does not matter if you are a man or a woman; it is not a gender issue. The writer of Proverbs is using a literary technique. He is just using the figure of a woman to illustrate the way wisdom affects our lives.

He begins with a woman of wisdom who speaks and declares at the city gates. He says we should listen to her. Then he writes about the adulterous woman who continually sins because she does not listen to wisdom. Then he culminates in chapter 31 with the ideal woman who shows what it looks like to walk in wisdom with God.

Faith and wisdom go together. You can see that in James where it says that if you lack wisdom, you should ask God who gives generously to all without finding fault. However, when you ask, you must believe and not doubt. Let's say that faith is the sail of the boat and catches the wind of God to take you somewhere. Let's say that wisdom is the rudder of the boat that helps you go in the right direction. So faith and wisdom work together, not in contradiction, because you need both of them to get to your destination safely.

What happens when I think I am being wise and bad things still happen? Let me respond to that question with three words: hang on longer. All of us look at the short-term perspective, and we have to look at the long-term perspective. There is never going to be a time when you look back and wish you had been unwise so things would have gone better. Wisdom will always be the choice if you want to get good results. You might not see them on day one or even day 100, but you can be sure that God is going to do something.

The Apostle Paul exhorts us to not become weary in doing good, for at the proper time, we will reap a harvest if we do not give up. Sometimes we just have to wait for God to show us what He is doing, even through bad times.

Are you ready to get wisdom for every aspect of your life? Let's do it together!

*For further study: James 1:5*
*Additional references: Galatians 6:9*

# HOW DO I GET WISDOM?

Proverbs 2:6, 4:5

Do you want to be a wise person? Would you like to make wise business decisions? Would you like to make wise decisions in your family? All of us want wisdom, but what do we mean by wisdom? Wisdom is the capacity to understand in order to live skillfully. It's not a haphazard thing; it's God guiding you skillfully.

I want to parent skillfully. I want to be a husband skillfully. I want to minister in the church skillfully. I want to be a friend skillfully. Students should be skillful in the way they interact in school. That is what wisdom is. So how do we get it? Let's look in the book of Proverbs where King Solomon invites us to get wisdom and understanding and not forget God's words or turn away from them. He is inviting us to get wisdom.

There are three ways we can gain wisdom. First, we get wisdom from the Lord. That could be the whole message. You would not need anything else. We get wisdom from Him when we read the scriptures because we know there is something higher and more significant that we need to know. It's something that is not earthly but comes from the heavens. So we pray for wisdom, we read about wisdom, we ask about wisdom, we think about wisdom. And in doing so, we will grow in Christ. As we grow in Christ, we are getting to know Him more.

It is essential to spend time in the Word of God—reading it, studying it, memorizing it. The Lord gives wisdom, and from His mouth come knowledge and understanding. When Jesus was a young boy, He grew up to be filled with wisdom. Now He has become wisdom for us from God.

The first place we should go for wisdom is the Lord. James advises us to ask for wisdom because God gives generously to all. That is something we should do every single day. I try to ask the Lord for wisdom every day. I have missed some days and have made some bad decisions because I am still human, but I keep asking God for wisdom and leadership. I want Him to lead me, and I want to be a good leader in my family and in my church. So remember to put wisdom (and wise leadership) on your prayer list.

*For further study: Luke 2:52*
*Additional references: 1 Corinthians 1:30*

# GETTING WISDOM

Proverbs 11:4

The second place we get wisdom is from other people. Wise counsel is greater than today's thought. You can look at the world and get many opinions about many things. There could be five subjects and 50 views, but wise counsel is greater than any of them. You can see ideas come and go, but society never apologizes and says, "Hey we had a bad idea about 20 years ago." Instead, it just shoves in the next idea.

So wisdom comes from wise counsel. Do you have men and women in your life, people surrounding you, from whom you are able to get wise counsel? Parents, let's incorporate people into our kids' lives who are able to speak wisdom to them, people besides us to whom our kids can go in order to hear wise counsel.

When you come to a place where you do not know what to do, you should have wise people in your life. You should be able to pick up the phone and say, "Can I ask you a question?" Wise counsel is so crucial. When I started pastoring 14 years ago, I set up a wisdom team. I had five guys, and I called a different guy every week to talk about what we were doing, decisions I had to make, situations we were facing, and so forth. Because wise counsel is better than today's thought.

The third place you get wisdom is from life. You learn from your mistakes, and you learn from the mistakes of others. Here's the bad news. Often you make good decisions by first making bad decisions. Often, life will teach you lessons because no one is perfect. We feel so guilty when we fail. "Why did I do that?" "Why did I not do that?" "How did I not see that coming?" However, here is what you have to understand: God is using those things to teach you. That is why the Word of God says that gray hair is the crown of wisdom. You get gray hair by having to make difficult decisions about things that happen. Experience comes from what we have done, and wisdom comes from what we have done badly. A wise man learns by the experience of others. An ordinary man learns by his own experiences, and a fool learns from no one's experience.

We want to learn from the Lord. We want to learn from other people, even in bad stuff. Pay attention when somebody has an affair—how did it go? Learn from that. Look when somebody makes a bad decision—learn from that. Learn from others' faults. Learn from other people's failures and other people's successes. And learn from life as life teaches you.

Are there people in your life you can count on? Are you paying attention to the lessons of life?

# A DECISION TREE

Let me give you a decision tree, because wise decisions are hard to make. Where do decisions begin? Decisions start by asking this question: What is best for me? That is the lowest level of decision-making. Unfortunately, that is really where our world lives—what is best for me. People usually only care about themselves.

Here is the next question to ask: What is right? What is right or wrong? What is moral, and what is immoral? Some of us as Christians think that God is a great umpire in the sky and that all He cares about is what is right. Just do what is right, do what is right! Well, that is true, but He also cares about your heart. He loves you. He does not want you to do what is right like a robot. He wants you to do what is right because you love Him and want to obey Him. So it is not just about what is right or what is best for me.

Then we need to ask this question: What is wise? Something may be legal and not wise. For instance, you can go to Colorado and smoke pot (I am not encouraging you to do that). But it is an unwise way to live your life. So where are you on this continuum? Are you just asking, "What's best for me? What's best for me?" Are you asking "Well, what's right and what's wrong? Could you give me a rule?" Or are you asking "What's wise?"

The ultimate place for decision-making, the highest place, the best question is this: What glorifies God? Parents, if you want to be teaching your kids how to make decisions, it is not just "What is best for me?" It is not just "What is right or wrong?" It is also "What is wise and what glorifies God?" And here's the secret: if you ask "What glorifies God?" first, then all the other things will fall into the right place. What glorifies God answers all the other questions. What glorifies God is what is right because He is the King of righteousness. And what glorifies God is going to be best for you. It might not be what you want, but it will be best because He has come to give you life and give it abundantly.

By first asking, "What glorifies God?" you will be seeking His kingdom and righteousness first. And all the other things—what is wise, what is right, what is best—will be added unto you.

*For further study: Psalm 37:23*

# GLORIFY THE LORD

In Proverbs, Solomon encourages us to not abandon wisdom because she will watch over us. We must love her, and she will guard us. He also tells us to love wisdom and obey wisdom. When you say you are going to love wisdom, that shows desire. But when you say you are going to obey wisdom, that means discipline.

In 2 Chronicles 1, the Lord comes to Solomon and asks him what he wants. What would you say to God if He asked you that? Many of us would say, "I don't want to pay taxes." Young people would say, "I want to be popular." A single person might say, "I want to get married." A businessman would say, "I want to make a bunch of money." And none of those would be good enough. Solomon said, "I want to be wise." He chose wisdom. He loved and desired wisdom. Would you choose to be wise?

Then Proverbs says to obey wisdom, because being wise requires discipline, not just desire. This is bad news, but it's true. Sometimes what is wise and what your emotions say may be at odds. You may emotionally feel something, and that might not be a wise decision. The secret is that we don't just live by our feelings, and that takes discipline. We live by the Word of God, and we walk in wisdom. So when you are feeling something and want it intensely, step back and ask yourself whether it is really wise. Many of us get in trouble because we walk according to what we feel instead of doing what is wise.

Does your decision-making process begin with the desire to glorify God? Are you obedient to wisdom in your life?

*For further study: 2 Chronicles 1:7–12*

# ELEMENTS TO GAIN WISDOM

Proverbs 9:9–10

There are some qualities that will bring wisdom into our lives. Reverence is one of them. So I acknowledge God and revere God. I fear the Lord. I say, "You are higher, You are better."

Humility is something that garners wisdom; it is a requirement for wisdom. You cannot be proud and wise. Humility brings wisdom. Think about teachable-ness. We need to be teachable and willing to learn. Consider diligence; it is the precursor of wisdom because you need to be careful and persistent and work hard in order to be wise. And then there is righteousness; you need to be morally right in order to act wisely. And finally there is faith; it is always needed to receive wisdom from the Lord.

Now, let's look at the opposite of all of these to see if they will bring wisdom. What is the opposite of reverence? If you say, "I do not revere God, and I am not going to respect Him at all," that will not get you wisdom. The opposite of humility is this: "I am cocky, and I know everything there is to know." That is not going to get you wisdom. If you are not teachable, you are a know-it-all. That is not going to work. To be lazy instead of diligent is not a way to become wise. When you say, "I am going to be crooked; I don't want to be righteous," that is unwise. To be faithless instead of faithful will not gain you wisdom.

Wisdom is like an all-day pass that allows you to enjoy all the rides and the fun at an amusement park. Can you imagine? You can ride as much as you want, wherever you want, and enjoy everything for free. Wisdom is that all-day pass for any ride you are ever going to be on in your life. It is a pass for parenting. It is a pass for singlehood. It is a pass for marriage and a pass for divorce. It is a pass for joy and a pass for grief. It is a pass for a business decision. It is a pass for choosing what college to go to. It is a pass you will be able to pull out and say, "I want this pass to be my entrance into every ride of life. So I am going to love wisdom. I'm going to obey wisdom. I'm going to be disciplined by it."

Get that pass for your life!

*For further study: Proverbs 11:2*
*Additional references: Proverbs 2:2, 9; James 1:5–7*

# THE COST OF WISDOM

Proverbs 4:7–9

For God, wisdom is supreme. He says you must get wisdom. Although it will cost all you have, get wisdom—get understanding. Cherish it, and it will exalt you. Embrace it, and it will honor you.

So you could say this: "I want to be as wise as Solomon." Maybe you will not achieve it, but you can ask the Lord for wisdom as Solomon did. Wisdom for every day, for the things you cannot handle. However, you need to know that wisdom will cost you something. And it will also bless you.

When Proverbs says to get wisdom, the author is using a word that means a business transaction, like when you pay for something you want. Wisdom will cost you. When you make a wise decision, you may pay a price for that. But the price you pay for wisdom will always be a trade up. The cost for sin is always a trade down; you will always lose when you choose to sin.

When you make a wise decision, it may cost you friends, it may cost you entertainment, or it may cost you time. When you get married, it will cost you to walk in wisdom. To be wise in parenting, you will not be able to do everything you want. You will not be able to do all the things you used to do when you did not have children because much of your time will be spent with them. So wisdom has a cost, and when you pay that price, you will find it is a trade up, not a trade down.

If you want to live your life honoring the Lord, seek wisdom. Remember, the Bible says that if anyone is without wisdom, they should make their request to God, who gives freely to all, and it will be given to them.

Finally, let me tell you that the wisest thing you could do is to trust Jesus Christ as your Savior. That decision will help you with all the other decisions you need to make in your life. He is the wisdom we all need.

# HARD TIMES IN GOD'S WILL

## Job 1:21

God's people don't get passed over when it comes to hardship. But hard times are the part of His plan we'd almost always choose to omit if the choice were ours to make.

The hard times might be easier to understand if we could always trace our pain back to our own or others' sinful choices. But often we have no part in the struggles that can and do befall us. Sometimes, the uproar of life is a natural result of choosing sin or selfishness, but just as often it is not. So how do we handle pain or heartbreak in a way that keeps us moving forward? Even if no 1-2-3 foolproof plan exists, can we at least hope in a higher way? I think we can.

In most miscarriages, nothing the parents did caused their baby's heart to stop beating. Right now, I am writing with my daughter, Valerie, in my lap. If we had not suffered a miscarriage, Valerie may not have been here. Obviously, conception is God's business. He is the giver of life. But in my and my wife's little microcosm of planning, the child now in heaven would have completed our family. We would not have tried again. Now this little blonde-haired girl sits on my lap with a fuzzy bear on her shirt and her hands on my keyboard—and I can't imagine life without her.

Her presence speaks to a truth we all need to grip for dear life and savor well. That truth is that God is working things out during those very parts of His will we do not want. He is crafting, shaping, and planning at a deeper level than we can see. He is looking on a line that stretches from eternity past to eternity future. We are looking through a straw at a tiny black dot on that line of life.

Note: In 2 Samuel 12:22–23, David said he would go to his child upon his death.

# STAY PUT—HE IS IN CONTROL

## Exodus 13:17

When Moses and the children of Israel stood at the edge of the Red Sea with the Egyptian army closing in, they made an almost unbelievable tactical choice: they stayed put. They just stood in place. Why? Because God was crafting a story that a bridge across the water could not tell. The Israelites would have to walk through the sea to tell God's great story of deliverance. Surely there were other routes, other plans of escape. Certainly, battles awaited them on shorter roads, too—but God wanted to take them the long way in a story that required an unprecedented miracle—the parting of the Red Sea.

"Our whole perspective changes," wrote Robert J. Morgan in his book *Red Sea Rules*, "when, finding ourselves in a hard place, we realize the Lord has either placed us there or allowed us to be there, perhaps for reasons presently only known to Himself."* His goal for the hemmed-in Israelites was not the dot of the moment Moses must have seen through his straw-like perspective. But it would be a timeless story of God's greatness that would be told and retold throughout history.

When you and I begin to look at the whole of God's plan instead of the tiny part—the small dot—immediately in front of us, trust opens up. We can trust our great God to see us through. He has been faithful to those who have come before us, and He will be faithful to us. The psalmist wrote, "Your faithfulness continues through all generations; you established the earth, and it endures" (Ps. 119:90 NIV).

Martyrs, widows, orphans, the impoverished, the forgotten, the persecuted, and the wounded have all found Christ faithful. With such a rich history, God is not going to ruin His reputation by hanging us out to dry. He doesn't just act faithfully; He *is* faithful. That is who he is, and it is all He can be.

"The one who calls you is faithful," Paul wrote to the Thessalonian church, "and he will do it" (1 Thess. 5:24 NIV). And to the church at Corinth, he wrote, "God is faithful, who has called you into fellowship with his Son, Jesus Christ our Lord" (1 Cor. 1:9 NIV).

*For further study: Psalm 119:90*
*Additional references: 1 Thessalonians 5:24, 1 Corinthians 1:9*

# TRUST DEEPLY

In the most difficult times, we can trust deeply that the parts of His will we don't want are the very things He will use to accomplish His eternal plan. He is faithful not to wound us at random; He is faithful to save us forever. Throughout our lives, we will surely experience pain and heartache, but they are not meant to thwart the mission of the Lord. They are meant to further it!

So keep standing. Keep trusting. Echo Peter's words as your declaration of truth in troubled times: "Lord, to whom shall we go? You have the words of eternal life. We have come to believe and to know that you are the Holy One of God" (John 6:68–69 NIV).

As Jesus drew closer to the cross and to His death, His disciples became more and more frightened and disoriented. They were hoping for something more secure. It's not surprising that some of His followers began to fall away. But Peter had it right. He understood that the best thing for them at the time was to press in even closer to Jesus than before. There was no better place for them to be.

Those times when we want to move just to keep from feeling trapped are the very times we need to be still and embrace His will. Don't leave— cleave! The more closely you walk with Christ in the uncomfortable of the unknown, the greater clarity of life you will experience. Are you confused? Hurt? Disoriented? Cling to Christ and His Word like never before.

Getting mad doesn't help, either. Anger is a secondary emotion. It doesn't achieve the will of God. In tough times, our anger and resentment might be simmering. We imagine that by drifting away or giving God the cold shoulder we can teach Him a thing or two. We look for an ally whom we think will love us better than God. Some see alcohol as a ready friend offering quick comfort. Others believe a church switch where "people really understand me" will relieve their pain.

Coping mechanisms and strategies for handling hurts and disappointments abound. But regardless of the action we choose, we're focusing on that tiny dot on the line of eternity. Maybe that realization is what prompted Peter to declare to Jesus, "To whom shall we go?" (John 6:68 NIV).

*For further study: Matthew 26:47–56*
*Additional references: James 1:20*

# CLOSER TO CHRIST

———— John 13:22–25 ————

The trials of life are meant to push us closer to Christ. The night Jesus was betrayed, the Apostle John had his head on his Master's chest. When Jesus announced that one of His disciples would betray Him, wouldn't John's reflexive response have been to quickly lift his head and draw back in shock? In my imagination, I see Jesus placing His hand gently on John's head to draw him near again.

Near Jesus is exactly where I need to be when troubling words or wounding circumstances come. That kind of intimacy can feel a little uncomfortable for some, especially men, but the physical image points to a deeper spiritual reality. When one of my kids wants to crawl onto my lap and press in close after a skinned knee or a scary dream, I can't help but be reminded of the tender love God has for His children. I am glad to be the one they run to. Think about it. There is a short list of folks who have an open invitation to place their head on your shoulder or chest. My list includes only my wife and two kids. No one else gets those kind of hugs because there is a depth of relationship that precedes such intimate contact.

When I am hurting, when I'm experiencing that part of God's will I do not want, He is the One I run to. The truth is, God has "rigged" this life to require Jesus Christ at its center. Faced with the part of God's will I do not want, He is the One I draw close to, trusting that He is crafting a plan—even when I don't understand it.

Through that difficult morning of loss and heartbreak through miscarriage, Kelly and I learned immeasurable lessons in trust. We chose to pray and believe that God was in control. We returned home from the hospital and cranked up some of our favorite praise songs—and we cried. We focused our attention on God and pressed into Him, hurting but knowing it was Him we needed most. We didn't like His will and did not want it, but He didn't ask us about that. He does not have to. He is the sovereign One. My job is to cling to Him in trust.

*For further study: Colossians 1:17*
*Additional references: Habakkuk 3:17–19*

# MORE THAN WE CAN HANDLE

## 1 Corinthians 10:13

Have you ever heard someone say, "God will never give you more than you can handle"? I'm guessing they're paraphrasing 1 Corinthians 10:13, which says God will not let you be tempted beyond what you can bear. But trouble and temptation are two different things. There will never be an instance when we are forced into sin with no way out.

Sin is always a choice, not the inevitable result of crushing temptation. But somehow that verse has been twisted to mean that we won't experience more trouble than we can bear. In fact, nothing could be further from the truth. God will often allow more than we can handle, but He'll never allow more than He can handle. My whole life is more than I can handle—that is why I need Christ!

I needed God to stay the course while I was in school. I needed Him when I was a single man who longed for a spouse. I needed Him when I needed a job. Now, with two kids, a marriage, friends, and a great church, I definitely have more than I can handle. I need God when my wife and I struggle to be two who became one and when we're arguing over which one of us we became. Only in His strength and wisdom can I know what is best for my family and whether or not my desires are selfish or pure. In marriage, it is possible to win the fight but lose ground, a lesson most of us have learned the hard way.

The bottom line is this: Life is hard. I need God every minute of every day because I am often faced with more than I can handle. Paul must have understood that when he wrote these words to the Corinthians:

*We don't want you to be unaware, brothers and sisters, of our affliction that took place in Asia. We were completely overwhelmed—beyond our strength—so that we even despaired of life itself. Indeed, we felt that we had received the sentence of death, so that we would not trust in ourselves but in God who raises the dead. He has delivered us from such a terrible death, and he will deliver us. We have put our hope in him that he will deliver us again.*

—2 Corinthians 1:8–10

*For further study: 2 Corinthians 1:8–10*

# SHINE

1 Peter 3:15

God will undoubtedly allow more than we can handle. Great pressure results in great reliance. Settle it, and rely on Him. The I-can't-do-this sweat of life is where we learn to trust Him most deeply. "Trials and troubles are dumbbells and treadmills for the soul," wrote Robert Morgan. "They develop strength and stamina."*

God has used the pressures of miscarriage and cancer to draw me closer to Him. They both looked as uncrossable to me as the Red Sea must have looked to Moses. But such challenges cause us to rely on God more deeply than we might otherwise. Sadly, if we could handle these things without Him, many of us would try.

When was the last time you prayed for the strength to take a single step? Today, someone in a hospital or a physical therapy clinic is asking God for that much strength. That single step to them looks impossible. It is more than they can bear. They need their God so they can shuffle just a few feet forward. And when they do, the resulting celebration will be even louder than when someone else finishes a marathon!

Those parts of His will that we do not want cause the volume of our faith to get turned up. C. S. Lewis wrote, "God whispers to us in our pleasures...but shouts in our pain: it is His megaphone to rouse a deaf world."† Not only do we hear God more clearly, but our attentiveness to Him can also cause the ears of others to incline toward words of hope.

When my wife endured a miscarriage and also the loss of her mom, she sought God like never before. You should see her Bible—ink-stained, pages curled, writing in every margin, torn cover. But the wear of her Bible also shows where the protection of her heart came from. Imagine a woman losing a child, caring for her cancer-ridden mother, and then speaking at her mother's funeral. It was more than she could bear. But she trusted God to bear it for her, and He did. She leaned into Him and not away, and once again He proved Himself faithful.

When God's will is not what you want, you have your chance to shine. So stay put and trust as you lean into Jesus. He will surely see you through.

# LIGHTS OUT

Bam! Zap! Pow! and all of the other Batmanesque cartoon words you can think of. They described the moment when the power went out on July 13, 1977. New York City came to a screeching halt. Subways stopped, Times Square no longer glowed with neon, the evening Mets game against the Giants was cancelled, and Wall Street closed its doors.

The largest city in the United States was in the dark, literally. The newspaper headlines the next day simply read "Powerless." That one word said it all. Even with all the state-of-the art technology and buildings reaching into the clouds, the lack of power resulted in thousands of people walking home from a shortened and purposeless workday.

New York City residents still had all of the appliances they had before the blackout, but they were useless. No power, no progress; just sit and wait. Then it happened again. Ironically, on July 13, 2019, on the 42nd anniversary of the 1977 blackout, New York City again went dark—it was powerless once more.

New York needed a power source, and so do we. If our power source is Christ, then every Christ-follower and every leader can rest assured that God's will has God's power behind it. God's power may be manifested in quiet, steady ways or in dramatic, you-have-to-see-it-to-believe-it miracles. Moses experienced both, but as he carried out his burning-bush assignment, he came to understand that God's will done in God's way has God's power. Always.

Moses made it his business to know the God of God's will. He followed his God from the back side of nowhere to the courts of Pharaoh the same way you and I are called to follow Him: one step at a time. And God did, indeed, demonstrate His power in spectacular ways when Moses came before Pharaoh. Why were those demonstrations needed? Because when Moses and Aaron asked Pharaoh for the release of the Israelites, Pharaoh resisted, just as God predicted he would.

It was that persistent hardness of heart that prompted God's mighty demonstrations of His power through a series of miraculous signs and terrible plagues. Some might argue that they were merely coincidental or caused by nature, but at least four factors mark the difference between a miraculous sign and a natural phenomenon: timing, location, purpose, and prediction. Those factors can determine what is a miracle and what is not. And those factors can also help us personally determine God's will. We can learn a lot from a quick overview of how we know the plagues were miraculous.

# TIMING AND PURPOSE

## Exodus 9

Let's look at those four factors again that mark the difference between a miraculous sign and a natural phenomenon: timing, location, purpose, and prediction. Those factors also help us personally determine God's will. Let's look at two of them.

*Timing:* When Moses declared the plague of flies, he told Pharaoh, "This sign will occur tomorrow" (Exod. 8:23 NIV), and it did. When he said Egypt would be devastated by hail "at this time tomorrow" (Exod. 9:18 NIV), hail came down at that very hour. This precise and accurate timing indicated not a natural occurrence but a divinely planned one.

We've heard it over and over and discussed it in detail already: God's timing is perfect. His miraculous timing rained down manna and quail from heaven to feed Moses and his sojourners. God in His perfect timing, through His magnificent power, accomplishes His eternal will in His time.

*Purpose:* The acts of God's power have a higher purpose that is missing from mere natural phenomena. When Jesus walked on water, He did not do so to prove He could float. He walked on water to demonstrate the power of God—that God could do anything He purposed, regardless of the laws of matter. When He rose from the dead, it wasn't a carnival trick but a permanent defeat of death and sin. God's miracles have a purpose—they are not just a freak show phenomenon. The *why* of the plagues and all miracles is to declare the greatness of God.

We must possess a personal understanding of this. The miracle of God's guidance in our lives is not simply to bless us. We can easily slip into thinking that God's guidance is solely for our own pleasure. But when God is at work opening and closing doors, our lives shine with His greatness for others to see. We aren't the recipients of the miracle as much as we are the vehicles for it. Like a boomerang, it comes from Him through us and then back to Him.

Miracles are a combination of a Father lovingly blessing His children and showing His power to others. We are thankful for the blessing but realize the purpose is higher than our perspectives. In fact, He said so Himself in the message He gave Moses to deliver to Pharaoh. He said the purpose was "so you may know that there is no one like me in all the earth" (Exod. 9:14 NIV).

*For further study: Exodus 8:23*
*Additional references: Matthew 14:25–27, 28:5–7*

# PREDICTION AND LOCATION

## Exodus 10

Moses predicted all the plagues. He clearly said the timing, the location, and the purpose of each miracle—before they happened. God uses the prophetic declaration of the future to establish credibility. More than 300 prophecies were stated about Jesus before He ever came. His birth, life, death, and second coming are all documented in the Old Testament hundreds or thousands of years before the manger.

Imagine if the news announced it would soon rain and that out of a dozen people on a certain sidewalk, rain would fall on only three of them. And then the news anchor would tell us which three they would be. If these things did happen as predicted, you would be less likely to attribute them to chance. Instead, you would likely think the news anchor possessed some supernatural power, and you would probably pay close attention to what was said next. The timing, location, purpose, and prediction of the 10 plagues show it was God's power at work through Moses.

The plagues were specifically predicted in location, not randomly experienced. They affected the Egyptians, not the Jews. The plague of darkness covered all Egypt for three days, but all the Israelites had light where they lived. With the exactness of a GPS coordinate, the missiles of each plague struck on a dime.

These things can give us assurance on our burning-bush journey. God is in the know, even when we don't have a clue. Right now, God is orchestrating opportunities for you to discover Him more deeply. Tomorrow and the day after that may present you with a choice to be selfless or selfish. A decision is headed your way that your last fortune cookie cannot adequately prepare you for. That decision is not a surprise to God. His timing, location, purpose, and knowledge are acting in unison to lead you forward another step. His will always comes with His power.

Moses trusted God's ability to predict the future. But will we take what we've seen and trust Him for our future? Corrie ten Boom wisely said, "Never be afraid to trust an unknown future to a known God."* The God we seek daily knows daily what is ahead. Understanding what makes a miracle miraculous helps us identify God's work in our lives. Personalizing these truths is the key to changing our day's headline from "Powerless" to "Powerful."

*For further study: Isaiah 53*

# WHERE IT ALL STARTS

## 1 John 1:1-2

1 John was written by the Apostle John around 90 AD. There are two big thoughts throughout the book: (1) God is light, and (2) God is love. Along those lines, the book takes a firm stance against Gnosticism, which was a common false teaching at the time. And yet John is very loving in the way he speaks to these believers.

John writes about light and darkness, love of God or love for the world, the Spirit of Christ or the spirit of the antichrist, righteousness or sin, and truth or falsehood. It seems John wants us to make a change in our hearts. In today's society, we need to learn how to combine these things—light and love—so we can stand strong against things that are not true and, at the same time, be loving.

John starts with these words: "What was from the beginning" (1 John 1:1). Have you heard that phrase before? The beginning? We find it in the first verse of the Bible, Genesis 1:1, as well as in the first verse of the Gospel of John, John 1:1.

The second thing I want you to notice is how John uses the words *heard*, *seen*, and *touch*. He wants us to live a life that is real. Now think about that for just a second. He speaks of what he had seen. What did he see? He saw Jesus Christ on the cross. He walked with Him all those days in His time of ministry on earth. He saw Him.

He also heard Jesus preach the Sermon on the Mount. He heard Him declare the blind man healed. He walked around with Him and broke bread with Him. He heard from Jesus. He touched Jesus. Who was the disciple that laid his head on Jesus's breast? It was John. So he could say something like this: "I heard His heartbeat. I've touched Him. I've seen Him for who He is. This is real. Jesus Christ is real."

And the real life of Jesus is what gives you real life. You're not just playing games. There is a real eternity. A real life. A real Savior. A real God who wants to affect your heart as a real person. Talk to Him. If you will, ask Him to touch your heart today so you can say with John, "I've seen Him, I've heard Him, I've been touched by Him; Jesus Christ is real."

*For further study: Genesis 1:1*
*Additional references: John 1:1, 13:21-26*

# WAS JESUS A GHOST?

1 John 1:1-2

When John wrote his first letter, one of his main goals was to counter the effects of a false teaching known as Gnosticism. It said you had to have a special knowledge in order to connect with spiritual things. *Gnostic* actually means knowledge, a special knowledge. Gnosticism had this main tenant: Physical things are bad; spiritual things are good. Therefore, if everything physical is bad and everything spiritual is good, then Jesus Christ must not have been a real man walking the face of the earth.

But Jesus had flesh. He was real. You could touch Him and feel Him. So they said no, He can't be the Christ if He was a physical man. We don't believe that. For them, Jesus had to be a spirit, but we have to be clear about this. The physical death of Jesus, the physical life of Jesus, the physical resurrection of Jesus—they are all pivotal to our faith. The central aspect of Christianity is not just the teaching of the principles of Jesus. It is that Jesus Christ was a real man who walked on earth, who lived a life we couldn't live, who died for our sins and came back to life again.

It says in Hebrews that He was tempted in all things, but yet He was without sin, so He could pay for our sins. He really went to the cross. Real nails went into His wrists and feet. The crown of thorns really hurt and drew blood. The spear went through His side. He really died. He really resurrected from the grave. That's why He said to Thomas, "Put your finger here and look at my hands. Reach out your hand and put it into my side" (John 20:27).

Why is this physical life of Jesus central to Christianity? Because you are a real person, too. You are going to walk this life and will die one day. You and I need a physical Savior who lived a life we couldn't live and died a death we should have died so we could know we will rise again and spend eternity in heaven with God. So John, from the very beginning of his letter, said he saw it, he heard it, he touched it. He said don't tell me He wasn't alive. I was there.

We all need a real encounter with Jesus. He is real. He is not a ghost flying around somewhere. Today can be the day you ask Him to come into your life.

*For further study: Hebrews 2:18*
*Additional references: Hebrews 4:15, 1 Timothy 2:5,*
*Zechariah 12:10, John 20:27*

# A REAL ENCOUNTER WITH JESUS

John 20:29

The Apostle John wrote a moving letter inspired by the Spirit of God. One of the first things he wanted his readers to connect with was the truth that Jesus is real. He wanted us to know that Jesus really lived, died, and rose so we can have a real encounter with Him.

John's journey with Jesus was physical, but our journey is through faith. It would seem perhaps that John's journey was easier, but Jesus said to John and the other disciples that those who have not seen and yet still believe are blessed and full of joy. Jesus told them it was to their advantage that He would go away so He could send the Holy Spirit to dwell in their hearts. If you have trusted Christ as your Savior, the Holy Spirit lives inside of you.

Going to church is great, but have you had a real encounter with Jesus? Do you really pray? Do you talk to Him about the ordinary things of life? Perhaps you are saying this: "Jesus, I'm nervous. God, I love you. God, I'm hurting. God, my marriage seems difficult. Lord, I'm so tempted by peer pressure. Jesus, I need you so badly right now."

Are you living a real life with Jesus? Do you really look into God's Word? When we read it, sometimes we don't understand everything. It's a difficult book at times. But it is of ultimate importance for you to be in it if you want to have a real encounter with Jesus. That's because Jesus Himself is the Word of God. It is sharper than any double-edged sword. It's able to pierce your soul and your spirit. It is alive and active. It doesn't return void. And it always accomplishes what it desires.

Are you having real fellowship with Jesus? Are you really trusting Him? When you get to heaven, nobody's going to ask you what denomination you were, what pastor you had, or what church you went to. The real question is going to be, "Did you have a real encounter with Jesus?"

Maybe you did many years ago, but it has gotten stale. Or maybe you have just been to church so much or you are so busy that you're not having real fellowship with Jesus anymore. Maybe you need to have an encounter with Him once again.

If you haven't trusted Christ as your Savior or if you want to renew your walk with Him, say, "Lord, I want You to forgive my sins. I want a real encounter with You."

*For further study: 1 Peter 1:8*
*Additional references: John 1:1*

# I WAS THERE

Have you ever seen or used virtual reality goggles with your cell phone? With the right app, you can ride a roller coaster or go to Hawaii through virtual reality. When you look up, it looks up. When you look to the right, it looks to the right. When you look to the left, it looks to the left. Down, it looks down.

It's really fun to watch when people put these on because they're like, "Let me touch something. Wow! This is incredible. This is amazing." The technology is just going to go further, and it is going to look more real. But even though they are called virtual reality goggles, they are not really reality.

Sometimes, you put on your spiritual virtual reality religious goggles, and you only look right when your pastor or your reading plan talks about looking right. And you only look left when you're told to look left, and you only look up when the right song comes on, and you only look down when you're trying to get through something. If you can relate to this, you may be living in virtual religious reality.

What God really wants is for you to have a real relationship with Jesus so you can say, "I've seen Him by faith. I've heard His voice through His Word and through His people. I've been touched by Him in the depths of who I am. And I have a heart that can say, 'I was there.'"

If you just do a few nice religious things, go to a certain church, and behave as you are supposed to, it's virtual reality. It's not reality. When you're walking around with virtual reality goggles, you don't see anybody else. When you move through reality, you begin to see everybody else in a totally different way, and you are able to share the good news you are a witness to.

Only when you can say, like John, "I was there" can you be a reliable witness to others. Nobody can tell you that it didn't happen—because you saw it, you heard it, and you were touched and transformed by it. And that's what we all want to say about our relationship with Jesus Christ. Salvation through Christ alone is reality. And then walking in the steps of Jesus Christ as He lives His life through you, touching and loving others—that's even more reality.

*For further study: Proverbs 14:25*
*Additional references: Galatians 6:7*

# PRAY. CARE. SHARE.

## 1 John 1:3

We humans long to share, talk with people, be known, and know others. We don't want an isolated life with nothing to share. We want somebody to call us and share with us their good and bad news.

If you have a real experience with Jesus, the most natural reaction is to want to talk to others about the One you love. The older generations shared Christ more freely. We have become more silent today because our culture has become more aggressive, so much so that when we talk to our friends, we combine Jesus with other philosophies or religions because we're afraid of what people will think or we fear losing our social status.

It is still biblical to share your faith and tell somebody about Jesus, to say "I saw it and heard it. Jesus walked on this earth, died, and rose. He is the way, the truth, and the life." The world is hurting like never before. People are so stressed out, burdened, and afraid. And we have Jesus Christ, the Prince of Peace. We can share Him with somebody.

A real experience can't be kept in. You know Jesus is real, so you want to share Him with your friends in a way that's loving and kind without being obnoxious. How can we make a difference in somebody's life?

*Pray.* This is the first thing you can do for somebody. It can be for a person you work with, someone you live near in your neighborhood, a friend, or a family member. Begin to pray for that person. Say something like this: "God, I'm praying for my friend and I'm asking that You just use me. Would You do something in my friend's life? Would You speak to my friend, who needs a real relationship with You?"

*Care.* What can you do to care for someone? How can you encourage them? Bring them cookies. Write them a note. Bring them some balloons. Be with them in the hospital. Earn the right to be heard.

*Share.* Just tell people the wonderful news about Jesus Christ.

What name do you have in mind? God has placed you in that neighborhood, in that job, on that ball team, in that band for a purpose—to be able to reach out and love people. They need someone like you who has had a real encounter with Jesus and who will love them well and share with them the Prince of Peace.

# FELLOWSHIP WITH ONE ANOTHER

Acts 2:1

When we have a real relationship with Jesus, we are going to have a real relationship with others. We will want to make a difference everywhere we go, not only with people we know.

There are people who need a word of encouragement or just a prayer. You will find them in simple interactions when you go shopping, sit in a restaurant, watch your kids practice sports, spend time in a waiting room, or even wait in line. You will see what the people around you are going through and seize the opportunity to chat with them or even ask for their permission to pray over them.

God wants to use you. Keep it practical, simple, and natural. Don't be obnoxious about it, and don't take precious time the person could be using to make another sale or one more customer happy.

Maybe they are not going to pray and receive Christ at that moment. Or they may not make a big deal out of it at all. But you surely can pray, care, and share with strangers, new acquaintances, and people all around you. You will make a difference in that little moment right there.

When we share our testimony, people can have fellowship with us. What's fellowship? *Fellowship* is a Greek word that means to share something or to connect. That's why you have a fellowship hall in church where you can share a meal or share life with one another. We long for connection. So we have fellowship with one another and fellowship with God.

We also need fellowship in our families. We need to plan what we want our fellowship at home to look like. If we don't stop and plan right now, before we know it, the year will be over and we will have spent no time with our kids.

Other people will raise your children, and there will be no connection with you as a family. Don't convey the idea that life is what happens outside your home. Get those kids around your table and spend time together as a family. Don't miss those years. Think about it now. Be involved in a ton of stuff. Don't let your dreams wither or die. Make sure you make time for fellowship with each other.

*For further study: Acts 2:41–47*
*Additional references: Acts 4:32, 1 Corinthians 1:9*

# FELLOWSHIP WITH THE FATHER

## 1 John 1:3–4

Today may be a lazy day, or it may be a busy day. No matter which direction your day may take you, the most important part of your waking hours is to have fellowship with the Father through Jesus Christ. That means to take time to share and connect with Him, trusting Him each moment of your day.

Do you have a real relationship with God? Do you read your Bible on days other than Sunday? You don't have to understand every word, but just by getting in it intentionally you will grow into having a real Bible study life, a real prayer life, a real faith life. And that will enable you to have a real family life, a real single life, a real married life.

That real fellowship comes from real fellowship with God the Father through Jesus Christ. Fellowship means to connect and have in common. What do you have in common with God? Absolutely nothing. And that's why He sent Jesus Christ—a real person who walked on earth, lived temptations, but never sinned—so He could die on a cross and rise from His grave so you and I as men, women, teenagers, and kids could have real relationships with God with whom we have nothing in common. But Jesus Christ, our mediator, brings it all together.

What will be the result of this? Our joy will be complete.

The whole thing is about our joy. If you don't live a real life for Jesus and never share Jesus, fellowship with others, or fellowship with God, you are never going to experience real, complete joy. It is that kind of joy that luxuries, possessions, real estate, or fulfilling dreams can't bring—at least not permanently. The Holy Spirit is telling you and me that we have purpose and a relationship with God the Father through Jesus.

If you don't know for sure that you know Christ and you want to come to know Him, pray this with me: "Jesus, I believe that You are the Savior. I ask You to forgive me of my sins. I believe You died on the cross and rose for me. I place my faith in You alone for salvation. I want a real encounter with You. Come into my heart and save my soul."

*For further study: Psalm 119:25–32*

# GOD IS LIGHT

### 1 John 1:5

One of the themes found throughout scripture is that God is light. Jesus said in the New Testament, "I am the light of the world" (John 8:12). In Matthew, at the transfiguration, Jesus's face shone bright like the noonday sun. And again, when Christ talked to John in Revelation, His face shone like the sun.

In the Bible, we see a contrast between light and darkness. Darkness is evil, and light is good. We can see that contrast in the way we talk about some things. If we see a movie and it is a dark one, it means there's likely some evil in it. But if it is a light movie, that means it has some goodness in it. God is light, and His primary attribute is holiness. God's holiness is linked to His light. He's bright. He's pure. He's without any blemish, without any darkness, without any smudge. His character is impeccable and perfect. He has never thought about doing anything wrong. His glory and His light are intrinsic to who He is.

That's different from us. Our glory is granted. It is not intrinsic. The more we know about who God is, the more we will understand about who we are and how to journey on this path.

That doesn't mean you are going to have a perfect life. You will have to go through trials, judgment, discipline, and the consequences of sin. But whenever you think that God is doing something mean or evil, just dismiss it, because you know that everything God does is from a heart of light.

*For further study: John 8:12*
*Additional references: Matthew 17:1–2, Revelation 1:16*

# LET'S WALK IN THE LIGHT

**1 John 1:7**

God is light, and there is no darkness in Him. Walking apart from God is walking in darkness—walking in sin. Walking in darkness brings self-deception and lies.

In many ways, our society walks in self-deception and lies. But before we blame society, we have to begin with our hearts. Why is society like it is? Because it is a reflection of the human heart. Of course, society influences the human heart. We can't say that is not the case. But what is the problem with the world? The problem with the world is me. That is the problem with the world. We are the ones who influence society. This is not to say we are the worst of the worst. That wouldn't be completely true, either. Hopefully, we are trying to influence for good. But society and our hearts mirror one another in many ways.

That leads us to think that it is possible that we live in self-deception and lies. But how did we get there? First, we have to realize this: As human beings, we have trouble admitting that we're wrong. If you don't believe that, just get married. There are many situations in marriage when one or both spouses know they are wrong, but then they try to figure out some way to make it seem like they are right and have always been. And that stirs up a little bit of a battle. That is a problem. We end up in self-deception and lies because we have trouble admitting we are wrong. Why? Because pride is in us. We are prideful people. The root of sin is pride. Pride produces sin.

Humility doesn't produce sin. Humility doesn't produce wickedness. Pride does. When we say, "I'm going to have it my way, in my fashion, in the way I want it, and nobody's going to tell me I'm wrong," we end up prideful. That's how Satan fell from heaven, because of his pride—wanting to be above God. It is impossible to simultaneously choose sin and humility. When we are humble before God, it is the antithesis of choosing sin.

We have to desire to walk in His light. The question is, do we desire to be walking in His light?

*For further study: John 1:6–8*
*Additional references: Proverbs 8:13, 11:2, 16:18*

# THE DARK SIDE

## 1 John 1:8

In the first chapter of the Apostle John's first letter, we see a fight between light and darkness. John says we are sinful and that we don't want to admit we are wrong. Sadly, the pride behind this condition is the path to deceiving ourselves. We end up creating a new reality so we can put together a world in which our sin is not wrong but normal.

Birds of a feather flock together—that's how we say it. Thieves like to hang out with thieves, drunkards like to hang out with drunkards, drug folks like to hang out with drug folks, cursers like to hang out with cursers, and this and that like to hang out with whatever they are. We encircle ourselves with those who are like us. What started as "I know this is wrong, I know this is bad" ends up as "Everybody does it."

This delusion ends up being a sinful and prideful place where we have created a new reality where sin is no longer sin. It's where we call darkness light and light darkness. It's where we plant a garden of our lives, pick weeds, and call them vegetables. We say no, this isn't wrong. Why is it not wrong? Because, we say, everybody does it. And we get around folks who do what we want to do, and we end up with a new alternate reality. We have self-deception, deceiving ourselves. Do you know what we call it? Here's what we call it: justification.

"I'm not materialistic. I just like nice stuff. Everybody likes nice stuff."

"I'm not selfish, I just like my way. I just like how I do things. I think that's the best way to do it."

Everybody likes their way. So what happens when we then create a self-deceptive place where we justify our sin? We slowly but surely begin to walk in the shadows, then in the dark until finally we circle ourselves with a group who will normalize our sin and make it no longer sin. Why? Because everybody does it. And that's how we define sin. So what's right or what's wrong in society, in our own hearts? The Bible tells us that when we walk in darkness, we walk in self-deception—and lies.

But our only hope is to walk in the light.

*For further study: 1 John 1:10*
*Additional references: Isaiah 5:20–23*

# DON'T GIVE UP!

## 1 John 1:6

I think some parents have given up. They say, "Well, boys will be boys, and girls will be girls. That's just what they do."

Hear me loud and clear. You don't have to look at pornography. You don't have to have sex before marriage. You don't have to party and get drunk. You don't have to cheat or lie. You don't have to cuss. You don't have to experiment with drugs. You can be a godly man or woman and walk with God.

Some of us justify all these things with an everybody-does-it attitude. No. Not everybody. That is a normalization of something destructive. In fact, if everybody is doing it, that might be the reason you shouldn't do it. Sin hinders our fellowship with God, and it hinders our fellowship with others. It messes with your relationship with our son, our daughter, or our parents because sin always rips apart relationships. No one in the history of the world has said, "My family is awesome because my dad had an affair. My family is incredible because my mom is an alcoholic. The disobedience of our kids has done more for our unity than anything." No. Sin always separates. It is the real joy-killer.

Yet we create this dysfunctional world, and we justify our actions. Some folks living in self-deception have separated personal holiness (walking with God in the light) from social justice (changing the world and making it better). Those two things have to connect.

The younger generation is more into opposing human trafficking than any generation before. And yet this generation is also more into pornography than any other generation. We think these two don't connect, but they do—pornography is funding human trafficking. Rejecting personal holiness while working for social justice is like rallying against a corrupt politician and then donating to his or her campaign.

We change the world when we realize that personal holiness and social justice are connected. The abolitionists who helped end slavery were believers in Jesus and realized that God had placed equal, intrinsic value in every person. Hospitals were started by believers who wanted to help and minister to people in their greatest needs. Believers started orphanages because they realized kids are precious to God.

Do not be self-deceived. God is calling every one of us to walk in the light. Every teenager can be a godly teenager and walk with God. Parents, the high calling that we have is to help them do that.

*For further study: Leviticus 20:7*

# WALKING IN THE LIGHT

1 John 1:7

Through Jesus Christ, God forgives our sins and washes us clean. He is the only way we get to God. That's why God sent Jesus to earth so He could be the substitute for you and for me.

When we walk in the light, our families and our friendships come together; our marriage and our dating are better. But you and I are pulled into the shadows over and over. What's the answer? To stand and say, "I'm going to walk in the light and trust Jesus who has cleansed me of sin."

Like the cross, there is a vertical relationship with God that makes our horizontal relationships better. So when we walk in the light, we are better spouses, better friends, better employees, better neighbors. And that's because we aren't walking in the shadows, trying to justify and deceive ourselves.

When Hurricane Harvey hit Houston in 2017, a lady filled out a request for help on the church's website. One of our staff members called her and found out she was a single mom in need of diapers and pajamas. Then the lady added, "Our car was flooded, too. If y'all got a car, that would be awesome." So the people in the church started working on how they could help her. Staff Member One hung up the phone and said to Staff Member Two, "We need to help this single mom get some diapers and clothes. And you're not going to believe this. She even said, 'If you have a car, that would be awesome.'" And Staff Member Two said, "Five minutes ago, somebody called to donate a car to a single mom!"

Staff Member One called back the single mom and broke the news to her. She began to cry. An hour later, the single mom called back and said, "Did I hear you right? Did you say a car?" And Staff Member One had the opportunity to lead this single mom to Jesus Christ.

When you walk in the light, you love others differently. When you walk in the light, you hear God differently. When you walk in the light, you get to be part of those kinds of stories. Is there any hero in the darkness stories? No. The light stories are where God is doing great things.

# HOW DO WE WALK IN THE LIGHT?

## Matthew 6:22

We all want to walk in the light. The question is, how do we do it? You can begin by asking yourself three things. First, what goes into your eyes? Jesus said that the eye is the lamp of the body and that if your eye is good, your whole body will be full of light. But He also said that if your eye is bad, your whole body will be full of darkness. So what are you looking at? What's going into your eyes? If it's good, your whole body will be filled with light.

Second, who do you run around with? Who are you hanging out with? Paul asks us not to deceive ourselves; bad company corrupts good morals. I know we think this verse is for somebody else. We say, "But I'm the designated driver. I just hang out with all the partiers. They do all that, but I don't do it." Just wait. If you keep going that direction too far, too long, you're going to end up like them.

Bad company corrupts good morals because we create a circle of an alternate reality where our sin is normalized. We make ourselves believe everybody is doing it, and we deceive ourselves. This is not to say that you shouldn't hang out with unbelievers. We as believers ought to hang out with people who do bad stuff. But we shouldn't be part of it. Do you see the difference? Choose your Friday night friends carefully. And while you are at it, there is no shame in hanging out a week or two with your family.

Third, what do you love the most? Don't love the world or the things that belong to the world. Because if anyone loves the world, the love of the Father is not in him or her. What do we love? We love Jesus. We love His Word. We love God. If we love the light, we are going to walk in the light, and it is going to be attractive for us to walk in the light. Walking in the darkness brings self-deception and lies. Walking in the light brings fellowship with others and God. It should be really easy to decide which one we want.

*For further study: 1 Corinthians 15:33*
*Additional references: 1 John 2:15*

# JESUS, OUR RESCUER

## 1 John 1:6

God is faithful. He is not fickle. He is truth and doesn't lie. But if we justify ourselves, we are calling God a liar. We might say, "Everybody else is saying it's okay. God, You say it is not. They're not the liars. You're the liar, God."

When we realize we have done that and walked in darkness, we need to repent and say, "Lord, I confess to You my sin. I've done wrong, and I am sorry."

C. S. Lewis wrote:

> Fallen man is not simply an imperfect creature who needs improvement: he is a rebel who must lay down his arms. Laying down your arms, surrendering, saying you are sorry, realising that you have been on the wrong track and getting ready to start life over again from the ground floor—that is the only way out of our "hole." This process of surrender—this movement full speed astern—is what Christians call repentance.*

People think they just need to be enlightened because they aren't that bad. That is different from realizing there is wickedness in their heart, and something has to die in them. Jesus died on the cross to pay for that. So I'm going to place my faith and my trust in His death on my behalf, and that's what's going to kill this in me—because now the Holy Spirit lives inside of me. He is faithful, He is righteous. When we confess our sins, He forgives us and washes us clean so now we can walk in the light.

We all need Jesus's forgiveness. If we say we haven't sinned, we have made Him a liar. Repentance brings self-understanding, fellowship with God, and fellowship with others. There is not a person who is without sin. If you think, "Well, that's me; I haven't sinned," you're sinning right then in your pride. I'm not perfect. You're not perfect. We all dabble in the dark at times. But when we confess it, Jesus Christ is able to give us light.

Spiritually, we are a house on fire, surrounded by floodwaters; we are on an island in need of rescue from this heart of darkness. Jesus is the only One who, in the spiritual realm, can rescue you and me. It is only Jesus, and He is the One you have to call on. He's the only One. So don't live self-deceived. Don't live in lies. Don't walk in darkness. Walk in the light of Christ.

*For further study: 1 John 1:9–10*

# WHAT IS CONFESSION?

## 1 John 1:9–10

What comes to your mind when you think about confession? Is it someone famous who got caught for something and then said in the news, "I did this"? If you are a Catholic, you may think it means to go to a booth and tell a priest about your sin. But is that what confession is?

Confession means to admit or acknowledge sin or wrongdoing; it also means to agree with someone or something. When we admit wrongdoing or sin, we pour out our hearts to God and to those we have wronged. When we recite a creed, we show agreement with a certain theology. Confession and theology go well together because when we confess our sins, we agree with God that He is right and that we have been wrong.

Doesn't it feel good when you confess? It takes some courage. But self-respect is better than another person's respect. Sometimes, when we need to confess, we think, "What are people going to think?" But it is better to just say, "Let me confess this. I'm sorry I wronged you."

The first time I felt this I was eight years old. My aunt and uncle loved to play tennis. When I visited them, we played a lot. I had a cheap racquet, but both of theirs were good. One day I borrowed my aunt's racquet. I started hitting balls against the wall. After a while, I began hitting rocks. Then I picked up a piece of glass and hit it. When I looked down at the racquet, I saw that the glass had cut the string. I panicked, put it back in the case, set it next to my aunt, and then walked away.

The next day, my aunt returned home and said she had broken a string on her racquet while she was playing. She took the racquet to be restrung. When we went to pick it up, she said, "They told me the string was cut. I did not break it playing." My face went red, but I didn't say a word.

She was gracious with me. But every time I thought about her, saw the racquet, or played tennis, I admitted to myself that I should tell her. For three years, I carried that. Finally, I told her the whole story. She said, "That's okay, Gregg. You could've just told me right then. I love you."

Secrets make you sick. When we confess our sins, He is faithful and righteous to forgive us.

*For further study: Psalm 32:3*

# A STATEMENT OF CHANGE

## 1 John 1:9–10

Confession is not just guilt release. It is also a statement of change. Think of all the scriptures that say something like this: "I want You, Lord, to make me different."

In Acts, the Bible says there was a group of people involved in sorcery who came and confessed their practices because they intended to change. They even burned their old magic books. When Paul says to confess with your mouth that Jesus is Lord, it is a statement of change. We are saying, "I am going to follow Christ, not my own ways."

When confession happens, it is intended to break the cycle of sin. When we confess our sins to the Lord and to somebody else and when we apologize, we feel guilt relief because we have gotten things right. But it is also a statement of change because now we have been placed under accountability for our actions.

Often, we would prefer to confess only to God and not tell anybody else. That option gives us a little bit of an out. Nobody knows except God that we were wrong. But when we confess our wrongs to the person we have wronged, we place ourselves in accountability for change. Andy Stanley says in his book *Enemies of the Heart*, "Remember the purpose of confession is not to relieve your conscience. It's to effect change and reconciliation."*

Who do we confess to? The two people we have hurt. We have hurt God because we have sinned against Him, so we confess to the Lord. Then we also confess to the person we have hurt. "I am sorry I did that. That hurt you. I apologize." Now we have been placed into accountability. So we say, "Lord, give me the strength to not do that again. I know it is wrong, so I am going to strive not to do it again."

Confession is not just for us to feel better. It is to restore a relationship. Keep your lists short. You don't want to be on your deathbed apologizing to every kid, cousin, grandchild, and person coming to visit you. If you say something that could be taken as an offense, instead of staying up all night worrying about it, just say, "I didn't mean that to sound like that." Make sure things are right between you, God, and other folks.

*For further study: Acts 19:18*
*Additional references: Romans 10:9–10*

# THREE CONFESSIONS

## Romans 10:9–10

Let's talk today about one more notch of confession. There is a confession to God that is unto salvation, a confession to continue the relationship with Him, and a confession to other people.

How does a person become a Christian? You confess with your mouth that you aren't in charge of your life anymore, and now Jesus Christ is in charge. Have you declared that to the Lord in a prayer like this?

Lord, I know I have sinned. I know I have done things wrong. Jesus, I know you are the Savior. It is not going to church, doing the right thing, or my willpower that is going to do it. I need a Savior. I need Your blood to wash me clean. I want to confess to You that I'm a sinner. I've done wrong. I have wronged You, God. In faith, I place my life in Your hands. I trust You to be my Savior. Wash me clean of my sins. God, save me. I want my heart to be changed.

Your only hope for forgiveness of sins is the resurrection and the cross. If you believe in your heart that God raised Jesus from the dead and confess with your mouth that Jesus is Lord, then you will be saved.

We also confess to God and to our fellow humans in order to restore and keep existing relationships so they can continue.

Let me give you an example. You wake up one morning a little grumpy. You get to the office and decide to let everybody else have it. What you have to do is go back in your own office and say, "Lord, forgive me that I have been grumpy. Help me to not be grumpy." Then, you walk out of your office and say to everyone, "I'm sorry I was grumpy."

What happened here is that you began throwing things out horizontally because you didn't first get it straight vertically. There has to be times in your life when you say, "Lord, right now I'm feeling angry (or greedy, lustful, jealous), and I want to confess it to You before I take it out on anybody else. I want to ask You to give me the strength not to make a mess."

There is one confession unto salvation when you become a Christian, one to continue that relationship, and one to make things right with others. Confession makes all the difference.

*For further study: Matthew 5:23–24*
*Additional references: Matthew 6:2, Luke 11:4*

# CONFESSIONS

James 5:16

When we don't confess our sins to the Lord and to one another, physical things can happen in our lives and we can get sick. People have heart attacks, high blood pressure, and ulcers because of unconfessed sins, undisclosed faults, or chronic guilt. But when we get it out to the Lord and get it out to others, things change.

How does God respond to our confession? With anger or wrath? No. God's response to our confession is faithful and righteous forgiveness. He will cleanse us of our sins!

How does our trash make it to the street? In some households we pull out the trash bag from underneath the sink, and before we tie it up, we make sure there is nothing else that needs to go in it. Then we tie it, put it outside the garage, and wait for one of the kids to pick it up and take it to the garbage can. Hopefully, a squirrel won't rip it open, find something to eat, and leave the rest all over the place. When it finally makes it into the can, the garbage company comes and picks it up. So it went from under the sink to the kitchen floor, from the floor to the garage, from the garage to the garbage can, and finally from the garbage can to the truck.

How does your horizontal confession work? Does it go something like this? "You know, I'm sorry if you felt like I said that in a way that was inappropriate." You just moved it to the kitchen floor. "Maybe I hurt your feelings, but I didn't mean...." You just moved it to the garage. "God, sure you're right on that, but everybody does it." You have moved it outside, but you haven't taken care of your sin yet. You just moved it a little bit further. Then it blows up and is a mess that it didn't need to be. Finally, the can gets dumped and emptied.

On the vertical side, let me tell you what Jesus does. He will take the trash away from underneath the sink of your heart straight to the dump at the bottom of the cross—instantaneously. Jesus is faithful and righteous to cleanse us from all our sin. Our forgiveness is based on His faithfulness and righteousness. Often our response to each other is retribution, but God's response to us is forgiveness and cleansing of all sin.

*For further study: 1 John 1:9*
*Additional references: Psalm 51:1-4, 10*

# CLEANSED AND MADE CLEAN

## 1 John 1:9

The Bible says that when we confess our sins, God forgives us and washes us clean. Do you know about King David? He said that while expressing anguish in prayer: "Completely wash away my guilt and cleanse me from my sin" (Ps. 51:2). John the Baptist in the Jordan River, while the people confessed their sins, said, "I baptize you with water for repentance" (Matt. 3:11). With a towel draped around his waist, Jesus said to Peter, "If I don't wash you, you have no part with me" (John 13:8).

When we confess our sins to God, who is holy and blameless, we agree with Him. We admit we are wrong, and He washes us clean. Even our consciences are washed clean. We are forgiven, made spotless and beyond reproach. We are holy in His sight. We are His children, and Jesus cleanses us of all unrighteousness.

So when you come to confess, you come to a safe place. When you come to confess, you're trying to restore relationships with other folks. But when you keep it in, it just burns you up inside. Secrets make you sick. But if you get it out, you can say, "Lord, take care of all my filthiness and sin. Cleanse me of all unrighteousness."

Juicing is one of the popular things to do nowadays. You take a bunch of fruits and vegetables and juice them. In one cup of juice, you're able to drink a huge amount of produce you wouldn't have been able to eat otherwise. But there are these things called juice cleanses that claim to clean your whole system.

Which do you think is harder to clean? Your insides, your stomach, your intestines, or your soul? Jesus is faithful to cleanse you of all unrighteousness; He will cleanse the soul. Does it mean we will be perfect? By no means. But He cleanses our souls in such a way that we can then say, "Lord, I'm just grumpy (or angry, jealous, lustful, greedy, selfish, anxious, nervous) today, and I want to get this right with You. I just want to confess it to You. I want to keep a short list, God, between me and You and me and other folks. I don't want to just be stuffing it." He cleanses us completely.

When you and I confess what we already know is wrong, He's faithful and righteous to cleanse our souls. Can you think of a better deal?

*For further study: Psalm 51:2*
*Additional references: Matthew 3:11, John 13:8, Mark 1:4–5,*
*Hebrews 9:14, James 5:16*

# WHO'S RIGHT—GOD OR PEOPLE?

## 1 John 1:10

If we say there is nothing we need to go to God with or nothing to confess, we make God a liar, and His Word is not in us.

The big question of life is this: Who is right—God or people? I believe that God is right. Therefore, instead of saying, "No, I haven't sinned. That wasn't that bad," I know in my heart when I am wrong. I go to Him and pray, "Lord, I am sorry. I don't want anything to hinder our relationship."

Parents, have you ever apologized to your kids? You should. There is no way you have ever been a perfect parent. What does that do when you apologize? It teaches them that even their parents don't always get it perfect. Do you apologize to your wife, your husband, your boyfriend, your girlfriend, or somebody you work with? Are there faults you want to hide or sins you have tried to make time wash away but know in your heart they are still there?

Some years ago, I went through a weird season. For six months, numerous people confessed to me that they had been talking badly about me behind my back. It troubled me, and I wondered what was causing it. Part of that just comes because leaders and speakers become like characters. It is easy to throw rocks at people on TV or on the Internet and say things we wouldn't say in person.

To every one of them I said, "I forgive you. It is okay." They received the forgiveness, and I received the confession. Sometimes, we will be on the receiving end. We won't always be the person confessing but perhaps the person someone confesses to. Our response, then, must be as gracious as God's response to us: "It is okay. I love you. It is fine." Then we will be able to make the connection that makes the difference.

If we confess our sins to God, He is faithful and righteous to cleanse us from all unrighteousness. But we have to confess our sins to one another as well when we have hurt other people. What happens is that this confession restores the relationship, and then we receive the cleansing that comes from Jesus.

Do you hide your sins and act like they don't exist? It is eating you up. You have the opportunity to confess them to the Lord. Let's get it out and make it right!

*For further study: Colossians 2:14*

# DIFFERENCE-MAKERS: PART 1

### Psalm 148:12-13

*Great Work: How to Make a Difference People Love* by David Sturt is a 2013 *New York Times* bestseller. It describes studies conducted by the O. C. Tanner Institute with Forbes Insights. The research found a fundamental mind shift in people who get groundbreaking results and achieve greatness. They have a specific mindset. Instead of seeing themselves as workers with an assignment to crank out, they see themselves as people who can make a difference and have an impact.

Are you one of those people? Do you have the potential to achieve greatness? In your vocation, do you see yourself as a worker with something to crank out? At home, do you see yourself as someone who is just checking items off a list? The lists are endless—dishes, laundry, cleaning, cooking, errands. How do you see yourself? Are you someone who completes a task, or are you someone on a mission? There's a huge difference!

What does it take to be a difference-maker? We want to be people who make an impact for Jesus. In our homes, in our schools, in our churches, in our neighborhoods, in our nation, and in our world, we need to be difference-makers.

We do not need to just elect or vote for people who can make a difference. We cannot just hire difference-makers or ask someone else to do it. We need to *be* difference-makers. God has a call and a plan for every believer. At every age and stage, and if God is sustaining you, then He has a difference for you to make. If you are older, you cannot dismiss His call by saying, "Been there, done that." If you are young and do not know what to do, God still wants you to serve Him. Everyone in Christ is called to do the good works He prepared for them to do, to bring glory to Him by making a difference in this world.

Here is a sample prayer:

*I was made for more than watching things happen. I have a history-changing, difference-making, life-giving, Spirit-empowered legacy to leave. Jesus, I ask You to work deeply in me and clearly through me as I pray, give, and go in Your love. I am a difference-maker. In Your name, amen!*

*For further study: 1 Timothy 4:12*
*Additional references: Ephesians 2:10*

# DIFFERENCE-MAKERS: PART 2

## Matthew 9:1–8

After Jesus traveled to Capernaum by boat, some men brought one of their friends to Him. Their friend was paralyzed and lying on a stretcher. What is the first thing Jesus said to him? "Have courage," He said. "Have courage, son, your sins are forgiven" (Matt. 9:2). Some versions of the Bible say "take heart" or "be of good cheer." What the Greek is getting at is that Jesus wanted the man to be courageous, to be cheerful, to be bold, to stand up and go for it. Difference-makers live with courage.

Christians often read this story and characterize it as a healing moment. But there is more to the story than that. Notice that Jesus starts with the heart. Before Jesus tells the paralyzed man to get up and pick up his mat, He says, "Have courage, son, your sins are forgiven." This has nothing to do with walking; it has nothing to do with being paralyzed.

The first thing Jesus does is declare to the man that his sins are forgiven. He uses the present tense. He is not suggesting the man's sins were forgiven in the past or that his sins will be forgiven in some distant future when he gets to heaven. No, the man's sins are forgiven right then and there when Jesus speaks. By forgiving the man's sins, Jesus declared that He was God in the flesh. This was a statement of deity. And so the man received Christ's forgiveness. Sin is always the problem, and a right relationship with God is always the answer.

We tend to think the wrong way about this. We tell ourselves something like this: I've got to go to church more. I've got to do more to be holy, and I need to sin less. If I get all my little ducks in a row, I'll be a good Christian. But being a Christian is not about what you do but about what your relationship is with God.

Jesus began with the heart. To be a difference-maker, start with your heart. Have the courage to allow God to work in you to begin your spiritual transformation.

Here's a sample prayer:

*God, make a difference in me. Give me the courage to allow You to work deeply in my heart. Forgive my sins through Jesus. Renew me through Your Holy Spirit.*

*For further study: 2 Corinthians 5:17*
*Additional references: Psalm 51:10–12*

# DIFFERENCE-MAKERS: PART 3

The Gospel of Mark also tells the story of the paralyzed man. It says his friends had to lower him through the roof to get him close to Jesus. Sometimes, we can help others get close to Jesus, as those men did. The paralyzed man's friends lowered him, and Jesus said to the man, "Have courage" (Matt. 9:2).

Difference-makers live with courage. We live in a society where there is a lot to fear. A week or so ago, I took my kids to see a movie. As we went out the door, my wife said, "Have fun at the movie. Be safe." The moment my kids and I sat down in the movie theater, I asked them, "Where are the exits? Who is around? What is going on?" Being aware of your surroundings is smart. We live in a dangerous place and time. In today's society, we need great courage.

Crime and strife are in the news all the time. But what if there were no sin? There would be no crime. Trouble and disease would disappear. Sin rips us apart, but God brings us together. Jesus forgave the paralyzed man's sins and told him to have courage. Difference-makers are forgiven sinners who have the courage to change as God works in their hearts and minds.

A triangle is a symbol used to represent the Trinity: God the Father, Jesus the Son, and the Holy Spirit. A triangle is also delta, the fourth letter of the Greek alphabet. In mathematics, a triangle stands for change. To help us change, God uses the Bible. He speaks to us through His Word. He speaks to us through His Spirit, and He speaks to us through His people—generally in that order.

Often, we ask His people for advice before we consult the Bible. We ask our friends, "What do you think?" When we hear the answer we like, we go to the Bible to look for a verse to justify what our friends said. That is not the way to rightly relate to God. Start with the Word. Ask the Lord to confirm His Word with the Holy Spirit. And then ask Him to confirm His Word and Spirit with the wise counsel of His people.

Here is a sample prayer:

*God, grant me the courage to walk according to Your Word, with Your Spirit, and with Your people.*

*For further study: Mark 2:1–12*
*Additional references: 1 Chronicles 22:13, Psalm 31:24*

# DIFFERENCE-MAKERS: PART 4

## Matthew 9:1-7

Imagine the paralyzed man on his mat. He was probably used to it. His friends were used to seeing him on it and helping him get around. Maybe the paralyzed man was even comfortable. But Jesus said to him, "Get up, take your stretcher, and go home" (Matt. 9:6).

Now think about the fear the man felt as he stood up for the first time. Would his legs give out? Would he fall flat on his face? Was this a joke? Would he be tricked? Would he be embarrassed? The man had to have the courage to get up and take up his mat.

All of us get comfortable with things that we know are not best for us. It happens to everyone, Christians and non-Christians alike. God says, "Get up!" Maybe I respond, "Hey, I like my mat. It's comfortable." God's Spirit prompts me to get up a little earlier, to have some quiet time, and I say, "No, I like my sleep." And God says, "Get up! Do something different." And I say, "No." We like the mat, even though we know it is not what is best for us.

Change is hard, but difference-makers know they have to change. They know they must have courage. They know they must take action. It is not easy. I try to eat right and exercise, but sometimes I rebel. I put a bunch of processed cheese and good old queso on my tortilla chips. There I am, shoving it into my arteries. There are times when I don't want to do what is right. I want to do what is wrong. I like my mat, and that's where I want to stay.

It isn't always about food. God speaks to us for our own good. You know what your mat is—it's that comfortable sin. Jesus tells us, like He told the paralyzed man, "Get up, take your stretcher, and go home." The man had the courage to obey. Do we? Are we living in faith, or are we living in fear? Are we getting up and walking with God, or are we comfortable on the mat? Do not stay in the comfortableness of sin. Take action. Get up.

Here is a sample prayer:

*Lord, give me the courage to change so You can make a difference through me. Help me put my sins and rebellion aside.*

*For further study: John 2:5*
*Additional references: Romans 6:11–13*

# DIFFERENCE-MAKERS: PART 5

### Matthew 9:7–8

In Matthew 9, Jesus forgave and healed a paralyzed man. The crowd saw that man get up, take up his mat, and go home, and they were awestruck. The Bible tells us that they glorified God, amazed at the authority He had given to Jesus, the Son of God.

By forgiving the man's sins, Jesus declared Himself to be God. By healing the man, Jesus confirmed that He was the Messiah. When the crowd saw what Jesus had done, they celebrated the Savior. They gave glory to God and were awed by Jesus.

The crowd was not applauding the paralyzed man's steps. Scripture does not say that the people cheered as he danced or that he ran a marathon and everybody thought he was awesome. They didn't select him to be on their soccer team because he would be the best runner and kicker. The paralyzed man walked, and the people glorified God.

For the man's part, he got up and walked with great courage. Difference-makers aren't concerned with their success; they are concerned with doing what Jesus asks them to do. That's what the paralyzed man did. If we are difference-makers who are courageous in faith, we need to let God have all the credit, and we need to glorify Him.

Difference-makers want to shine with their Savior. Jesus is not a route to fame or riches or success. Jesus wants to shine through you. You cannot work for your salvation, but you do have to step forward in faith by God's grace to follow His leading.

We are all streaked and stained with our own desires and need for recognition, and we all want pats on the back. Sometimes, we want some credit, but we need to let God have all the credit and be glorified. If we lack courage, if we refuse to get up, if we want the credit that properly belongs to God, we're not going to make a difference for eternity. Difference-makers have the courage to live for God, not for themselves.

Here is a sample prayer:

*God, help me know my own heart. Reveal the sins that hold me back, and help me to live for You. Help me shine for my Savior.*

*For further study: Luke 9:23–24*
*Additional references: Matthew 5:16*

# DIFFERENCE-MAKERS: PART 6

---

### Matthew 5:14–16

---

In Kenya, there is a place called the Maasai Mara. It's a national reserve, a grassland area where there are no billboards, no fences, no power lines, and very few people. Instead, there are lions, elephants, zebras, giraffes, cheetahs, baboons, and many other creatures. It is a very beautiful place. The reserve borders the Serengeti National Park in Tanzania.

A difference-maker went on safari there. He discovered that his guide, Thomas, was not a Christian, so he led him to Jesus. Thomas realized he had a call for his life. He began preaching under a tree and led half his tribe to Christ. Now, every Sunday, 200 people show up to the church that an American congregation helped him build.

A mission trip was organized to support this work of God. Pastor Thomas received speakers, an amplifier and sound system, a screen, a projector, and even a motorcycle. Now he goes out to all the surrounding villages with a pile of equipment on his motorcycle and shows films that teach others about Jesus. Pastor Thomas is making a difference.

A school was built. Now, more than 300 children are being taught to read and write. Then a ministry team came to dig a well to give the people clean water. Each day, 1,000 people go to that well. Excess water goes to a pool where cows can come and drink. None of it is wasted. People bring their buckets and fill them to get clean water—and they hear about Jesus, the living water.

That all happened because one man on safari decided he was going to make a difference and shared the gospel with his guide. God can use you and me to make a difference far beyond what we could expect or imagine. As we allow Jesus to give us courage, letting Him change our hearts and minds so we live for the glory of God, we can make a difference.

Here's a sample prayer:

*God, give me courage. Help me take up my mat and walk so others might see and give glory to You. I have a history-changing, difference-making, life-giving, Spirit-empowered legacy to leave. Jesus, help me be a difference-maker in Your name.*

*For further study: Matthew 28:18–20*
*Additional references: John 4:13–14*

---

# DIFFERENCE-MAKERS: PART 7

## Matthew 9:9–10

No one likes tax collectors. No one says, "The IRS is my best friend" or invites tax collectors over for dinner and asks them to peruse their 1040s. In our day and age, we know tax collectors have a job to do, and we respect that, but it is not desirable.

In Jesus's time, the Roman Empire would conquer an ethnic group or people and from that group choose individuals to collect taxes. It was such a heinous job that it was literally considered punishment. Tax collectors would not only collect money from their own people, but they would also take a little on the side for themselves.

Jesus called a tax collector—Matthew—to follow Him. Matthew had been very far away from God, but Jesus was willing to go to his house, eat dinner with him, and be associated with him.

While Jesus was reclining at Matthew's table, many tax collectors and sinners came as guests to eat with Jesus and His disciples. Sitting at the table is a moment that says, "You're part of the group." Even in our culture today, those folks who eat with us are different from those we say hello to when walking down the street. The people we invite into our homes receive a higher level of hospitality than those we meet at a coffee shop or at the mall.

Jesus and His disciples are in Matthew's home, dining in great diversity. They are in a sinner's home, speaking about the Savior's heaven. Difference-makers dine in diversity and speak with clarity. So what does it mean to be difference-makers? You and I are called to dine in diversity. We are to be with people who are not the greatest believers in Christ. No one is outside the pursuit of Jesus Christ; no one is outside God's desire to be present with them, to dine with them, to love them.

Jesus Christ is pursuing you and me in absolute love. He wants to sit with us, dine with us, and converse with us.

*Jesus, please work in me as I seek to learn how to be a difference-maker in Your name.*

*For further study: Matthew 5:46–47*

# DIFFERENCE-MAKERS: PART 8

## Matthew 9:9–13

Difference-makers dine in diversity while speaking with clarity. There are two parts to this statement. It is amazing to dine in diversity. But it is also important to speak with clarity so we can step out and make a difference in a great way.

Jesus and His disciples were dining at Matthew's house. Notice the diversity of Jesus's dining partners. The disciples may have been a bit nervous, but they dined with Matthew and the other tax collectors and sinners. Then Jesus did something extraordinary. He spoke clearly. He did not condemn or condone those around Him.

Jesus came not to condemn but to save. You and I sometimes dine in diversity without condemning, but we do condone. We act like everyone's chosen lifestyles are all great and wonderful: "Hey, come on to the table! We all make mistakes. It's okay. It is just great that you are a tax collector. Of course, ripping people off is just part of your job."

But Jesus didn't do that. He kept a wonderful balance. The Pharisees, however, thought that by sitting at the table, Jesus and His disciples were turning a blind eye to sin. And they questioned Him.

How did Jesus respond to the Pharisees, these keepers of the law? He declared truth to them. He spoke clearly. He said He did not come to seek the righteous—as if the Pharisees were righteous—but sinners. Difference-makers speak with clarity. They declare truth.

All of us need to realize that God loves us, no matter where we are or what we have done. Jesus Christ loves you. Jesus loved the disciples; He loved sinners, the Pharisees, and even Matthew the tax collector.

Matthew went on to have a tremendous, earth-shaking ministry. He was a tax collector who was changed because Jesus spoke with clarity about the powerful topics of love and righteousness.

*Jesus, help me not to condemn or condone but, instead, speak the truth in clarity, with love and righteousness.*

*For further study: Ephesians 4:25*

# DIFFERENCE-MAKERS: PART 9

## Matthew 9:9–10

You are in Matthew's house. The dinner table is right here. Where will you sit? Which group are you in? Are you sitting with the disciples, in Jesus's group? Are you in the group of sinners and tax collectors? Are you outside, one of the Pharisees? Are you walking with God, ministering with Him and His followers, or are you a ministry for them?

Which group is Jesus's inner circle? It isn't the sinners and tax collectors. It's not the Pharisees. It is the disciples. Jesus walked in full obedience to His Father. His inner circle shared His desire to walk in God's will. If you are young in life or in belief, pay attention: Your inner circle should be people who share your same heart for Jesus. Choose your friends very carefully. Who you hang out with on Friday nights will affect how you live out the rest of your life.

Difference-makers dine with diversity but speak with clarity. They get mixed up. They tell themselves that Jesus ate with the tax collectors and sinners, so we can do the same. But it is important to have an inner circle of friends who can challenge and encourage you to pursue God's heart in those situations.

A cloudy heart brings a cloudy mind; a clear heart brings a clear mind. Do your friends enable you to minister, or do they confuse you to the point that you become just like them and don't even know what clarity is anymore? Many who dine with diversity can fail to speak with clarity.

Others are like the Pharisees. They can speak with clarity but never dine in diversity because they are judgmental. They don't want to be around "those people." The longer you walk with God, the harder it can be to dine with diversity because you have made a lot of Christian friends.

Christianity is when you put the two together—when you dine in diversity and also speak with clarity. So eat lunch with everyone, hang out with people all the time, but stay close to Jesus. If you are dining with diversity, are you still able to speak with clarity? If you're speaking with clarity, are you still dining with diversity?

*Jesus, help me dine with diversity, speak with clarity, and be someone who shares Your heart.*

*For further study: 1 Corinthians 15:33*

# DIFFERENCE-MAKERS: PART 10

---

### Matthew 9:9–13

---

Difference-makers care what God thinks. They care more about what God thinks than what people think.

The Pharisees who were watching Jesus thought He was doing the wrong thing. They pulled the disciples aside to question them, but Jesus heard them. He told the Pharisees that those who are well do not need a doctor. Only the sick need a doctor. Jesus did not care what the Pharisees thought about Him, that they did not like to see Him dining with tax collectors and sinners. Jesus cared more about doing God's will than about looking holy and righteous in front of the Pharisees.

It can be hard to tell others that we don't care what they think. And that is appropriate to a certain level. But in fact, we do care what people think. If we don't care, then guess what? News flash: Nobody likes you. They see you as impolite and just not nice. So there is a balance. We care about what other people think, we are polite, but we care more about what God thinks.

The commandments are in the right order: "Love the Lord your God with all your heart, with all your soul, and with all your mind," and then "Love your neighbor as yourself" (Matt. 22:37, 39). Don't get them reversed. Keep the mindset of a difference-maker—not caring what the Pharisees think, caring more about what God thinks, and then caring enough to love and care for others.

Does caring for sinners mean that we blow our witness? Does it mean that we start dealing drugs to try to reach drug dealers? No. Difference-makers care about what God thinks. They share His heart for sinners. They dine in diversity while speaking with clarity.

Remember what Jesus did. He reached out to a tax collector in such a way that Matthew became a disciple. Jesus was clear. He wasn't condemning or condoning. Jesus was secure in His identity and purpose. He knew, and declared, that He had come to seek and save the lost.

*God, help me prioritize Your desires over my need to be liked by others. Help me keep the mindset of a difference-maker.*

*For further study: Mark 12:30–31*

# DIFFERENCE-MAKERS: PART 11

## Matthew 9:14–17

John's disciples came to Jesus, asking why He and His disciples did not fast. Jesus used the imagery of a wedding to answer them. The groom was Jesus, and the bride was the church. While the groom and His disciples and followers were together, they would feast together. The disciples rejoiced while Jesus was with them. Then, the ascension came, and Jesus was taken from them (Acts 2). Then they fasted. Jesus is not with us physically; He is in our hearts. So now, the church fasts. For the period Jesus is gone, however long it may be, we long for Him.

For the Pharisees, fasting was a badge. It said, "Look at me. Look how spiritual I am. See how I pray and fast. Look at my downcast face." But Jesus taught that when you fast, you should wash your face, look like you have taken a bath, and look happy. Fasting is a discipline to help you attain spiritual depth. It is a cry, not a badge. It is a prayer: "Let the ache in my belly be my ache for You, Jesus. I want to ache for You."

Don't be like the Pharisees. They had long faces so people would ask them what was wrong. And they would say, "I'm fasting for God." A Pharisee is like Eeyore in *Winnie the Pooh*, who moped around waiting for someone to ask what was wrong. That's what the Pharisees did when they fasted.

We Christians sometimes act like Eeyore or the Pharisees. We need to be honest about our emotions and not seek attention for doing what God says. Christians are Jesus's greatest testimony; and Christians can be His greatest hindrance. When we walk around with our spirituality as some kind of badge, it is because we do not have spiritual depth in our lives. We are wearing our spirituality on our sleeves because we do not have it deep in our hearts. We haven't been on our knees, we haven't been studying the Bible, we haven't been worshipping, and we haven't been to church.

Difference-makers go deep with God. To have a wide ministry of dining in diversity while speaking with great clarity, you need to go deep with God.

*Lord, I long for You. Deepen my walk with You.*

*For further study: Matthew 6:16–18*

# DIFFERENCE-MAKERS: PART 12

———————— Ephesians 3:14–19 ————————

In his book *When a Nation Forgets God*, Pastor Erwin W. Lutzer wrote:

I believe that the spiritual climate of America will never be changed unless we have....ordinary people living authentically for Christ in their vocations, among their neighbors, and positions of influence. We cannot look to a man [leader] or even a movement as much as to the common person who is committed to Christ and living for Him.*

I love the thought that it is ordinary people, not just leaders like a Billy Graham or Christian music artist, who are the difference-makers. You do not have a public ministry that is really good and true if you do not have some private depth. In my own life, my prayerfulness on my knees has a greater effect than any message I preach or any witty things I say. To be difference-makers, we must have a wideness but also a private depth. We must be in deep relationship with the Lord in order to be effective for Him. Difference-makers impact widely because they live deeply.

In his book *Orthodoxy*, G. K. Chesterton wrote, "It is always simple to fall; there are an infinity of angles at which one falls, only one at which one stands."† You can fall backward, forward, or sideways, but there's only one position where you can remain standing. The disciples stood only with Jesus. Our strength, our gas in the engine, is not the wideness of our ministry but the depth of our life with God.

Do you see what difference-makers do? They dine with diversity but stand in love and great clarity. You don't have to condone. You don't have to condemn. But you do have to be clear about Jesus, especially in an ambiguous, crazy society.

God did not put you in your workplace so you could just make some money. He put you there so you could make a difference. You will likely spend more time at the office than anywhere else, so don't waste your time there. Wherever God has placed you, make a difference. And remember, difference-makers impact widely because they live deeply. Go deep in your relationship with God.

*Jesus, even though I am an ordinary person, help me live authentically for You.*

*For further study: Psalm 25:4–5*

———————— **MAY 16** ————————

# DIFFERENCE-MAKERS: PART 13

## John 15:5

Reporting for *On the Road*, a segment on CBS Evening News, Steve Hartman shared the story of a difference-maker here in the United States. Jaden Hayes lost his father when he was four; his mother died in her sleep two years later. Jaden was heartbroken, but the orphan decided he wanted to make sad people smile. He asked his guardian to buy toys so he could give them away to others, to cheer them up.

What would you do if a child gave you a rubber ducky or a dinosaur? You would probably do what the people in downtown Savannah, Georgia, did. They smiled. And some may have given Jaden a hug.

This orphan decided he wanted to make a difference in someone's life. Instead of focusing on his misery, he chose to make it his ministry. That little six-year-old boy decided he was going to make a difference, and he stepped out and did it.

As Christians, we aim for smiles of the soul, not just smiles on the face. That is what is so great about being a believer in Christ: We get to make a difference by putting a smile on someone's soul. And we get to put a smile on God's face.

A church member who is in the oil business shared with me about missionaries in the Middle East. She wrote:

> They leave their home countries and their families behind because they are dedicated to sharing the love of Jesus in closed countries and in some of the world's most remote areas. The difference-makers I've met are insightful, hard-working, humble, and incredibly courageous people with a passion for the lost. I've watched them persevere under tremendous pressures as they live like Christ in the toughest of circumstances.*

Difference-makers reach out. They are about their personal Savior, not about their personal successes. They want others to know the difference Jesus can make in a person's life.

*Jesus, help me be a difference-maker in Your name.*

*For further study: Colossians 1:10*

# KNOW THAT I AM GOD

Psalm 46:10

In Houston, we are famous for energy, NASA, and the Astros—when they are whipping every other team. These are awesome things to have going for us. What we are not really famous for are sunrises and sunsets. You do not really see those in the City of Houston. Once in a while, people who live out in the suburbs might catch a glimpse of one, but not if you live inside the Beltway.

The best sunrise or sunset you will see is when you are on an overpass going somewhere. When you are heading to Katy and I-10 just crests on a hill, you may get a quick look at a sunset—so gorgeous! We are not really known for them, though. You have to go out in the country to get rid of distractions so you can really see a sunrise. There are too many buildings, billboards, and other things in your way.

The same is true for our relationship with God. We have so many distractions that we do not know how to be still. How do I be still and know that He is God in my life? How do I really rest in Him and see the beauty of the sunrise in my darkness? I am looking at the buildings and the billboards.

Our phones and our fears also keep us from seeing the beauty of God. Our hurry and our worries keep us from seeing the sunrise of God in our lives. Now let's consider what "be still" means. We'll remove the distractions so we can see the sunrise of God in all the circumstances of our lives.

Deep people are still people. They understand that God is in control of their pain in cancer as well as their pleasure when it is the greatest day in the world. In all our hustle and bustle, all our buildings and billboards, we can see the sunrise and know that He is God and that He is right there with us.

Do you need to see God more clearly? Do you need to rest more deeply? Are your fears and your phone keeping you frazzled and keeping you from staying on task? Are you running so busy that your hurry and worry are wilting your soul? God has a word for you today:

*Be still, and know that I am God.*

—Psalm 46:10 NIV

Stillness will allow the sun to rise in your life.

# BEING STILL

Stillness deepens our hearts and our lives. Deep people are still people. But when Monday morning comes, we all hit the pavement running because we have a lot of work to do. There is a rhythm to our lives—an ebb and a flow. There is a put-the-pedal-down and tap-the-brakes mentality. Our lives have a neutral, a park, a reverse, and a drive.

Many of us are caught with the pedal down in drive, and we never rest or slow down. I am not talking about one e-mail—it's about 100 e-mails. It's not one project at work—it's 100 projects at work. It is not one busy day—it's about 100 busy days in a row. It is not one phone call or text message—it's a life of phone calls and text messages.

Stillness is what we need because we need to deepen our hearts in order to deepen our lives. When we really get still, we finally begin to understand who we are and what we are really feeling.

One of the reasons we do not want to be still is because deep down we do not want to face what we are feeling inside. Maybe our anger, our hurt, our wounds, or our fears are too deep. If we slow down or get very still, we'll have to look at that sunrise in the face, and we're not only going to see the beauty of it, but we'll also see its brightness. The brightness of stillness reveals in our hearts what we are thinking, feeling, and going through.

We often get extremely busy and keep the noise and adrenaline flowing because we do not want to deal with what is going on. If we keep going and going, we're convinced we won't have to deal with it. We will not have to see the brightness of the sun. We can glance up and see the beauty every once in a while, but not the brightness.

What do you really think about the things of God? What are your thoughts about your purpose in life? The hurry and the worry will keep you from recognizing God's thoughts toward you.

Deep people allow stillness to happen so they can truly see what they are feeling and thinking and understand who they are. Let's learn to be still.

*For further study: Jeremiah 29:11*

# DEEPENING OUR HEARTS

— Psalm 46:10 —

Have you ever needed a vacation after you got back from vacation? That happens because we never stop to rest. We need to have a sabbatical mindset where we let our hearts rest. We need a Sabbath day to get away from everything and think about our lives.

Stillness deepens our hearts and lives; it deepens who we are. Stillness deepens our relationship with God; it deepens our relationship and understanding of the weariness, joy, hurt, or anger that we have when we really, really reflect.

When my wife's grandmother turned 100 years old, her100th birthday celebration was absolutely amazing. My family and I were sitting in the living room with Oma, as we call her, when I saw a pillow on her couch that had Psalm 46:10 on it: "Be still, and know that I am God" (NIV).

I said, "Oma, would you tell me the story about this pillow?"

She said, "Oh, yeah. I remember when Opa [her husband] got diagnosed with cancer. He went to sleep that night and acted like he wasn't worried about a thing. I walked the floor all night long, worried about him having cancer. What would happen? What would take place? And then, in that midnight hour, as I was just walking the floor praying, I heard this verse in my mind: 'Be still, and know that I am God. Be still, and know that I am God.' There's no way it could be anything else but the Lord speaking that to me." She continued, "I didn't even know the reference of it or where it was. I just knew I'd read it somewhere before. Be still, and know that I am God. I heard that verse, and then I got into bed, and I slept like a baby."

God will deepen your heart. The deepness and peace of the Lord come not just at 2:00 in the afternoon; they come at 2:00 in the morning, at 4:00 in the morning, at midnight. They don't just come at a 100th birthday celebration; they come when there's a cancer diagnosis.

*For further study: Isaiah 30:18*

# GET TO KNOW GOD

Psalm 46:10

God wants to deepen your relationship with Him, and stillness deepens it. Psalm 46:10 does not just say "be still." It is not transcendental meditation. It is not a Caribbean vacation. It says, "Be still, and know that I am God" (NIV). It is a spiritual discovery. It is Christianity. It is saying, "Lord, I want to know You, and I want to get to know You better."

Be still. Cease striving. Be still. Stop fighting.

I love this verse in The Message version of the Bible. It says, "Step out of the traffic." Step out of traffic, and take a look up. See the sunrise. See the beauty of the Lord in the heavens—what God is able to do. Our stillness lifts Him higher because now we are still before Him. We are able to see Him lifted up.

In my life, I want to walk in depth. So I put my phone and computer aside. I quit running errands and sit with Him, allowing Him to speak to my heart so I can fully understand what I am feeling. What am I actually going through? What am I truly joyful about? Why am I hurting?

We need to be still and know that He is God. And then it says, "I will be exalted among the nations, I will be exalted in the earth." He will be exalted everywhere. Missions begin with stillness. Our world will be different, not by doing something about it but by sitting still with true prayer.

I wonder if God sometimes thinks this:

If y'all would just get out of the way, I could do so much more. Y'all are asking Me to bless your ideas. Why don't you come discover My ideas? My ideas already have My blessing and My purpose. My ideas have your parenting and your marriage in its hand. My ideas have your singleness in its hand. As long as you keep trying to give Me your ideas to bless, you're going to miss it. Just let Me rise the sun in your life. Let Me set it in another chapter. And when you walk the floor at 2:00 in the morning, let me be the One who you'll hear say, "Be still and know that I am God." And then I will be exalted in your world.

*For further study: Exodus 14:14*

# OUR GOAL

God is the goal. That is what exalts Him in the nations and in the world so He can do His work. Our stillness lifts Him higher. How do we get still? It happens daily, weekly, monthly, and quarterly. Daily, we spend time with the Lord. Weekly, we have what is called a Sabbath.

All this begins with desire. Do you want to walk with God at a deep level? Do you really want to know what is going on in your heart and in your life? Do you want to know that He is God? Is it really your desire?

There are three words that have become very special to me. I learned them from the book *Love is Stronger than Death* by Peter Kreeft. Here they are: Stranger. Enemy. Friend. Here is what they look like:

*Stranger:* "Oh, going to church. I should go more."

*Enemy:* "Oh, I don't want to go this week. It's raining."

*Stranger:* "Oh, I'd love to have some time where I could really think and ponder."

*Enemy:* "I'm bored. Let's go to the mall. Let me check my messages. What else is going on?"

*Stranger:* "Boy, I wish I could have time to just rest."

*Enemy:* "Oh, I don't like this quietness."

But if you break through the Stranger and the Enemy, you get to the *Friend:*

"Oh yeah, I need to give. Oh man, I don't know if I really want to give that much. Ah, I could think of nothing greater than the friend of giving."

"Oh, I should go on a mission trip and make a difference in somebody else's life. But I sure love my pillow. Oh, goodness, to go around the world and tell people about the Lord? What a joy and what a pleasure."

As an extrovert of all extroverts, I have loved and finally learned to become a friend of solitude. And I am an extrovert full tilt. It was a stranger for years in my life. It was an enemy because I had FOMO—Fear of Missing Out. I would say, "What's everybody else doing?" Solitude is now my friend.

# STILLNESS IS A DISCIPLINE

## Proverbs 8:35

Stillness is something we all need to learn. And the way to start is first to have a great desire for it.

Then move on to application—with discipline. Begin with one day. Start small. Fifteen minutes with God one day this week. Just spend time with the Lord.

Spending time with the Lord might be very familiar to you. Just let that be part of your sabbatical heart, to just rest for 15 minutes one day this week. Then take that 15-minute time with God and move it to 15 minutes every day for a week. Then you might say from your heart, "You know what, Lord? I really desire to have an entire Sabbath day with you."

For me, my Sabbath is not Sunday. That is the biggest workday of my week. So when I sabbath on another day and just rest, my soul is restored. It doesn't mean you can't do things or be part of things that day. Just do things that refill you. Then you might say, "Oh, if I could just sabbath for a month." Let me tell you something. You wouldn't know what to do with a month if you don't know what to do with an hour, a week, or a day alone with God.

Let a sabbatical heart happen on your Sabbath day. Honor the Sabbath and keep it holy. It is the only one of the Ten Commandments that uses the word *holy*. And throughout the City of Houston, the Sabbath is probably the biggest Ten Commandment that's broken. And we are wilting and dying. We have not seen a sunrise or sunset of the Lord or the beauty of the heavens of God in a long, long time.

What if you gave God your heart the same way you give 40 to 60 hours to work every week? Put it on the calendar because guess what? If you do not put it on the calendar, it will not happen. I have it on the calendar every month that I spend a day with the Lord. One day a quarter might work for you. And do you know how many things battle for that day? When I put "Time with God" on the calendar, everything battles for that day. Persevere. Break through that enemy.

*For further study: Psalm 1:2*

# WHAT DOES IT LOOK LIKE?

―――――――――― Philippians 3:8 ――――――――――

So what do you do on your Sabbath days? Well, you take your Bible. You take a book you are enjoying. You take your journal. You take your headphones. You just get away and tuck away all your other distractions, all your billboards and buildings that distract you. And you sit with God and just say, "Lord, I want to know."

I know God, and I know who I am and what I really feel. And knowing who you are and what you feel—and knowing God—that's crazy! Let me tell you, in today's society, that is crazy. To actually have emotions and actually understand life a bit—yes, it's crazy.

I want to be that kind of crazy. My kids and my wife need me to be that kind of crazy. I need me to be that kind of crazy because my fears and my phone will wilt my life. Everybody has to put "Time with God" on their calendars because that is when it will happen. If you don't do this, the exterior pace will rob your interior peace.

When you are able to get that break and that peace, when you are able to let go, to see the sunrise, to step out of the traffic and let God do some work, then you will rest in the gospel.

What is salvation except resting in God?

Lord, I rest in Your finished work on the cross. I rest in Your blood that You shed for me. I rest in what You have done in my life. I want You to use me, God. I want You to empower me. Amen.

I challenge you to put "Time with God" on your schedule. You will be blessed. Allow God to still your life and your heart. Then Psalm 23 will become a reality for you:

> *The Lord is my shepherd;*
> *I shall not want.*
> *He makes me to lie down in green pastures;*
> *He leads me beside the still waters.*
> *He restores my soul.*

—Psalm 23:1–3 NKJV

*For further study: Psalm 1:2*
*Additional references: Psalm 23:2–3*

# SING TO THE LORD

## Psalm 47:6-9

As you travel around the globe, you will see many different things in every culture and every place, but there will always be music and singing. Do you know that we need to sing? Singing is not just for good singers; it is for everybody. Our hearts need to sing—especially in the summertime when people love to go to concerts. They experience singing their favorite songs out loud together with a venue full of strangers.

There is a higher aspect of singing, though. There is Someone we sing to.

In today's verses, we hear the psalmist say the word *sing* five times. Sing praise to God! Throughout the Old Testament, we see praise after praise. It is important that we do not just think or listen but that we also sing to the Lord. When we sing praise to Him, it makes a difference in our lives.

A battlefield in the church in previous decades was praise, worship, and singing. Have you ever heard the phrase *worship wars?* Have you heard about churches splitting over the music? In the 1800s, Charles Spurgeon called the music department in his church the *war department* because everybody had a preference—a lot of different thinking about how they should praise.

So you can understand where we are as a church right now, I'll give you a history review over the next two days. We'll go all the way back to the Old Testament where there are heaps of songs. They include today's verses in the book of Psalms—the songbook of the Old Testament. About 7 percent of the Old Testament is songs that were recorded in Psalms.

In Genesis 4, we learn that Jubal was the father of those who played the lyre and pipe. In Exodus 15, Moses and the people of God sang about the Red Sea going over the Egyptians. In Nehemiah, there are choirs walking on the wall that sing out the praises of God to rebuild the city of Jerusalem. In the Old Testament, Moses and David were songwriters—which conveys the intimate relationship they both had with God. Throughout the Old Testament, there is a lot of singing—declaring the praises of the Lord—which brings us back to one of today's verses: "Sing praises to God" (Ps. 47:6).

God already knows what's in your heart, but He still loves to hear your praise.

*For further study: Romans 8:28*

# MAKE MELODY IN YOUR HEART

## Psalm 144:9

Both the Old Testament and the New Testament declare worship songs to the Lord. In all eternity, singing is taking place right now; the angels are singing out to God.

In the New Testament, the Apostle Paul, in his letter to the Ephesians, writes about "singing and making music with your heart to the Lord" (Eph. 5:19).

Right after the Lord's Supper, the Gospel of Matthew tells us that they sang a hymn and went to the Mount of Olives. Then Jesus Christ died and rose from the grave. And the church was persecuted for about 300 years. The early church encountered Roman emperor after Roman emperor with persecution upon persecution. So the Christian church was a house church. Very small. They could not simply sing out as loud as they wanted because they would end up being killed for their faith. Many of the first Christians did die for their faith—and they were not embarrassed about it.

In 313 AD, Constantine, the emperor of Rome, signed the Edict of Milan, which allowed Christians to worship freely. Everything that had been stolen from the church was going to be given back to the church. All the house churches could come out of hiding, which they were excited about it. Over the next 1,200 years, Christians built beautiful cathedrals because they were so excited. Unfortunately, many of those beautiful building are tourist attractions today instead of houses of worship.

From the 300s to about the 1500s, the church was singing psalms in a Gregorian chant fashion. In 1517, the year of the Protestant Reformation, Martin Luther began to reclaim the teaching of the scriptures. He preached Matthew verse by verse. The church began to understand the scriptures and sing songs about them. They took melodies from the barrooms of Germany and put Christian lyrics to them, which became very scandalous. They were no longer just singing psalms; they were writing songs. That was mind-blowing.

Have you ever sung to the Lord from your heart? Maybe there is a song or poem in there waiting for you to sit down with pen and paper and let out. Make a melody in your heart for the Lord.

*For further study: Matthew 26:30*
*Additional references: Ephesians 5:19–20*

# MUSIC IS TO UNIFY

Psalm 72:17–19

Today let's go through the 1600s, 1700s, and 1800s. Most of our hymns were written in the 1700s and 1800s but then fell off in the 1900s. We didn't have as much hymn writing because in the 1920s there was prohibition, flappers, the Roaring Twenties, the speak-easies, the bootleggers, and such. As a result, the church stiff-armed the world and separated itself from it.

That brought us to the '50s with rock and roll and Elvis, who was the so-called worst thing that ever happened to the United States of America. However, if you listen to today's music, you would probably say, "Bring back Elvis!"

In the '60s, everything changed. We can look at US history as before the '60s and after the '60s. It was a watershed moment for the culture of the country. The Jesus Movement began in the late '60s and early '70s, and worship songs were like campfire songs played with one guitar.

Then, in the '70s and '80s, there was a huge worship war because part of the church was saying, "We want the 1870s hymns," and the other part was saying, "No, we want 1970s songs."

They battled for a while, and now the battle is not going on as much. Everyone still has preferences, although it's not quite like it was in the '70s and '80s. And that is a basic history of church music.

Music is for the Lord. Music is to unify us. Isn't it interesting that Satan has assaulted the family and the music in the church? That's because music brings us together—and that is why he put it in his crosshairs.

There are four reasons why it's important to sing to the Lord. Let's look at just the first one today. Singing grows our vision of God. He increases, and we decrease. Have you decreased at all this week? Has spending on yourself or thoughts about yourself decreased at all? Has your conversation about yourself, your attention to yourself, or your pride decreased at all so He can increase?

When we sing praise to the Lord, it increases our vision of Him and decreases the vision of ourselves. Think about this prayer:

*Lord, You are amazing. You are eternal. I'm just me. I'm singing to You. I want to be humble before You as I sing, as heaven is singing right now. Amen.*

*For further study: John 3:30*

# A FAIR AND LOVELY GIFT

Remember? There are four reasons why it is important that we sing to the Lord.

As we saw yesterday, number one is this: Singing grows our vision of God.

Here's number two: Singing softens our hearts and firms our resolve. In my own life, as I worship before I am about to speak, it softens my heart and firms my resolve. There have been times when I was about to share, and as I sang, I was able to say, "Lord, this is going to be a difficult or controversial message. I'm not sure how it's going to go. But Lord, I want to firm my resolve that I'm going to teach Your Word even though it's a difficult passage. Lord, I want You to use me. I've got a lot of stuff prepared. I'm ready to go. But God, if I don't do this with love, then I'm like a clanging gong or a tinkling cymbal. Lord, I allow Your love in my heart and my life."

Martin Luther, the leader of the Protestant Reformation, said this when he was asked him to recant what he had written: "Here I stand; I can do no other. God help me."* His faith had a firm resolve.

Luther also commented on music:

Music is a fair and lovely gift of God which has often wakened and moved me to the joy of preaching....Next after theology I give to music the highest place and the greatest honor....My heart bubbles up and overflows in response to music, which has so often refreshed me and delivered me from the dire plagues.†

God softens our hearts and firms our resolve. In the book of Acts, Paul and Silas are singing in the jail cell at midnight. Maybe you have gone through incredibly excruciating, difficult times in your life, and I bet God has given you a song you can sing in your midnight hour of pain. God takes us through our hard times with a song in our hearts before Him in order to firm our resolve. Here's a prayer:

*Even though I do not understand what You are doing, God, I am still going to walk with You. I know You are with me. I want a soft heart before You. Amen.*

*For further study: Psalm 23:4*
*Additional references: Acts 16:25*

# THE RIGHT THING TO DO

Psalm 47:8

There are four reasons why it's important to sing to the Lord. We've looked at the first reason: Singing grows our vision of God. The second reason is that it softens our heart and firms our resolve.

Now let's look at reason number three: Singing is the right thing to do. That seems foolish to say in America these days, because we do what we want to do. However, praising God through song is the right thing to do.

The book of Revelation says the Lord is worthy! If you are going to be a good husband, a good wife, a good friend, or a good employee or employer, you are going to have to do things because it is the right thing to do—whether you feel like it or not.

You show me employees who only work when they want to and not when it is the right thing to do, and I will show you some sorry employees. You show me a parent who does not do things just because it is the right thing to do but only when he or she wants to, and I will show you a sorry mom or dad. The Lord is worthy of your praise. Period. We need to be adults about it. We are going to do what is right, even if it is not easy.

The fourth reason we sing is that it unifies us as a people and as a church. After the disciples took the Lord's Supper, they sang a hymn and went to the Mount of Olives where Jesus was arrested. They were unified in their singing as they went out to a troublesome time.

Think about a baseball game. The seventh-inning stretch. Everybody stands up and sings "Take Me Out to the Ball Game." At an Astros game, we sing "Deep in the Heart of Texas." The Red Sox fans sing "Sweet Caroline."

It is a unifying event that has a purpose in each game. You may go to a college football game, and when they sing the fight song, you suddenly feel part of a greater calling. Everyone is there to support their team.

Singing together with your church might not make you think alike, but it will open your eyes to see that you are part of the great kingdom of God.

*For further study: Revelation 4:9–11*

# MY IDENTITY IN JESUS CHRIST

Psalm 47:6

As the people of God, we can come together and sing praise to God and be unified. We can conquer any worship war.

In the Old Testament, Abraham, Isaac, and Jacob—grandfather, father, and grandson—had the same job, wore the same clothes, lived on the same piece of land, and sang the same songs. That is not how it is today. I might not like the same thing you like. The chances of liking our grandkids' music are very small. As a grandson, you do not have the same job your grandfather had for more than 40 years.

We are called to sing *to* God, not just *about* God. We do not go to church to have Christian karaoke; we go to church to sing to God—sing to Him with all we have. It requires us to go beyond our personalities to our identities in Christ. If you are a believer in Jesus Christ, He has given you a song in your heart and praise to give back to Him. It is the right thing to do.

God has wired all of us differently. Some of us grew up singing every moment. Some always have a song in their hearts and whistle it while they work in the garden or doing dishes and always with the radio on. Some of us could take music or leave it. It is not really our deal.

You have to move past your personality to your identity in Jesus Christ—to your heart—your spirit. It does not matter if you are a good singer. I am talking about praising. I am not talking about vocal cords. I am talking about the cords of your heart. If you are a bad singer, who cares? But if you are a bad worshiper, that is a problem. If you are a bad keeper of a melody and a harmony, who cares? But if you do not give praise, it will affect your relationships, your marriage, and your way of life. It is about your heart as you are before the Lord, singing *to God*, not just *about* God or to other people.

Sing to Him. Get past your personality and to your true Christian identity. We are not all great singers, but we can all be great worshipers, and that is what God is calling us to be.

*For further study: Psalm 22:27–28*

# SING A SONG OF WISDOM

## Psalm 47:7–9

All music should have no other end and aim than the glory of God and the soul's refreshment; where this is not remembered there is no real music but only a devilish hubbub.*

—Johann Sebastian Bach

At the top of all his compositions, Bach wrote "J.J.," *Jesus Juva*, which meant "Jesus help me." At the end, he wrote, "S.D.G.," *Soli Deo Gloria*, which meant "To God alone be the glory." He was composing instrumental music and saying, "I want to praise God."

Worship is about what your heart is saying. Be a great worshiper before Him and sing a song of wisdom. Connect your head and your heart. Understand what you are singing, and feel what you understand.

There is a lot of music out there, and you could be singing songs of praise that have a great melody but are incorrect theologically. I want to encourage you to not sing those songs, because what you sing is what you end up believing. For example, if you think the Holy Spirit comes and goes, you are going to miss that He indwells you and lives inside of you. In your deepest, darkest pain and in your greatest joy, He is with you.

Jesus said it like this: "Worship in spirit and in truth" (John 4:24). We need to sing with wisdom as we walk with God. As we get to know Him better, we sing to Him wisely with an understanding of who He is and what He is doing.

Psalm 47 says that the leaders of the earth *belong to God*. Songs of praise remind us of *whose* we are, not *who* we are. If our world's leaders were to realize that they belong to God and worship Him as such, we could end world hunger, poverty, trafficking, and more. Great leaders entrust themselves to the greatest leader. And great leaders, great mommas, great daddies, great husbands, great single adults, and great employees and employers praise God—not themselves. They sing *to the Lord*. Here's a sample prayer:

*Lord, it is You I am entrusting myself to. I'm going to sing praise to You. I want to walk with You and trust You always, for Yours is the kingdom and the power and the glory. Amen.*

*For further study: John 4:24*

# DREAMS

## Psalm 126

We have been studying the Psalms. The first series was based on Psalm 46 where we discussed our need to rest in the Lord. In the second part, we looked at the power of worship, of singing to the Lord as described in Psalm 47. We saw that you could be a terrible singer and an awesome worshiper, making a joyful noise from your heart to the Lord.

This third part is based on a psalm that is not really famous. But I will tell you this: It has become one of my favorites. Psalm 126 is about dreaming big, and I am not referring to the dreams at night when you go to sleep. I am talking about dreams that make you think out loud, "What if this were to happen? What if that took place? What if God did this? What if the Lord moved in this way?" This psalm deals with the spectrum of emotions that we have in life—from joy and laughter to weeping and pain. It talks about how we can be part of the dreams of God.

As Americans, dreams are extremely important to us. One of the most famous speeches in American history is "I Have a Dream" by Martin Luther King, Jr. He repeated over and over, "I have a dream. I have a dream. I have a dream." It changed the course of our nation.

At the end of your student career, when you get to graduation, the speaker is going to stand up and say, "Follow your dreams." And your parents are going to be behind you saying, "Make sure you can pay for your dreams."

We are a dreaming culture, and that is a great thing. But the key is that we need to be about God's dreams—not getting God behind our dreams. We need to get on board with His dreams and let His dreams be what comes out of our lives. Then we will see what it means to truly dream something and see it come to life.

Does God have a dream for you? For your kids? Does God have a dream where you play a part in the kingdom? Yes, He does, and He cannot wait for you to get on board.

# THE DREAMS OF GOD

================== Psalm 126:1–3 ==================

What does it mean to truly dream something and see it become a reality? How does it happen?

Keep dreaming of what God can do. God can do amazing, incredible things about who you are in your life and in your family's life. He can use you to do incredible things, so keep dreaming of what God can do. Psalm 126 says that when the people were dreaming, their mouths were filled with laughter and joy. The greatest joy and laughter comes when you get to be part of God's dreams.

His dreams have to become our dreams—we have to want to do what He wants us to do.

Historically, today's verses are talking about the time when the people of Israel were released from Babylonian captivity after being enslaved for 70 years. They were released and could go back and rebuild Jerusalem. When they were released, Psalm 126:1–3 says they were like those who dream. They might have said something like this: "What could God do now? I can't believe we're free. This is like a dream!" There were smiles and laughter.

God has not freed us from Babylonian captivity, but He has done something even more extravagant. And it is almost like a dream. God has forgiven us of our sins through Jesus Christ, who died on the cross for you and for me and rose from the dead for us. When we place our faith and trust in Him, He washes us clean and gives us the right to be children of God. Wow! That is a dream come true.

I am free. I am rightly relating before the Lord. I can connect with God. I can talk to Him. He can talk to me. I do not get it all right all the time, but He always gets it right, so I just keep following Him. It is like a dream. The psalm says that they began to laugh and had joy. What can God do? If He can free us from captivity and save our souls, what can God do in our lives, in our city, in our schools, in our friendships, and in our families?

They were "like those who dream" (Ps. 126:1). Are you like those who dream? Keep dreaming about what God can do.

*For further study: Psalm 53:6*

# GOD'S DREAM FOR YOU

---

Psalm 71:19

---

As you get older, you laugh less; life gets more serious, more stressful. When you are 12 or 13, you laugh all the time. Things always seem funny. But when you get to be 42, 52, and so on, life is not as funny as it once was. We laugh less. We begin to say things like, "Let's do something fun tonight."

When you are a teenager, fun just happens. Fun is where you are. It is a party wherever you go. When we become adults, we get serious and begin to lack joy. Is that not peculiar? We have money to do things, we know who we are, we know what we do, and we understand all these things. There is a lot of security in our lives, but we are lacking joy because we have lost the ability to dream.

We should dream bigger now. We know what our gifts are, where we have been placed, and what we are to do. We should be living light because we are trusting deep—fulfilling God's plan. There is a deep joy when we can say, "God, I will stop trying to talk You into being part of my plan. I want to be part of Your plan." The gospel sets us free from the captivity of our pride—of what we want—and we are able to be people who dream God's dreams.

I was at a board meeting when the person leading it began by saying, "If God answered every one of the prayers you're praying, what would happen?" That question really convicted my heart of this: I am not praying specifically enough in my life. I am praying ambiguously. It also showed me what my dreams are. What am I really dreaming for God to do?

So if God answered every prayer you prayed, what would happen? Whose lives would be changed? God wants to use you in a great way. He has a dream for you. It might be to start an organization, club, or event. Or maybe it's just to introduce you to one person you are going to minister to and love on. It could be a new way of living that you have never experienced before. Once you are free, God will move forward with His dream for you.

*For further study: Genesis 21:6*
*Additional references: Job 42:10*

# DREAM BIG

Psalm 139:17

Do you have an idea? Do you have a thought? Let's jump out there and be like those who dream. What could God do if you took a step to go out there?

Let me share a couple of examples from my own life. When my kids were in middle school, some dads and I decided to have a Bible study once a month before school. We called it Dudes and Dads. Sons and fathers. A dad would bring a devotional, and another dad would bring donuts. We had two rules for the boys. They had to sit by their dads, and they had to hug their dads when they left.

For three years, it was one of the blessings of my life. It was also a blessing to the other dads and the kids as well. When their high school years began, some dads got together and said, "Hey, what if we get together as dads and pray?" Now, once a month, we meet at a little restaurant and have eggs, waffles, and all the syrup our wives won't feed us at home. Then we have a time of devotional, and we pray that God will do something great at the school. Often, we end the time writing thank you notes to teachers and coaches or administration. In their inbox, they get an encouraging note saying something like this: "I'm praying for you, and I appreciate you."

Then some families got together and had a wonderful idea. What if they kicked off the school year after the first week of school on a Sunday night? They decided they were going to meet in the front parking lot of the school for a time of praise and worship, a time of prayer, and say, "God, we're praying for the school. We're asking You to do great things here." They let everybody be part of it.

Then parents from another school said, "Hey if they are doing that there, what if we do it here?" What if 40 schools next year had a time of prayer to kick off the school year? What if every parent realized that their kid's school is also their mission field? Let's make a difference, and let's be dreamers of what God can do.

I once had a dream, and it was called a Little Bitty, Small Bible Study. Three decades later, it is still reaching thousands upon thousands of students. Do not despise the days of small beginnings. Dream big.

*For further study: Philippians 2:13*
*Additional references: Luke 12:31–32*

# GRACE

Psalm 126:2–3

Psalm 126 says that the Israelites' mouths were filled with laughter and their tongues with joy. Then the nations around them saw the blessing and said, "The Lord has done great things for them" (Ps. 126:2). The people of God responded, "The Lord had done great things for us; we were joyful" (Ps. 126:3). The blessings and the source will become apparent to others and to us.

Are you aware of how many great things God has done in your life? How faithful has the Lord been to you? If God never did another thing for you, He has already done too much.

That is a whole different worldview, is it not? If God never did another thing for me besides releasing me, not from Babylonian captivity but from the weight of my sin, He has already done too much. I have been set free by Him! Yet from His abundant love, I still receive one gracious blessing after another.

And now He has given me the ability to dream, to think, and to be part of what His plan is. I can say, "Lord, You will do great things through me." Can you say it out loud? "The Lord has done great things for me." Now close your eyes and say it to the Lord: "Lord, You have done great things for me, and I am filled with joy."

One of our ministries in Asia rescues young girls from the brothels where their moms are prostitutes. If these little girls do not get out, they will end up in the same vocation as their moms. They are trapped. The ministry organization adopts these girls as their own after their moms give them up for adoption. The organization helps them with school and everything else.

We visited this place once, and one of these girls said thank you because she had been rescued from a brothel where her mom is a prostitute, and now the girl is headed to college at a university in the United States of America. When I think about her, I see a joyful dreamer. As she cried, we cried, and then the other girls who are not going to the United States cried with her, hugged her, and celebrated that she was going.

That is dreaming. That is working. And that is saying, "The Lord has done great things for me."

*For further study: John 1:16*

# SEEDS OF JOY

## Psalm 126:4–6

Psalm 126 reminds us that after the Israelites were filled with joy, they cried out to the Lord to restore their fortunes like the rain restores the water to the streams in the desert. They knew that even though they had sown in tears, they would reap with joy. Keep planting in hard times. We started this psalm with laughter and joy; we are ending with weeping and sorrow. That is the spectrum of life we will face at one point or another.

The Negev is a dry desert in Israel where there is nothing but crevices. But in the rainy season, at a time unexpected, a storm rolls in, and the crevices fill up with water. The desert miraculously turns into raging rivers.

That happens in our lives as well. The healing and the finances come. The business deal happens. Mom was infertile and got pregnant. We did not know it was coming, but the rain fell, and the living water filled up the water in our desert. God does immeasurably more than we could ask or imagine.

Salvation is very much like that. We did not earn it. We trusted in the living water of Jesus Christ to fill our dry and cracked hearts. Then streams of His living water flowed from us as believers.

This psalm also speaks of hard walking. "Those who sow in tears will reap with shouts of joy" (Ps. 126:5). Somebody with a bag of seeds is throwing them out, weeping in their pain as they walk. Do not waste your pain. Invest your pain. God will take your misery and make it your ministry. God will use you to give sheaves of joy.

A family from church had a dear family member die. That person was an organ donor. Later, the family got a letter from the person who received the donated organ. They met and talked, and this family received great joy. Out of great tragedy, they walked and planted seeds, even in the midst of their grief. God can do amazing seed planting when it is watered by our tears. He can bring a harvest as you have never seen before.

Stand up and say, "Lord, step by step in my tears, I'm going to continue to throw out the seeds." And the joy will come.

*For further study: Deuteronomy 30:2–4*

# JOYFUL DREAMERS

—— Psalm 67:1–4 ——

We are joyful dreamers who thank God and work faithfully. The Lord has done great things. Even in the midst of pain, we work faithfully. Even in the midst of joy, we work faithfully. We let God do something through us. God has a dream for you, your marriage, and your family. He has a dream for the schools you represent and for your business. God has a dream for you to be His dreamer on earth, thanking God and working faithfully.

I am not calling you to start a big ministry or a new event. I am calling you to be a difference-maker, to dream and say, "God, You've placed me here. What's Your dream for this place?"

If you are a parent, perhaps the dream is that you may be a prayer warrior on your kid's campus and realize that God has placed you there for a reason during this season of your life. Then you will march out as a joyful dreamer who thanks God and works faithfully.

Have you trusted Jesus as your Savior? Has the living water from heaven filled your heart and your soul? If your heart and soul are filled with Jesus, are you letting the river rage wherever He wants it to, or are you just building little dams to keep the course going the way you want it to?

The Lord has done great things for me. As the water courses fill the Negev, as we sow in tears and reap in joy, we walk faithfully with the Lord. Pray this prayer:

*Jesus, I love You and thank You because You are God, and You are the giver of dreams. I don't want to spend my whole life climbing a ladder and end up with it leaning against the wrong wall. I don't want to be tremendously successful and not joyful. I don't want to get You on my dream schedule. I want my life to be about Your dreams. I know I will be filled with Your joy and laughter. Use me in the place You've placed me to be a difference-maker in huge ways. I love You, Jesus. Amen.*

*For further study: Ephesians 2:10*

# GOD IS LOVE

## 1 John 4:7–12

Regardless of what version of the Bible you choose to read, the word *love* is found many times there. You can find it everywhere—from creation to creation, from creation to Creator, and from Creator to creation. And it can be described in many different ways.

Have you ever asked yourself what true love really is? Have you ever felt it? Have you ever really loved? We are going to focus on the love of God in this series. We will discover some aspects of the love of God toward us, toward others, and toward Him.

First, let's define what love is according to the Bible. A perfect definition of what true love really is and means is found in 1 Corinthians 13. Love is not just a feeling or an emotion or even a reaction to someone else's actions. Love is. It is not something that is attached to actions. True love does not change according to what the object of affection does or does not do. It just is.

God is love. Everything He does and everything He did is because of love. He is the purest form of love. He is the true measurement of love. Love was made by Him, for Him, and through Him. It is not until we get to know God that we can truly understand what love is.

God shows His love for us in many ways. He gave His Son as a sacrifice for the forgiveness of our sins because He loves us so much. He makes everything work together for our good because He loves us. He created everything for us to enjoy because He loves us. It does not matter what we do or do not do, God is love. And because He is love, He cannot go against Himself. It is who He is; it is based on His character, not on our actions. So no matter what we do, He still loves us. Because love is Him, He is love.

My prayer for you is that you will get to know God in a deeper way, that through knowing Him more, you will feel a love like you have never felt before. I pray that you can understand what true love really is and that your life and the lives of those around you will be changed forever. What the love of God touches cannot remain the same.

*For further study: Genesis 1:27–30*
*Additional references: 1 Corinthians 13:4–8, Romans 8:28*

# THE LOVE OF GOD IS STEADFAST

## Romans 8:38–39

We live in a world where everything changes, where one day one thing is cool and the next day it is old-fashioned and ridiculous. I remember a few years ago when the egg yolk was almost forbidden to eat because it was so bad for our health. And now it is okay to eat it because scientists have discovered so many health benefits that come from the yolk of the egg. There are many things like that throughout history. Everything changes and keeps changing.

There is one thing, though, that will never change. That is the love of God for us. His love is steadfast. It is firm. It is unwavering. It is forever. It is always faithful. It will not change no matter what, because God stays the same forever. He is love. He promises us His steadfast love many times in the Bible.

It might be hard for us to fathom the reality of the steadfast love of God—a love that endures forever—because nothing around us lasts forever. We are not used to thinking about things lasting forever in our lives, in our families, or in society. We do not want things that last forever because we want everything to move fast so we don't get bored. We don't want to buy furniture that will last us forever anymore, because we know we will soon get bored with it. We buy our cell phones knowing that in two or three years, we will be upgrading them for newer models. We buy our shoes not because of their amazing lasting quality but because of their design. We know they will not be in style for a long time, so we might use them for a year and then move on to other styles.

If we really think about it, how amazing is it to know that the love of God is something that will never change, no matter what? It will not change if we change. It will not change if we do something or do not do something. It will not change with time. It will remain firm forever.

*Thank You, God, for Your love. Thank You for loving me with a love that will last forever and will not change, no matter what I do. Thank You for the security that is found in Your love. Thank You for a love I will always be able to depend on. Thank You for a love that always is and always will be.*

*For further study: Deuteronomy 7:9*
*Additional references: 1 Kings 8:23; Psalm 25:10, 85:7–13, 136:1*

# GOD'S LOVE IS IRREVOCABLE

## Exodus 34:6–7

Have you ever wondered about something that could be done to make the world a better place? To make it more peaceful? Have you asked yourself what makes the world such a chaotic place?

The chaos of the world is because we have shunned the love of God. We have told God that we do not want His love and do not want to operate in His love or even experience it. We want to do things our own way with our own wisdom and for our own gratitude. That is the reason for all the chaos in the world. Because of that, there is not one thing we can do as human beings to make the world a peaceful place. It has to be through the love of God operating in the people of God to shine with the love of God. It is a love that is irrevocable, no matter what anyone else does. It does not depend on anything or anyone, only God Himself.

Human-to-human love is revocable; we are constantly taking back things we give, say, or do—always revoking things. But heaven-to-human love is irrevocable. The love of God for us is irrevocable. His love for us is not conditional; it does not matter what we do or do not do.

*Irrevocable* is a legal term. It is something you cannot take back. It is something beyond recall—binding, changeless, definite, factual, final, indestructible, permanent, stable, certain, conclusive, ironclad, unavoidable. That is what the love of God is for us. It is based on His character, not our actions.

We often think that when we do something wrong or make bad decisions, God no longer loves us. We believe His love changes toward us and that now He loves us differently. But the love of God does not work that way. It's not only because God is our Father; it's because it goes against who He is and all the promises He made us.

His love will never change, and He will never take His love back. That is a truth we must learn to accept and understand. There is nothing we can do to change it. God gave us His love to enjoy and take advantage of for the rest of our lives. It is His irrevocable love.

*For further study: Ephesians 3:17–19*
*Additional references: John 3:16*

# GOD'S LOVE IS FORGIVING

Psalm 78:38

There is a painting by Rembrandt that has always caught my eye. It is called *The Return of the Prodigal Son* and is believed to be one of Rembrandt's final pieces. The painting perfectly depicts the forgiveness of a father toward his son, and it is based on the parable of the prodigal son in the Bible. If you look at the painting closely, you can almost feel the love of the father by the way his hands are placed on his son's back and by the expression on his face.

The parable talks about a son who asks his father for his inheritance, and then he leaves and spends it all. It tells of the forgiveness of the father when the son returns. The son has no other expectation except to become one of his father's servants. But this father's love offers unexpected forgiveness and grace. It's the same for the love of God for us. Even when we least expect to be loved and forgiven, He still loves us and forgives us, repeatedly. That is who He is.

The forgiveness God gives us through His love is not the same as human-to-human forgiveness. God throws our sins so far away that they cannot affect us anymore; He forgives us and never holds a grudge against us. His forgiveness is complete. It is a forgiveness that forgets all wrongdoing. It is a forgiveness that goes deeper than what we can expect or imagine. And that is not because of us or because we did something to deserve such a forgiveness. It is because of who God is and the love He has for us. It is a forgiveness that restores and brings life, purpose, meaning, hope, and grace.

We as human beings are used to forgiving but not forgetting. However, God is not like us. My prayer for you is that you will be able accept the love and forgiveness of God in all its fullness. Know that it is not and will never be about you; it is about who He is. Know that our actions will never be greater than His character. Know that one day you may find yourself loving and forgiving others in the same way that God loves and forgives you every day.

*For further study: Micah 7:18*
*Additional references: Luke 15:11–32, Exodus 34:7– 8;*
*Psalm 145:8, 103:12*

# GOD'S LOVE BRINGS WORSHIP

## Matthew 4:10

Worship is an essential part of our Christian lives. We worship God in our prayers, in our songs, in our living. We worship God as a sign of thankfulness and awe of who He is and because of how He loves us. Worship is a response from our hearts and souls and spirits to God's goodness and faithfulness. It is a response to who He is, to His character. He is the only One deserving of our worship.

As human beings, it is a natural need and instinct to worship something— not necessarily God. Many people who do not know God worship other gods or other things. Sometimes, we may not even realize it, but we are worshiping other things instead of God. We might be worshiping our jobs, our families, money, success, or material things. We may not be bowing down to them or singing songs of praise to them, but in our hearts, they hold a place that is meant only for God.

Worship is a condition of the heart. If we understand the love of God for us, that He will always love us no matter what, then our hearts will always be filled with worship toward Him. It is like finding out someone did something good for you, something unexpected. Your heart gets all warm and fuzzy and happy, and all you can do is thank that person and say nice things about them. You acknowledge what they did for you. The same goes for God. He loves us with an undeserving, inexplicable, unchangeable love every day of our lives. So it is only natural that our hearts are filled with worship for Him.

Take a moment and think about the love of God in your life and all the ways you can thank Him and worship Him with your life. Your worship is not only through songs and music but by the way you live your life, the way you treat people, the way you are with your family and friends, the way you talk, the way you act at work or school, the way you drive your car, the way you shop at the supermarket or mall. Think of practical ways you can worship God with your whole life.

*For further study: Psalm 136:1–9*
*Additional references: Jeremiah 20:13, Psalm 103, 100:1–5*

# GOD'S LOVE IS OUR COMFORT

## Psalm 119:76

What would you do if you knew there was an easy answer for all your problems? Would you take it without consideration? Would you stop and consider the pros and cons? Would you consider other options? Sometimes, when things seem too good to be true, we tend to stay away from them, disregard them, and not even consider them as a possibility.

The truth is that the more we know God, the closer we are to Him. We start to realize that in Him, we have all the answers, all the security, and all the comfort we need for every area and every circumstance of our lives. But it sometimes seems too good to be true, right? And it asks us to trust without reservation. It's sometimes hard to have faith in a God we cannot see and believe blindly and deeply that everything will work out for our good, even when things are not going well in our lives.

God promises us that He will always be with us. He promises us a love that is faithful, steadfast, and irrevocable. No matter what we do, no matter what the chaos of our lives looks like, He loves us with a faithful love. It is a love that is not fickle because we cannot be comforted by a fickle God. From the faithfulness of God comes the comfort of God. His promise is that He will always love us and comfort us.

To give comfort is to give strength and hope to someone. And that is what God has promised us. It does not matter what goes on around us—He will always be with us, strengthening and comforting us. In Him, we will always find safety and security. He is our shepherd; He will always protect us and guide us along the right paths. In His comfort, we can find rest and happiness.

God never intended for us to live lonely, sad, or worried lives on our own. He did say that in this life we will encounter affliction and bad days, but He also says that He wants to be with us through it all. He wants us to feel His warm embrace and His comforting love all the days of our lives. He also sent us a comforter, His Holy Spirit, to guide us and be with us. He gave us an easy way out of all our problems and afflictions. It is time for us to take advantage of what God offers us and start living our lives to the fullest, knowing that we will always have God on our side.

*For further study: Psalm 23*
*Additional references: 2 Corinthians 1:3; Psalm 46:1–3;*
*Isaiah 54:10, 43:2; John 16:33*

# LOOKING FOR COMFORT

— Psalm 119:75 —

What I am about to say may sound strong and negative, but it is a universal, undeniable truth. Suffering comes with living. Every living thing goes through some sort of suffering in the duration of its life. Animals suffer, plants suffer, humans suffer. It is part of life. And it is also an undeniable truth that we as human beings look for some sort of comfort to ease that suffering. Every person has looked for comfort. Everyone is looking for comfort or will look for comfort. There is no way to escape it. No matter what we believe in—and even if we don't believe in anything—we all need comfort.

We were made to need comfort. We seek comfort all the time, even when we do not realize it. Sometimes we look for comfort in shallow, quick things. We might go to food for comfort. Some of us go to shopping, technology, TV, movies, pornography, noise, or addictions for some form of comfort. Maybe that quick fix of fake comfort gives us some sort of control over our lives.

But do we value immediate comfort over real comfort? Do we go to the quick things instead of the deep things? Even when we turn to God for comfort, are we looking for something quick, or are we seeking something eternal? C. S. Lewis said that the end goal of Christianity is not personal comfort but a relationship with God. And from that relationship comes the deepest and most real form of comfort we could ever dream of.

We have all been hurt. We are all wounded and lonely. We have all felt guilty. We all make mistakes and lack control over so many things in our lives. But we can submit all of that to God, and in return, He promises us His faithful love that comforts us. We can think of His love as the rope that rock climbers use. It is there whether they need it or not. The same thing goes for the love of God in our lives—it does not matter if we succeed or fail, whether we are in joy or in pain, we will always need the rope of the comforting love of God.

*For further study: 1 Peter 5:10*
*Additional references: John 16:33, Psalm 34:19*

# WHERE IS YOUR DELIGHT?

### Psalm 119:77

To delight in something is to find great pleasure, happiness, and joy. There are many verses in the Bible that say we find joy when we go through trials and hard times. I often wonder why that is. It sounds somewhat contradictory to find joy while going through a hard time or circumstance. But in the kingdom of God, we are going to find many contradictory things that meet each other on common ground. That is because we have a God who promises us that His eternal love will always give us comfort. He is a God who says that if we focus on Him, He will take care of everything for us.

There is a hope that comes with trusting God when we are going through a hard time. It is a hope that comes from knowing that the love of God gives us comfort. It is a hope that is the result of delighting and rejoicing in God's promises. It may not be easy to find joy or happiness when we are going through sufferings, but we must know that we are never alone in those sufferings. The Bible says that we have the Holy Spirit with us as our comforter and that He will be with us forever. It tells us that everything we go through is meant to make us grow as individuals in our faith and help others who will go through the same thing we are going through.

When we delight in something, we want to spend time with it. It may be a TV show, music, the company of friends or family, a good meal, a sports show—whatever it is that brings us joy, we want to spend time doing it. Would you consider taking time daily to enjoy the Word of God and His promises? Think about all the times the comfort of God has given you hope and joy during the hardest moments of your life.

As we learn to delight in the promises of God, as we learn to find joy during trials and hard times, we know we have the promise of His eternal, faithful, comforting love. Remember that God also delights in us with shouts of joy. How wonderful is His love for us!

*For further study: 1 Peter 1:6–9*
*Additional references: Psalm 40:1–11, Philippians 4:4,*
*Romans 5:3–5, Zephaniah 3:17, John 14:16–18*

# SUBMISSION BRINGS COMFORT

## Psalm 119:73–76

Comfort is not earned; it is received. We do not have to earn it. We can seek it by seeking God, but it is something God gives us in His love, and we receive it. It is a gift and a promise from God to us.

According to Psalm 119:76, we receive the comforting love of God as His servants. To be a servant is to submit to someone else's authority, to accept their authority over us. We submit to the One who created us; we agree that what has afflicted us is just and fair in His eyes. We know He is building us up and giving us perseverance through the trials we might go through. We trust that going through these hard times will bring something good into our lives.

As human beings, we are going to find that we have to submit to many things during our lives. We have to submit to laws and regulations, to our parents when we are young, to our teachers when we go to school, to our governing authorities as citizens of the country we live in, and many other things. Do you find yourself more secure when you submit to certain rules and regulations? If your answer is yes, you are right. That is because those were meant to make us feel more secure. They are meant to help us live our lives with a certain order and comfort.

When we submit to the love of God, we will find comfort. If we look at the story of the prodigal son in the Bible, we will find that when the son came back, he submitted to his father, and in that submission, he found love, comfort, forgiveness, hope, and joy. The father did not leave him standing there alone; he met him halfway. The same happens when we submit ourselves to the love and forgiveness of God. He meets us halfway; He gives us the gift of His love and comfort. He gives us back our joy and happiness.

My prayer today is that you will learn to submit to the will of God and accept that whatever sufferings or trials you may face will bring you closer to His love and comfort. My prayer is that you might be able to understand that submitting to God does not mean you lose part of your freedom. It means you gain freedom by living completely surrendered to His love and comfort.

*For further study: 1 Peter 5:10, Luke 15:20–24,*
*Luke 22:42, Titus 3:1*

# SERVING HANDS

## 2 Corinthians 1:3–7

We were made to need comfort, but we were also made to give comfort to others. We have the capacity to give and receive comfort. Psalm 119:79 says, "Let those who fear you, those who know your decrees, turn to me." Do you know what that means? It means that our misery becomes our ministry. Our servant hearts become hands that serve others.

God takes our pain, and we go through it with the comfort we receive from the love of God. Then God takes our misery and makes it our ministry. No one is better to care for someone in a painful divorce than someone who has gone through a painful divorce and submitted it to the Lord. No one is better to care for a person in grief than someone who has experienced grief and given it to the Lord. No one is better at comforting someone going through suffering than the person who went through that same suffering.

During her reign, Queen Victoria heard of a lady who was a common laborer, just a peasant, who had lost her baby. Queen Victoria had experienced deep sorrow herself, and she felt moved to express her sympathy. So one day she called on the bereaved woman—the grieving woman—and asked her to spend some time with her. The lady came and spent time with Queen Victoria. When the lady went back to her house, her neighbors were excited and waiting for her at her door. They asked her what the Queen had to say. And the grieving woman told them that the Queen had said nothing. She had simply put her hands on her hands, and they had wept silently together.

We know. Why? Because we have been there. We understand. We know what it is like. And we are going to comfort someone else. You can let God use your misery to make it your ministry and let your servant heart become your serving hands.

I pray that today you can receive the comforting love of God in your life in a way so deep that you feel the burning need and desire to share it with others. I pray that you can be a comforter to others through the comfort that God gave you first. I pray that you may be able to understand that every suffering you went through was not pointless but had a divine purpose.

*For further study: Romans 15:1–2*

# SUPERNATURAL THIRST

Creatures are not born with desires unless satisfaction for those desires exists. A baby feels hunger, and, well, there is such a thing as food. A duckling wants to swim, and there is such a thing as water. People feel sexual desire, and, well, there is such a thing as sex.

King Solomon, who succeeded King David to rule Israel, was famous for his wisdom. Like his father, who wrote many of the psalms, Solomon's writings are also part of the Bible. He wrote Proverbs, Ecclesiastes, and the Song of Solomon.

Solomon was wealthy. He was educated. He was accomplished, able to govern and make alliances. He supervised the construction of magnificent buildings, including his own palace and the Temple in Jerusalem. He obtained whatever gave him pleasure. He had 700 wives and 300 concubines. He had everything he desired—power, sex, money, knowledge, accomplishments, popularity, and fame. Yet he felt that pursuing all these things was like chasing the wind. It was meaningless. He was not satisfied. He was still thirsty.

When you have desires that you realize are not going to be satisfied through sex, marriage, money, fame, or anything in this world, that is an indication that you've been created for another world. Solomon came to that conclusion and concluded his meditation on the meaning of life by encouraging people to remember their Creator.

Acknowledge your thirst. Whether you are young, old, or somewhere in between, you've probably felt that thirst that is larger than life, that longing for something or someone you can't name, that desire that shows you still haven't found what you're looking for.

Put aside your need for accomplishment. Put aside your need for ownership, security, and attention. Put it all aside. The world cannot satisfy your thirst. You need Jesus. We all need Him. He invited all who are thirsty to come to Him.

*For further study: Ecclesiastes 2:10–11*
*Additional references: Ecclesiastes 12:1*

# THIRSTY FOR GOD

Luke 16:22–24

The human body has three stages of dehydration: mild, moderate, and severe. The first is ordinary thirst. Your mouth is dry, and your brain tells you to drink some water. If you don't drink, your thirst intensifies. In that stage, you experience headaches, dizziness, fatigue, confusion, and more. In the third stage, drinking water is no longer enough; medical intervention is necessary.

Two guys were driving through the desert, and their truck broke down. You can imagine what they thought! They were stranded and had no way to reach someone to help them. They were alone in the heat and in the sun. After a while, they drank all the water they had. They decided to lie underneath the truck to get some shade from the sun and maybe bring the temperature down a few degrees. They got thirstier and thirstier.

The thirst of these men was like the thirst of the rich man in hell who longed for relief and asked Lazarus for just one drop of water on his tongue. The stranded men were so thirsty that they decided to drink the liquid from the truck's radiator. It was poisonous and lethal.

We can get so thirsty in this world that we will take our legitimate need—a thirst for God—and try to satisfy it in ways that won't work, that are even deadly for us. This world is full of broken cisterns where we try to slake our thirst but can't. Some of these are success, fame, money, pleasure, and fulfillment. But Malcom Muggeridge, a British author, said this:

> I may, I suppose, regard myself, or pass for being, a relatively successful man. People occasionally stare at me in the streets—that's fame. I can fairly easily earn enough to qualify for admission to the higher slopes of the Inland Revenue—that's success. Furnished with money and a little fame even the elderly, if they care to, may partake of trendy diversions—that's pleasure. It might happen once in a while that something I said or wrote was sufficiently heeded for me to persuade myself that it represented a serious impact on our time—that's fulfilment. Yet I say to you—and I beg you to believe me—multiply these tiny triumphs by a million, add them all together, and they are nothing—less than nothing, a positive impediment—measured against one draught of that living water Christ offers to the spiritually thirsty, irrespective of who or what they are.*

Jesus is the living water. He is the only way to satisfy your spiritual thirst.

# LIVING WATER

John 7:37–38

Jesus invited all who are thirsty to come to Him and drink. Jesus is not like a trickle or a drop of water about to vanish. It is not a gulp or a mouthful; it is much more. Believing in Jesus does not mean you receive temporary reprieve for your thirst. In fact, Jesus said that those who drink of His water never thirst again.

Jesus said He would give people who believe in Him water from the spring of life—that they would experience Him as a spring of water continually bubbling over in their hearts. He also said that whoever believes in Him would have rivers of living water flowing within them.

Springs and rivers are not stagnant. They flow from their headwaters to the sea. They plunge over cliffs, gurgle through the woods, carve channels in the hardest rock, meander over the countryside, rush under bridges, roar as they gain strength and volume, and finally reach the shore. They provide habitats for living creatures and bring sustenance and refreshment to all in their path. Life with Jesus brings abundance and joy.

Do you want that transformation? Drink of Jesus, the living water. Christ is the thirst quencher of the soul. There is nothing and no one else who can satisfy the human soul like He does. Salvation doesn't depend on how often you go to church or read the Bible. It doesn't mean you believe Jesus is a nice guy. It isn't saying that you've always known about Jesus or that you grew up in a Christian home. It doesn't mean that you will never struggle with sin or that your life will be perfect. You will still have to deal with your schedule; your family is always going to be your family.

But Jesus is the thirst quencher for the soul. To believe in Christ means to rest your full weight on Him, to have confidence that He is the One who will save you. It means that when Christmas is long past and you're deep in the February funk, you still know that the only way to be saved, the only way to walk through the pearly gates is by believing in Jesus. He is the Shepherd, the teacher, the King of Kings, the Lord of Lords, and the living water we thirst for.

*For further study: John 4:13–14*
*Additional references: Revelation 21:6*

# JESUS MEETS OUR NEEDS

Nehemiah 9:20

Do you remember the story of the Israelites? They were enslaved, crying to God for help because of the harshness of their masters. God sent Moses to deliver them from Pharaoh who did not want to let the people go. God sent plague after plague to change Pharaoh's mind. Finally, Pharaoh relented. Then he changed his mind again and chased the Israelites with his army. The Israelites were trapped between Pharaoh's army and the Red Sea, but God made a way of escape. Moses raised his arms, and the sea parted. The people of God escaped, and their pursuers drowned.

Moses led the people through the wilderness. It was a harsh and rocky desert. How did Moses and his people get food and water so they could survive in that difficult environment? God sent the Israelites manna every day. When the people longed for water, God told Moses to speak to a rock. But Moses did not do what he was told. He struck the rock instead, which angered God. Yet God still gave water for the people to drink.

The rock that Moses struck represents Christ. He is our spiritual food and drink. At the Passover meal before Jesus's arrest, Jesus held the bread before His disciples and said that it was His body, which would be broken for their sake. He held the cup and said it was His blood, which would be poured out on their behalf. Then He was stricken for our sins. He was beaten on the way to Calvary and nailed to a cross. When He died, He was pierced with a spear, and water and blood flowed from His side. Because of His sacrifice, we can be forgiven of all our sins. Because He rose again, we can have new life. When we believe in Jesus, He sends the Holy Spirit to dwell in our hearts.

Jesus knows what we need. He forgives our sins. He frees us from our fears. He brings life. He brings continual nourishment and refreshment so we can have communion with God through the Holy Spirit. The Spirit reminds us of all Jesus taught and did on earth. He helps us travel through the wilderness and deserts we face until we reach the Promised Land. Jesus meets all our needs.

*For further study: Deuteronomy 8:15*
*Additional references: Psalm 107:8–9, 1 Corinthians 10:3–4*

# AN URGENT INVITATION
### John 7:37–38

It was the last day of the Feast of Tabernacles, and Jesus stood up and loudly declared that anyone who was thirsty could come to Him and drink. He added that whoever believed in Him would have rivers of living water from within. Why did Jesus issue that invitation? Why did He wait until the last day of the week-long feast?

It's important to know what happened before that. Jesus had been declaring that people who believe in Him shall not perish but have everlasting life. He preached to all he could. He performed miracles. He extended Himself to those who would abuse Him. In John 5, Jesus experienced conflict. Leaders began to persecute Him because they did not think He should claim to be the Savior. In John 6, despite more miracles, people who had supported Him began to leave Him. They found His teaching too hard to accept. Jesus even asked His disciples if they wanted to leave.

John 7 begins with Jesus's brothers. They are going to the feast. They tell Jesus that if He wants to have this public persona as a savior, superhero, and the most popular guy in town, He should attend the feast, too. They did not say that because they believed in Jesus; they said it to mock Him. They were making fun of Him. Is it possible to miss Jesus on the way to a religious feast? Is it possible to miss Him on the way to church, while listening to Christian radio, or while doing good deeds? That's exactly what His brothers did. In the midst of all their activity, they missed the Savior.

At the Feast of Tabernacles, the Jews celebrated God's faithfulness to them in the wilderness. The priests who led the celebration would go to the Pool of Siloam each day to draw water. They would walk back with the water and pour it on the altar. On the last day, they would go around the altar seven times. Sometime later, Jesus healed a blind man by telling Him to wash in the Pool of Siloam. But at the Feast of Tabernacles, on the last day after the priests had poured out the water on the altar, when the greatest number of people had gathered and people were watching even from the rooftops, when He would get in even more trouble with the Jewish leaders, the Savior issued His invitation.

Jesus declared that all who were thirsty should come to Him. He stood and said in a loud voice that whoever believed in Him would have streams of living water flowing within. Will you accept His invitation?

*For further study: John 9:1, 6–7*
*Additional references: 2 Corinthians 6:2*

# WATER FLOWING WITHIN

John 7:38–39

You are thirsty for something better and something deeper in your life. Your thirst is not for short-term satisfaction but for the truths of scripture to be true in your life. Jesus's invitation is wide open. He says *whoever*. He says anyone who is thirsty. Everyone can come to Him.

Belief in Christ is what quenches our thirst. Believe that Jesus is the living water. Believe that His grace is enough. Believe that He is the One who gives us true security. He is the One we can trust. He is the One who sings the song of victory. He is coming again. He is not coming to take sides but to take over. His attention is the only attention that matters.

Whoever believes in Jesus, as the scripture says, will have streams of living water flowing from within. When Jesus promised that, He meant he would send the Holy Spirit to those who believed in Him. That would happen after Jesus died on the cross, laid in the tomb, rose from the dead, and ascended into heaven. Before then, Jesus had not yet been glorified. But now Jesus has been glorified, and all He promised is available to all who come to Him to slake their thirst.

When you trust Jesus Christ as your Savior, the Holy Spirit of God dwells in your heart. He lives inside you and empowers you so the living water can flow through you to others.

The Holy Spirit's indwelling results in living water flowing. God's love is poured into our hearts through the Holy Spirit. He is our advocate and teaches us the truth, reminding us of all Jesus said and did. He comforts us when we are sad or worried—when we experience the ups and downs of life. He builds us up. He equips us. He gives us gifts to serve God and serve others. His power flows through our lives. He energizes us. And He helps us bear fruit to please God. Pay attention to what He is prompting you to do this day. Listen to Him.

*For further study: Romans 5:5*
*Additional references: John 14:26, Ephesians 2:22*

# FILLED TO OVERFLOWING

## Colossians 2:6–7

The water Jesus gives is like a spring bubbling up within us for eternal life. It never stops. It does not run dry. Living water flows like rivers within our hearts. And that flow cannot be contained! It spills over in our speech, and it spills over through song. Our hearts are so full that we look for ways to express our gratitude to God. We praise Jesus's name to those around us.

People everywhere are thirsty. They want to see the spigot turned on. Their parched hearts want living water. And we can share it with them. Through the indwelling of the Holy Spirit, their lives, like ours, are transformed. Where nothing grows and the land is scorched and cracked, God can make green shoots of new life appear. Where there are only weeds and husks and dry stalks, He can make flowers and ferns and forests grow. God transforms barren ground into gardens.

Before God created the first human being, streams watered the ground. When the Lord formed Adam and Eve, He placed them in a garden surrounded by rivers. Many years later, the prophet Isaiah recalled the abundance of this first garden when he talked about the King who will reign in righteousness. That King is Jesus. The book of Isaiah says the righteous King will share His glory. Others will reign with Him. They will be like shelter from the wind, a refuge from the storm, shade in the sun, and streams in the desert. That is an amazing promise! All who Jesus invites to come to Him, no matter how thirsty and humble and powerless and ordinary they might be, will become rulers with Him—and thirst quenchers and bringers of blessing.

Thank God for His wonderful plan. Thank Him for His mighty deeds and great promises. He satisfies all who are thirsty. He satisfies all who are hungry. Christ is our spiritual food and spiritual drink. He meets all our needs. Thank God for His unfailing love!

*For further study: Colossians 3:16*
*Additional references: Psalm 107:8–9, Isaiah 32:1–3*

# LIVE BOLDLY BUT SPEAK KINDLY

## 1 John 2:1

The first thing John says in 1 John 2 is "my little children." He uses this phrase throughout the book to speak to us. He is now an elder who is pleading with us to receive what he has to say. He is speaking kindly. Then, without being harsh, he boldly declares, "I am writing you these things so that you may not sin" (1 John 2:1). What we learn in these opening verses is to live boldly but speak kindly. We want to live confidently in our faith, pray for people, share Christ, and take risks in obedience to God. Nobody has ever wanted to live timidly.

But sometimes we can live so boldly that we forget to speak kindly. Husbands, you need to be men of ambition, going forward in leadership in your families, but don't forget to speak kindly to your wife and children. At the same time, when we make a decision, we shouldn't worry that someone will think we are wrong or that we want to hurt anyone's feelings. If we do, we will never do anything. Being bold will sometimes mean acting in obedience to what we have heard or learned from God.

Have you noticed that we live in a world where we do not speak kindly? Do you ever turn on the TV and everybody looks like they are fighting? To speak kindly but live boldly sets a different tone. It does not include being sarcastic, belittling, or humiliating others. It is far from disrespecting authority, tearing down, or putting people down. It has everything to do with speaking the truth in love, building others up, and being the example of what we would ask of anyone else. God has a plan for you, and when you follow His heavenly advice, you are partnering with Him to bring life.

The beauty of Christianity is that you can be an amazingly loving person and also live boldly and speak strongly. To be able to put those two things together is very important.

*For further study: Ephesians 4:15*
*Additional references: 2 John 1:3*

# GOOD TEACHING

1 John 2:1

Have you ever wondered why someone is telling you something? Some people just start talking, and instead of going straight to the point, they take you for a ride. There is never a more comforting thing to hear in those conversations than these words: "I'm telling you this because...."

In 1 John 2, John gives us a startling reason for why he is writing. He has already told us, "My little children, I am writing you these things." But what are "these things"? They are that Jesus Christ is the atonement for our sins and that we have to confess our sins to one another and to God. Then he goes on to say, "I am writing you these things so that you may not sin."

Most of us are going to sin. We are not going to get up today and never sin again. It is not going to happen. We can sin less, but we will never be sinless. So what is John trying to say?

Good teaching is intended to keep us from bad living.

We need good teaching in our lives. Many of us are taking in whatever the media and the news give us; our minds are being shaped, formed, and molded by the things that are happening in the world. Digging into good teaching is really a challenge, particularly for adults. Students are challenged this way all the time. They get it so much that they get tired of it. Adults have to look for it. Why? Because we are not usually in a learning environment.

Where do you get good teaching? Where does it come from? From your reading plan. From your Bible reading. From mission trips. From the music you listen to. Maybe you listen to podcasts from pastors. At church, we receive godly input from the weekly sermon, conferences, or presentations. In some churches, adults sign up for Sunday school or Bible classes. There are many options. But you just can't expect to have good living without good teaching. It is not going to work. We need good inflow to have good outflow.

Spend time in God's Word. Take notes. Get something out of the scriptures. Sin destroys direction, kills joy, and shreds relationships. But good teaching gives us direction, fills us with joy, and helps us in our relationships. Do you see the difference?

*For further study: Romans 3:23*
*Additional references: Romans 3:9–10*

# UP AND IN THE RIGHT DIRECTION

—————————— 1 John 1:8, 10 ——————————

Have you ever wondered when we will stop sinning? The bad news is that we are all going to sin. There is no question about it. But what we don't want to do is practice sin, which means we should stay clear of continual or habitual sin.

We may never get rid of sin in our lives, but we don't want to end up sinning over and over again every day. We may use our condition to be able to relate with others and understand that we all need a Savior, but we must also be able to make some progress and let good teaching result in good living so we can journey on together.

Compare this to your finances. What do you want them to do? You probably want them to go up and to the right. You invest a little bit here, and you want to see some growth or an increased rate of return over time. It's the same thing with your faith. Faith pulls your obedience forward as it increases, and your obedience pulls your faith forward. Faith and obedience both need to grow at the same time.

Some folks say they have a lot of obedience, but they don't have a lot of faith. They are just like the Pharisees in the Bible; they are self-righteous and legalistic. Some other folks have a lot of faith, but they think their faith is personal and don't do much with it. The Bible says that faith without works is dead.

We don't want to be a Pharisee or somebody with dead faith. We want to be people whose faith pulls our obedience forward and whose obedience pulls our faith forward. As I walk with God, every step of obedience is followed by a step of faith. If you don't know if you can obey, just take another step of faith, and your obedience will follow. If you don't know if you can have enough faith, just take a step of obedience, and your faith will follow. They go hand-in-hand, and they pull one another onward.

Now here's the truth: Nobody is perfect. We go up and down every day. Hopefully, we are going more up than down—and in the right direction!

*For further study: James 2:14–26*
*Additional references: Ephesians 2:10*

# WE HAVE AN ADVOCATE

━━━━━━━━━━━━━ 1 John 2:1 ━━━━━━━━━━━━━

God our heavenly Father is good beyond our wildest imagination. He has us covered in every aspect of our lives—spiritually, fiscally, and intellectually. We can't help but marvel at His love. In 1 John 2, the Apostle John tells us not to sin. But he did not stop there. He went on to say that if we do sin, we have an advocate. His name is Jesus.

Even when we do everything we should, we struggle, and eventually we will slip and fall. In that moment, it is important to understand that we can bounce back because Jesus has fully paid our debt. We live in a courtroom drama. We are on trial, and God the Son, Jesus Christ, continually steps forward as our defense attorney. He is our righteousness and our payment in the eternal heavenly trial.

Our assurance is not placed on which denomination we belong to or our efforts to increase our church attendance, do good works, or just be nicer people. No. If we ever sin, we have Jesus to advocate for us. When we struggle with sin, we just need to turn back to Him. That increases our faith, which in turn increases our obedience. And as we obey more, we sin less and keep on walking. That is what it means to walk with God. Just as your investments don't skyrocket overnight, neither does your Christian walk. Growth is the cumulative effect of journeying on this path with God every day.

But Jesus, as our defense attorney, doesn't declare us innocent. What a farce it would be if Jesus stood before God and said, "No, no, no. He is innocent. You are taking it all wrong, God. That's not what he meant." In this courtroom drama, you agree with God that you are guilty, because you are the only one to blame. That is what confession is all about. But the Advocate steps in on your behalf and pays the price for you. He is the atoning sacrifice.

You become a person who is forgiven by God through Jesus Christ who paid for your sins. That is how you become a Christian. You know Jesus as Savior by pleading guilty before God and letting Jesus step in on your behalf to pay the price.

*For further study: Job 9:33*
*Additional references: Job 19:25; Hebrews 7:22, 9:15*

━━━━━━━━━━━━━ **JUNE 28** ━━━━━━━━━━━━━

# WE WILL NEVER BE ALONE

## 1 John 2:1

In the second chapter of 1 John, the Apostle John says that in Jesus we have an Advocate. *Paraclete*, the Greek word for advocate, means one who walks alongside of. It conveys the idea that Jesus Christ, through the Holy Spirit, walks alongside of us for the rest of our lives.

Thanks to the permanent company of the Holy Spirit inside of us, we know that we always have a friend in Jesus. He bore all our sins and grief. It means that He is right there in the heavenly courtroom saying, "This man, this woman is redeemed because of My blood that was shed for their sin."

Every one of us has felt alone at one time or another. Did you know that 40 percent of adults in America report feeling lonely most of the time? More and more Americans report that they don't have one close confidant or friend. In spite of all the social media and all the connections we now enjoy, people are feeling lonely. Single adults? Lonely. Married people? Lonely. Widows and widowers? Lonely. Old and young? Lonely. You can go to the mall and be surrounded by people, but you still may not have even one friend.

We need someone who cares about us to walk alongside of us. Jesus never leaves us alone. If today you are feeling lonely, without any friends or anyone who cares if you are still breathing, heaven is bringing you a message: Jesus is the One who walks alongside you.

When Abraham Lincoln died, in his pocket he had five things. Among them was a worn-out newspaper clipping about a speech in which someone said, "Abraham Lincoln is one of the greatest men of all time." In the midst of a difficult season, Lincoln must have felt encouraged by knowing somebody was on his team.

If you're a believer in Jesus Christ, in your heart you carry more than an encouraging quote. As we walk on this journey of life and the seasons of loneliness come, we can know that Jesus is right there with us.

*For further study: John 14:16–18*
*Additional references: Matthew 28:20*

# WE HAVE AN ACCUSER

## Job 1:8–11

If you have ever watched a good courtroom drama on TV or at the movies, you know that it isn't complete without a prosecutor. In the heavenly courtroom, not only do we have an Advocate, but we also have a prosecutor, an adversary, an accuser—Satan. And he is a real spiritual being.

The Bible describes how Satan accused Job, smearing Job's motives for his devotion to God. In the book of Zechariah, the author reveals that Satan stood at the right side of Joshua, the high priest, to accuse him before God. The book of Revelation says that Satan accuses us before God day and night.

Some of us don't like to talk about these things. But it is important to realize that there is an accuser. However, God is greater. When accusations fly at us, God refers the devil to our Advocate, Jesus, who crushed Satan's head at the cross to save us and paid for our redemption with His own blood.

The accuser hates you deeply. He hates your family, your future, and your joy. He will try to keep on lying to you, saying: "You are not a good mom," "You are a sorry dad," "You are single because nobody wants you," "If this is marriage, get out," "God is not good; look at all He withholds from you."

In Revelation, we read that the saints will overcome Satan by the blood of the Lamb and by the word of their testimony, which elaborates on how they were saved by Jesus. There is a praise song that goes like this: "Let the devil know, 'Not today.'" Maybe we could borrow those words as we are walking with God, taking steps of faith and obedience. When the accuser tries to stop us, we can let him know, "Not today. Today, I have an Advocate, I have faith inside my soul. I'm not good at everything. I don't make a lot of great decisions. But Jesus Christ is in my heart, He shed His blood for me, and He has crushed you."

Maybe your walk with God is a jagged line. But in Christ, you are heading upward and to the right. It is time you believe you have a strong Advocate before God. He paid the price for your redemption with His blood. He is your strength, and He lives inside your heart.

*For further study: Zechariah 3:1–2*
*Additional references: Revelation 12:10–11, Colossians 2:15*

# JESUS IS MY PAYMENT

## 1 John 2:2

Jesus can change your life. He loves you. He is the atonement for your sins. He died for you. He wants to change your life and be your atoning sacrifice. But at the same time, He is global. Jesus not only died for your sins, He died to pay for the sins of the whole world. That does not mean that everyone is saved, but it means that everyone can have the opportunity to trust in Jesus Christ as Savior. We could preach everywhere around the world, but each person must place his or her faith in Christ for salvation. Do you see the difference? It is not that everybody is saved, but now everybody *can* be saved.

Back in 1929, a man robbed a mail carrier. He not only robbed him, but he killed him. The man was sentenced to death, but he received a presidential pardon. And here's the dilemma: the man rejected the pardon. The issue went all the way to the U.S. Supreme Court with this question: If the President of the United States pardons you, can you reject it? The Court responded, "A pardon rejected is no pardon at all. Unless the recipient accepts the pardon, then the pardon cannot be applied."*

A pardon has two sides: the giver and the receiver. Jesus Christ has given us a pardon through His death on the cross, through the shedding of His blood. To be saved, we must receive that atonement and say, "Jesus, I trust in You." We are all guilty, but Jesus provides us with innocence through His death on the cross. If we place our trust in Christ as our Savior and the Holy Spirit comes to live in our hearts, we will never be alone. We take a step of faith. And we take a step of obedience. Our lives can become a little topsy-turvy, but in the long run, we move up and to the right. We grow in this relationship with Jesus. We will never be sinless, but we can strive to sin less as our faith in Jesus Christ pulls us forward in obedience to look more like Him.

*Father, I thank You that the accuser is crushed and the Advocate stands for me. I thank You, Lord, that in the midst of many accusations, You fight on my behalf. You fight my battles for me.*

*For further study: Matthew 26:28*
*Additional references: Romans 5:8; Hebrews 9:22, 10:19-22*

# SECRETS TO GROWING

## 1 John 2:3–4

As people who love the Lord Jesus Christ, we want to deepen our relationship with Him, and we want our lives to show it. This is not as difficult as it may seem. Spiritual growth is marked by two interdependent indicators: our faith and our obedience. Our faith pulls our obedience up. And as our obedience grows, our faith grows. Sometimes, when you don't feel like you have enough faith, you just take the next step of obedience. And when you don't feel like you have enough obedience, take the next step of faith.

Faith and obedience work interactively to our spiritual benefit. We shouldn't neglect one while championing the other. If you have a whole lot of obedience but not a lot of faith, that is self-righteousness. At the same time, if we claim we have a lot of faith, there should be some evidence of it in our lives.

We have some good days and some bad days. Not every day is perfect, and we don't do everything right. That is why we have an Advocate whose name is Jesus Christ. God is going to stand in for you and for me through Jesus Christ so we can have forgiveness. Grow your faith, and obedience will begin to take care of itself. If you are not sure how to grow your faith, take a step of obedience, and you will see God working in your life.

Growing in faith and obedience starts by knowing Jesus Christ. Knowing should result in growing. If you say you know Him and don't keep His commandments, you are fooling yourself. Do you think that people should do what they say? Yes, of course. If not, they are inconsistent.

If you say you know Him and then do not follow His commandments, the gap between your words and your actions is too big, and you are a liar. When you say something, you should do what you say. When you say you are going to be faithful, you should be faithful. When you say you're going to be there, you should be there. When you say you are going to do something, you should do it.

No one does everything perfectly. We are sinners. We struggle. We will never be perfect until we get to heaven. But as we grow in our relationship with Christ, what we say and what we do should get closer and closer together.

*For further study: Hebrews 11:6*

# CHECKING YOUR HEART

## 1 John 2:3–4

When we are studying a book of the Bible such as 1 John, sometimes it is important to zero in on the text so we can squeeze from it some not-so-obvious meaning. In 1 John 2:3, we find the word *know*. In Greek, it is in what is called perfect tense. That means there is some action that has taken place in the past, an action that is already completed.

If knowing Jesus was completed in the past, then these verses of scripture are not talking about salvation but about intimacy with God. John is focusing on the bigger picture of our Christian walk rather than on its individual pixels. If you think salvation goes on and off according to our present actions, then we would be going in and out of salvation all day long.

By this word *know* in the perfect tense, John is talking about how to have an intimate, growing relationship with Jesus Christ. Therefore, he calls us "little children" and "brothers and sisters." If you have placed your faith in Jesus, you have become a member of the family of God. And the only way to prove that is to live it out.

If we, as members of the family of God, don't keep His commands, we are lying. We are lying to God, which is the dumbest thing we can do because God knows everything. We lie to other people because we are trying to put forth an image that is not us. And we are lying to ourselves.

Self-deception is a big deal. That is where we can get in trouble as believers in Christ. We might think that if our morality is intact, then the authority issues between us and God don't really make a difference. You may be tremendously rebellious in your heart before the Lord and living independent of God, but you are still making it all look right and good. God loves you, He cares for you, and He wants you to come back like the prodigal son.

*Heavenly Father, I want to be honest with myself. Where am I with You, Lord? What am I saying, and what am I doing? What am I claiming, and how am I acting? Where is my faith, and where is my obedience? If I am really Yours, am I living it out?*

*For further study: 2 Chronicles 29:11*
*Additional references: Ephesians 2:19, Luke 15:17–19*

# JESUS CAME FOR YOUR HEART

## 1 John 2:3–4

We all love the rodeo in Houston. Here's how the rodeo begins: Everybody comes out carrying flags in a little parade and circles the arena. Everyone is dressed really nice. The horses are all pretty with bejeweled horse tack, looking perfect.

Imagine for just a second that one of those horses at the beginning of the rodeo—the one with the sparkles, the pretty saddle, the mane, and the brushed tail—is a horse from the bareback riding competition. You can't get on it. It looks beautiful, but the heart of the horse is one that will not take authority.

When we lie to ourselves, we become like that horse. We have everything happening on the exterior when people are watching and listening, but our heart is really like a bareback bronco. We don't want anybody to tell us what to do. We don't want God to tell us what to do. We don't want to be useful. We want to do our own thing. That is the difference between a horse that is useful and a bronco that bucks authority. When we don't do what we say or walk according to who we are, we are lying to ourselves, even if we are moral.

Rewind in American history to a time when everyone was considered a Christian. Remember those days? Everyone was a Christian. But that really wasn't true, was it? They all just kept it together a little bit better, and maybe they were more apt to go to church. But the issue is not the exterior; the issue is the heart.

The great news is that Jesus Christ came to change your hearts. When your heart changes, it changes who you are. Then you are not lying to God anymore. You are not lying to others anymore. You are not lying to yourself. You are walking with God, and He puts you on a journey of growth so what you say and what you do are consistent. I have been on that journey for more than 30 years. Even though I am still not perfect, I am a lot further along than when I started.

Where are you on that journey of growth with the Lord? Do your words and actions show that you are increasingly useful to the Lord, or is your heart still rebellious?

*For further study: Psalm 32:9*
*Additional references: 1 Samuel 16:7*

# KEEPING GOD'S COMMANDS

### 1 John 2:5

Guarding a prisoner. Keeping a military secret from falling into the wrong hands. As strange as these tasks may seem, God thinks you are the one for the job. In 1 John 2:5, we find the phrase "whoever keeps his word." The Greek word for *keep* means to hold or protect something of importance. It was a word used for guarding a prisoner. How important was that for the guard? Extremely important.

That same word is also in a couple other verses of scripture you may be familiar with. Peter says in his first letter that we have an inheritance that is imperishable, uncorrupted, and unfading, *kept* in heaven for us. And in 2 Timothy, at the end of his life, Paul said that he had *kept* the faith.

When John says "whoever keeps his word," it means that God's Word is important, real, and true. We keep it as we would guard a prisoner or the most valuable thing we can think of. And when we do that, the love of God is perfected or completed in us. When what we say and what we do connect, an amazing thing happens. We begin to walk with joy in the power of God. We come to realize He is in us, and we are in Him.

If you have never trusted Christ as your Savior, consider what has been offered to you. Come to this relationship. Jesus died on a cross for you. When you keep His Word and walk in intimacy with Him, your life will be complete.

Jesus said that if we have His commands and keep them, we love Him, and we will be loved by the Father. Do you see intimacy here? He also said that if we keep His commands, we will be loved by Him, and He will reveal Himself to us. Keeping God's commands will bring intimacy to our relationship with God. And walking in faith and obedience will keep us closer to Him.

If you feel like you don't have an intimate relationship with Christ, say this: "I am going to keep His commands. I'm going to trust Him." In doing so, you will be able to have greater intimacy with Him.

*For further study: 1 Peter 1:4*
*Additional references: 2 Timothy 4:7; John 15:5, 14:21*

# BEING LOVED BY HEAVEN

## 1 John 2:5

The goal of Christianity is not that you quit cussing, that you are nicer to people on the street, or that you quit doing this or that. The goal of Christianity is a love relationship with Jesus. You begin to express back to the Creator the love He has for you. When that happens, this beautiful circle starts turning: I am loved by heaven. I love heaven. I am loved by heaven. I love heaven.

Paul said that for him to live is Christ, but to die is gain. It is as if he were saying, *I am hard pressed on whether I should stay here with you or go to heaven, because it is far better to be in heaven.* We begin to long for a relationship with Jesus. It is not stuff on earth that drives us anymore. It is hearing this: "Well done, good and faithful servant." Imagine hearing that in heaven!

This is our core motivation: I am loved by God. Because of that love relationship, I am going to keep His commands. They are the best for me, so I am going to walk them out.

Why am I faithful to my wife? I am faithful to my wife because I love her and because I said I would be faithful to her. But the day that I am only faithful to my wife because I said so, not because I love her, is the day that our marriage has intimacy problems. With God, we have a love relationship. We are faithful to God because we love Him. That is the number one thing—not just because He told us to be faithful but because we love Him.

Think of this as two sides of a circle. On one side, we have our love. On the other side, we have our life. What is our love for Jesus? How do we love Jesus? What is our heart? At the same time, what is our life like? How are we living? In other words, our intentions lead to real actions. There shouldn't be a disconnect between them. If you keep God's commands, then your life will be complete.

My love and my life are connected. That is Christianity. I want to be caught up in a circle of loving heaven and being loved by heaven. I love Jesus, and I live it out. And as I live it out, my love for Jesus grows.

*For further study: Philippians 1:21–26*
*Additional references: Matthew 25:21–23*

# THE JOY OF INTIMACY WITH GOD

1 John 2:5

The joy of living out what we believe is that we grow in intimacy with God, and He reveals Himself to us. You are not going to find intimacy when you are obedient but have no faith, or when you say you have faith but don't have obedience. You will only find intimacy through faith and obedience as you get closer and discover more in Him.

What happens now is that we keep the commandments because of our love for God. We experience His love for us. Now we are completely surrendered to Him and useful for His glory. We trust Him. And He directs us with every single step because we have experienced and seen His faithfulness over time. That makes us better husbands, better wives, better employees, and better employers. It makes us faithful.

Some folks from our church put "what I say" and "what I do" together. Words and actions went together. They went to North Carolina on behalf of our church to help with hurricane relief and to clean up houses. They had credibility because they were from Houston and had experienced the devastation of a hurricane. The group told of a man in Home Depot who didn't know how to mud-out his home. One of our people simply told him how. Then he shared Jesus Christ with that guy right there in the aisle at Home Depot and was able to tell him about the love of Jesus that can help him through any disaster.

That team has also served thousands of meals to people. It was an awesome thing as part of the body of Christ. They are together as a team. People pray for them. They pray for others. They worshiped God by getting sheetrock out of a house. That is a say-and-do coming together.

They did not go because they had to or because it was mandatory. There was no draft. The government didn't say every church had to send people. They went on their own to say, "I want to be there." Two of the group could tell the people of North Carolina, "I know what it's like to be in a house just like this." That was a huge thing.

Do you know the joy of bringing words and actions together to love Christ by helping others?

*For further study: Matthew 25:31–46*

# WWJD

1 John 2:6

Once in a while there comes our way a nagging question: How do I follow Christianity? The answer is as easy as an old cliché. We just ask ourselves, "What would Jesus do?" or "WWJD?" The Bible says that those who claim to follow Christ should walk as Jesus walked. But how did Jesus walk?

Jesus walked slowly, having time for relationships. How many of us bought our house thinking about the people we were going to invite over? But now, we are so busy that we just pull in, close the garage door, and hope nobody comes over. We have a welcome mat, but we don't mean it. The time has come for us to walk slowly and invite people over. Don't you love it when you see somebody whose first priority is relationships?

Jesus walked toward the needy, not away from them, to help them. Let's walk to the least and the lost. Let's be part of their lives. Let's connect with people. Suburban America is not heaven on earth. There are needy people everywhere we go. Let's be friendly, extend a hand, and say, "We are so glad you are here and so glad you are in our lives."

Jesus walked securely in God's love and His plan. If we begin to walk securely in God's plan, there is going to be a depth in our lives that will bring a sense of connection and completeness. This deep growth will hold us true and strong, moving in God's direction.

In the northern oceans, sailors frequently observe icebergs traveling in one direction, even though the wind is blowing strongly in the other direction. How does that happen? Well, we only see the tip of the iceberg. The deep current of the water is stronger than the wind on the surface.

When we follow the commands of God, when our "say" and "do" get closer and closer, when our love and life connect, when our faith and obedience are working in tandem to help us grow, we become people of depth whom the current of God can take against the winds of this world. The Lord and the intimacy of God determine your direction.

*For further study: Mark 1:32–34*
*Additional references: John 4:5–7*

# BE WISE

Women can typically be compared with flowers. Most women love flowers because they are delicate and beautiful; they have life, and they are colorful. Now let's think of a comparison for men. What about a media center with five remote controls? Let's look at that in the context of a Proverbs 31 man.

Proverbs 31:1–7 gives us our first remote control, which is to be wise. Those seven verses actually talk a lot about drinking, which I'm sure made a lot of you nervous, but what the passage is trying to get across is that we need to be wise. Men are given two things to look out for: women and wine. All of us have seen men fall for those two things.

Men have a propensity to fall for women because they are stimulated visually. They begin by looking, and then they are tempted and drawn in. It may be through pornography, through a wrong relationship, or through dating. The same is true with wine. Wine symbolizes an escape. Often, men have a lot of pressure, and they are looking for an escape. That can be alcohol or drugs.

The temptations are so predictable, so obvious, that God warns men to be on the lookout for women and wine. In order for men to maintain their purpose of walking with God, they must be aware of those two areas of temptation.

Consider this regarding drinking: The more responsibility you have in your life, the less alcohol needs to be part of it. Proverbs is talking about kings here. Nobody wants to see a pilot at the bar before getting on the plane. Nobody wants to hear a surgeon come in and say, "Hey, we are ready for this heart surgery; I usually have a beer or two just to relax." The more responsibility you have, the less you need to be influenced by alcohol or drugs. They give you a lack of clarity in your life.

Everyone knows somebody whose life has been wrecked by alcohol. In our homes, our kids and grandkids are watching us. We must model a positive way of living life.

Men, be wise about these two obvious temptations. We have seen it with David and Bathsheba, with Solomon and his wives, with our friends. Do not let pleasure destroy purpose in your life. You will find that if you follow the purposes of God, you will discover the delights in your life to be far more in-depth than anything you could have imagined. Be wise. Read and apply Proverbs in your life. Open up the Bible, read a chapter a day, and use it to lead and guard your life.

Are you being wise about temptation?

# SPEAK UP AS PROTECTORS

### Proverbs 31:8–9

"Speak up for those who have no voice, for the justice of all who are dispossessed" (Prov. 31:8). Men, we must speak up as protectors. This does not dishonor women at all; rather, it honors them. Honor women by protecting them, because that is what God has wired men to be: protectors and warriors for good.

That is what is lacking in today's world. We lack men standing up as protectors and providers. It is time for us to be real men. A man nowadays is not a hero; he is a bumbling fool. Consequently, we do not have anyone as a model of what it is really like to be a man. Sadly, men have moved from protectors to predators. What has been said repeatedly is that sex is something you have to get, not something you have to give. Now, sex is about lust and passion, not about love and commitment. In just the past year, more than 200 celebrity men have been accused of some sexual impropriety.

Men, we need to rise and speak up for those who cannot speak for themselves. We have to be men of God who say, "No, this is wrong! This is not how we are going to be in this house. This is not how we are going to be at work. This is not how we're going to be in our society." We do not have to be obnoxious or rude about it, but we do have to step up.

Do we want to be passive predators? If you are connected or addicted to pornography, you are part of the harming of women. Get help with that problem. I understand it is a tricky thing, but we must rise and speak up as protectors if we don't want to become passive predators. God has created you to be a warrior for good.

This is the kind of man single women should be looking for. This is what a married woman should be praying for her husband.

Are you raising your voice on behalf of people in need?

# MEN OF GOD HONOR WOMEN

## Proverbs 31:10-11

"Who can find a wife of noble character? She is far more precious than jewels. The heart of her husband trusts in her, and he will not lack anything good" (Prov. 31:10–11). Men of God do not look down on women. They do not try to get something from them; women are not mere sex objects. That is why the most significant contributor to women's rights is Christianity. God has called husbands to die for their wives, to protect their wives, and to honor them in a significant way. That is what men are to do.

Trust is the foundation of any relationship of any value. If you cannot trust someone, you do not have a relationship. How do we have a relationship with God through Jesus Christ? We place our trust in Jesus as our Savior. We trust that He died on the cross. We believe that He is the man He said He was, that He is the Messiah. We trust that the scriptures are true. We trust that He rose from the grave.

The heart of the husband trusts his wife, and she should trust him. Men should honor women. Do you honor women? Do you daily listen to them? Do you daily respect them? Do you receive their wisdom? Do you speak to them in the right tone? Sometimes, we are harsher with the women we love than we are with women we do not know. We are kinder to somebody who passes by than to someone in our own home.

This king, Lemuel, is very interesting. First, he is not mentioned in any of Israel's history, so he is not an Israeli king. Maybe he is a foreign king. Perhaps Lemuel is Solomon's pen name. The name Lemuel means devoted to God. So the one who is devoted to God is going to be wise, is going to be a protector, and is going to honor women. Men, if you see a woman being harmed, go to the mat on her behalf.

Do you honor women in your life? Are you teaching your kids to honor women?

# BE RESPECTABLE

## Proverbs 31:23

You do not get respect just because you are a man or because you are the husband or the dad. Your respect is earned over years and years.

A woman who has a good man in her home should not disrespect him and cut his legs out from under him over and over again. In doing so, she is creating something she does not want. She may get her way, but in the end, it will weaken her marriage. Men need respect and encouragement.

To be a man of honor is to be a person who makes wise decisions. To become a man of respect, you need to fly with eagles, not turkeys. You have to be around the right groups of people. Maybe you do not have a good role model in your family. Find a man, somebody in the church, you can look up to, respect, and imitate. Find someone who is respectable—someone you can be like.

In the days when Proverbs was written, all the business took place at the city gates. Men sat there and acted like the legislative branch of the U.S. government. They decided who got in, who did not, and what laws applied. They were the decision-makers. They made the difference. If you are going to be a difference-maker, you have to be a decision-maker. You must step forward in difficult times, make wise decisions, and stick with them.

Respect requires responsibility. A lot of us men are trying to avoid responsibility. But respect comes during difficult times, through sleepless nights, from headaches and how you solve problems. You will not get respect because you have a band saw or a gun. Respect comes from how you respond to responsibility at work, at home, at church, and in life. Do you want to gain respect? Make wise decisions.

Are you gaining respect or demanding it?

# BE AN ENCOURAGER

**Proverbs 31:28**

How do you speak an encouraging word? How do you give a kind and clear word of encouragement daily to your wife, your kids, your friends, your employer, your employees, or the person on the street?

Encouragement is best from people who know you the most, and nobody knows you more than your own family. Men, when you give that word of encouragement, it makes a huge, huge difference. Be an encourager. Write notes. Say positive words daily. There has never been a woman who has walked into a marriage counselor's office and said, "I am so sick of this. He tells me I'm beautiful all the time. He tells me he would marry me all over again. He tells me I'm the greatest thing in the world. I'm precious like jewels. I want to be out of this." That never happens. What she really says is this: "He doesn't say anything. He sits in that chair, and I don't know how he feels anymore."

Men, your wife, your kids, the people around you, they need to hear a word of encouragement from you. They do not need to hear complaints or how they have failed or how they have not succeeded in the past. Being a woman is hard; being a man is hard; being a teenager is hard. Positive words are powerful for everyone.

Gentlemen, I am calling you to make a difference in our world. Are your words encouraging? Or are they discouraging?

# THE BOOKENDS OF PROVERBS

---
Proverbs 1:7
---

You have probably seen some crazy bookends out there. I have my little bookends of the cross. I went on the Internet and found all sorts of bookends, including a crazy one that looks like dinosaurs are chasing you. If you are a comics fan, you can get one with Superman and Batman fighting—who is the greatest?

There is also a bookend in the book of Proverbs. You can find it in Proverbs 1, and it ends in Proverbs 31. There are many verses in the book of Proverbs about the fear of the Lord. Chapter 1 talks about what the proverbs are intended to do in our lives. Near the beginning of the chapter, it says, "The fear of the Lord is the beginning of knowledge; fools despise wisdom and discipline" (Prov. 1:7). The last chapter says, "A woman who fears the Lord will be praised" (Prov. 31:30). These concepts of the fear of the Lord and wisdom are the bookends of Proverbs.

If there is something we need in this generation, it is the right knowledge along with the wisdom to apply that knowledge to our lives. Remember, knowledge is just information. In this era of technology, we have tons of information. But only in God can we find the truth. Knowledge without wisdom is just information in our brains. The only way to apply that information wisely is through the fear of the Lord in our lives. That will lead us to do the right things.

The foundation of life is the fear of the Lord. You can build a skyscraper, but it is not going to work unless you have a foundation that goes deep. You can have an awesome, beautiful tree, but if you do not have roots that go deep into the ground, it will fall down. You must have a foundation. You must have roots—something that goes deep into your life and gives you stability. That something should be the fear of the Lord.

What is your source of knowledge? Is it God? Are you applying this knowledge wisely to your life?

# SEEING GOD WITH AWE

### 1 Corinthians 3:12–15

What is the fear of the Lord? Should we be afraid to talk about that fear? Does it have something to do with hell or judgment?

If we define the fear of the Lord, we could say that it means we should regard God with reverence and awe. Now, there is also a fear of the Lord that involves judgment. The Bible says that one day we will stand before God to be judged. However, if you have trusted Jesus as your Savior, God will see Christ instead of you when that time comes. He will know that Christ is within you and you are in Him. He will not see your sin. He will see His Son and His righteousness. That is what was traded at the cross. God traded your sin for Christ's righteousness. He rose from the grave to stand before God on your behalf. And then there is the judgment of our works. The Bible says that our works will be like gold, silver, or costly stones. So yes, we must fear the Lord.

Do you see God with reverent awe? Do you realize that God knows every hair on your head and every star in the sky? He knows everything that you and I are going through. He is grander and bigger than any life we could ever live. He knows every person who has ever lived and every person who will ever live. We can come before this magnificent, vast God. He knows our names, our hurts, and our fears. He deserves our reverent awe.

Where does that reverence of God begin? People usually think that everything starts with them, that they are the center of the universe. That is why they are aggravated when they get into traffic jams. They assume that other people can experience traffic jams, but they should not. If there are no parking spots, they think there should be a parking spot for them. When bad things happen, they get upset. We all know that bad things do happen, but when they happen to us, there is a problem with the world. When your worldview begins with yourself, your happiness, and your joy, God becomes an afterthought. He only exists to bless you, and that is all you expect Him to do.

Do you think God is there just to bless you and your plans? How can you show the Lord your reverent awe?

# GOD, THE ALPHA AND OMEGA

Genesis 1:1

Would you like a God who does everything but requires nothing? That is what we have created in our society. Consequently, humans are in the middle, in the center, and God is their servant. The whole thing is about us and what God should do for us. That is the world's view, and Christianity has become a psychological self-help movement with Jesus tagged on at the end. That view does not conceive of Christianity as the power of God through the Word of God and through the people of God changing lives for Christ. Humans are the center.

What is the biblical worldview? God is at the center of it all. He is eternal. He is the Alpha and the Omega. We were created, and He is the Creator. See how Genesis begins: "In the beginning God" (Gen. 1:1). It doesn't say "In the beginning humans" or "In the beginning I." God is the central focus.

When you believe there was no Creator and you just came into existence, you think you are amazing because you are the center of the universe and the greatest thing that has ever happened.

But when we realize that God is the best thing that has ever happened, we have reverence and awe for Him. We can say, "Lord, you are incredible. You love us, and You care for us. The foundation of our life is based on You." This is such good news. It is not self-help. It is not willpower. It is not your intellect or strength. It is God's help, God's power, God's strength, God's will, God's desire.

Do you still think you are the center of your life? What can you do to make the Lord the center of the universe—the center of your life?

*For further study: Revelation 1:8*
*Additional references: Revelation 22:13*

# FEARING GOD BRINGS LIFE

Proverbs 10:27

I want to show you four things in the book of Proverbs—in the middle of the bookends of Chapter 1 and Chapter 31. These four things will give you an understanding of what can happen in your life when you have the fear of the Lord.

The first thing is that real life is found only in the fear of the Lord. Proverbs 10:27 states, "The fear of the Lord prolongs life, but the years of the wicked will be short" (ESV). It is a fountain of life that will let you live in such a way that you will sleep satisfied. You will be able to lay your head on your pillow knowing you are a man or woman of integrity. God has everything under control. You know that evil cannot touch you. It is said that Stalin had eight bedrooms, all with locks on them because he was so afraid somebody would kill him in the night. He certainly did not have peace.

True life is found in Jesus who came to give you abundant life.

Everyone is breathing, living, and doing things, but living well is not possible when you are the center of your world. Living well happens when God is at the center of your universe.

Are you enjoying the abundant life? Would you like to have that kind of life?

*For further study: Proverbs 14:27*
*Additional references: Proverbs 19:23; John 10:10, 14:6*

# THE SOURCE OF CONFIDENCE

**Proverbs 14.26**

The first thing the fear of the Lord does is give you real life. The second thing the fear of the Lord does is give you genuine confidence in the Lord. Proverbs says that in the fear of the Lord is strong confidence and that God's children have a refuge. It is better to have a little treasure with the fear of the Lord than to have a great treasure that brings you turmoil. You would be better off if you were broke but honored God than you would be if you had everything you could ever want or wish for but dishonored Him.

In Christ, we can have confidence that He is higher and greater than any circumstance you face. Someone who fears the Lord says something like this: "I humbly revere you, Lord. I am yours. I love you. I revere your judgment; I revere your great grace, your great love, your great kindness, and your excellent guidance." This is where you will find confidence.

Confidence without Christ is veiled arrogance. Why? Because it is a belief based in yourself and who you are. Confidence is found in the Lord.

As a pastor, I am used to speaking in front of people. They come to me and say, "We feel so sorry for you. How do you do that? How do you get up in front all those people all the time?" And I respond, "Well, first of all, they are very nice people. It is not as if they are against me. It is not as bad as you think it is. I like it. It is fun." However, let me tell you something. My confidence does not come from my competence. I pray, "Lord, I do not want my competence to come from my personality or my confidence from my experience."

After preaching three times a week for more than 25 years, I can say that I have done a lot of public speaking. However, I do not rest in my experience, and I do not rest in my competence. My confidence is based on believing that God has a word for His people. He has a message. He has a Bible that far outlasts me, outlasts the men and women who have preached it before me, and outlasts the men and women who will preach it after I am gone. God's Word has lasted throughout all of history and has been taught throughout the entire world. That is where my confidence comes from. If your confidence is in your personality or in your experience, at some point that will not be enough.

Is your confidence based on you or on the Lord? How can you increase your trust in the Lord?

*For further study: Proverbs 15:16*

# HONEST AND SKILLFUL LIVING

## Proverbs 8:13

We have seen that the fear of the Lord brings real life and confidence. Now let me tell you the third thing the fear of the Lord brings: holiness and humility. Proverbs declares that the fear of the Lord is to hate evil, pride, and arrogance. That's not just disliking them; it's hating them. Whenever God says He hates something, you need to pay attention. He hates all those things because He wants to be glorified, and He wants us to live in a way that honors Him. Throughout the book of Proverbs, we find the importance of integrity. That means being honest, not having unbalanced scales, not taking from somebody, not stealing.

The fourth thing the fear of the Lord brings is skillful living. Solomon wrote, "The fear of the Lord is the beginning of knowledge; fools despise wisdom and discipline" (Prov. 1:7). A fool despises skillful living.

Knowledge is not necessarily wisdom. Many people have a great deal of knowledge. They know a great deal, but they are great fools. You can be Mr. Smarty Pants all you want, but if you do not have the knowledge of the Lord and the fear of the Lord, you may be a bigger fool than anyone else. That happens if we do not have a reverent awe of God. Remember, He is God; we are not.

I am in Christ, and Christ is in me. From that place of holiness and humility, I have confidence. I am experiencing real life. Now I have a skill for living in order to go through this journey because God is guiding me and doing His work. Then from that place of trusting in Him, I can step out to make a difference in other people's lives. Remember, you are not the center; God is. And when God is the center of your life, you will make a difference in the hearts of other people.

Are you living honestly and skillfully? Is the Lord the source of your knowledge?

*For further study: Proverbs 1:7*

# THREE KINDS OF FOOL

**Proverbs 1:7**

We can embrace the fear of God, or we can be fools. The Bible says that by despising wisdom and discipline, by saying something like "I do not want to hear all that stuff," we are fools. There are three Hebrew words in Proverbs that the writer uses for the word *fool*.

The first word means dull and closed-minded, a thickheaded or stubborn person. That word is used 49 times in Proverbs. If you are that kind of fool, you are the kind of person who says things like, "Hold my beer and watch this," "I could jump off that," "Give me that motor." That is what we are talking about here.

The second word for fool refers to someone who lacks spiritual perception. Those fools may know everything in the world but not understand how things really work. They see the tree, they see the fruit, but they are not able to see the root from which they come. They lack spiritual sight.

The third kind of fool is arrogant and flippant, coarse and hardened in his or her ways. That word is used 19 times in Proverbs. In Proverbs 1:7, that fool—that arrogant and flippant person—despises wisdom. What does despise mean? It means you disdain, hate, and throw off something, saying, "I do not want any of it." When we despise wisdom, we become fools—arrogant, flippant, and hard-hearted. We say, "Hey, I am just going to do it my way, Frank Sinatra style." And what happens when you do it your way? You get what your way can produce. For some, that might be remarkable, but it is only going to be remarkable for a short time because you are at the center.

When we say, "Lord, I want to do it Your way," true life, true confidence, true humility, true holiness, and skillful living will come to you. That does not mean that your life will be perfect or easy. It means that you have connected, that you have jumped into this river, this stream, this flow. Instead of swimming upstream, let God take you in His power and His strength. Lift up your feet, keep going, and let God do His work.

Can you see farther than material things? Or do you prefer the Frank Sinatra style?

# DESPISING WISDOM

## Proverbs 31:30

The last chapter of Proverbs says a woman who fears the Lord will be praised. If we fear the Lord, we are praising Him, and we are able to have a life of praise.

The Apostle Paul says that Christ became God-given wisdom for us. Paul also said that in Christ are hidden all the treasures of wisdom and knowledge. Consequently, when we embrace Jesus, we are embracing wisdom. When we embrace wisdom, we are embracing Christ. Thus, we do not want to despise wisdom by despising Christ.

In his letter to the Thessalonians, the Apostle Paul tells the church that he sent Timothy to encourage them so they would not be shaken by the trials they were bound to face. Paul was afraid the enemy had gotten the best of them, but since their foundation was Christ, he also declared that the enemy had no place there. God knows what you are going through, just as He knew what the Thessalonians would face. God knows what is happening in your life.

What should we do, then, when trials come? We go to the Lord in prayer to find His help and keep the enemy from taking advantage of us in our difficult times. Everything is resolved in prayer. What will hold your life together is you on your knees before God. In poverty or wealth, sickness or health, you must say, "Jesus, I've got a very short time on this planet, and I want to live skillfully. I want to pray so I can live with a reverent awe of You."

Do you appreciate wisdom? Do you go in prayer to the Lord in your trials?

*For further study: 1 Corinthians 1:30*
*Additional references: Colossians 2:3, 1 Thessalonians 3:1–5*

# HOW DID WE GET HERE?

━━━━━━━━━ Proverbs 5:1-2 ━━━━━━━━━

When we talk about sexuality, I want you to know that Jesus Christ can forgive us and change our lives if we have made any mistakes. If you are struggling with sex, I want you to know there is hope in God. You can find forgiveness in Christ and learn from the Lord.

How did we get to where we are when it comes to ideas about sex? Have you noticed that in the last 50 to 60 years, things have turned upside down? Before the '60s, talking about sex in church would have been a scandal. Before the '60s, here was the order: marriage, sex, family. You were scared to have sex because you might end up having to get married. In a sense, abstinence was fear-based because you did not want to end up shaming your family. What happened that made a significant change? Well, one thing happened: birth control.

Birth control separated sex from pregnancy. You could have sex, and there was no risk of becoming pregnant. We also began to have great urbanization in our society. Instead of being in small towns growing up where everybody knew everybody, people started moving to big cities where nobody knew them.

Then, in the '70s, we had no-fault divorce. In 1969, Ronald Reagan, governor of the State of California, signed the first law allowing no-fault divorce. It made marriage a simple contract instead of a covenant. Fatherless homes began to grow at a rapid rate.

Ninety percent of homeless and runaway children are now from fatherless homes. Seventy-five percent of rapists with anger problems come from fatherless homes. Seventy-one percent of high school dropouts come from fatherless homes. And single parents? Well, they have to work harder with their kids.

In the '90s, the Internet grew like crazy, and so did Internet pornography. Forty million Americans regularly visit porn sites. Thirty-five percent of all Internet downloads are related to porn. The Internet made pornography accessible, affordable, and addictive, which led to the rise of rape, sex trafficking, sexual abuse, and more.

In 2015, same-sex marriage became legal; marriage is no longer exclusively between a male and a female. We have taken the biology out of it. Is there such a thing as a male and a female anymore? I could list a thousand other things, but this is basically how we got where we are today.

Are you alarmed by these facts and statistics? Do you think they break God's heart?

# DEFENSE AND OFFENSE

## Ephesians 6:10–15

In yesterday's devotional, we had a quick review of how we got where we are today in our ideas about sex. Now think about this: Does God have something to say about it? What is the right thing to do now? What is the truth?

In every sport, you need a good defense and a good offense. In basketball, you go from defense to offense in a matter of seconds. We are going to look at the defense and the offense of God's plan for sex.

First, we need a good defense. What is our defense? In 1779, talking about the military, George Washington suggested that a good offense is the most excellent defense.

Sex is everywhere. It comes to us a million miles per hour all day long. Advertisers use sex to sell stuff that does not have anything to do with sex. King Solomon said that an immoral woman's lips drip with honey. Though her lips are smoother than oil, they are poison. Her mouth is a double-edged sword. She is headed straight to the grave. She does not even know that her life is crooked and going in the wrong direction.

We must have a great defense and realize that a short-term gain brings long-term pain. Unfortunately, I have been in some conversations with folks who have committed adultery, and the tears and the sobs are not worth the pleasure that lasted for a few brief moments. There is not an adulterer I've talked to who would tell you it was worth it; the pain afterward was just too deep.

That sums up Solomon's advice: "So now, sons, listen to me….Keep your way far from her. Don't go near the door of her house" (Prov. 5:7–8). We are called to flee temptation. When you see sexual temptation in the scriptures, you will always see God's people fleeing from it—taking off, running away, and getting away from it.

Do not scroll down to see if that picture on the Internet is what you think it is. Do not click to do a little investigation to see what the story is about. Do not answer that call. Do not respond to that message. We have to flee those temptations. Our defense begins with not allowing ourselves to be involved in situations that could make us fall.

Have you ever been in such a situation? Did you flee from it?

*For further study: Proverbs 5:3–8*
*Additional references: 2 Timothy 2:22*

# THE BILLY GRAHAM RULE

**1 John 2:15–17**

Billy Graham, the famous evangelist, had a rule in order to avoid sexual temptation. It was this: Never be in a situation with a woman by yourself. That does a couple of things. First, it keeps you free of accusations. Second, it keeps you free from temptation as you hold yourself accountable.

I know some of you have to travel for business, and you have to meet with people of the opposite sex. But let me encourage you to do everything you can to not be in a situation where you are alone at dinner with another person who is not your spouse. You men are not strong enough to share a meal with those ladies at the office because they are good looking, they are dressed up. And when you get home to your wife, she has a scrunchie in her hair and a kid on each hip because she has been taking care of your family. And all of a sudden, the temptation gets stronger.

So, men and women, sit down with your boss and say, "I will meet any person in his or her office, but I do not need to be alone at dinner with them. I am not going to be there." If you keep the Billy Graham rule, you will not have a problem, because you will have accountability. It is better to be considered rude than interested in others you have no business being interested in.

It is also very important to know your weaknesses. You may need to use filters on your computer and your phone. Put your computer in a public place. Parents, your children should not have computers in their bedrooms. They should not have technology in private places. You as a parent must have access to every password, every app, everything. Just because your children get a phone does not mean they need an Internet browser on it. They can talk and text all day long. Handing our kids that kind of technology is like handing them an encyclopedia with a *Playboy* magazine in the middle and then saying, "Do not read what is in the middle."

Do you control your kids' screens? Are you accountable for your own issues in this area?

# SELF-CONTROL

When we talk about fleeing temptation, the most important and crucial element is the fruit of the Spirit. Galatians 5 describes it as love, peace, patience, kindness, goodness, gentleness, faithfulness, and self-control. How do you battle sex temptations? Fall in love with Jesus and let self-control, a fruit of the Spirit, flourish in your life. I am not telling you to try harder; I am telling you to love deeper. It is important to have great filters and accountability. At the same time, you should not miss the spiritual part of loving God and being satisfied with who Jesus is and what He can do.

Remember, we are looking at the defense and the offense regarding God's plan for sex. Why is a good defense so important? Because the price of being careless is higher than your life can afford. It is more than you want to pay. We have to be on the defense because temptation is everywhere.

Now, let's talk about the offense. Let's make some baskets and score some points, not just play defense our whole life. How do we move forward in the offense? When Solomon talks about drinking water from our own cistern, from our own well, and that our stream should not flow into the streets, he is talking about the satisfaction of sex we must find only in our marriage. Remember, our greatest defense is our offense. You have everything you need in your home with your spouse. There is no need to spill the fountain of your pleasure on the streets or the public squares. You do not have to share it with strangers. Enjoying the love of your spouse is your best counterattack against the enemy.

Do you know that those who are happily married are 61 percent less likely to look at porn? That does not mean you are not going to struggle in your marriage, but it does mean that in a satisfied relationship, there is great protection from the adversary.

Are you manifesting the fruit of the Spirit in your life? Are you enjoying love with your spouse?

*For further study: Galatians 5:22–23*

# TRUE PLEASURE

## Proverbs 5:15–16

Regarding sex, whatever you have seen on TV, heard in a song, or seen in a movie has all been wrong. If it had been right, it would not have been done in front of anyone else. That is what is called privacy. Remember, your streams should not overflow in the streets. I want to give you an equation for real pleasure: Privacy + purity = pleasure.

Television industry statistics state that since 1998, sex scenes have nearly doubled, and 70 percent of television programming now includes some sexual content. Ninety-two percent of the top ten songs are about sex. So if you have heard it, if you have seen it, you have seen it wrong. That is not how God wanted it to be. Why? Because true pleasure comes from privacy and purity in marriage.

Today, many believe that pleasure is when you take out privacy and purity and do whatever you want whenever you want. Sex is more than physical, and it is more than virtual in pornography. It was intended to be spiritual, soulful, and safe.

Parents, we should talk about sex with our children, early and often. Our kids are going to figure out the biology of it, no doubt about that. However, in order for them to understand the theology and the emotional aspect of sex, we must talk with them.

Something we need to understand about human sexuality is that men and women have different needs and responses. Women must cross an emotional bridge first, and then they can pass to the physical part. Men cross a physical bridge first, and then they are ready to cross to the emotional part. It does not mean that women are not physical and men are not emotional. Their differences are just the way God made men and women and put them together to make a balance. Sex is something more than physical activity; it is an interaction that is soulful and spiritual with the person you love who has committed their life to you in marriage.

Do you agree with the equation for pleasure? Do you apply it in your marriage?

# PRACTICE SAFE SEX

Almost everyone knows what safe sex is. But for Christians, it is more than just prevention from some disease or pregnancy. Safe sex is when a guy takes a gal out on a date and treats her great because he considers her the most precious thing in the world. He takes her on date after date until finally he has saved up enough money to buy her a ring. He gets down on one knee and humbly says, "I am going to protect you and provide for you. I am going to give my life for you. Will you marry me?" If she says yes, he takes the ring and puts it on her finger. Then they celebrate with both of their families, pick out dishes, and plan the wedding.

Later, they get married before God, their families, and all their friends. Eventually, they may become parents. They will be together through thick and thin, and the expression of their love will be a physical blessing of God because the two will experience great pleasure, great privacy, and high purity.

All that can happen for you. It can happen even if you lost your virginity before marriage, were into pornography, or were abused. God can redeem and change all those things.

If you practice safe sex—God's way—you will get into this safe zone with your spouse, and you will have intimacy. You know your spouse is not comparing you to anyone else, that nobody is judging your body, that you are being embraced and cared for, and that you have not been wronged or taken advantage of. That is how safety comes into a relationship.

Have you noticed that the world calls it making love? However, God would call it expressing the love that already exists. You are not going to create love from sex. Women tend to use sex to get love. Men tend to use love to get sex. When you are in love and married, a great offense and a great defense come together.

Are you having real safe sex? Would you like to enjoy that kind of love?

*For further study: Hebrews 13:4*

# INTIMACY AND MARRIAGE

## Proverbs 5:18-19

We have talked about enjoying our sexuality in the safety of a relationship based on love—a place where truly safe sex can happen. King Solomon said that our fountain should be blessed and that we should take pleasure in the wife of our youth. Sex is intimacy without insecurity. It means to be satisfied in a relationship of sexual intimacy. That is our best offense.

Proverbs refers to the woman as a loving deer and a pleasant dove. How do you approach a deer? You do not chase a deer yelling, "Hey! Get over here, deer. Come here. Come here!" If you do that, it is going to run! A woman is going to run if someone approaches her like that. You must approach a deer gently and kindly. Men, women are looking for more romance in their marriage than husbands are giving them. They are looking for more kindness and gentleness. It is not just a physical thing; it is wooing. It is caring. It is pursuing. Sometimes in our marriages, we begin to slow down on that and not do it quite as much.

However, as wives are looking for more romance, most likely husbands are looking for more frequency. When both romance and frequency increase, good things begin to happen. You can love one another and care for one another instead of taking advantage of one another. Then you can come together and find satisfaction.

Fifty-six percent of divorces are now based on Internet pornography. Let's ask the Lord for His blessing, praying, "God, we want to walk in our marriage with greater romance, greater frequency. We want to be satisfied in one another." God created sex, and He has a plan. If you think that God's plan is wrong and the world's plan is right, look at the results. The world is in chaos. However, there is forgiveness, faithfulness, and fulfillment in Jesus Christ. God can take your pain and your brokenness and restore the years that the locusts have eaten.

I am not calling you to get better filters on your computer. I am inviting you to come to Christ, to let the forgiveness of Jesus wash over you and let Jesus be the strength in your life and your guide in loving your spouse.

Husbands, are you treating your wife tenderly? Wives, are you being a pleasant dove?

*For further study: 1 Corinthians 10:13*

# LET'S BUILD A FIREPIT

Proverbs 6:27–29

A friend of mine at Breakaway Ministries uses this illustration: Let's compare sex to a fire that heats and burns. If you go to the Internet looking for that fire, you will get an image that you will see, and you will even hear the crackle. But if you tried to get warm by getting close to that kind of fire, that would be crazy, right? The screen is not going to warm you. Virtual sex and pornography are just like that. There is no heat, there is no intimacy, and there is no gathering. You only see it and hear it.

What about casual sex? It is like lighter fluid. You have a moment of flames, but you will end up with burned and charred embers. That is what hooking up with someone is. Dating a few times and then having sex may be very exciting, but just like lighter fluid, it is highly flammable and temporary.

What is God's idea? The Lord wants to put that fire within the right parameters and in the right spot. He takes the firepit of marriage and puts sex there, where it is contained. Then you, as a married person, can say, "I am going to put some logs on the fire" and work on our romance, frequency, and intimacy to make things burn and work again. Sex is contained in marriage, in the firepit. There is a flame there that we can stoke. We can care for it, and we can help keep this love burning. And knowing the fire is lit and burning, you can walk from this firepit into the world and find strength to face temptation because you are coming from a place of satisfaction.

That does not mean your marriage is perfect. It does mean that you do not have to walk in need but in fulfillment. Instead of walking in lust, you can walk in the world from a place of love and care. We are in a world that is in chaos, but we have a great defense and a great offense. Let's teach those things to our children and live them out in our own lives.

Are you containing and feeding your fire in the proper place?

# PARENTING GOALS

Proverbs 23:15–16

Think about the influence parents have on their children. I decided to do a little research with my own family. I sat everybody down around the dining room table and said, "I want you all to tell me the one thing you are going to remember that we always say as a family and that you are going to take away with you." We have some phrases that we often repeat, like "Be a leader for good, be a leader for God." I also say this: "It is not how you react when you do not get anything but how you react when you do not get everything." The idea is that they are never *not* going to get anything. However, there will be times that they do not get everything, and their reaction when that happens evidences their character. I also say, "Your heavenly Father loves you, and so do I."

So I asked my kids which saying they are going to remember most when they leave the house. The reply was, "Do not use all the hot water." That was what they said! I think that is a good one. Also, "Close the door," "Shut the refrigerator," things like that. I know they will remember something else as well. There are many things we are trying to get across.

So we are going to look at parenting, and as we do, we are going to throw off parenting guilt. We are going to throw off parenting stress. We are going to hear what the Lord wants to tell us about how He wants to move in our families and how He wants to shape our lives.

Let me ask you a question: What do you think our goal is as parents? King Solomon teaches us that our parenting goal is character, not accomplishment. It is not about what our kids do; it is about who they are. Our relationship with Christ is the same. It is not about what we do for God; it is about who we are with God and our relationship with Him.

So we parent for character, not accomplishment. It is not about how many home runs they hit; it is not about how many A's they get. It is not about how they are first chair or second chair in the band. It is not about how pretty or popular they are. The most important thing is who they are.

What is more important to you? Character or accomplishment? Why?

# DO NOT BURN OUT YOUR KIDS

— Proverbs 10:1 —

Why is our kid's character the most important goal as parents? Because it will take our kids into marriage and into life, and it will serve them a whole lot better than accomplishments.

Let me give you two accomplishments that are battling against character in our kids' lives. One is a good education. We promote a good education, sometimes bribing them to get a good education. We pay them for grades. You get an A, you get this. You get a B, you get that. It is great when they succeed in school, but the focus can be so intense. It is not like when we went to school. To tell the truth, they study more in a week than most of us studied in a semester. We want success and discipline for them, but their education is battling for accomplishment over character.

The second accomplishment that is battling for character is specialized skills. We want our kid to be the greatest cheerleader, the greatest baseball player, the greatest football player, the greatest soccer player, the greatest band member. We want our kid to be able to say, "I am a specialized skill person," "I got a coach for this," and "I have a trainer for that." They do all these things, and those specialized skills begin to steal them away from family because they take so much time and make life so hectic and busy.

Many parents are so busy running around with their kids in so many different directions that they're eating from a fast-food drive-through all the time. The family is seldom together and never around the same table. Everyone else is raising our kids instead of us. The goal is character, not accomplishment.

*Time* magazine's cover article in September 2017 was this: "Crazy Travel. Crazy Costs. Crazy Stress. How Kid Sports Turned Pro." The article stated that kids' sports are now a $15 billion industry. I have a friend who is a trainer. He trains Major League Baseball players and NFL athletes. He trains at the highest levels. I asked him his thoughts on kids' sports and the direction they are going. He said, "For every Tiger Woods, there are a million kids who hate their dad and a half a million kids who hate the sport."

Parents, instead of pushing your kid to be a professional athlete, you may be better off just going with your kid to watch a game, buying a couple hot dogs, and drinking some soda so you can just spend time together. Do not jump into that kids' sports river and go down it because you will miss church every Sunday, your kids will have no connection with the church, and they will never be part of the things the church is doing. Moreover, they will never be home. Allow them to grow in their relationship with Christ.

# TEACHING CHILDREN

## Proverbs 23:17–21

There are four traits parents need to teach their children in order to develop their character.

Trait one: Teach your kids to choose their friends and their spouse well. Do not underestimate the power of peers. Talk with your kids about the type of friends they should hang out with. Talk with them about what to do. Pray for your kids, for that godly wife or husband. Set their minds toward what they are looking for in a spouse. It is not about beauty; it is about godliness. Pray not only for your kids but also for their friends.

Parents, at some point, you are going to have to tell your children that they are not going to hang out with a particular group. You will have to tell them they are not going to go somewhere. But they should also know that if they ever get in a situation where drugs or alcohol are involved, they can call you at any moment, and you will give them a ride home, no questions asked, and you will not give them a sermon on the way home.

Teach them the way to choose friends. Put them in the right circle of peers so they will have the right people in their lives. It is better to have four good friends than 40 bad ones.

There are different stages of parenting. You begin as a caregiver. You take that little baby and make sure he or she is okay. You are a caregiver. Then you become a cop: "Do not do that," "Do not touch this." Then you move on to the teenage years and become a coach and then a consultant as they leave home. But you cannot stay a caregiver as your kids get older. You have to move on so you can help them make good choices, pick the right people to date, choose the right spouse. Remember, the power of their peers is huge.

You must also consider who *your* friends are—those people you spend time with. What kind of people are you putting into your kids' lives? You must model the right way to choose friends. Are you doing that?

# TEACHING CHILDREN RESPECT

### Ephesians 6:1–3

As parents, we must be teaching our children four critical traits. We already looked at the first trait—choose friends and companions wisely. The second trait is this: Walk in respect and humility.

"Honor your father and your mother" is the fifth commandment, but it is the first commandment that includes a blessing—"so that you may have a long life" (Exod. 20:12). So honoring and respecting mom and dad is the key. It is crucial. Disobedience and disrespect receive punishment. Children should respect their parents. They should respect their elders. Let me give you a few of words that will open more doors for them than anything else: "Yes, ma'am," "please," and "thank you." If we do not teach proper respect and humility, our children will be ungrateful, and they will want anything they see.

We have to teach our sons to respect women, and that comes with us saying, "You are not going to talk to your mom like that," "You are not going to treat your sister like that," "You are not going to treat your friend like that," "You are going to be a man of God who respects and honors women."

Let me give you a thought on humility. You, the parent, need to realize that your kid is not the center of the world. The Duke of Wellington once said this: "The thing that impresses me most about America is the way parents obey their children."*

You do not have to pay for your children's college; it is fine if they get a job and learn to work for that. Some of you have been saving for that, and if you can bless them that way, great. But they should not be the center of your universe.

We should not be running all over the place to keep them satisfied and then feel parental guilt if we do not give them everything or aren't at every single thing they ever do. As a parent, be there as much as you can. But you will have a business trip or something will come up, and you will not be able to be there. That is okay. If you make them the center of the earth, they are going to be fired from a job someday because nobody thinks they are the most important person in existence. They are going to take a class, and they will get an F because nobody thinks they are the center of the world.

Are you raising humble and respectful children?

*For further study: Proverbs 23:19–21*

# CELEBRATING RIGHT THINGS

### Proverbs 23:24–25

We have discussed the importance of teaching our children to make wise choices in friends and companions. We have talked about the need to raise them so they will have humility and respect. And here is the third trait: Celebrate the highest things. King Solomon says that the father of a righteous child has great joy, and a man who fathers a wise son rejoices in him. What is the father rejoicing over? That his child is walking with God. What are you rejoicing over? That your child played a sport successfully? No, the rejoicing should be over character. The best thing you should want for your children is to love Christ. We want our children to love God. Parents, cheer for that!

Let your kids know how pleased you are when they love God. They are tuned in to what they sense will please us, and they want to please us. If a girl senses that her mom is proud of her because she is pretty—she gets the right clothes, everything is perfect about her—she is going to go on that route. However, if she realizes that what pleases her mom's heart is that she has a relationship with Christ, then she will focus on that.

Therefore, encourage your children when they are kind. Encourage them when you see godliness coming out in them. Encourage them to pray, and pray with them—not just for them. Discuss God's work at home. When you get to your table, tell them, "You will not believe what God did today," or "Let me tell you about a verse I read today." Make that a point of conversation. Do you read Luke chapter two when it is Christmastime at home? Or do you just depend on your pastor to read it? Do you talk about Easter at home? Do you do some little projects with your kids to talk about the meaning of Easter? If you do egg hunts, do you talk about the empty egg representing the tomb that was empty after Jesus rose from the dead?

Joshua put it like this: "But as for me and my household, we will serve the Lord" (Josh. 24:15 NIV). Jesus said, "Seek first his kingdom and his righteousness, and all these things will be given to you as well" (Matt. 6:33 NIV). Your kids could be on many different teams and in many activities, but when anything starts to mess with your family time, you need to be very careful. You should not sign up for anything that has a Sunday morning attached to it, because that takes you out of the church. Do not show your kids that you only walk with God when there is nothing else to do. Celebrate the highest things.

Do your kids know that the Lord is more important than anything else?

*For further study: Joshua 24:15*

# SAFE PLACES FOR KIDS

---

Proverbs 23:26

---

As a father, King Solomon said, "My son, give me your heart, and let your eyes delight in my ways" (Prov. 23:26 NIV). When your kids do something wrong and think you will kill them if you find out, you may need to consider whether you have created a safe place for them at home. That doesn't mean you shouldn't discipline. Just make sure they are safe at home. So trait number four in parenting is that we need to provide a safe place for our children.

If your teenager goes out one night, you have to be able to sit down with him or her on the couch the next day and say, "Tell me, how did it go?" "What's going on?" "Who was there?" You need to talk about these things together and create a safe place. Then your teenager will be able to say, "You know what? I think I did something wrong." Rather than being upset and horrified, you can listen and say, "Okay, let's think about that. Let's pray about that. What can we do to make that right again? What can we learn from that?" Creating a safe place will help them turn to you as a consultant and will allow you to be a godly example.

Creating a safe place starts when they are little. It starts with reading good bedtime stories. When they get older, it becomes, "Hey! Let's go get a Starbucks together." "Let's get ice cream together." "Let's go on a trip together." Learn to be together and create safe places for them.

We must also set a godly example for them. We are not to be travel agent parents who say, "Go live in that land of righteousness, but I will stay right here." We are to be leaders, walking out our righteousness so they can look at us and see what it looks like to be a godly man or a godly woman. We must be able to say, "I want to walk with God myself."

Show your kids how faith and life merge. Is anybody perfect? No. Throw off parenting guilt right now. Throw off parenting pressure and realize that you are not going to be perfect. Nobody is perfect. That gives our kids a reason to need Jesus. Point them to Jesus, and they will see the need to go to Him for an example of perfection. And they will see the need to find Him and have a relationship with Him.

Let your kids catch you praying and reading the scriptures. Take a look at your own walk with God. Do you let God do His work through you? We all know there are godly parents with bad kids, and there are bad parents with godly kids. But we can pray, "God, do your work" and trust that our children will turn to Him for all their decisions.

---

# CRAZY LOVE

1 Peter 4:14–16

True love can make you seem crazy. It can make you do crazy things. Think about the first crush you had on someone. Think about when you first started dating someone. Everything you saw made you think of that person. You saw a lamp, and it reminded you of that person. You were writing poems and drawing hearts on every piece of paper you could find. Did you find yourself acting in ways that were unfamiliar to you? That is what love can do. It can change you; it can make you seem crazy.

That does not mean that the love of God will make you do something illegal or wrong. On the contrary, it makes you act in a good, positive, legal, life-giving way, in a way that for some people might seem crazy. We do things like read a 2,000-year-old book or "talk to the ceiling" when we pray. The love of God causes us to have faith that things will get better even when there seems to be no way out of a bad situation. It causes us to have faith in God and all His promises and to have faith that the blood of Jesus makes us clean as snow and that we will have eternal life with God in heaven. It might seem crazy to some, but that is what the crazy love of God does in us.

This is the crazy kind of love we receive from God: that He sent His only Son to die for us so all of us could be saved and live in heaven, with Him, forever. He made us in His image and gave us all living things as a gift for us to take care of and enjoy. We find endless demonstrations of the crazy love of God for us in the Bible. And we are constantly finding evidence of His crazy love for us in our daily lives. Only someone who is crazy in love would leave 99 sheep alone to go find the one that got lost. That is what God does for us. He is so crazy in love with each one of us that He would do anything to be with us.

When we know and receive the crazy love of God in our lives, we start living out that crazy love ourselves. As the love of God infiltrates our lives, our actions will not seem logical to others. That love compels us to do things that are no longer about us but about others. And it makes us live crazy lives for God and His kingdom.

*For further study: 2 Corinthians 5:13–15*
*Additional references: Luke 15:3–7, John 3:16*

# COMPELLING LOVE

## 2 Corinthians 11:23–28

The love of God in us is a force that moves us into action. It is not passive, but active. The love of God pushes us out of ourselves. It motivates us to do things—to compel us to powerfully urge someone along a line of conduct, to convince someone, to make someone interested in something.

The love of God compels us to live our lives outside of ourselves. It compels us to live crazy lives for Him, like the Apostle Paul did. Before knowing God and receiving His love, Paul had an ordinary life. However, once He met God and experienced His love, Paul's whole life changed. The love of God compelled Paul to live a crazy life—a life that was no longer self-focused but about God's kingdom and God's people. Paul was moved into action.

When someone does something great for us, we feel compelled to be grateful. We do good things out of gratitude for that person and for what they did for us. When Jesus died for us on the cross, it was the greatest act of love anyone could ever do—to lay down their life for someone else. Knowing that He died out of love for us, to save us, should automatically make us live our lives in eternal gratitude. That is the kind of love that compels us. It is the love that compelled Paul to live a crazy life for God.

Paul had truly experienced the love of God in His life. Once we experience that same love, it is impossible to keep it to ourselves. The true love of God, experienced, transforms into the love of God, expressed. It is a love that is too wonderful to keep to ourselves. We have such good news to share that we have a burning desire to share it. The love of God is so great, so different than what we are used to in this chaotic world, that we feel compelled to share it with others.

Would you keep quiet if you knew the secret to making the world a better place? Would you keep quiet if you knew a way to make the lives of everyone around you better? Why would you keep quiet when you know the crazy love of God for all humanity?

My prayer for you today is that the crazy love of God compels you into action. My prayer for you is that you can start sharing the great news of God's crazy love with everyone who crosses your path.

*For further study: 2 Corinthians 5:14*
*Additional references: Romans 8:31–39*

# KNOW GOD

Martin Luther once wrote, "Learn to know Christ and Him crucified. Learn to sing to Him, and say: Lord Jesus, You are my righteousness, I am Your sin. You have taken upon Yourself what is mine and given me what is Yours. You have become what You were not so that I might become what I was not."*

One of the most important things in Christianity is to know God. We cannot believe in someone we do not know. We cannot trust in someone we do not know. We cannot accept and receive the love of a person we do not know. For us to believe, trust, and accept God and His love for us, we must first know Him.

Knowing God can be a feeling as much as it can be an understanding. We come to know God through His Word, through attending church, and through growing in our relationship with Him. As it is with any human-to-human relationship, so it is with our relationship with God. The more time we spend with Him—praying, praising Him, worshiping Him, reading the Bible—the more we get to know who He is.

The entire purpose of the Bible is to help us know God. The Bible reveals who God is. It reveals His character and His plan for humankind. It is through knowing God that we can receive His love.

Imagine being in a relationship with someone you know nothing about. Would you be able to trust that person or receive that person's love and affection? Consider how you would feel not knowing where they came from, their middle name, their likes and dislikes, or what makes them happy or sad. That is not a good way to keep a relationship. Our relationship with God is the same. We cannot have a relationship with God unless we know Him.

When we know God, when we start seeking Him, He starts revealing Himself and all His promises to us. The more we get to know Him, the more we understand Him and discover His perfect love for us and the plans He has for our lives.

*For further study: Jeremiah 9:23–24*
*Additional references: John 1:12, 17:3; Psalm 118:4; Jeremiah 29:13*

# TRUST IN GOD

## Proverbs 3:5–6

To trust someone is to become vulnerable. When we trust someone—a friend, a parent, a sibling, a spouse—we give that person control over a certain area or situation in our lives. When you trust your sibling to take out the trash you were supposed to take out, you are giving them control over the bag of trash and trust they will take it out before your parents come home. When you trust your best friend with a secret, you are giving them control over it. You trust that they will not say anything to anyone about it, but you cannot control them. All you can do is hope that they will not betray that trust. You decide to trust them because you know them.

We cannot trust someone we do not know. We cannot trust in something we know nothing about. Thanks to the Internet, it is becoming easier than ever to trust a brand or a product. We have all the information we need about a specific product before we buy it. We want a new washer and dryer, so we open the Internet and search for product reviews, comparisons, characteristics, and all the information necessary to decide which washer and dryer to buy.

The Bible is our source of information about God and His love for us. It is through reading the Bible and having a real relationship with God that we can get to know Him. His crazy love for us compels us to trust Him. However, there is no possible way to trust Him without knowing Him first.

Trusting in God does not mean that everything in our lives will be perfect and that we will have everything we want. It means that we trust God in spite of, not because of. Trusting God may not be common sense for most people nowadays, but it is a consequence of the crazy love of God infiltrating our lives. The way God loves us does not make sense, but we do not have to understand it. What we must do is trust Him and enjoy His love and His plan to give us a great future and hope!

*For further study: Jeremiah 29:11*
*Additional references: Jeremiah 17:7–8, Job 2:9–10,*
*Isaiah 26:4, Psalm 56:3*

# WHAT IS REALLY IMPORTANT

## Psalm 37:4

What is important to us right now might not be important in eternity. In truth, what is important to us today might not even be important to us in a few years. Sometimes we focus on things that seem like a huge deal to us at the moment, but after a while we realize we could have used our time differently and more efficiently if we had shifted our focus to something else.

When my grandfather was alive, he was devoted to taking care of his front yard. He would spend countless hours every day caring for his plants, the soil, and the water he used for his plants. He worried about the weather and how it might affect his flowers. We would all be inside having family time, and he would be outside taking care of his plants. I loved that about him—his passion for his garden. He would tell me everything about a certain type of flower and how to take care of it. When he passed away and our family sold the house, the new owners did not take care of the front yard anymore. The plants died, and the front yard transformed into something that would have broken my grandfather's heart. What was important to him was not important to someone else.

Sometimes we get wrapped up in what seems important to us—running errands, cleaning the house obsessively, working 24/7, being right all the time—and miss what is really important in life. We miss making a difference in someone else's life. We do not enjoy life anymore. Some other person will take over our business; someone else will live in our home; someone else will buy our car; other people will have our jobs. We need to focus on what actually matters.

Some say that love is the most powerful force in the universe. The love of God is the greatest love. His love is not something He wants to give to just some of us; he wants to give it to everyone. It is a love that compels us. It compels us with such force that we no longer want to live for ourselves but for Him! I pray that this crazy, compelling love will compel you to live for what is really important!

*For further study: Proverbs 16:9*
*Additional references: 1 Corinthians 13:1–13; Matthew 6:33–34, 6:25;*
*Colossians 3:23–24*

# BE A DIFFERENCE-MAKER

## Matthew 23:11–12

Many of us are coping with life instead of being compelled into life. When we cope, we turn inward, making everything about us and what happens to us. When we are being compelled by the crazy love of God, we look outside of ourselves and start serving others, making a difference in their lives.

People love difference-makers. When Michael Jordan was playing basketball, he changed the game. He was a difference-maker, and many people loved him. Steve Jobs changed cell phones forever; he was a difference-maker, and many people loved him. Martin Luther King, Jr. was a difference-maker, and many people loved him. Mother Theresa was a difference-maker, and she was loved by many people regardless of what they believed in.

As believers, we have the love of God, which makes us different from the rest of the world. We have a light shining inside of us that makes us stand apart. We have that crazy, compelling love that forces us to be different and make a difference wherever we are. As believers, we are called to be difference-makers.

Jesus was the greatest difference-maker of all time. He taught us that love conquers all and that grace triumphs over judgment and sin. He taught us that the greatest person is the servant, and that the proud will be humbled. He did everything out of love for us. His love is a crazy, compelling, everlasting, irrevocable, faithful, and steadfast love.

We find many difference-makers in the Bible. Think of Daniel and his friends in the time of King Nebuchadnezzar. Think of the Apostle Paul and everything he did to change the course of history for believers everywhere. Think of Moses, Elijah, Queen Esther, and countless other people in the Bible who made a difference forever.

May you be a difference-maker through the crazy, compelling love of God in your life. May you find yourself living a life greater than yourself. May the love of God shine through you like never before! May you live a life of serving others with the same love you received from God.

*For further study: Hebrews 6:10*
*Additional references: Galatians 5:13, Philippians 2:4,*
*3 John 1–6, John 15:12–13, 1 Peter 4:10–11*

# GOD LOVES US TO DEATH

Hebrews 2:9

Christ loves us so much that He laid down His life for us. He literally loved us to death! He died so we could have eternal life and live with Him forever in heaven. Think about it: He loves us with a love so deep that He not only gave His life for us but He wants to spend eternity with us.

Every step Jesus took to the cross on Calvary meant "I love you" to each and every one of us. His love was intentional. It was there since the beginning of time; it was not something that grew with time. His love was always meant for us.

Have you ever done something crazy for the person you love? Jesus did the craziest thing. He changed the course of history for you and for me. He gave up His life for love. He went through a lot of suffering for us. He was beaten, humiliated, denied, and abandoned because He loved us with an irrevocable, steadfast, everlasting, crazy, and compelling love.

His love for each of us is personal. He has our names written on the palms of His hands. He does not love us because we are great people or because we do so many great deeds. He loves us because He is love. He loves us because He made us to love Him. His love does not decrease or increase when we do something wrong or when we do something right. It is always there, given to us without reservation and without limits. We will never be able to pay for the love of God; we can never do anything to earn it or deserve it.

He loves us so much that He paid our debt on the cross. And He does not require repayment or charge us interest. All He asks of us in return is to love Him back. And His love is so crazy that even when we choose not to love Him back, He still loves us the same.

My prayer for you today is that you will feel loved by God in a way you have never felt before. May you feel compelled to love others with that same love—a love that does not require anything in return, a love to be enjoyed and given away as a precious gift.

*For further study: 1 John 3:16*
*Additional references: 1 John 4:9–11; Romans 5:8; Isaiah 49:6, 50:6*

# GOD'S PLAN VS. OUR PLAN

Luke 15:11–19

Luke 15 tells the story of 100 sheep and one that gets lost. The Bible goes on to talk about 10 coins and one that was lost. A little bit further into the chapter, we read about two sons, and one of them gets lost for a while. This chapter in the Bible shows God getting more personal as He talks about His love for us.

For the next few days, we're going to go deep into the story of the prodigal son. A prodigal is someone who spends money in a reckless, extravagant way and later makes a repentant return. If we think about the prodigal son, a number of words may come to mind: disrespect, impatience, lust, deception, unfaithfulness, selfishness, carelessness, and recklessness. We see someone whose selfish vision led to a sinking life.

The prodigal son had this thought that we often think as well: My plan is better than my father's plan. Sons and daughters may think this about their parents, and people can think that about God. My plan is better than my Father's plan.

We may someday face this fork in the road of our lives where we have to decide if God's plan is better than our plan. We can see ourselves standing there at the fork, wondering which way to go. Are we going to follow God's perfect plan for our lives, or are we going to follow our own plan and ask God to just bless it?

C. S. Lewis said, "We are not necessarily doubting that God will do the best for us: we are wondering how painful the best will turn out to be."* Maybe the prodigal son did not want to stay with his father because he thought that being on his own would be more relaxing and more fun. Maybe he thought he wouldn't have to work so much and could enjoy life the easy way.

We always know in our hearts that God's plan is better, yet somehow, we do not always want to do things God's way. Sometimes, we just want to do what we want to do and hope that God is not paying attention to us.

God always has a plan for our lives. May we finally come to the realization that His plans are always better than our plans.

*For further study: Jeremiah 29:11*
*Additional references: Matthew 6:31–33, 1 Peter 1:3–4,*
*Proverbs 3:5–6*

# THE GRASS IS GREENER

## 1 John 2:15

The prodigal son chose his own plan instead of choosing his father's plan for his life. His older brother, in contrast, always followed his father's plan to work and take care of things at home. Maybe the prodigal son thought the grass was greener somewhere else, outside of what he was used to—far from his father's plan.

We can all look at somebody else's life and think, "I wish I had their car. I wish I had their house. I wish I had their life. I wish I had their job. I wish I had their spouse. I wish I had their kids. I wish I had their gifts. The grass is greener over there. If I only had that, I would not have this, and I would not feel like this."

We often think the grass is greener on the other side. That is probably what the prodigal son thought. "All this stuff I have with my father, but if I were to go to a distant country...." But that distant country is a mirage. It is a mirage of thinking. "If I only had that job. If I only looked like that. If I only had that notoriety, that fame. If I only had that kind of money. If I had all of those things, I would finally be satisfied."

John D. Rockefeller was once asked how much money it takes to make a person happy. He said, "Just one more dollar."* We always want this mirage of going out to greener pastures. We do not realize that life is life, that things may get hard sometimes, and that truly the grass is not greener in some distant country. We always want more, but sometimes we have more than enough and are not able to see it.

God always gives us what we need. He is always taking good care of us and has the best plans for our lives. He knows what we need and when we need it. He also knows what other people need and when they need it. What others have may be great for them, but it is not what is best for us.

May we always be grateful for what we have, knowing that whatever we have was given to us by God. He knows what we need before we even realize we need it.

*For further study: Galatians 6:4–5*
*Additional references: Philippians 4:19, Matthew 6:25–34*

# THE JOURNEY BACK HOME

Luke 15:14–20

The prodigal son's journey back home started the moment he left. The day he gathered all he had and left home, he started coming back home. He may not have realized it at the time, but the truth is that when he left, he started losing. He started losing his money, spending it on things that were not important, on people who did not love him, on selfish and shallow things, trying to fill a void that could not be filled with any of those things. He lost all the comfort he had at home, he lost touch with his family, and he lost sight of what was truly important in life.

When he lost everything he had, he realized he needed to come back home. He did not think he was worthy of his father's love and affection again or worthy of his forgiveness, but he knew he needed to go back home. Back to where it all started. Back to where he felt safe and had everything he needed. Back home where he had taken everything for granted. After venturing into the distant country and spending all his money, he realized that being home was everything he wanted.

Have you ever ventured into the distant country away from God? We all have one way or another. Some of us may have ventured deeper and others not so much. Maybe we turned away from God because we did not get what we wanted. Maybe it was because of a difficult situation in our lives, or maybe because someone we trusted hurt us. Maybe it was because we just wanted to see what was out there and have things go according to our plan and not God's plan. Whatever the reason, throughout our lives, we have all wandered away from God, venturing into a distant country, just like the prodigal son.

After spending all his money and being left alone, hungry, cold, and tired while feeding pigs, the prodigal son decided it was time to go back home. He had to hit rock bottom to realize that since the moment he left, he was actually on his way back home. He needed to go back home where he had everything he wanted and needed. He had to go back to his father's plan for him.

God is always pulling us closer to Himself, even when we do not realize it. May we always feel Him pulling and decide to go back home to Him and to His perfect plan for our lives.

*For further study: John 15:5*
*Additional references: Isaiah 55:1–3*

# THE OLDER BROTHER

## Luke 15:25–32

Maybe we have been the kind of people who have always followed God and never drifted away from Him—never ventured into the distant country. Maybe we are like the older brother. He did everything the father wanted, but with a hard heart. An obedient life with a hard heart is totally empty. Maybe we have been following God and doing the right thing for decades because our mom and dad and our grandparents did it. Maybe we have always gone to church. We have all the right things checked on our lists, but there is a distance in our relationship with God.

Often, our hearts are not soft toward God. We have rules, but we do not have a relationship with the Father. We do all these things right, but we are not spending time with God. We are not praying; we are not fasting; we are not reading the Bible; we are not yearning for a relationship with God. We are good people, but we have a hard heart. We are wondering why our lives feel so empty.

What we often miss in the story of the prodigal son is that the older brother also took his part of the inheritance. He was just as greedy as the prodigal son. In Jewish culture, whenever you had two sons, two-thirds of the assets went to the older son, and one-third of the assets went to the younger son. The older son got more than what the younger son wasted. However, because of a lack of relationship with his father, the older son had bitterness hidden in his heart, despite his outward obedience.

How does that happen? It happens when we begin to lack gratitude. Instead of being grateful for all he had, the older son was bitter because he did not get one fattened calf and a party. Whenever we lack gratitude, we begin to have entitlement. We are not grateful for what we have and feel entitled for what we do not have. We expect things should be done for us and given to us, just like the older brother thought.

The older brother did not know that everything his father had was already his. He could not be thankful for what he had, he could not be happy with his father, and he could not love his brother—because his heart was hard.

We are all God's children. Jesus gave His life for all of us. All He wants in return is for us to love Him with all our hearts—soft hearts—and for us to love each other with the same love He first loved us. May we always be grateful and celebrate what He celebrates with joy!

# THE LOVE OF THE FATHER

### Luke 15:20–24

The real change in the life of the prodigal son happened in the arms of his father. The father's embrace broke down every barrier. It erased every feeling of shame and fear the son had. Everything he was planning to say to his father fell apart when he was met with his father's embrace.

Imagine being in those arms. Imagine feeling guilty, unworthy, dirty, shameful, unforgiven, alone, hungry, cold, and undeserving of love and forgiveness. Imagine having all those feelings and being met halfway home by a father embracing you with such love and grace that all those feelings started to fade and disappear. Imagine an embrace like that.

The father saw the son coming home and ran toward him, hugged him, and kissed him. He did not let his son finish saying what he had planned to say because that was not part of the father's plan. The father's plan was for his son to come back home and feel loved, forgiven, and welcome. It was the same for the older son. When he was angry because the prodigal son was back and they were having a party for him, the father went out to where he would tell him that he loved him. He told him that everything he had was his. He loved both sons the same.

God's love for us is like that father's love. God loves us no matter what. He never stops loving us. He loves us—every single one of us—with an irrevocable, steadfast, everlasting, crazy, and compelling love. He does not care about our past decisions or the things we did or did not do. He wants us to get closer to Him so He can get closer to us.

All the prodigal son needed to do was come back home. God wants us to do the same—to come back home. He will meet us halfway.

We can rest assured that we have a Father in heaven who loves us unconditionally and will always wait, with open arms, for us to come back home. No matter what we do, He will always love us!

*For further study: Psalm 145:18*
*Additional references: James 4:8, Revelation 3:20,*
*Psalm 86:15, John 14:23*

# PETER: THE MAN AND THE TIME

## Mark 1:16–18

In 1 Peter, the Apostle Peter teaches about God's greatness—what He has done for us and how He has done it through Jesus Christ.

But who was this Peter? He was a fisherman who left his nets when Jesus called him to be His disciple. Eventually, he became the spokesman for the disciples, which sometimes was good but occasionally wasn't because from time to time he spoke before thinking.

Three times, he denied Jesus, and that was his worst moment. So we know that Peter was not perfect. Like Peter, you and I are going to do things that, in our hearts, we do not want to do. But the great thing about that episode in Peter's life is that he was restored three times by Jesus. What a lovely God we have! He can take you out of the pit you are in, the hole you have dug, and restore and rescue you.

Peter was going to be used in a great way as a leader. He was going to give the first Christian sermon at Pentecost, and thousands were going to come to Christ. He needed to be restored for that.

He wrote the epistle of 1 Peter in about 63 AD. It was about how to make it through difficult times. At least 15 times in his letter, Peter referred to suffering. He used eight Greek words to do so. He was saying that there is hope in the pain.

There is no question that you are going to go through pain. The question is whether you will find hope in Jesus Christ when that happens. So why did Peter write about pain and suffering? What was happening when he was writing?

It was a dangerous time for Christians. Jews did not have to worship the Roman emperor as long as they prayed for him. So Christianity was safe from persecution as long as it was considered part of Judaism. But when Peter wrote his letter, Christianity had separated from Judaism. That was a problem because Christians would not worship the emperor. And they were persecuted without mercy.

In 64 AD, Nero burned Rome so he could rebuild it to his liking. He blamed the fire on the Christians. In 67 AD, Roman authorities took Peter and Paul. Many historians believe they were executed that very same day in Rome. In 70 AD, the Temple in Jerusalem was destroyed by the Roman Army.

Are you going through difficult times? Have you found hope in Jesus Christ?

# STRANGERS PASSING THROUGH

==================== 1 Peter 1:1 ====================

Now that you know who Peter was and the context in which the epistle of 1 Peter was written; let's talk about its content.

Peter identified himself as an apostle—that means one sent out with a message. His message was one of hope in Jesus Christ, and it was for those who were in Pontus, Galatia, Cappadocia, Asia, and Bithynia. These people were 500 to 800 miles away from Jerusalem. That is a long way from where Christianity started in Israel. Christians were strangers and aliens, and they felt like strangers and aliens, which is fine because our citizenship is not on earth. As believers in Jesus Christ, our citizenship is in heaven.

In this crazy world we live in, there is going to be more craziness. It is not going to be perfect. There is going to be much sin. That is what happens when people are doing their own thing.

Remember, you are not home yet. You are a stranger, an alien, a temporary resident. You are just passing through. That is why there is going to be some awkwardness in this life. However, we are called to bring heaven to earth and shine with the gospel of Christ. We find our security in the Lord. Many of us are struggling to try to make earth a place of comfort, and that is not going to happen. This is a place of pilgrimage.

If you do not know Jesus Christ as your Savior, let me invite you to be a stranger and an alien on earth because it is better to be a child of the Father and a citizen of heaven than to be a child of this world and a stranger in heaven. But I do not want to be what I call a double stranger. What is a double stranger? It is when you are already a stranger because this is not your home, and you are also not living for God.

All of us have the temptation to mimic other people instead of imitating Christ. Please do not do that. Do not lose sight of who you are; be yourself for God. Many of us are so confused about who we are. We do not know our spiritual gifts and do not honor Jesus as we should. But you will find great freedom in being yourself for God.

Here is a powerful declaration: I am seated in heaven, and my identity is found in Jesus Christ. I am not going to be a double stranger. I do not care what anybody else thinks. I am going to honor Him as a stranger and alien in this world because I am just passing through.

*For further study: Philippians 3:20*

# THE FOREKNOWLEDGE OF GOD

## 1 Peter 1:2

Where do you look for security in difficult times? In family, government, money? Peter reminds us that we can find security in the foreknowledge of God, the filling of the Spirit, and the blood of Jesus Christ. Your safety is in the Trinity, not in society.

If you want to find security in society, you will wait a very long time. Society does not have places that are worthy of placing our security. They cannot hold that weight. Your security must be placed in Jesus. What Peter is saying here to the believers who are 500 miles from their homes that God knows who you are. He has chosen you, and He knows you from the foundation of the world. It does not matter that you are 500 miles away from home. Our all-knowing God is very aware of where you are, even if you are not in Rome or Jerusalem.

God knows everything. You do not have to turn to a horoscope, a talk show, or some political pundit to tell you what the future is. You do not need to have your palm read because His palms have been pierced, and He knows the future. God knows yesterday, today, and tomorrow, and He will never, ever change.

One of the sweetest times as a parent is when your kids think you know everything. A moment will come when they realize that you do not know it all. However, there is never a moment when you will realize that God does not know everything. We can always have child-like faith in the Lord. We can always trust in the fatherhood of God.

I have the identity of a stranger on this earth, but my deeper identity is a son—a child of the Father. Then I do not have any problem being a stranger in this world. Being a child of God gives me confidence and security. Everyone does not have to like me. I do not have to be invited to every party; I can be a bit odd at times. I can be who I am. I don't have to be a double stranger.

God knows everything. Be comforted.

Are you trusting God in every circumstance no matter what? How do you feel understanding that God knows everything about you?

*For further study: Romans 8:29–30*

# SECURITY AND SANCTIFICATION

### 1 Peter 1:2b

We have learned that our security is based on the omniscience of God. The Apostle Peter then said that our security should be placed in the Spirit. When you trust Jesus Christ as your Savior, the Holy Spirit comes and lives inside your heart and changes you. You are different; you are set apart; you are unique. So how does He change us? What happens?

You are filled. You are not empty and searching anymore. You walk into a strange situation, and you are secure among the children of the King. Men and women do not walk into a relationship looking for love; they come into a relationship already having found love in Jesus Christ. Women, God has touched you, so no other man needs to. He has touched your heart and your soul. When somebody says, "Hey, fill yourself up with these drugs, fill yourself up with this alcohol," you do not have to do it because you are already filled with the Holy Spirit of God. You do not need other stuff. You do not require the approval of others. You are not searching. You are a believer in Jesus Christ and a child of the King.

You have walked in as a believer through the Holy Spirit, so you are set apart, and you are complete. You have joy instead of jealousy. You do not need what the world has because you have what God has given you. You trust Jesus Christ to be your joy so you do not have to look at other stuff with jealous eyes. You are guided in your life instead of guessing where to go. Your circumstances might not all make sense, but you can trust that step by step, God is going to lead you, and you will be a faithful follower.

God welcomes you into His joy. He welcomes you into His guidance. He wants you to find His will. And His will is about who you are more than about what you do. So if you are a child of God who lives filled with the Spirit, you do not have to live empty. It is the Holy Spirit who fills you. You have been set apart for obedience, which is a fruit of the Spirit. The Spirit will help you obey the Word of God; He is your helper. He sanctifies your life in such a way that nobody can touch you.

Are you aware of the presence of the Holy Spirit in your life?

*For further study: 1 Corinthians 1:30*
*Additional references: 1 Corinthians 6:11*

# THE BLOOD OF JESUS

### 1 Peter 1:2

Our security is in the foreknowledge of God and in the sanctification of the Holy Spirit. And if that is not enough, our security is also in the blood of Jesus Christ. The Trinity gives us security. The Apostle Peter said that we are sprinkled with the blood of Jesus Christ, and that changes everything. We know it was not just a sprinkling of blood on the cross; it was a dousing. Jesus died, and His blood was poured out.

Peter went back to the purification rites of the Israelites in the tabernacle and the Temple where the priests would sprinkle the blood of lambs and goats to obtain purification for the Jews. Then Jesus stepped forward and became the Lamb of God who was slain, shedding His blood for our sins.

Every one of us is looking for somebody to sacrifice themselves for us. Kids are looking for their parents to sacrifice by buying stuff they want and showing up to their events to cheer them on. Girlfriends are looking for a boyfriend who will sacrifice for them. Boyfriends are looking for a girlfriend who will sacrifice for them as well. In our marriages, we are called to sacrifice ourselves for our spouses.

But no one has sacrificed himself or herself for us like Jesus Christ did. No one but Jesus has poured out His blood; no one else has been falsely accused; no one else has gone to the cross; and no one else has had His palms pierced to give you and me a future. That is what Jesus did to rescue humanity, to save us. He welcomes us. He wants us to be rescued by His blood.

To seal our security, we have grace, which multiplies peace in our lives. If you are looking for peace, you first need to discover God's grace. In His grace, you will find the kind of peace that surpasses human understanding. That peace is not going to be simply added to you, but it will be multiplied for you. It will be given abundantly to you in Christ.

I saw these words in a card from a friend: "Life is a test, a trust, and temporary." Your faith will be tested, but you can trust God with your life because you are a stranger and an alien just passing through. Let's be like Peter and say to God, "I want to be your child."

*For further study: Hebrews 9:19–22*
*Additional references: Hebrews 11:28*

# THE EXAMPLE OF LOVE

1 John 2:7–9

In the second chapter of his first letter, John tells us to love our brothers and sisters. He says this is an old command, and it is true. More than likely, we have all heard this before. The first place we see this command is in one of the oldest books of the Bible, Leviticus, which was written at least 1,400 years before John was born.

Then John says he also has a new command for us. John is trying to tell us something new about the things we have already heard before. It is a review, as when someone goes back over a class he or she already took in order to understand it better from a different angle.

If an adult were to take a fifth-grade math or science pop quiz, chances are the score would not be as high as a fifth grader's score. Even though the adult might have proficiently solved similar problems before, most people lack practice in these subjects and would need a thorough review.

We have heard about loving our brothers and sisters before, about loving those we disagree with and showing them Christ's love, but maybe in our culture, some of us lack practice on really loving each other well. So we need to come back for a review. We need to go through the class work one more time and give it a new try. That is what the Apostle John is asking us to do.

What makes this age-old commandment new? What is new about Jesus Christ's love?

Jesus Christ is the only person to walk on earth who is the perfect example of love. To know how to love someone well, we can look at His example. He is not a prophet, a teacher, or just a nice guy. Jesus is the Son of God who came to earth to live a sinless life—to show us exactly how to love.

Over the last decades, we have removed Jesus from public conversation and kept Him out of the public square. We have replaced Him with celebrities. We can learn a lot from successful people, from intelligent people in education and the arts. But they are fallen human beings, just like us. They don't provide a good example of what it is like to love someone. Who is the example of love? Jesus.

*For further study: Leviticus 19:18*

# AUTHENTIC LOVE

## 1 John 2:8

Who do you think about when someone says we must love one another? The people around you? Your friends and family? Your Christian brothers and sisters? In the second chapter of his first letter, the Apostle John talked about loving one another, and he took the idea of love a little bit further. He talked not just about one's family, but about one's village.

As we learned yesterday, when it comes to loving one another well, Jesus is our ultimate example. And what did He do? He taught something like this, in a way we might say it today: "You have heard it is good to love your neighbor, but I tell you to love your enemy, pray for those who persecute you, love those who skip past you when greeting others, and love those who never wave back at you." We are called to love our enemies.

The Pharisees, the leaders of the Jewish religion in Jesus's time, were astonished at Jesus. They said, "This guy has dinner with sinners!" Jesus answered that He wasn't sent to the righteous or to the self-righteous, but that He was sent precisely to sinners. We, as well, are called to love sinners.

Peter and Paul in the book of Acts said to not just love the Jewish people. They were going to the Gentiles, the non-Jewish people. We are called to love those who are different from us in ethnicity, religion, and culture. We are called to love even those from nations, states, cities, communities, and families who have historically been enemies of our nation, state, city, communities, and families.

Love is not just a flickering feeling. In marriage, it is not so much about feelings or emotions, because those can change gradually or suddenly. Love and marriage are all about choice—our choice to be faithful, stand strong, and build a good relationship together. When we make that choice, then feelings and emotions flow from it. Jesus didn't feel like going to the cross, but He chose to go to the cross. He died on the cross to pay for our sins. The love He demonstrated was deeper than a feeling. And through His death and resurrection, our souls are cleansed. We are called to choose to love.

Are you showing the love of Jesus Christ to the world? To people who are different from you? We get to be part of God's plan—His plan to show His love to the world. We get to be included in that. That's an amazing, incredible thing!

*For further study: Matthew 5:43–48*
*Additional references: Matthew 9:10–13*

# A LOVE WITH HANDS AND FEET

Luke 14:16

Our world is tremendously diverse. The different nationalities have their own way of expressing themselves even when they are doing the same things. You can find these differences in the same city or community. How can we go about reaching people of different nationalities? We can learn from the experiences of many who have gone to the field before us. Here are a couple of tips we can put to good use.

Do what is important for the culture to reach its people. A morning brunch? A late evening meeting with cake? No food? Lots of food?

Go where they are, where they live. Jesus came to us. Now it is our turn to go. Many would rather wait for them to come where we are, but the wisest move is to go where they are. Where does their community love to gather? Are there places we should avoid?

Invite the people who need to be there, who would be interested in learning something new, or could use some help. Invite everybody. Don't forget homeless people. As it says in the scriptures, invite everybody to the banquet; do unto the least what you would do unto the Lord; go and save the lost. Invite whoever wants to come.

Dress like they would dress. Get good advice from the locals and don an outfit they would identify with. That way you might avoid being the center of attention or at least you could soften the difference your appearance may strike. Like our Lord, show understanding and concern for ordinary people. And then just pour into their lives. Nothing gets better than that. It is awesome.

Try to get into their world. Ask them questions. Talk about topics you may have in common. Ask them how much they know about your culture. Enjoy their company, have a great time, and just love them. Sit and eat with them. And do you know who will receive the biggest blessing? You and your team.

Praise the Lord in their language.

Share the gospel as clearly as you can.

Show love to all the community with a simple service that may benefit everyone and not just those you are ministering to. Shovel the snow off their sidewalks. You never know where that could take you or who might be touched because you are doing something for their community.

We get to be part of it!

*For further study: Matthew 25:40*
*Additional references: Matthew 18:11*

# OUTRAGE AND HATE

— Matthew 24:12 —

The Lord said that in the last days, the love of many will grow cold because the lawlessness around them will multiply. To some extent, that is already happening. Sometimes we are filled with darkness and hate instead of the love of Christ.

John is telling us to love our brothers and sisters. Love the people around us. Today we have a challenge. There are so many people around us that we end up hating them while trying to love others.

Have you ever had that feeling? You see someone on TV who says something completely opposite of what you think. And in your heart, you begin to form not disagreement, but hate. We can disagree all day long, but when hate begins to develop, that is a whole different ballgame.

If we allow hate in our hearts, we can begin to form aggression and darkness toward the people who oppose us. Our hearts begin to gnaw, and we don't do what John told us to do. He said to walk in the light in a way that we can really shine with Jesus. He wants us to show the love of God.

The Greek word for *hate* means to spit at one's heart in disgust. In our society, the media would like to keep us in a place of outrage, tension, and hate. When we keep stoking the fires in our hearts, someone just has to disagree with us on any issue, and the fire of hate comes out of us to char them. But what Jesus is saying through John is that He wants us to love them.

If you love people, does that mean you never disagree? No. Of course, you disagree. Does that mean you never fight for what is right? No, we fight for what is right, but we fight right. Do you see the difference? We fight right.

As believers in Christ, we can actually love people we vehemently disagree with and show them the love of God. To do that, we have to be able to say, "Lord, I want to love people with your love despite completely disagreeing with them. Jesus, You have to do it through me. I want to walk with You, and I want You to live life through me."

*For further study: John 13:34–35*

# MAKING A WAY FOR LOVE

---------------------------- 1 John 2:8–9 ----------------------------

Ed Stetzer is a church planter, pastor, editor, radio host, author, dean, and Billy Graham distinguished chair for church, mission, and evangelism at Wheaton College. An article in the October 4, 2018, edition of *Outreach* magazine quoted him as saying, "A lot of people have lost their lives to outrage and are losing their ability to relate to other people. People are being discipled by their cable news stations. They are being shaped by their social media feeds, producing more and more waves of division."*

Are we being dragged by those waves? Where do we stand on love? If you are married, where is your marriage right now? Are you getting pulled into tension and outrage with your spouse? Your family? Your brothers and sisters? Your church family? Your friends?

We can allow the love of God to do something in our lives so we are able to love well. We need to love our spouses, our families, our fellow believers, our friends, and even those who are outside our normal, little circles in which we live.

What can we do in a practical way? The first thing we can do is get rid of the gnawing in our hearts and then receive healing. In the Lord's Prayer, we ask God to forgive our trespasses as we forgive those who trespass against us. That means we must forgive those who have wronged us. Forgiveness is our best bet to keep our love flowing strongly. Our obedience will restore our own well-being and our ability to love. Once healed, we can move on and love freely again. That way, we let God do His work in our lives, and we can walk in the light and share God's love.

When God's people walk consistently in the light, sharing His love, others will experience the love we show, and that will shape our minds to know that our love is real. Little love gestures can go a long way into other people's hearts. Give them a Bible or go out of our way to bless them by letting them use our parking space or sharing the gospel with them. That will have a cumulative effect that sometimes will lead the person to give their life to Jesus. It doesn't matter how different they may seem from us or our background and life experiences.

To walk in the light in a great way is only possible through Jesus Christ!

*For further study: Matthew 6:12–15*
*Additional references: Colossians 3:13*

# LOVE CHANGES EVERYTHING

## 1 John 2:10–11

What happens to us when we begin to walk in darkness and live with a heart of hate? We don't like anybody but us. Darkness and hate begin to inhibit our relationship with God and our relationship with other people. Darkness brings blindness; we lose clarity of direction and start stumbling like when we stub our toe while wandering through the house with the lights off.

Whenever you sense that a disagreement is turning into a feeling of hate, whether it is toward someone on TV or someone around you, get back into the light. If we walk in the light and in love in an active relationship with Jesus Christ, we begin to see the path clearly. Then we trust God to fight for us, and we allow Him to do His work in our lives.

When the world is trying to keep us in hate, Christians look different because, through the cross of Jesus, we want to remain in the love of God. Love is defined in Paul's first letter to the Corinthians. Love was shown by God sending His only Son to give us everlasting life. Love is produced by the Spirit who lives inside of each believer.

When we are friends with nonbelievers, even if they stand on the other side of things, we will have many opportunities to shine the love of Jesus on them. Maybe we can even get to pray with them, letting them experience God personally. Loving nonbelievers doesn't mean we have to negate our faith or compromise and believe some universalistic idea. Jesus will work in their lives in an amazing way. Let's go with the love of Christ and the light of Christ and not let hate form in our hearts.

Is there hate in your heart toward someone or something? Are you staging fights in your mind in kind of a fantasy fight with others? Maybe what you feel doesn't go all the way to hate, but it is getting closer and closer. Would you take just a moment and confess your sin?

If the grade on your love test isn't what you want it to be, here is the deal. Jesus has already taken every test for you, and He got 100 percent in all subjects. Let's just say this: "God, I'm still going to stand for what is right. Would You love others through me?"

*For further study: 1 Corinthians 13:4–8*
*Additional references: Galatians 5:22–23*

# LIVING RIGHT

The book of Acts was written by a doctor named Luke in about 63 AD. It is a continuation of the book of Luke. In the first 12 chapters, the main human character is the Apostle Peter; in chapters 13 through 28, it is the Apostle Paul.

In chapters 1 through 7, the story moves like an earthquake from the epicenter, Jerusalem. Then it moves to Judea and Samaria for chapters 8 through 11. Finally, it goes to the ends of the earth for chapters 12 through 28. Like an earthquake, it moves out geographically. This progression is also seen with people groups. First, the gospel goes out to the Jews; then to the Samaritans, who are half Jew and half Gentile; and then further to the Gentiles. It is said that we should study the book of Acts at least once every five years.

In this devotional, I want you to see that it is possible to live right in a culture gone wrong. We do not have to live away from the culture; we must live right and go out into the culture. Some cultures are telling us that, as Christians, we cannot fit in with them. We, as believers, should be able to invite people in those cultures to be with us, even if they do not believe what we believe.

Definitely, the world in the time of Acts was very different from the world today. In the book of Acts, the divide between the culture and God's people was even worse. Paul shows us what we are supposed to do in that situation. When he saw all the idols people had, he knew it was not right because idolatry is sin, and there is no good for anyone when you disobey God. Sin is very expensive—you have to pay a great price for it. We live in an era when the world celebrates sin and intimidates righteousness. Sin is always loud and repetitive, but it is without reason and without foundation.

God has given us His Word that speaks about the redemption He has provided for us. The Word shapes our worldview. We should not be intimidated by the world but be able to move further in the ways of the Lord.

What is your worldview? Is it that we have a small God and a big world? Or do you believe that we have a big God and that this is His world? The way you see this, your worldview, will make a significant difference in the way you behave in this crazy society we are living in.

# WE HAVE A BIG GOD

## Acts 17:6

If you believe that we have a small God and a big world, you are going to hide out or give in. If you hide out, you will be afraid of everything and will remain only within the walls of your house or your church. If you give in, you will end up doing the same things the world does. You will agree with sex without marriage, with abusing drugs, and other sinful behaviors because you will go with the flow. Do you want that for your kids? Do you want to do that? Neither hiding out nor giving in is the right thing.

If your worldview is that we have a big God and this world belongs to Him, you will walk in faith and hope. God knows what is happening to everyone everywhere. He is big enough for the whole world. He is the Creator of the universe. That is the size of the God we have.

Can anything of this world intimidate God? No. He is not dead. And this world, even though it seems to be lost, is still His world. So you can walk in faith, in hope, and in strength. Paul stood in the middle of all the idols of Athens and felt troubled, and that made him speak boldly about Jesus to the people there.

J. B. Phillips, a famous British Bible scholar and translator, said this about the church in the book of Acts:

> This surely is the Church as it was meant to be. It is vigorous and flexible....These men did not make "acts of faith," they believed; they did not "say their prayers," they really prayed. They did not hold conferences on psychosomatic medicine, they simply healed the sick. But if they were uncomplicated and naive by modern standards, we have ruefully to admit that they were open on the God-ward side in a way that is almost unknown today....these men have turned the world upside down.*

But perhaps because of their very simplicity, perhaps because of their readiness simply to believe, to obey, to give, to suffer, and, if necessary, to die, the Spirit of God found that He could do His work in them and through them.

A.W. Tozer, a noted American pastor and author, wrote, "The man who comes to a right belief about God is relieved of ten thousand temporal problems."†

Your worldview and my worldview will shape the way we interact in this world.

# NOTHING INTIMIDATES GOD

Acts 4:18

How do you see yourself? What is your internal and external view of yourself? Are you more than a physical being? In the world, people think that everything is just carnal. They encourage you to get whatever you want materially. The whole goal of their lives is to stimulate their nerve endings. If you feel good, they say, you should do everything you want.

But you are more than mere physical beings; you have a soul. That is why you are sad when your pets die and grieve when your spouse dies. There is something in you that is different from what your body looks like, something that is deeper. It is your soul, the fingerprint of God. How does evolution evolve a soul? How does evolution give a personality? You have a personality because we have a personal God.

Is life just about you? Can you do whatever you want, or are you called to live dependently on the God who created you? You should live depending on God, a resource that is higher than your very small resources in the world. That is our God, who is bigger than the world—a world that belongs to Him because He created it.

The culture in the time of the book of Acts was even worse than today's culture regarding the worldviews people had. There was violence; Stephen and James were killed. The disciples were silenced; the Jews did not want the disciples to speak in the name of Jesus. They were jailed; three times they were put in prison. But there were several prison breaks. God broke the chains and made them free. You may feel like you are jailed, but God can break your chains, and bring you freedom in Jesus Christ.

Humanity's sin nature pushes against God. People push away the One who loves them the most. People call evil good and good evil; they have darkness for light and light for darkness; bitter for sweet and sweet for bitter.

But the world cannot intimidate God. When people fight against the Holy Spirit, they will always lose. God always wins. They may seem like they win, but their end is destruction. They will lose for eternity because fighting against the Holy Spirit is called blasphemy, and that will never be forgiven. They are guilty of an eternal sin. Please do not fight against the Holy Spirit!

*For further study: Philippians 3:19–21*
*Additional references: Mark 3:29*

# AMAZING THINGS STILL HAPPEN

Acts 3:1–8

Even though the culture in the time of the book of Acts was against God, Jesus still did amazing things through the disciples. That is why when Phillip heard the Ethiopian reading scripture, he was able to tell him the good news about Jesus—Jesus is the good news. There is hope for you no matter how bad the world is treating you.

Jesus healed the sick; He healed the lame man who was at the gate of the Temple. Jesus healed the mind of the Ethiopian who was reading scripture without understanding. Jesus healed the heart of a persecutor of the church called Saul of Tarsus on the road to Damascus.

Jesus unified communities. There was great joy in Samaria when the crowds heard Philip and saw the signs he performed in the name of Jesus. Jesus unified families. All of Cornelius's family received the Holy Spirit and were baptized when Peter was brought to speak about Jesus.

Jesus saved sinners. He came to earth to die on a cross to save us. Thousands were saved by Jesus due to the preaching of the disciples.

The world will never stop the work of God. He is still in control and is doing amazing things. Nobody can intimidate God.

If you are like me, perhaps you like to see the seen. I know that God works in the unseen, but I want to see His work in the seen. I want to see people coming to Jesus; I want to see the healing when people pray for it. It is hard to see what God is doing, but I have to trust that He is working. You have to believe that He is working in your heart. He is working on your children. He is working on your spouse, even if you cannot see any change.

If you turn to the culture today, you will think God does not even exist. But He is still working. Can you trust in God's work without seeing it? Are you aware that nothing can stop God's work?

*For further study: Acts 8:26–39*
*Additional references: Acts 10:44–48*

# IMPACTFUL ACTS

## Acts 4:32–35

It is important to trust in God's work even though we do not see what He is doing. How can we see Him moving? Consider the ingredients of impactful Acts.

When the disciples were asked by the Sanhedrin to stop speaking in the name of Jesus, they did not pray to the Lord for protection or for revenge against their enemies. They prayed for three things.

First, they prayed for bold love. The disciples loved each other so much that they said something like this: "If I have something you need, it is yours." Today, the world should know we are Christians by our love. We must love people who believe in Jesus and those who do not believe in Him. We must love the person we agree with and also the person who disagrees with us about everything. That is the difference in Christianity.

Second, the disciples prayed for bravery in their clarity. They were clear in their work. They were clear about what they needed to pray for. They were clear on their message. They had just one message, and it was Jesus. There was no confusion about that. They persevered and pushed back against the culture. We have to push back against our culture as they did—not in anger but in love.

There are going to be jokes at your office that you must not laugh at. There are going to be things that everybody is going to do, but you are not going to do them. Many times, you will have to go against the current. If people can be bold about their sins, which wreck their lives, why can't we be bold about Jesus, who saves our lives?

And third, the disciples prayed to be true in their devotion. They were not playing a Christian game. They were living for Jesus. Do you just repeat the same things over and over when you pray? Pray with your heart, not your lips. Have you ever fasted? Have you ever turned off the TV to spend time in the Word? Have you ever made a sacrifice to be with Jesus? Be genuine in your devotion.

If you get these three things—love, bravery, and devotion—you will see life from another perspective. You will know that God is at work, and nothing can intimidate Him. You will see that it is possible to live right in a culture gone wrong.

*For further study: Acts 11:27–30*

# DIFFICULT PASSAGES

Some teachings are addressed to the heart, to touch your emotions. Others are addressed to the feet, to encourage you to take some action. And still others are addressed to the head, to make you think and affirm your beliefs. Today, we will appeal to your head because we will discuss a passage from scripture that may be difficult to understand. There are many portions of the Word of God that could be hard to comprehend, and if you have not faced any of them, perhaps you are not reading your Bible enough.

Before getting into the scripture we are going to study, let me give you five instructions on how you should approach a difficult passage.

1. Is the passage intended to be descriptive or prescriptive? For example, we know that Moses went to a burning bush, but that does not mean that every time God speaks, we have to see a burning bush. Joshua and the people of Israel killed a lot of people in the Old Testament, but we are not called to kill people who are not believers. Those stories are descriptive of the journey of the nation of Israel, but not prescriptive for the people of God.

2. Is this an unusual incident or a biblical theme? For instance, Moses led the people out of Egypt to freedom. Freedom is a biblical theme, but how he did it is not necessarily how it is going to be done today.

3. What is the context in the biblical book or in the Bible as a whole? For example, the book of Jeremiah is different from the book of Ephesians. But there is also context; we must pay attention to how a scripture fits with the whole Bible. Does it appear in different parts of the Bible, or is it occasional?

4. Dig deeper. Look at the grammar and sentence structure. You might need to look at the Greek or the Hebrew. Some verses are very clear, but others need more attention. Do not stay at a superficial level.

5. Use clear texts to understand confusing texts. Mark Twain reportedly said: "It ain't those parts of the Bible that I can't understand that bother me, it is the parts that I do understand."* Many things are very clear in scripture, and we can use those clear things to then study the unclear things.

Have you ever applied any of these rules to biblical passages? Are you willing to dig deeper into the Word of God to know your Lord better?

# CONSIDERING CONTEXT

Now that we have looked at how to interpret a difficult passage, let's study the story of the Apostle Paul and the disciples who had not heard about the Holy Spirit. This story marks the beginning of Paul's third missionary journey.

First, Paul went to the city of Ephesus. Cities are a place for impact. In the book of Acts, the disciples were continuously going to cities. So we should not run out of them, but into them. The United Nations says that by 2030, 80 percent of the world's population will live in cities. Cities are very important places to spread the gospel.

The city of Ephesus was not a small place. The Temple of Artemis, or Diana, was there. It was 425 feet long and four times the size of the Parthenon in Athens. It is well known as one of the Seven Wonders of the Ancient World. Ephesus was the fourth largest city in the world by that time, with 250,000 people.

Second, Paul directed his life and influence toward Jesus. This story is not about the Holy Spirit or spiritual gifts. It is not about baptism. It is about believing in Jesus. These disciples said they had never heard about the Holy Spirit, which is hard to believe because, in the Old Testament, the Holy Spirit is mentioned plenty of times. In creation, He was moving upon the face of the waters. In the book of Psalms, David recognized that he could not get away from the Spirit. Zechariah declared that the work of God must be done by His Spirit. Now remember, Paul's listeners were Jewish. They were also disciples of John the Baptist, who was always pointing to Jesus. John even told his disciples that Jesus was going to baptize them with the Holy Spirit and fire. How could they have not heard of the Holy Spirit before?

So Paul noticed that if they did not know about the Holy Spirit, they surely did not know about Jesus. How did that happen? We do not know. Paul pointed to Jesus, not the Holy Spirit or baptism. It is important to know that John's baptism was pointing forward to the One who was to come, whereas a Christian's baptism points back to Jesus who already came. John's baptism was linked to repentance; Christian baptism is linked to regeneration. John's baptism was the promise of the Spirit to come; Christian baptism is the promise of the Spirit who came.

So when you study a difficult passage, be clear on what the main topic of the text is so you won't be distracted with other things that are not relevant.

Have you ever approached a difficult passage? Is it helpful to know this rule when studying a difficult passage of scripture?

# DEALING WITH DIFFICULTIES

Acts 19:6

The coming of the Holy Spirit on new believers is another controversial topic. We find it in the story of the disciples of John the Baptist and Paul in Ephesus. Does the Holy Spirit indwell the believer at salvation? Or is there a time for salvation and then, later, a time to receive the Holy Spirit as a second blessing? I believe that the Holy Spirit indwells a believer at salvation. It is an oxymoron to have a Christian without the Holy Spirit; there would not be any difference between a Christian and a non-Christian.

Regarding the relationship of the believer and the Holy Spirit, scriptures say this:

1. No one can enter the kingdom of God unless they are born of the Spirit.
2. God saved us by the renewing by the Holy Spirit.
3. Our body is a temple of the Holy Spirit.
4. If anyone does not have the Spirit of Christ, they do not belong to Christ.
5. The Spirit testifies to our spirit that we are children of God.
6. We are sealed with the Holy Spirit.

To be a Christian without the Holy Spirit is biblically incoherent. Therefore, this story must have been an incident and not a biblical theme. Another difficult issue in Acts 19:6 is related to speaking in tongues. Many believe tongues are a sign that a second work of the Holy Spirit has taken place in the believer. Tongues have been so divisive. We must be careful about dividing the body of Christ into the ones who went to seminary and the ones who did not, the ones who speak in tongues and the ones who do not.

Remember that members of the body of Christ are side by side to do the work of God. The hand cannot say to the foot, "I do not need you." You have as much of the Holy Spirit as a new believer in Christ, or as Billy Graham, the famous evangelist, had. Maybe the ways our gifts come out are different, but that does not mean that some believers are better than others.

In the book of Acts, whenever Luke said the disciples were filled with the Spirit and spoke in tongues, that filling always had some connection with the gospel proclamation or some specific service related to outreach—it was a method of proclamation. Remember, in those days there were not many multilingual people, so this event was not an ecstatic utterance but an event where the Holy Spirit enabled believers to speak a known language to make the message understandable to everyone.

# DIGGING DEEPER

Tongues in the book of Acts were a gift of the Holy Spirit to proclaim the gospel to every nation. How do we know that? Let me give you six biblical reasons:

1. The word for *tongues* is a Greek word used for *language*.
2. There was no interpreter present, which is necessary when someone speaks in tongues, according to the teaching of Paul to the Corinthians.
3. Ephesus was very diverse, and there were few bilingual or multilingual people.
4. This was a place of proclamation, not a place of prayer.
5. This is the last mention of tongues in the book of Acts, so they did not go on further.
6. The laying on of hands was done for commissioning for the ministry, not for the impartation of the Holy Spirit.

A challenge we often have is that we prefer personal experiences to public proclamation. And when we do that, we privatize our faith too far and negate our purpose. We tend to make our Christian experience more and more private when God wants our Christian experience to be more public.

Here is what happened in Acts: The Apostle Paul encountered some folks who did not have clear theology. We know the Holy Spirit was present throughout the Old Testament, and we know despite John's constant pointing to Jesus, Paul had to tell the Jews in Ephesus about Him. Those who believed were baptized in the name of Jesus. Paul laid hands on them, and the Holy Spirit came. This had happened before. In Acts 2, the Holy Spirit came upon people of different nations; in Acts 8, He came on the Samaritans when the disciples laid hands on them; in Acts 10, the Gentiles began to receive the Holy Spirit. Why did this happen? The incorporation of new people groups into the body of Christ was given apostolic authority when the Spirit came.

Jewish believers who saw that would understand that the other groups, the Samaritans and the Gentiles, would not be inferior to them. There would not be a junior varsity, and the Jews would not be the varsity team. For there is no difference between Greek, Jew, or Samaritan; slave or free; male or female. Remember that the book of Acts is a transition from the Gospels to the epistles. It is not the place to base all of your theology, because it is descriptive and not prescriptive.

Can you see the reason for tongues in Acts?

# SUMMING UP

Can a person be a Christian without the Holy Spirit inside of him or her? As we have seen, the answer is no. Is this gift of the Spirit a prayer language or a proclamation tool? We saw that the believers in Acts received the Spirit and then proclaimed the gospel.

Steven Smith, our worship pastor, said this: "We have to be able to worship God past the endorphins and the adrenaline in our brains." That means that we should not worship the Lord only when our emotions are high.

The goal of the gift of tongues was that the believers in the early church would be able to proclaim Jesus.

Let's recap the five questions we must ask ourselves in order to analyze this difficult passage:

1. Is this passage intended to be descriptive or prescriptive? I would say it is descriptive.
2. Is this an unusual incident or a biblical theme? It is an unusual incident, not a biblical theme. These Jews did not know about John's pointing to Jesus, and they did not know about the Holy Spirit.
3. What is the context in this book and in the Bible? In the book of Acts, there are a lot of different things happening because we are legitimizing the early church, and that includes the coming of the Holy Spirit to all those groups coming into the church. The message of salvation was being spread to the world, not just to Israel, which implies a big transition.
4. We dug deeper. We looked at the grammar and the original language. We saw that the tongues in Greek are known languages, and we understood the difference between John's baptism and Christian baptism.
5. We used clear texts to understand unclear texts. We saw that many verses confirm that the Holy Spirit comes to believers who trust in Jesus so they can proclaim the gospel through the use of spiritual gifts.

So everything in this passage is about proclaiming the gospel and declaring that God can do His work in our city, our nation, and our world.

Are you proclaiming the gospel? What can you do to reach your city, your nation, or your world?

# PHYSICAL AND SPIRITUAL

**Matthew 9:35**

Jesus went out to towns and villages to do two things. First, He preached and taught. He prioritized spiritual needs. Second, He healed people of their sicknesses and diseases. He met their physical needs. What Jesus did is what difference-makers must do: Minister to both physical and spiritual needs.

The Bible also teaches this in James. It warns us not to say, "God bless you!" to a hungry man and then not give him some food. If you say, "God is with you" and talk about the Lord but do not give that hungry man the food he needs, he is not going to listen to you.

Meeting physical needs allows us to meet spiritual needs. They go hand in hand. Do not pray before the meal and then tip only 6 percent. Be a person who blesses others. The more you meet others' physical needs—the more you care—the more you can make a difference in people's lives.

The other day, my little daughter came up to me at home. I guess we had the air conditioning on a little too low because she said, "Daddy, I'm freezing. Can I snuggle with you?" For dads, that is a dream moment. Yes, my prayers had been answered, right there, for my daughter to ask to snuggle with me.

We started snuggling. I had my arm around her. I was rubbing her arm a bit, trying to warm her up. She said, "Oh, Daddy, it feels so good. I'm getting warmer!" Then she said, "You are a difference-maker!" I said, "You've been listening in church! All right! Way to go, girl!" What happened in that little microcosm, that little scene, is that her physical needs were being met as I snuggled with her.

When we minister to and care for people when they have physical needs, at that moment their ears begin to perk up. It is then that a Christian is reaching out with the kind of love that Jesus showed. It is then that people will ask, "Tell me more about this Jesus." Jesus makes a difference in us so we can make a difference in someone else.

*Jesus, open my eyes to the needs of those around me and help me make a difference in Your name.*

*For further study: James 2:14–17*

# HELP FOR HEAVEN

## Matthew 9:35

Some of us are trying to do enough to be Christian. That is the wrong order. You become a Christian through faith in Jesus Christ. You lay your life down for His. You make an exchange of His life for your sinful life. You put your faith in His death and resurrection. You ask Him to be your Savior. And then, once you are a Christian, you live as one. You walk out your actions. Our identity precedes our actions. We have a phrase we use around our church: "As we go." It means that what we do flows out of who we are.

What actions should flow from our identity? As Christians, we help people go to heaven. Difference-makers meet both physical and spiritual needs. Our ministry is not limited to helping people with their physical needs. Our goal is not to make earth a better place to go to hell from.

It is not enough to just help people. Everybody can be well fed and have access to clean water. They can have all the clothes they need, shoes, whatever they want. But having one's physical needs met does not change one's soul. If it were true that having everything you need makes it heaven on earth, then suburban America would be perfect. We have more than we need. But we know there are just as many divorces, addictions, pornography, and sin there as anywhere else. The world is a bizarre place, quickly becoming crazier and more chaotic. It cannot continue like that. It is not sustainable. Something has to be different.

As Christians, we help people. Yes, of course! But that is not all we do. We do not just engage in social activity but in soulful activity. The world says life does not matter. It says a human being is just a freak of nature and that we are no better than a dead dog when we die. But Christians know each person has a soul. You were knitted together in your mother's womb. Each and every life matters to God.

We help people, and by meeting their physical needs and declaring truth to them, we help them go to heaven. As we go, we become like Jesus.

*God, fill me with Your love so I might not just help, but help people go to heaven.*

*For further study: Titus 2:14*

# COMPASSION FOR SINNERS

### Matthew 9:36

Jesus felt compassion for the crowds because they were weary and worn out, harassed and helpless. If we are going to be difference-makers, we must ask this: Do we have compassion for the crowds?

I confess that sometimes, when I am watching the news, I don't have compassion. I think, "This is chaos. This is crazy. I am aggravated with you people. Why can't you get a clue?" At other times, I get ticked off. I hope it is a righteous anger. I say, "I'm sick of this." But the Lord wants us to have compassion. Sometimes I think, "If I had grown up like that, I might have turned out that way, too. Who knows where I would be? Let me have compassion. Let me love that person."

Of course, no one should break the law. I am not saying that in the least or trying to be soft on crime. But people do make crazy decisions because they are hurting, wounded, or confused. They have been molested; they have had all sorts of problems in their lives. We must recognize this and have compassion even as we stand for truth.

Sin makes people worn out and weary. There is a truth to that. Sometimes, people who sin think it is the sin that is making them cool. Maybe they can drink more than anybody else. But in just a few decades, their bodies are wrecked. Sin literally wears them out. It creates a weariness. It can lead to medical problems.

The Bible teaches that sin brings death. It makes us worn out and weary. I met with an adulterer, a man who had cheated on his wife. He said, "It is exhausting." He said it was a relief to be found out because the sin of his double life was exhausting. Sin is exhausting, but following God is exhilarating.

We all sin, but there is forgiveness in Jesus Christ. Many in our church have made decisions that they are not proud of in a lot of different areas, but Jesus has the power to forgive sins. He has compassion for us. There is hope in Jesus Christ. He makes a difference in us so we can make a difference in His name.

*Jesus, please give me a heart like Yours, full of compassion.*

*For further study: Romans 6:23*

# JESUS OUR LEADER

Galatians 6:7

Moved with compassion for the crowds, Jesus said they were weary and worn out; they were sheep without a shepherd. People without a leader do not know their purpose. They do not know where they are going, what to do, or where to go.

If you do not have direction, you will wander into fields where you should not go. That is why we ask in the Lord's Prayer for Him to forgive us our trespasses as we forgive those who trespass against us. We have walked into the wrong field. We have begun to feast on what was not ours to feast on. We have trespassed across a boundary line.

Jesus said the crowds were sheep without a shepherd. They did not have a leader. He stepped forward as the Messiah to say He was their leader. He was not chosen by the Sadducees or the Pharisees but by God the Father.

God sets up the government, the church, and the home. He sets up authorities and establishes laws. We must respect the leaders with authority in our society. We must honor them, stand behind them, and pray for them. When there is an election coming up, whether it is to elect the mayor or the president, we must decide what kind of people we want to elect. Will it be a leader with some good ideas or a leader who is also following Jesus?

God is the supreme leader, but we have removed God as leader. We are in chaos because we do not know who we are following. But God will not be mocked; we will reap what we sow. Leaderless equals purposeless. We have this chaos and confusion. We have racial issues, moral issues, security issues, and all sorts of things. But when you fall in love with Jesus, you realize the color of your skin does not matter. It can be black, brown, white, or even blue or purple! It does not matter; what matters is the soul and what God is doing to change it. God does not look at the exterior; He looks at the heart. If you want to relieve racial tension, get your eyes on Jesus.

Leaderless equals purposeless. Difference-makers have a leader. They have a purpose. To be a difference-maker, make sure you are following Jesus.

*God, help me to follow You.*

*For further study: Matthew 6:12*

# KIND OF PEOPLE

**Matthew 9:37–38**

Jesus said that the harvest is abundant, but the workers are few. The problem is not with the harvest. Many people realize they have a need of the soul. The problem, according to Jesus, is that there are few workers. He says to pray that God would send out workers into His harvest.

Jesus tells us to pray for difference-makers. They are people who say yes to God. They are the ones who stand up and pray, "I want You to call on me, Lord. I want to be the one who makes a difference in my city, my nation, my world. I want to be a yes person."

There are not enough yes people. There are not enough people who are stepping forward to say, "Yes, yes, I'm in. I want God to do something in me and through me."

Many Christians are not yes people; we are "kind of" people. We are kind of committed to the Lord. When asked to give, we answer, "You know, I've given in other ways." When asked to go, we say, "I'm for missions, but I'm not going to go on a trip. I like my pillow. I like my blanket." If asked, "Are you going to share your faith?" we answer, "It is just so hard; at work we cannot really do that; no." If asked, "Are you going to teach your kids about God?" we say, "Well, I do not want to force anything on them. I just want them to choose for themselves one day."

We are kind of people. We are kind of in it, kind of out of it. We are a little bit scared and a little less faithful until finally we become hiding people.

But to follow Jesus, we must see the crowds with compassion, not hate. We must recognize that they are weary and worn out. They have no shepherd. And we, who have a Shepherd, must pray.

*Lord, I want to be a yes person. I want to follow You. And as I follow You, Lord, You will bring people in my path whose physical needs I can minister to and care for. I want to share Your greatness with them. I trust that You will have a harvest, Lord, as You work through me.*

*For further study: Luke 4:18–19*
*Additional references: John 20:21*

# PRAY FOR OTHERS

## Matthew 9:37–38

How do you become a yes person? You pray for others. Praying for others brings a yes to you. Interestingly, in this scripture, Jesus does not say, "Okay, let's all step out, let's go for it." He doesn't command, like a military leader, "Everybody, charge!" What Jesus says instead is something like this: "I do not want you to reach out before you have looked up. I do not want you to go out before you have gone up. I want you to pray. I want you to pray that God will send workers out in the field." Jesus is not asking you and me to pray for ourselves; He is asking us to pray for somebody else.

Pretend you are in business and that you pray, not for yourself, but for other men and women in business this week, that they would make a difference through their work. So you pray, "Lord, I want to pray for all the business people. I want to pray, God, that they will make a difference, that they will realize it is not just about making money, it is about You placing them in a position of influence. I pray that business people will take the opportunity to share Jesus Christ when it is appropriate and bless their associates. I pray for the business community in this city to be difference-makers for good and for God."

When you start praying that way, as a person in business, guess what happens? You ask, "How can I pray for everyone else to do this if I am not doing it?"

If you are a teacher, pray for teachers. If you are a principal, pray for principals. If you are an administrator, pray for administrators. As you begin to pray, you will want to be part of it because your heart is moved. Pray for missions, and you will end up going. Pray for America, and you will vote. Pray for your family, and you will grow in love. Pray for your church, and you will begin inviting people there. Pray for the harvest, and you will begin to share.

Do you see what God does? When you begin to pray for yes people, you can become a yes person. You can be a difference-maker.

*Lord, stoke my heart through prayer.*

*For further study: Colossians 4:2*

# BE A YES PERSON

**Matthew 9:37–38**

Are you a yes person, or are you a maybe or kind of person? A few days ago, I went to the funeral of a deputy who was killed near here. He was a white officer who was killed by a black man. I sat in the service with other pastors from our community. We sat as a pastoral block, representing all different races, to say we love Jesus. We do not care if you are black, white, brown, green, purple—it does not matter. We sat together in unity.

It was a powerful funeral. The crowd was mostly made up of uniformed police officers, guys and gals with guns, sitting at the funeral of a comrade. There were also first responders there and people in suits.

The preacher said something like this: "If you are going to stand against evil and we are going to trust you to continue to protect, then we want you to stand right where you are so we can pray for you." Those men and women stood up right away. There was no hesitation. They could not get up out of their seats fast enough. And those of us who are not police officers, who are not in the line of fire, were inspired. We had goose bumps on our arms. It was powerful. When those officers stood up, I wanted to stand with them. I was sitting there thinking, "This is what yes people look like. Yes, this is what yes people look like."

Jesus calls us in the same way that preacher called those officers at the funeral. He calls us to make a difference. He calls us to meet others' physical and spiritual needs. Does He call us to be obnoxious? No. Does He call us to be winsome? Yes. Does He call us to be harsh? No. Does He call us to be compassionate? Yes.

As Christians, we help people, and we help them go to heaven. We walk as difference-makers in a world that is in great need.

*Jesus, help me be a difference-maker in Your name.*

*For further study: Colossians 1:9–11*

# LIVE HEART-HEALTHY

### Isaiah 1:1–4

My daughter gave me a milk chocolate peanut butter cup. She said, "Daddy, it is *healthy!*" The wrapper had the word *organic* on it, so it must be good, right? Organic makes everything okay: the sugar, the fat, and more.

We love buzzwords. If something is organic, hybrid, biodegradable, or gluten-free, that makes it okay. One of the big phrases on all sorts of foods right now is *heart-healthy*. God wants us to be heart-healthy. He wants us to have hearts that are spiritually healthy. Physical health is important, too, but if you live organic and gluten-free and all those cool words but don't have God, you're missing it.

To look at what God says about being heart-healthy, we are going to study Isaiah, the 23rd book of the Old Testament. Isaiah is amazing in that it mimics the whole Bible; it is like a Bible within the Bible. There are 66 books in the Bible, and Isaiah has 66 chapters. The Old Testament has 39 books, and there are 39 chapters in the first section of Isaiah. The New Testament has 27 books, and there are 27 chapters in the second section of Isaiah. They even focus on the same themes: God's righteousness, justice, and holiness in the Old Testament and the first part of Isaiah; God's glory, compassion, and grace in the New Testament and the second part of Isaiah. The name *Isaiah* means *the Lord saves*, and that is also the message of the Bible.

The book was written between 740 BC and 700 BC. Isaiah 1:1 tells us that the prophet saw this vision during the reigns of Uzziah, Jotham, Ahaz, and Hezekiah. His ministry spanned 40 years throughout the rule of four kings.

In Isaiah, the word *holy* comes up 33 times—compared to 26 times in the rest of the Old Testament. Isaiah emphasizes that God is holy, and that because He is holy, God is serious about love and sin. The more you get into God's love, the less desirable sin is going to be. And the more you get into sin, the less desirable God's love is going to be.

To stand up as difference-makers, we need to be heart-healthy.

*Lord, heal our hearts so we can put away sin, love You, and be holy.*

*For further study: Isaiah 1:16–20*

# COLD HEARTS

What does a loving parent do? Does he or she say, "Hey, kids, go and play on the freeway. It is not a problem. Do whatever you want—whatever you think is right." Now that is crazy. That's not love. Or does that parent say, "Stay away from the street. Look both ways. Cross at the crosswalk. Make sure the light is red and the sign says it is okay to walk."

God is our parent. He is serious about the dangers of sin and loving enough to warn us. Isaiah 1:2 says that God raised up children who rebelled against Him. God did everything for them. He raised them, provided for them, and blessed them. Yet they turned their backs on Him. They refused His goodness and said they wanted to do their own thing. They preferred sin. We have done the same thing. And sin hinders love.

When we sin, our hearts grow cold. Can you feel that in you? I feel that in me. A cold heart is not heart-healthy.

All of us are overwhelmed with bad news. We get bad news from the Internet, the TV, and the radio. We hear about bombs going off, people getting shot, and others being killed. I do not even want my kids to watch the news. Bad news is everywhere, anytime, all the time. Our hearts grow cold because we cannot handle all the negative news. It is just all too much emotionally.

So instead of praying about the tragedies and being broken for the sin and pain we see, we watch news that is entertaining. We want to see what happens in the scandal. We want to follow the bombing and see what takes place next. The news becomes an entertainment drama instead of breaking our hearts. Our hearts grow cold.

It has been said that if you live in a graveyard too long, you will stop crying when someone dies. Am I saying we should cry over every news report? No. We do not have the emotional capacity to do that. But am I saying that we should not have cold hearts to people dying? Yes, I am. We should care when people die. We should care about the tragedies going on in our world. And we should care about the sin that brings them about.

*Lord, make us sensitive to the dangers of sin.*

*For further study: Psalm 119:65–72*

# HARD HEARTS

**Proverbs 21:23**

If you glorify God, you mortify sin. If you rebel against God, you welcome sin. You get used to it. It no longer breaks your heart. You get a cold heart. Then it becomes a hard heart.

It happens in our relationships. It happens in marriage. Every marriage has friction. Some seasons are easier than others, but there is always friction. My wife, Kelly, and I have this saying: "The two became one, and now we are arguing over which one we became." I think *we* became *me*. If I want something and she wants something else, well…let's do what I want.

As the sin of selfishness sets in, the feelings of love decrease. You begin to push for what you want. When you don't get it, you get a little upset. You start using phrases like *she always*, and *he never*, and *we used to*, and *we need to*, and *they always do*, and *we never do*.

Next, your tone changes. Your tone is a big deal in marriage. It begins to be a different big deal. Your words are more cutting; you give subtle jabs. You become a real expert at it. You begin to just go after each other because you are fighting over which one of you the two of you became when you became one.

Here is what you need to learn: You think it, but that does not mean you should say it. When you are young, you think it is best to be honest, no matter how much you hurt your spouse. But that is not the best thing; that's the dumb thing. You need a filter. After 18 years of marriage, I have learned that everything I think does not need to be said; neither does everything Kelly thinks. Our desires need to be laid before the Lord. We need to say, "I am not going to be selfish," and we need to mean it. Sin will hinder the love in marriage, but love will hinder the sin of selfishness. You see how it works?

God wants you to love Him. A relationship with God is not about trying to do the right thing but about falling in love with the Father, the Son, and the Holy Spirit. Then our hearts become healthy and whole, not cold and hard.

*Lord, help me to love You more; help me to not want to sin anymore.*

*For further study: Proverbs 12:18*

**SEPTEMBER 16**

# HEARTS THAT HIDE

## Isaiah 1:11

Sin makes your heart cold. Then it makes your heart hard. A third thing that sin does is cause us to hide. Instead of embracing God and others, we hide.

Sin isolates you. With some sins, it is far easier to sin in solitude than it is to sin in a group. Sin moves you into the dark. It is much easier to sin at midnight than it is to sin at noon. You drive past places in our city that are seedy, gross, and terrible. In the daytime, they look like a dump, but at night, they look different. We think, well, now that it is dark, maybe we can enter in and nobody will know. It gives us a hard heart. It gives us a cold soul. We hide instead of embracing God and embracing others.

When you are alone, the enemy comes and takes out your knees. When you are in a place of darkness, he comes and takes out your life. God, in contrast, wants to bring you to the light and to the community of the people of God.

Isaiah tells a vision about the people of Judah and Jerusalem. They were sinning against the Lord, and they knew it. So what did they do? They began with their own works. They tried to get rid of their guilt and trouble by making sacrifices to the Lord. But Isaiah 1:11 shows us what the Lord thought about their efforts. They were useless. They were detestable.

The people of Israel said something like this: "Let's just go to church more. We have a heart problem, so let's just try to do some spiritual things." All of us have lived that facade before. We have pretended when we know that our hearts are cold and hard.

But God says something like this: "No, no, no, no, no. I am not asking for your exterior. I am asking for your interior. I want to make a difference in who you are, because who you are will affect what you do." God wants to warm and soften our beating hearts. He wants to bring us to the light and to the community of the people of God. And then He wants to fill us with life and love so love can become the basis for our actions.

*Lord, do not let me hide. Make my heart healthy.*

*For further study: Isaiah 1:16–20*

# STOP DOING EVIL

Isaiah 1:16–20

No one has done you more harm in your life than you. I know it is the cool thing today—it has been for a long time—to blame it on somebody else. The practice goes right back to Genesis. "Well, who gave you the apple?" "My wife did." "Who gave *you* the apple?" "The snake did." "Who made the apple tree?" "God did." "The fault is not mine. Somehow, the fruit got eaten."

Do you know what the number-one killer is in the United States? Every year, 610,000 people die of heart disease. One out of every four deaths is due to heart disease. It is the leading cause of death for both men and women. We are dying of heart disease because we are eating a bunch of junk. Adam and Eve ate the apple.

We are dying physically, but we are also dying spiritually. God has the solution. He told the people of Judah to stop doing what is evil and start doing what is good.

Stop doing evil. If it is not glorifying God, if it is not giving you passion for Him, if you wouldn't do it in front of your mamma or your daddy, if you wouldn't want all of us to know, then stop. Quit looking at that, doing that, going there, acting like that, thinking that. Just quit it. Just stop. That is how you begin to live heart-healthy. Stop doing evil. John Owen, a Reformed theologian, said it like this: "Be killing sin or it will be killing you."*

Jesus Christ died on the cross to pay for our sins. Trust Him, and His blood will make you pure in God's sight. Christianity is an exchange. You take your ugly heart and exchange it for the righteousness of Christ. Have you made a trade with Jesus? Have you been born again?

Sin brings death, and love brings life. If we are going to be heart-healthy, if we are going to be difference-makers, we must repent of sin and stop doing evil. Only then can we walk with God.

*Lord, I am sorry for my sin. Help me get my heart right.*

*For further study: Genesis 3:8–13*

# START DOING GOOD

Isaiah 1:16–20

No one has done you more harm in your life than you. No one has done you or me more harm than what we have done to ourselves. Our own decision-making is what has brought us the harm. Romans 6:23 says that the result of sin is death.

No one has done more harm than yourself, but at the same time, no one has done you more good than God. He has given you and me a bounty of love, a feast of righteousness, and all kinds of blessings. He provides our every need—not every want, but every need. God has given us everything, just as He gave it to the people of Israel and Judah. And yet they and we have turned our backs on Him. Our nation has received blessing upon blessing. Just look at the hand of God on our history! Yet we continue to sin. God's first command through Isaiah is to stop sinning. Stop doing evil.

God's next command is to start doing good. God is very clear about this. Isaiah 1:17 not only tells us to do what is good, but to learn it, to seek justice, to fight against oppression, and to defend and help those who need it.

You see, it is not enough to just say, "Stop doing evil." That's like telling a hungry man to quit eating. If you do not eat, you starve. The thing is, you do not need to starve. To avoid heart disease, you need a healthy diet. Instead of a hamburger, eat a pizza made with cauliflower crust. I am eating as heart-healthy as I have ever eaten in my life, and my wife is cooking healthier than she ever has. We are enjoying it, and it is good.

Sin hinders love, and love hinders sin. God does not just say, "Don't sin." He offers an alternative. He does not just issue a negative command; He wants positive action. He wants that cold, hard heart to change. He wants it to be soft and warm and beat with purpose. He wants you to become a difference-maker.

*Lord, I want to invest my energy in doing good and not evil. I want to make a difference.*

*For further study: Titus 2:11–14*

# SERVE ORPHANS AND WIDOWS

## Isaiah 1:16–20

Loving the orphan and the widow is not an option for the Christian. There are things that are kind of optional. You are good at hospitality; well, I am not. You do this; I do that. God has given everyone different gifts. But all throughout the scriptures, we find God commanding us to care for the widow and the orphan. At different times, the prisoner and the stranger are thrown in there, too. The point is, God cares about people who are defenseless. He wants us to defend them.

I am not saying that widows or widowers are not strong people. Because they have faced hardship, they may be stronger than any of us. But I am saying that God has called us to work on behalf of the orphan and the widow. They need us, as the body of Christ, to be their defenders.

So God gets really specific. He commands the people of Israel, and us, to care for the orphan and the widow. God has been blessing our church for 175 years. I think our emphasis on supporting widows and orphans has brought us a deeper blessing of God.

We help widows. Every one of our deacons has a widow assigned to him that he connects with, cares about, and makes sure is doing well. We also have a ministry to widows to help them with whatever is needed. Every so often, we organize a day for the men in our church to serve others. Our men come together, put on T-shirts, and show up at widows' houses with power tools. They paint, they fix, they do what is needed. Our budget includes giving to our denomination's retirement program, which helps widows.

We help orphans. We have been part of more than 100 adoptions, providing assistance for special needs cases. We help orphanages and orphan ministries. We have a full-time staff member at our church who is in charge of adoptions and orphans.

Part of living heart-healthy is being a person who is not selfish, but selfless. Living heart-healthy means not focusing on ourselves, being defensive, or protecting our turf and our stuff. It means stepping forward to defend somebody else.

*Lord, I want to make a difference. Help me stop doing evil, start doing good, and help widows and orphans.*

*For further study: James 1:27*

# BUT GOD

Ephesians 4:21–24

What we most deeply desire as human beings is something people characterize as very Christian. That is because God has put a thumbprint on every human life; we have been created for God and by God. We are never going to be satisfied with anything less than God. Therefore, our deepest desires are not desires for sin. They are desires for the things of God.

We are born in sin, but when we accept Jesus into our lives, when we embrace the new life He brings within us, we begin living new lives as new men and women in Christ. We stop walking like sinful creatures and accept the new life, new hearts, and new minds that God gives us.

When we start walking with God, we are changed. We can all live lives of sin and far away from God, but God shows up and changes everything. "But God" is such a powerful phrase. It is what changes all things in our lives. When God shows up, He makes a difference. He comes and makes us new so we can start walking in a new way.

We can live our lives minding our own business, worrying about things our way, living dark and meaningless lives, but God shows up, and He makes everything different. He turns our lives upside down and gives us purpose, a new life, a new way of walking, and a new way of seeing life.

God shows up, and nothing stays the same. He changes our old self into a new one, our old way of walking into a new way of walking. He leads us into a new life. That is the truth that is Jesus. That is the truth of the cross—Christ dying for our sins, for our old nature, and resurrecting us into new people, transforming us into new men and women through His sacrifice.

When that "but God" moment comes, nothing can stay the same. "But God" changes the course of our lives forever. As we begin to live new lives as new men and women, God transforms our way of thinking. We begin to see things differently, we begin to speak differently, and we treat people differently because we start seeing things the way God sees them.

I pray that while reading this devotional, your "but God" moment will come and change your life forever!

*For further study: Romans 6:6*

# THE OLD SELF AND NEW SELF

## Ezekiel 11:19–20

We need to understand what the Bible calls the old man and the new man. All of us are born in sin; all of us are born with our own desires. The old man, or old self, means walking in my strength, on my path, for my glory. There is no room left for anyone else but me. The new man, or new self, is completely different. Living life as a new person means walking in God's strength, on His path, for His glory. It is living our lives for God, completely surrendered to Him. It is leaving sin behind and following in Jesus's footsteps.

There is an old self, the natural man of Adam, and a new self, the spirit man of Christ. The difference between the two is faith in the cross and the resurrection of Jesus Christ. It is not just going to church or doing what is right. It is not getting shined up. It is understanding that once we were lost, and now we are found. Once we were blind, and now we see. Once we were in the dark, on the broad road of destruction, and now we are on the narrow road of life. Once we were without God, and now we are indwelled by God through Jesus Christ. Do you see that?

We might believe that it is enough to just stop cursing in order to live life as new men and women in Christ. Yet we can have the purest language and not know God. There is a difference between the old self and the new self. We are not just the same person with a different coat and a new pair of boots. We are no longer who we were. We talk differently, we walk differently, we treat people differently. We understand the sacrifice on the cross and start living our lives with a different mindset. We walk as Jesus walked.

It is when we really know God and understand the sacrifice of Jesus on the cross that we start living new lives. It is through faith and through having a real, honest relationship with God that we begin to walk in a new way, leaving our old way of life behind.

Understanding the difference between the old self and the new self will help us grow as believers in Christ and in our relationships with God.

*For further study: 1 Corinthians 15:47–49*

# GROW UP

There comes a time in our lives when we need to put aside the old self, the old way of thinking, our sinful nature, and grow up spiritually into new men and women in Christ. We need to realize that we are not who we used to be. There comes a time when we need to leave the old self behind and know that, as we abide in Christ, we need to start releasing what is within us.

What is our old way of thinking and sinful nature? According to the Apostle Paul in Ephesians, it is pointless thinking, darkened understanding, exclusion from the life of God, ignorance, hardened hearts, and callousness when we lose the capacity to feel shame. It is being promiscuous, impure, and greedy—with a constant desire to want more and more of the things that do not come from God. It means having an appetite for sin.

Sin is an appetite, and the more we eat from it, the more we are going to want it. That is why it is so important for us to leave our sinful nature behind. Christian author and evangelist Ravi Zacharias put it this way: "Sin will take you farther than you want to go, keep you longer than you want to stay, and cost you more than you want to pay."*

Whenever we begin to have the sinful appetites of our old self, we need to remind ourselves that is not what we really want and not who we really are. We do not want sin if we are believers in Christ; and even if we do not believe in Christ, we do not want a life of sin, either. There is a famous quote that says: "The young man who rings the bell at the brothel is unconsciously looking for God."† Even the most sinful person is looking for God.

Can you imagine the owner of a business saying that he wants his employees to be ignorant, impure, greedy, hard-hearted, and always thinking about pointless things? Even if he is not a Christian, he will want his employees to be like the new man or woman in Christ, not like the old one.

I pray that you may put aside your old sinful nature and grow up spiritually. Embrace your new life in Christ, leaving sin behind and following in His steps.

*For further study: Ephesians 4:17–19*

# RENEW YOUR MIND

## Romans 12:1–2

The Bible tells us that we need to renew our minds. Have you ever wondered why that is? It is because what we think is what we become. In the Old Testament, it says, "For as he thinks in his heart, so is he" (Prov. 23:7 NKJV). What we think about is what we are going to yearn for and what we will become. René Descartes famously wrote, "*Cogito, ergo sum*," or "I think, therefore I am."*

What we think about is what we will be worried about; what we worry about is what we are afraid will happen, and that will become our idol. What do you think about? Do you think like a Christian (taking every thought captive to obey Christ), or do you think as the world thinks and just add a Christian tagline or motto to your thoughts?

When we renew our minds, we start to think in a Christian way. This changes the way we do things. It changes the way we parent, how we treat our spouse, how we talk and act in our workplace, and how we live our lives. It is not enough to just keep thinking the same way we used to think before, adding a few touch-ups and shining it all up. That will not make a difference. We need to renew our minds entirely.

It is so important for us to understand that the way we think affects our lives. It is the difference between living a life of sin and death and living a life of freedom and peace. I want to encourage you to read the scriptures and fill your mind with the Word of God. Worship and listen to preaching. Fill your mind with the things of God, so it will be renewed in a godly way, and then you will respond to things in a godly manner.

*For further study: 2 Corinthians 10:5*
*Additional references: Philippians 4:8*

# PUT ON THE NEW SELF

## Galatians 2:20

God has made us new, not improved. A lot of things can give us a new suit, but only Christianity can give us a new person inside the suit. Put on the new self, and then God will do something amazing. Release what God has put in your life through the Holy Spirit. When you put on the new self, you allow God to work through you.

When we put on the new self, we are being transformed into the likeness of God, who created us perfect in His image. But we chose our own path for our own will and glory. We walked along that path for a long time, and then we came to the cross. Hopefully, we accepted Jesus Christ as our Savior and put our faith in His death and resurrection. Now we have a new self. God wants to make us as He made us way back when we were pure, when He first created us. He wants to wash us clean. He wants to dwell in us. He wants to walk with us as He did in the garden with Adam and Eve before they sinned.

The new self is God doing something on the inside and our salvation coming out. God puts a desire for Himself in our hearts and minds when we begin walking as new men and women in Him. The Bible says, "Take delight in the Lord, and He will give you your heart's desires" (Ps. 37:4). As we put on the new self, God gives us new desires and renews our minds. He gives us a new appetite for the things of God.

I pray that you may begin to walk in a new way, as the new person God intended you to be. May you embrace salvation through the sacrifice of Jesus on the cross and start living and thinking in a completely new, godly way.

*For further study: Colossians 3:10*

# FULLY KNOWN

## Psalm 139:1–6

Psalm 139 is a very poetic and famous psalm. David declares in this psalm that God is everything. He is all-powerful and everywhere for every time and every moment. We are to lay our lives before Him.

God is also all-knowing and all-interested. You might say, "Yeah, I know God's all-knowing. Of course. He's God!" But do you know that God is not only all-knowing but also all-interested? He not only loves you, He likes you. He not only cares for you, He wants to be part of what is going on in your life.

This is so important for us because every human being desires greatly to be known and to have friendships. All of us, introverts and extroverts, long for different levels of friendship, but everybody wants to have a friend. Everybody wants to be known. Everybody wants to be cared for.

One of my best friends since sixth grade and I have this phrase that we use together: "Fully known; fully loved." That is the way we describe each other. I know everything about him. He knows everything about me. I fully love him, and he fully loves me. It is the same with the Lord, just at a deeper level. He fully knows everything about you, and He fully loves you with everything He is.

We crave to be known. It may be through selfies on social media. We may be looking for fame through acknowledgments of our accolades, our accomplishments, or our trophies. Everybody wants to be known, and God says, "I know you, and I like you."

It does not matter how many followers you have on social media; it matters who you have as your leader. If you have Christ as your leader, knowing Him will give you more satisfaction than a million followers will ever give you.

God wants you to know that you are fully known and fully loved by Him.

*For further study: Hebrews 4:13*

# WALKING IN THE LIGHT

### Psalm 19:14

One of the worst feelings a human can experience is feeling ignored. I listened to a podcast from a retired CEO of Ritz-Carlton, and he made this statement: "We train our people so when they're walking down the hall, if they get within six or seven feet of a customer, they are supposed to say, 'Good morning, Sir. Good morning, Ma'am.'"*

The employees are trained to look at customers in the eye and acknowledge them as they pass them in the hall. They understand the psyche of men and women because they understand that the worst feeling is to be ignored. Have you ever been ignored? Sure you have!

Have you been to a party and it seems like everybody else knows each other? Have you walked up to somebody and they have turned the other way? All of us have been in a spot where we felt like we were just blending into the wallpaper instead of being part of what was going on. Everybody has felt ignored, and being ignored is one of the worst feelings we can experience.

God is saying to you, "You'll never be ignored by Me, because My eyes are on you, and I know right where you are."

God's knowledge of us is intimate knowledge, but His intimacy does two things: It invites us, and it also repels us. It invites us when we understand how God knows us, and we respond by saying, "Yes. I want to be known by my Creator and God. I need a place to pour out my deepest thoughts, a place for forgiveness of my sins. I need a place to connect." I am invited to understand that He searches me and knows me. He knows when I leave, what I say, and what I do.

But if God knows everything, then it also repels me because it is a little scary to think, "If He knows everything, I don't know how close I want to get; He may start changing things. I want Him to know 'these' are the changeable things and 'these' are the unchangeable things."

Everything is on the table before Him. God can see anything. Even the things that I think are in the dark, God can take those and change them. His love invites me to trust Him.

*For further study: 1 John 1:6–7*

# WHAT ABOUT THE PAIN?

### Psalm 139:7–12

God's intimate knowledge of us invites us, but it also repels us—it moves us back. If God knows everything, then I am safe and satisfied. But if God knows everything, how do I reconcile the pain and the tragedy in my life? What do I do with that? And when I don't know what to do with that, can I lean further in, or will the pain and tragedy push me further out?

In John 11, Lazarus dies. The Bible says two days passed before Jesus went to Lazarus, whom He loved. He waited two days. Why did He delay like that? He delayed so He could show the glory of God in an even greater way. Mary and Martha—and you and I—do not like God's delays.

I do not like the moments when I feel like I must say, "God, You should be doing this." I am not sure how to adapt that into His sovereignty. There is part of the sovereignty of God that actually repels me when I say, "Why does this happen?" And then there is the part of God's sovereignty that motivates me to say, "God, You know that it's happening, and I've got no other place to flee."

We are going to see that same tension with David in the next devotional. David is thinking about fleeing. You might not have seen this before in the scriptures, although you might have considered fleeing.

David's thinking might have been something like this: "I don't know if I want to stay here. What would happen if I fled? Well, if I go to Mars, He's there. If I got to the bottom of the ocean, He's there. Golly...wherever I go, He's there!"

This knowledge is actually going to comfort us eventually. God is always present and always powerful. It does not matter where you are, where you're going, or where you've been. God is always present and always powerful. David ponders fleeing, but he realizes that it is impossible. God is omnipresent—everywhere. He is omnipotent—all-powerful. David says, "I can't go anywhere. God is already there."

So wherever you are hurting, quiet your heart and find Him there. He is God. His name will be glorified in your situation.

*Lord, even in the midst of my pain, walk me through it. Amen.*

*For further study: John 11:5–7*

# GOD'S HANDIWORK

Psalm 139:13–18

David discovers that God is everywhere because God is the Creator. God is not the same as His creation. Creation symbolizes the characteristics and the glory of God. We do not look at and worship a tree or look at a sunset and say, "Oh, there's God over there."

God is everywhere, and He is the Creator of all we see. The heavens declare His glory. The skies declare the skill of His hands. David said, "You knit me together in my mother's womb. I praise you because I am fearfully and wonderfully made" (Ps. 139:13–14 NIV).

Psalm 139 can answer so many questions that we have in our culture right now. People have removed the Creator from society and have lifted up creation. Many are looking for the fruit of the Spirit without the Spirit. People want to have love and to be kind, patient, gentle, and faithful, but they do not want to receive the fruit of the Spirit from the Spirit. If we remove the Creator, we cannot tell everybody to be nice to each other.

Global warming will not be the motivation for a black person to love a white person. Saving the seals is not going to get the job done to make a white person love a black person. It is not going to happen. Love happens when we realize there is a Creator who has put His fingerprint on our lives. He is saying something like this: "I am the Creator, and I want you to learn to love Me first. Then you can learn to value and love others."

We all have value because we have been knit together by the same loving Father in heaven. Our skin color does not make any difference; I can love you, and you can love me because the same God who loves us has knit us together.

When we love God as He loves us, we are able to step forward and love across racial lines. My heritage is from South Louisiana. Don't you think there is some prejudice in my heritage? But let me tell you this: There is no prejudice in my heart because Jesus can change hearts. He can make things brand new. God wants to do that for all of us.

It is not willpower. It is the power of His love in me saying, "I want to follow through on the fingerprint of God."

*For further study: Psalm 19:1*

# PRECIOUS VALUE

### Psalm 139:13–14

Psalm 139 answers this question: When does life begin?

Life begins when it is knit together in a mother's womb—in that place—as sperm and egg come together. God knits us together as male or female. God's knitting is so intricate that Sir Isaac Newton said, "In the absence of any other proof, the thumb alone would convince me of God's existence."*

God said He has put a fingerprint in you and on you. That is why humans are valued. What brings value to anything? An exterior statement brings value to something. Gold is worthless unless everybody wants it. Land is worthless unless somebody is going to build a shop or a house on it.

God has put His fingerprint on us and has said that we are created in His image. That is why you can drive past a dead possum on the road, but you would never drive past a dead person on the road. It is different. All creatures are not the same. God's image is on you and me.

This knitting that comes together in a mother's womb reveals our great value. God can do great things in us. He can move through us and move our minds and our hearts so we can love people whom we didn't love before.

God can do more than we can think of or even imagine. We can walk in the paths that He has prepared for us to live out His plan. God is at work; it happens through the knitting. You have been intricately created by God, and that gives your life a precious value.

We also have His most valuable gift of love, which comes through Jesus Christ and what He has done for us. When we understand how valuable we are to Him, His thoughts will be our greatest treasure and will enable us to walk in His ways.

God, You knit me together so wonderfully! Move my heart and my mind to follow through on the continuation of Your plan and Your will for my life. I am ready to follow Your fingerprint. Amen.

*For further study: Psalm 138:8*
*Additional references: Ephesians 2:10*

# EVERYTHING IN US

Psalm 139:16–18

In Roman culture in the first century, baby girls were born and unwanted. The parents would take the baby to the outskirts of the city and leave her there. People could hear the baby cry from the city, and two groups would run out to get the baby. One group consisted of brothel owners; the second were believers in Jesus Christ. Early Christians would run, rescue, and care for that child.

If you look at the end of slavery, you find the church there. Look at the history of the Civil Rights movement in our country, and you will find the church. When you see people with the cross in their heart, you will see people who sacrificially care for their brothers and sisters. This care comes from their understanding of the scripture that says we have been knit together by God, and we are therefore valuable.

Where does value come for humans? What makes us different from a cat or a dog? It is the fingerprint of God. Not only does He love you, He likes you. He created you and has a plan for you. His thoughts about you are as numerous as the grains of the sand of the sea. Nobody else thinks of you that much!

Have you heard this phrase? "You wouldn't worry what people thought of you if you knew how seldom they did." It is true! But God is telling you something like this: "As the sand of the sea, so are My thoughts toward you. That's how much I love you. In the midst of the pain, My thoughts are toward you. In the midst of joy, My thoughts are still toward you. I have thoughts toward you because I have been weaving you together since day one."

Everything in us is crying out, "I want to be known... please notice something special about me!" Where does that come from? It comes from a Father, God, who knit you together, who is still thinking about you this very moment. He is so in love with you.

God knows who you are; He sees how special and valuable you are. He has a plan for your life, and He is at work. Trust Him.

*For further study: Isaiah 43:4*

# THE EXAMINED LIFE

Psalm 139:19–24

David begins the last part of Psalm 139 by separating himself from awful people. He says something like this: "God, I despise your enemies. I'm not like them; I'm completely on Your side."

Then, in verse 23, David tells the Lord to search him and know him. Let's compare verse 1 with verse 23. Verse 1 says, "Lord, You have searched me and known me." That is a fact, just the way it is. Verse 23 is an invitation that stems from humility: I want You to "search me, God, and know my heart."

It is exactly what happens in our lives. When we begin to understand that God is everywhere, all-knowing, all-interested, ever-present, and that we are precious in His sight, created by Him in His image; when we understand that there is something different about us that is not in a cow, a monkey, or a dog, then we understand the intrinsic value God places on us. When all of this knowledge begins to sink in, we begin to respond to the Lord with requests and respect.

Here is my request: Lord, search me and know me. Test my heart. See if there's any anxious way in me, and lead me in the path of everlasting life. I want You to speak to my heart, God. What's in there? I can't even rightly judge myself, Lord. Where am I off? Where are my lusts becoming something I'm trying to justify? Where are my prejudices coming out, Lord? What still needs to be crucified in me? I'm requesting that You would do that, Lord.

Here is my respect: God, because You are a loving Father who thinks about me more than I can fathom, speak to my heart and reveal Yourself to me. I respect Your leadership in my life. I'm going to follow You even when it's not convenient or I don't necessarily like it.

It is called living the examined life. He knows everything about me, and He does not want my heart to get away with sin. He is interested in me pursuing the dreams He has for me as I trust that He is God. I know He can fill my heart with praise and joy and my mouth with laughter as I give Him everything that is in my heart.

*For further study: Psalm 139:1, 23*

# REAL LIFE

My first missionary journey that opened my eyes to the nations was a trip to China. We were able to talk to people who were in English classes and answer questions about America. I wrote on the board that I was from Texas. The students started yelling words like *cows*, *horses*, and *hats*! They asked me if I had horses, and I explained that we don't all have horses in Texas. I added that I was a minister at Texas A&M University and that our mascot was an Aggie. They did not grasp that at all, so I explained that it had to do with agriculture and farmland. They all got together, and after much effort on their part, they translated the word *aggie* to *peasant*, the lowest rung of society who works in the field. For an Aggie, that is kind of offensive, I know, but we just went with it because we were not there to teach them about Aggie football.

I use this illustration because I want you to see how sometimes we take God as the gardener of our hearts and souls and move Him down to the lowest rung. He only gets to garden where we give Him permission. We are above Him, and we want Him to tend to what *we* want. We never actually say this, but we live like this: His gardening happens only when He has been given approval by "the big boss"—you and me.

Whenever God gardens in ways we don't agree with, we get offended and say, "God, I want the blessing that this person has" or "I don't want the trial that I have; I don't like it." "Lord, here is the fruit that I want you to plant. I want you to water it on Monday, Wednesday, and Friday, but I want you to leave it alone on Tuesday and Thursday." We make God into a peasant—one who follows our orders—instead of us following His orders.

In John 14, Jesus gets us ready to trust the Gardener by talking to us about the Holy Spirit. Jesus tells us that the Holy Spirit is our Counselor, our *Paraclete*—one who walks alongside. He is part of the Trinity. So with the Counselor's help, we are able to say, "Lord, You prune, clip, and plant as You want." In doing this, we will find real life.

*For further study: John 14:15–17*

# OUR UNION WITH JESUS

God uses the garden illustration to help us understand that He is God and not a peasant:

- He wants to have a right relationship with us as we abide in Jesus Christ.
- He also wants us to have a right relationship with other believers.
- He wants us to know that as we walk in Christ, things are going to come against us. When we abide in Christ, we have communion, which will help us handle the persecution.

The books of the Bible connect with each other to prove God's points. In the first chapter of John's Gospel, John the Baptist tells us the first *I am* statement about Jesus when he says that Jesus is the true Light. What is the first thing God created? Light! Genesis and John just connected to prove God's point.

Then in John, chapter six, Jesus makes *His* first *I am* statement when He says, "I am the bread of life" (John 6:35). What did the Israelites eat when they were in the wilderness journeying through the desert? Manna—bread from heaven. Jesus says He is the true bread, and when we eat of Him we will never go hungry again.

Jesus makes another declaration in chapter 15. He says, "I am the true vine" (John 15:5). This is the seventh and *last* "I am" statement from the book of John.

When we come to the table for the Lord's supper, we have bread and wine—the fruit of the vine. From the first to the last statement, we declare who Jesus Christ is—He is God, not a peasant.

When Jesus tells His disciples He is the vine, He is saying, in essence, "I am a huge connection point to you." In the book of Isaiah, we learn that the Lord is given a vineyard, and Israel is supposed to be the true vine that blossoms with His fruit. Israel failed. Jesus took the place of Israel, claiming to be the perfect vine. Israel's redemption comes from Jesus. His obedience bears the fruit of righteousness. Salvation comes through Him. He is not a peasant.

When we declare in our culture that Jesus is the true vine, it means He is the only way to heaven. He is not *a* vine, He is *the* Vine. He and the Father are one.

*For further study: Genesis 1:3*
*Additional references: John 6:48–51*

# PEASANT OR GOD?

John 15:7–8

Is God the gardener who can tend to your soul, or is He one that needs your approval? Is God the one you hire to be your yardman, or is He the one you give your field to so He can own it? These are vastly different roles. If you hire Jesus to be your yardman and do some things for you, through His grace, He will show you some things.

However, when you give Jesus your land, you might say, "Lord, I don't like tomatoes, so please don't plant tomatoes." And when He plants tomatoes, you realize, "I love tomatoes!" When He says, "I want to make this a pecan orchard," you say, "I'm not really into pecans...but I am going to trust Him." In doing this, we say, "Lord you are the true Vine!"

The greatest blessings in my life were those things I was afraid to give up. I was so afraid as a teenager to give my life to Jesus because I did not want to lose my friendships. Now, I have so many friends that I cannot remember everybody's name.

God had to peel my hands off of my dream to be a businessman, which is a great calling. But God said, "No, vocational ministry is what you are going to do." What a blessing it has been! Now I am able to say, "Lord, my life is Your field. You are not my worker; You are not my yardman; You are not a peasant. I am Your bond slave; I am Your indentured servant; I am Your son."

This is easy to say on Sunday at church but not so easy on Monday morning when the Gardener cuts off the branches that bear no fruit and prunes the branches that do bear fruit. The Gardener does this with two kinds of storms in our lives: correcting storms and perfecting storms.

Correcting storms take the vineyard vines out of the ground and train them to run along the trellis so they can get the right amount of sun. The perfecting storm is for the vines that are bearing fruit, but the Gardener wants to produce more fruit in them.

Whichever type of vine you are, storms are coming, and that is why it is important to abide in the Vine.

*For further study: 1 Corinthians 10:16–17*

# FRUIT BEARER

## Matthew 13:21

If you are not bearing fruit, you are in the muck of life. The Gardener wants to come and lift you up and put you in a place where you can grow. You will never be satisfied in your life until you are on the trellis and out of the mud. A believer in Christ, indwelt by the Holy Spirit, is not meant for the mire or the muck off the trellis. We are meant to bear fruit. Whenever we see our lives dragging in the dirt, we need to realize that is not what we were meant for. God wants to lift us up. If we think He is a peasant and we are the boss, we will never let Him do it. If we allow Him to lift us up, He will then place us high up where He can show us off for His glory. As He places you there, He will say, "This is what I meant for you, my child."

Jesus is the true vine, and the Father is the Gardener. The Gardener takes those who do not bear fruit and lifts them up out of the muck. He knows that grapes do not grow well on the ground. Pumpkins and squash might, but grapes don't. Believers don't. Would you allow Him to lift you up and place you on the trellis of growth? That is where you will get the sunshine you need.

Both types of believers—those who bear fruit and those who do not bear fruit—will have an aha moment when they say, "Why am I doing this? This might work right now, but it doesn't work for the long run!" At that moment, wake up and let the Gardener lift you up.

Believers who are bearing fruit are in need of perfecting storms. They are on the right path, and on that journey, they are being perfected, made better and stronger. They are given the opportunity to grow and exercise faith. When the Gardener prunes, we say, "Lord, don't prune away the leaves. Take the thorns instead." We get nervous about the pruning because we love today's leaves more than tomorrow's fruit.

How is He shaping you? How is God showing you that He is not a peasant? He is doing that by showing you that if you love tomorrow's fruit more than today's leaves, you will begin to be perfected in Christ.

*For further study: Hebrews 10:10*

# BLOSSOM WITH JESUS

John 15:3–5

God might not start picking at the leaves; He might start picking at the petals. When He does that, we really get upset. Sometimes, God prunes the whole thing. And in those moments, you say, "Lord, why?! Do you even love me?" There have been times in my ministry that I have felt like I was holding stalks and stems, and I have had to go back and remember that He prunes because He loves. And every branch that is fruitful He prunes so we can become *more fruitful*. He is not pruning because He is upset with us. He is perfecting us. He has a trade coming for you. Your stem is about to become a bouquet that is a pruned heart that begins to blossom with Jesus. When He allows you to blossom with Him, God is able to do His work in ways that you never expected.

The Gardener is doing His work. He is not a peasant. Do you see Him as a peasant? Do you see Him as mean? Or do you see Him as the Gardener of your soul? Pray this: "God, my heart is Your field, and I give You everything I have. I lay it down before You so You can do your work in me." If that is true for you, it will hurt when today's leaves are gone, but you will love tomorrow's fruit more. Choose the fruit.

Are you bearing fruit? If you are not, would you allow the Gardener to lift you up and put you back on the trellis? If you are bearing fruit, would you stand firm in the pruning? Allow God to prune your heart and your life. It is painful but purposeful. Which group are you in? Correcting storms or perfecting storms? Either one has the same Gardener. Allow Him to do His work in your life.

*Jesus, I give You great thanks. God, make my heart into a garden. Tend my soul. Speak to me, Lord. To those who are not bearing fruit, who are in the muck, speak to them and work in them so they will let You lift them up. For those who are bearing fruit, let Your discipline be a perfecting storm. May my faith grow even though it hurts. Do things in me, Lord, that I do not want You to do in my flesh but that I trust You to do in my spirit. In Jesus's name, amen.*

*For further study: Hebrews 9:13–14*

# WE ARE WASHED CLEAN

## John 15:1–5

Just like roses are not made to be in the mud, a vine is not supposed to be in the muck. Grapes are not meant to grow in the mud as pumpkins do; they are made to be lifted up on a trellis. Christians are not made to live in the mud, either, because Jesus lives inside of them through the Holy Spirit. Their lives are meant to be lifted up from sin.

We have times for pruning. The Gardener takes things away so we can be more fruitful. We learn to love tomorrow's fruit more than today's leaves. He prunes us so we can be on display for His glory.

In John, chapter 15, Jesus gives us a vineyard illustration with vines growing, and He presents us with the choice of abiding or not abiding in Him. If we do abide in Him, our lives will bear fruit; if we don't, our lives are going to be worthless—we will accomplish nothing.

Jesus begins by saying that we are already clean by the word He has spoken to us. We are forgiven in Jesus Christ. Our identity in Jesus is key to understanding the part about abiding in Him. If we just jump to abiding without realizing we are clean, we are going to work to try to earn our salvation and His blessing.

Many people think incorrectly about what it is to become a Christian. They think that a relationship with Jesus is on an installment plan. But when they pray the prayer of forgiveness and ask Jesus into their hearts, at that moment they are washed clean—completely forgiven.

We begin our walk as Christians, and yes, we make mistakes. But all we do then is ask for cleansing. When we receive forgiveness, it is not like this: "Now that I have a little bit more forgiveness, I am cleaner." This thinking is incorrect. Cleanliness does not come in installments. Forgiveness and cleanliness are a one-time deal. When we receive Jesus Christ as our Savior, we are made clean—righteous. We trade our life for Jesus's life. Our sins are given to Him, and His righteousness comes to us. We are not earning cleanliness by abiding in Him. We are responding to who we are, and that changes what we do. We are clean in Christ.

*For further study: 2 Corinthians 5:21*

# CLEAN FEET

## John 13:10

If you are a believer in Jesus, you are not a sinner who does saintly things every once in a while. You are born again. You have been made new. Jesus Christ, through the Holy Spirit, lives inside of you. You are clean. You are a saint who at times sins, and when that happens, Jesus gives you a way out—confession leads to being completely clean.

As believers in Jesus Christ, our greatest desire is not to sin anymore. If you are in Christ, you have been born again, and what you really want is righteousness. I want to do things that honor God. I want to know God better. That understanding is different from saying, "I know I shouldn't do bad things, but I really want to." Where is your want? Understand that you have been made clean.

God is a holy God. He has never thought about doing anything wrong. He is completely pure. He made us in His image. We were made without sin, but we chose the wrong path; we lied, and we sinned. Now we have a holy God and sinful people. What did God do? He sent His Son Jesus Christ to die on the cross for our sins so everyone could be made clean in Him. It is not in us but in a relationship with Him that we are clean. That is how we begin our journey—this Christian walk of abiding. We do not have to earn our salvation; we do not have to get clean on our own. He has given us cleanliness in Jesus.

That is what it means to be a Christian—forgiveness of sin and Jesus living in our hearts. All we have to do is respond and say, "Lord, I know I have done things wrong. I want you to come into my heart and make me clean." When that happens, change happens in your life. Picture a bride dressed in her clean, beautiful, white gown or a military sailor dressed in the cleanliness of dress whites. In Jesus, we are dressed in white, and we are clean. We are made clean in Him. We are not trying to earn a new nature; we already have one. From that knowledge and understanding, we then step into abiding, connecting to the Source.

*Lord, thank You. In You, I have been made clean. Now I can rest in Your love.*

*For further study: 1 John 1:9*

# GOOD SOIL

## John 15:4–5

A story has been told about a school that had a fire. When the alarm went off, the kids thought it was a fire drill, so they were excited to miss class for a while. As they got out of their classrooms, they realized that smoke was coming through the hallways. They went out into the parking lot, and the teachers began to count noses. The principal then realized that some of the kids did not make it out. They did not survive the fire.

The principal and the teachers vowed to rebuild the school and set up a state-of-the-art sprinkler system so this would never happen again. As time went by, a janitor was walking around the newly remodeled school doing some inspections. He realized that even though they had a sprinkler system that could put out a fire at any moment, they had failed to connect it to the water source. They had everything in place but had no connection to the water!

I give you that illustration as we talk about abiding because you also can have everything in place but not be connected to the source—Jesus Christ—and nothing is going to work. Life is never going to satisfy you because sin can never satisfy. No accomplishment can satisfy.

Jesus extends this invitation to us: "Abide in Me, and I in you" (John 15:4 NKJV). To abide is to experience a restful residence and a desperate dependence. We rest in the Lord. We trust in God that He is the vine and we are the branches. We are just a conduit, a pipeline for His glory and for what He wants to do. It is not our choices that matter; it is His choices. We yield as the vine takes His glory to the fruit. We are just the branch that it comes through. We are desperately dependent upon Him and restfully resident in Him. He has made us clean.

We are not encouraged to bear fruit but to abide. If we abide in Christ, desperately dependent on Him, restfully residing in Him, then the fruit will take care of itself. If we focus on bearing fruit, we will not abide in Christ. We may die trying to bear fruit, and we won't get to know Jesus any better in the process. It is in abiding that we find out who we are in Him.

*For further study: Matthew 13:22*

# ABIDING VS. ACHIEVING

## John 15:5–7

Let me take the bull's-eye of abiding and put two rings around it to illustrate the concept. The first ring is the difference between abiding and achieving. We are called to abide, not to achieve. When we abide, we trust God and allow Him to do His work through us.

We live in a culture that is very achievement-driven. We drop our kids into the "achievatron" because we never want to see any potential left on the table. That is why many of us are addicted to our cell phone screens, checking our email in the midst of conversations with people we love, wanting to find out if an acquaintance has anything for us to do. Our thinking goes something like this: "Let me not spend time with my spouse in order to get with someone I barely know and see what they need." Do you see the fallacy? Do you perceive the addiction? Don't seek achievement; seek abiding.

The addiction trickles down, and we put it on our kids. We put headphones on a pregnant woman's belly, trying to teach the baby an appreciation of music. As soon as a baby can eat Cheerios, we count them in Spanish because we want the baby to learn a foreign language. By the time the baby is six, he or she gets a tutor; by eight, he or she has specialized in a sport and has a former pro athlete as a trainer. These are not bad things in themselves, by all means. But often, we focus on achievements and accomplishments instead of training children in character. We are trying to achieve great kids.

The goal is not to achieve but to abide. As I abide in Christ, my godliness will make me a better father, and then I will be able to achieve greater things with my kids. If I abide, I walk with Christ and honor God. I live restfully resident in Him, desperately dependent upon Him. That makes me a better husband, employer, or whatever it is that I do. I have been made clean. I am attached to the Vine, and He is just coming through me to bear the fruit.

C. S. Lewis said, "Put first things first and we get second things thrown in: put second things first and we lose *both* first and second things."*

Remember those two rings around the bull's-eye of abiding? The first ring is this: Are you just trying to achieve? Or are you aiming for the bull's-eye of abiding in Christ?

*For further study: Matthew 6:33*

# MY IDENTITY IN CHRIST

### John 15:3–5

Let me once again make abiding the bull's-eye and put two rings around it to illustrate the concept. The first ring around our bull's-eye is the difference between abiding and achieving. Ring two has to do with the difference between our roles and our identities. Your identity is that you are a son or daughter of God by being a believer in Christ. Then you have your roles: You can be a spouse, a father, a mother, a grandparent, an employer, or an employee. If your whole identity is wrapped around your vocation, then when you retire, you will not know what to do with yourself because your role has become your identity.

Everyone calls me Pastor Gregg, and I love it! But there will be a day when I will not be a pastor. My identity is that I am a child of God through my faith in Christ; my role is that I am the pastor of a church. Do you see the difference? If I get to where I think my identity is being the pastor of the church, I am going to miss out on my true identity in Christ. My identity in Jesus keeps the role of the pastor in the right place.

Our identity as a child of God makes us a different kind of person as we walk in our role or vocation. We mix up our role and our identity because we seek to achieve rather than to abide. We lift up our role because we don't understand our identity. Then, when our vocation comes to an end or someone else comes along and takes the baton in our vocation, we are left without a sense of identity.

In an interview with *Good Housekeeping* magazine, Oprah Winfrey once said something like this: "I discovered that I didn't feel worth anything, certainly not worthy of love unless I was accomplishing something. Suddenly I realized I never felt I could be loved for just being but only for achieving."*

In an interview with *Vanity Fair*, Madonna said, "My drive in life is from this horrible fear of being mediocre. And that is always pushing me, pushing me. Because even though I have become somebody, I still have to prove that I am somebody. My struggle has never ended and it probably never will."†

When we do not understand our identity, we will not understand our role. As children of God, Jesus calls us to abide in Him, and then we will bear fruit.

Aim for the bull's-eye, then you will achieve.

# RESTFUL RESIDENCE

John 15:6

What does abiding look like when it is done effectively? You have a big meeting this week, so you stay up late preparing your PowerPoint presentation, making everything happen. Then you go to the meeting, knowing that if you don't get that deal, you are not going to get that money. So you say, "Dear Lord, bless all my efforts." After the meeting, you are insecure and don't know what is going to happen—you did it all in your own strength.

Or you can say, "Lord, I give you this meeting. I want to trust in You for all the preparation because this is a big deal for our company. So I give it to You, Lord. I want to begin by spending time in Your Word. I want to see and understand my identity in You. I am clean and forgiven, and nothing can ever be taken away from me. Even if I lose this deal, I am dependent on You. I rest in You, Lord. I give you this meeting; please show me how to prepare for it."

Tuesday at the meeting: "Lord, I am nervous right now, but would You make this greater than my purpose and speak through me and witness to these people? It is not about my achievements, it is about growing in You through this meeting." Then allow God to speak through you and use the preparation He gave you. After the meeting, you can say, "Lord, I trust in You as my provider. I am not looking for a prince to provide because I have a King! I don't want to earn anything; I am already clean. I just want to be for Your glory."

A parent wakes up in the morning, and the whole day is about getting the children's shoes on and making sure they get to their activities on time. Or the day can be about nurturing, about growing children who love Jesus when they realize their parents love Jesus and that Jesus loves them, too. So as parents, we are able to say to our children, "These are the kind of trophies we get in this family—trophies of character, not accomplishments at all costs."

That is what experiencing restful residence and a desperate dependence in Christ looks like.

*For further study: Isaiah 30:15*

# COSTLY STONES

1 Corinthians 3:11–15

Understand that you are clean, that you belong to Him, and that you are not the Vine. You don't have to be worried about the fruit; you are the branch. The fruit will take care of itself. If you abide in Christ, fruit will come. If you understand your identity, you will walk further in your roles. If you focus on seeking achievement in your roles, you will never be on a firm foundation. You will never be the parent or the husband or the wife you should be.

Make a choice: Will you abide in Christ or not? If we do not abide in Him, we are like a state-of-the-art sprinkler system that is not connected to the water source. *Nothing* of eternal value will be achieved in your life. You may rule the world, but when you die, it will be over. You will not have an eternal legacy.

I saw an article about stars with no talent, about people who are famous for being famous. The same is true of believers in Christ who do not abide. They are spending a lot of effort on life for it to just be gone in a flash.

Today's verses remind us that the fire will test each person's work. On the judgment day, we will stand before the throne, and everything we accomplished will be tested. If we did not abide in Christ, like a puff of air it will all be gone! If I'm not abiding in Jesus, I am not passing down eternal things. I will accomplish nothing.

True achievement comes from true abiding. I am going to abide in order to achieve. I am going to rest in my identity in order to fulfill my roles so I can accomplish great things for the kingdom of God. My kids will be blessed by eternal things, not just temporary things. The eternal fruit will come through abiding; it will change how we influence the people around us. Then we will stand on judgment day and say, "Lord, here are my gold, silver, and costly stones."

If we miss the target of abiding in Christ, we will accomplish nothing. Someone else will replace us, and we will lose our sense of purpose. But if we abide in Christ and hit our bull's-eye of loving Jesus, we will achieve great things as we rest in Him and depend on Him.

# UNINTENDED CONSEQUENCES

John 15:5

The budget does not allow for new furniture, so you decide to rearrange your living room to meet the need you have for change. You push the sofa, causing the end table to move and the lamp to fall off and shatter. You think, "Wait a minute. All I did was push the sofa. How did the lamp smash on the floor?" You keep moving things and decide to move the dining room table. When you do, it moves the bed in the bedroom, and it goes cockeyed. You begin to look more closely at things and realize that in between each piece of furniture is a rope. When you pull the rope, it pulls on something else. Everything is interconnected, and you learn a new concept: *unintended consequence.*

You didn't mean to push the sofa and break the lamp—that was an unintended consequence. You didn't mean to move the bed when you moved the dining room table. It was an unintended consequence. That term might come in handy when it happens at your next family gathering. Everybody in your family is going to bring some food. You've never liked broccoli, so you're bound to walk up and say, "I don't really like broccoli." You're then going to hear Aunt Thelma say, "Well, I don't really like you" (she made the broccoli). You didn't know that when you pushed the broccoli away, there was a rope connected to your aunt's heart that pulled her to react the way she did. It was an unintended consequence.

There is an unintended consequence when we do not abide in Jesus Christ. Jesus tells us that if we do not abide in Him, we will accomplish *nothing.* Do you intend to accomplish nothing for your family, coworkers, or friends? No! We intend to accomplish great things.

To truly raise your kids in the way of the Lord, you have to abide in the Lord. Mom and Dad are great parents when they're abiding. When we don't abide in the Lord, we end up with unintended consequences. We want our kids to be involved in clubs and sports, so we don't eat dinner together as a family on a regular basis. Their involvements have become more important than sitting together around the dinner table. When we abide in Christ, we spend time with the Lord. He gives us the wisdom to say, "If we do this and lose that, then let's not do this."

Are we going to be people who live by unintended or intended consequences? It is a choice.

*For further study: John 10:10*

# ABIDE IN ME

## John 15:7

Jesus gives us the first intended consequence of being restfully resident, desperately dependent on Him: *Prayers become intimate and are answered.*

Here is part of a 1,500-year-old prayer called St. Patrick's Breastplate:

Christ with me,
Christ before me,
Christ behind me,
Christ in me,
Christ beneath me,
Christ above me,
Christ on my right,
Christ on my left,
Christ when I lie down,
Christ when I sit down,
Christ when I arise,
Christ in the heart of every man who thinks of me,
Christ in the mouth of everyone who speaks of me,
Christ in every eye that sees me,
Christ in every ear that hears me.*

Does that sound like an abiding prayer? When we say, "Lord, I want to abide in you," He refines our prayer life. It is no longer about our comfort but about His kingdom. We realize there is something higher than our comfort. Our discomfort will be to God's advantage. The more uncomfortable I am, the more I need God—the more I must trust in Him.

A second refinement of our prayer life is that it begins to move from being about needs to being about our relationship with God. When we go out to eat, I like to tell our waiter, "We're about to pray for our food. Is there anything that we can pray for you about?" Waiters usually say, "I'm good; I don't need any prayer." That is how many Christians think about their prayer lives—"All is well. I don't need God…until I need Him."

God wants to move us from need-centered to relationship-centered prayer, to where we ask for what He wants. Then He can say, "Ask whatever you wish." It is not giving a five-year-old a list and asking, "What do you want for Christmas?" It is giving a new bride a list and asking, "What more do you want from your husband?" She will tell you, "I don't want stuff—I want him!"

*Lord, I am abiding in You. I want to walk with You and get to know You deeper, better, and more intimately. You can answer my prayers however You please because I have You, and You are better than stuff.*

# TO GLORIFY GOD

## John 15:7–8

Saturday evenings I look over my sermon. I lie down on the floor in my home office with my Bible, computer, and notepad. Sometimes I have worship music on. I look over my sermon outline, and I pray. I have done that for about 30 years now, ever since college. I was reminded of my prayer 30 years ago: "Dear Lord, I'm going to speak to a bunch of people tomorrow. Don't make me look dumb. In Jesus's name, amen."

That used to be my prayer, and sometimes, to be honest, I still pray that. But this past Saturday, my prayer was this: "Lord, thank you that I get to speak to people; let me know more about You. Let me understand more about You. Let me walk in You. Let me abide in You. I am so thankful that I've been able to sit down here with a notepad and an outline, and I've found You faithful every time. I know You. You're Jesus. You're the Savior. You're faithful. You've gifted me. I just want to rest." Those types of relationship prayers are different from "God, do something that keeps me from being uncomfortable."

The first intended consequence of abiding in Christ is that our prayer life is based on a relationship with God. Our prayers become intimate, and the answers flow as we understand that it is all about Him. It's not about getting God on our program. That is not prayer. It is about us getting on God's program. That's prayer!

The second intended consequence of abiding is that *it* glorifies God. If you abide deeply, you are going to bear fruit greatly—achieve greatly. You are going to be a better mom, dad, son, daughter, husband, wife, and friend. You will be better at whatever you do for a vocation, and you will achieve greater things. If you abide deeply, you will achieve greatly. We worry, "But wait a minute. If I don't spend enough time at the office, if I don't get there early and stay there late, will I really achieve?" You might achieve an unintended consequence—if you get there early and stay there too late, you won't have a family!

Jesus says that if we abide in Him, we will glorify God and bear *much* fruit. Now you have the right order.

*For further study: John 14:13*

# AGREEING WITH GOD

## John 15:5–8

Glorifying God is a vast concept. What does it mean? There are many definitions, but let me share this one with you: We glorify God when we stand in agreement with God. We say, "What Your Word says, Lord, I believe. I'm going to live my life like that." That brings Him glory. "Everything God says about Himself, I believe." That glorifies God.

I stand in agreement with God. And when I glorify God, He teaches me His disciplines—He makes me a disciple. Jesus says, "showing yourselves to be my disciples" (John 15:8 NIV). Discipleship is a continuous process of agreeing more and more with God. You might go to a Bible study, and you might learn to agree to a greater extent with God. You hear a message, and you agree with God. Glorifying God then results in bearing fruit.

In college, I took a class in botany, the study of plants. I want you to know that I can identify an orange tree spectacularly if there are oranges hanging from the branches. I can look at an apple tree from 30 yards away, and if there are apples hanging from the branches, I can say with confidence, "That's an apple tree!"

We are great at identifying the tree correctly if we see the fruit connected to it. Dear Christian, you will be identified as a disciple of Jesus if you bear much fruit. People should be able to look at a believer in Christ and see the fruit of the Spirit: love, joy, peace, patience, kindness, goodness, gentleness, faithfulness, and self-control.

People should look at you and say, "Look, it's a Christian." But what is really confusing is when somebody says, "I'm a Christian" and there is no evidence—no fruit. They hear "Christian," but there is no fruit to show for it.

Jesus says that you will bear much fruit, and people will know that you are His disciple. You don't have to announce you are a Christian, although it is good sometimes. You can show it with the fruit of Christ's life in you. People can identify His disciples from 30 yards away and say, "I see great peace in him; I believe he is a Christian." "I see great joy in her; I believe she is a Christian." That brings God glory.

*For further study: Galatians 5:22*

# THE FATHER'S LOVE

## John 15:9–11

The last intended consequence that Jesus wants us to experience is the Father's love and joy. In John, Jesus tells us, "As the Father loved Me, I also have loved you; abide in My love" (John 15:9 NKJV).

He is *not* saying that you are going to lose your salvation if you do not abide. He is saying that when you abide in Him, you are going to understand just how deep the Father's love is for you. Jesus wants us to know this so our joy may be complete. He is such a good brother to us! Abiding achieves love and joy. We understand and experience the love of the Father and the love that Jesus gives us when we abide.

God wants to bring joy, *deep joy*, into your life. That is the intended consequence of abiding. If our earthly parents know how to give good gifts, how much more does our heavenly Father know how to give us good things. The intended consequence of abiding in Jesus is that you get to know Him in prayer and glorify Him in fruit. It's abiding deeply to achieve greatly. Then we become His disciples and experience His love and His joy so we can respond something like this:

> Christ be with me,
> Christ at the dinner table,
> Christ at the ballfield,
> Christ at school.
> Christ at the office,
> Christ in my marriage,
> Christ in my singlehood,
> Christ in my friendships,
> Christ in my church.

The joy of abiding in Jesus! Will you live intentionally or unintentionally? Will you continue to see unintended consequences and accomplish nothing because you didn't abide? Or will you abide and experience the intended consequences of resting and letting Jesus move through you? The choice is all yours.

*Dear God, I want to know You better by living restfully, trusting fully, bearing copiously, and bringing You glory. I trust You to make a disciple of me as I abide in Your Son. In His name, amen.*

*For further study: John 17:22–23*
*Additional references: Romans 8:29*

# GREATEST SACRIFICE

**John 15:12–17**

Abiding is to be restfully resident and desperately dependent upon Jesus. He is the Vine, and we are the branches. If we just abide in Christ and allow Him to flow, we will have great fruit coming through our lives. The call is not to bear fruit; the call is to abide deeply. In doing that, we will achieve greatly. I am not talking about worldly success but about bearing eternal, lasting fruit.

We have to abide in Him, trust in Him, and rest in our identity in Christ—not in the roles of husband, wife, or student. We must rest in the identity we have through a relationship with Jesus Christ, whom we received when we trusted Him for salvation. As we abide in Christ, the fruit will come in our lives. It is a natural outflow.

When we do not abide in Christ, there is an unintended consequence—we accomplish nothing. When we do abide in Christ, we allow the love and joy of the Lord into our lives.

Jesus wants us to love each other as He has loved us, with sacrificial love. Great love shows itself in great sacrifice. While we were still sinners, Jesus died and paid for our sins. He sacrificed Himself for us so we could each be called a friend of God. Because of the great sacrifice Jesus made for us, what we do in response isn't really a sacrifice. When we forego things and give them away for Christ's sake, we receive so much back from the Lord.

Jesus is letting us know that we have friendship with God through the sacrifice He made on our behalf. Our friendship with God is shown through our friendship with others in making great sacrifices for them. Sacrifice and love go hand in hand. If you are not sacrificial in your actions, in your way of thinking, in the things that you do, then you really don't have love.

Deep love is shown best in deep sacrifice. Those we love the most, we sacrifice for the most. Parents with children know this because there are days when the whole day is spent doing kid stuff. There is also great sacrifice in marriage. We sacrifice for one another, saying, "I choose to put your interest before my interest."

Jesus, "who for the joy that was set before Him endured the cross" (Heb. 12:2 KJV), put our interest first—the greatest love, the greatest sacrifice.

*For further study: Hebrews 12:2*

# SACRIFICIAL LOVE

John 15:9–13

There were a few 14-year-old girls hanging out on boogie boards on a lake in Florida. All of a sudden, an alligator bit the arm of one of the girls and dragged her underneath the water. She began to pry herself loose from the alligator with her other arm. She popped out of the water and saw that every one of her friends had left in panic—except one, her best friend Amanda, who pulled her to shore as the gator followed them. If Amanda had not chosen to stay, the alligator would have killed her friend.

In the Greek language, there are three words for *love*:

*eros* – romantic love
*phileo* – friendship, brotherly love
*agape* – God's love

John 15 uses the word *agape* for deep feeling, but it begins with a decision. Does it mean there is no emotion? No, it does not. However, we need to understand that God's love is a decision.

In marriage, we decide to stick together through thick and thin. In the midst of sacrifice, it is the decision that holds you in it. Maybe you know that because your spouse has cared for you in a tough time, and it has been his or her decision to do it. Jesus Christ says, "Greater love has no one than this: to lay down one's life for one's friends" (John 15:13 NIV).

The greatest possible love is Jesus Christ on the cross. In John 15, the resurrection is coming in a few days. Jesus is saying something like this: "I'm going to the cross, and you need to know that I love you greatly. Remember that as I give my life for you." If our friend named Jesus had not died, we would never have been able to be in a relationship with the Father.

A friend sacrifices for another friend. I want to be the kind of friend Amanda was. Sacrificial love might look different for you and me. Maybe we have to decide to go sit at a different table, not with the cool kids. Maybe we choose to stay in our marriage or workplace even though it is difficult to do so.

The gator is following us, but I decide to remain a friend who sticks closer than a brother. No love is greater than someone who lays down his life for his spouse, kids, friends, coworkers, neighbors, and Savior. I want to experience *agape* love.

*For further study: 1 John 3:16*

# A FRIEND OF GOD

John 15:14–15

Jesus Christ can meet my innermost need—love. I decide I am going to keep my life pure for Him. Leaving sinful things behind is not a sacrifice, though it may feel like it when I am letting go. But I lay them down because I want to know the greatest love there is. Jesus Christ laid down His life for me. When I realize the love of God, renouncing things is really not a sacrifice.

In John 15, Jesus is saying something like this: "I'm moving you from 'servant' to 'friend,' from 'private' to 'pal.'" We move through salvation in Jesus Christ by going from relating to Him as servants to friends.

If Jesus says "Jump!" we as servants answer, "How high?" But as friends, we say, "Yes, I'd love to because I love and care for You. My love brings about action." A servant says, "You give me the command, and then I act. I don't have to think about love, know why, or understand. I just act." A friend says, "I act because I love and understand, and I'm going to take a step forward."

Jesus, the Son of God, calls us friends. That is amazing! Why? There are only two people in the entire Old Testament whom God called friends: Abraham and Moses. Jesus gives a blanket statement to us, Jews and Gentiles (all of us): Through Jesus Christ, each one of us, every one of us, can become a friend of God.

Moses and Abraham walked in relationship with God. Everyone else just went to the synagogue and kept the Law the best they knew how. They did not have a friendship with God. Jesus said He was going to lay down His life for you and call you His friend. The reason He can call us *friend* is because He made it possible for the Holy Spirit to dwell in our hearts through salvation.

In Him, we have the power to walk in love and leave behind our sinful nature and all the things that came along with it. They have no place in our lives anymore. We get to walk in friendship with God.

God's friends: Abraham, Moses, and _____ (insert your name here)

*For further study: Isaiah 41:8*
*Additional references: Exodus 33:12*

# GOD CALLS ME FRIEND

John 15:14–16

God calls you and me friend. This happens when you come to a place in your life where you realize you don't have a relationship with God through Christ, so you ask Jesus to forgive your sins and wash you clean. The Holy Spirit, who is part of the Trinity, comes and lives in your heart. Then you get to be called a friend.

We might understand being servants, but do we really comprehend being friends? We are more comfortable with the concept of being servants of Christ than friends of Christ. Please receive this: God not only loves you, He likes you. He is and wants to be your friend.

There is no better friend than Jesus Christ. He is the best friend you could ever have. You discover it the most when you lack friends the most. Student, will you sit at home on a Friday night because everybody else is doing something that will not honor God? Will you choose to stay home and say, "Jesus, You're better." If you do that, you'll find in Him a friend. How do I know? Because I did it many times in high school and college. If you choose Jesus to be your friend, He will be the best friend you could ever have. You are not just His servant; you are also His friend. Friends are fully known and fully loved. He knows you fully and loves you fully.

Jesus doesn't owe us anything. He chose us and wants us to be His friends. I experience His great love—*agape* love—because I am His friend. Now, the greatest thing I can do is serve Him. Friendship does not do away with service; it empowers it. A friendship with God allows me to serve in a way that I can truly abide. I am not serving to earn His love or please Him to gain some kind of benefit. Jesus and I are already friends, so I am completely secure in my relationship with Him, and now I serve from it. That is abiding in Jesus.

I want to sacrifice in my friendship with my wife so I can show God's love in the way I serve her. God is not asking what you can do for Him, because that will simply accomplish nothing. God wants you to see what He can accomplish *through* you, by the power of the Holy Spirit who inhabits you, because that will accomplish lasting fruit.

*For further study: 1 Corinthians 2:16*

# DISCOVERING GOD

## John 15:15

Jesus says, "I do not call you servants anymore...I have called you friends" (John 15:15). I know I'm saved because I've trusted Jesus dying for me; I'm not earning my salvation—now I'm a friend. If I am a friend, I will know my Master's business, and He will tell me everything I need to know. "I have made known to you everything I have heard from my Father" (John 15:15). My Friend and I know God's business.

Why do we so often pray, "Lord, what is Your will? Is it a right turn or a left turn? Is it speak or remain silent? Is it do this or do that? This car or that job?" If we are supposed to know the Father's business, why are we so confused about so many things? We have missed defining that the Father's business is not what we do, it is who we are.

Who are we? We are children of God. What are we supposed to do? Abide in Jesus. That is the business of God. We often want the specifics of the doing, not the generals of abiding. We want the specifics of the mission so we can execute it on behalf of God instead of the general aspects of the task being God's. Choose general abiding over specific doing. The call is not to bear fruit but to abide. That requires faith, not sight. We trust that if we abide deeply, we will achieve greatly. The goal is not answers from God, but a relationship with God. And if you discover God, you will discover His will. Find the God of God's will, and you will find God's will.

If you know the Father's business of resting in Him, then you will know who you are—His friend! If you are a friend, you will know what to do and how to serve. If you are only about what to do, you will begin to think, "God, you owe me something. You have to tell me something, God, because I am still a private and don't have a relationship with my Sergeant, so I just want orders." Jesus then says, "I did not die on the cross to make you a private; I died on the cross to make you my pal, and I've called you friend. If you get to know Me, you will know who you are in Me, and you will know what to do."

*For further study: Luke 12:31*
*Additional references: James 2:22–23*

# FRUIT THAT LASTS

## John 15:5

You and I, standing in friendship with Jesus, will bear fruit for our families, our lives, in everything we do. People will say, "I know God is holy, but I know you—you are not. How did you two get together?" You will say, "There is no love greater than someone laying down his life for his friends. That's what Jesus did for me." From the strength of our relationship with Jesus, we are able to walk in our lives—in marriage, in singlehood, at school, in our neighborhoods, in service.

When we stand next to the Son of God because of His grace—knowing we sinned but His death paid for our sin—we are making a huge statement about Christ. Being about the Master's business is being about abiding in Jesus Christ. We are friends with God, so we live out this relationship serving Him with all we are and have.

If you don't know Christ as your Savior, you are in the sinner category. If you know Christ, you are in the saint category. Saints still sin, but we are not defined by that. We did not choose the Teacher; the Master chose us, and He asked us to abide. Jesus says something like this: "If you walk in this friendship with Me, you will have fruit that will last. Abiding will turn into fruit. Walking in friendship with Me will yield fruit that lasts. Love and friendship leave a lasting legacy."

Jesus Christ is the best friend you and I will ever have because He laid down His life for us. He did that so the Holy Spirit could live in our hearts and He could call us friends. By being His friends, we get to know Him and love Him. As we love Him, we serve Him. We abide deeply so we can achieve greatly. Don't get these two mixed up. He is not asking what you can do for Him, but what He can do through you. Then you can rest in Christ and watch Him do His work.

Then guess what happens. You are the friend that stays when the gators of sin come. You are the friend who stays when your buddy has been shot down at the office. You're the one who shines with Jesus. Your life will have a lasting legacy.

You can be a friend of God!

*For further study: John 15:16*
*Additional references: Hebrews 2:10–11*

# THERE IS MORE

———————————— 1 John 2:12 ————————————

Since you're reading this devotional, chances are you want to grow spiritually. Hopefully, nobody forced you to read this. Something inside is telling you, "There is more."

We all need to grow spiritually. Our walk with God is not linked to our natural, physical age. Becoming older doesn't mean we are more spiritually mature. Some teenagers are more spiritually mature than their parents or other adults. As we grow older, shouldn't we be growing more spiritually mature at the same time? Shouldn't we be different than when we first started, more mature after walking with the Lord for years? John is going to show us, through the symbolic representations of a child, a young man, and a father, the different stages of spiritual maturity.

Imagine a graph where the vertical values represent obedience, and the horizontal values represent faith. Hopefully, our faith is pushing our obedience up. We are not perfect, but we are moving up and to the right. When we don't a lot of faith, we take a step of obedience, and our faith follows. When we really don't want to obey, we take a step of faith and trust God. That is how we begin to walk with God. We step in obedience and walk in faith.

John starts the second chapter of his letter with these words: *little children.* In the Greek, those words mean *born ones.* In his Gospel, John talks about being born again. He is addressing those who have trusted Christ as their Savior. Our relationship with God starts with forgiveness through Jesus Christ. To obtain forgiveness, we first need humility, because we must admit that we have sinned. Why would we not want to admit that we have sinned? Basically because of pride.

We must realize that we have not done everything perfectly or lived a holy life—we have sinned. Then we humbly come to the Father, the One we have displeased, and ask for forgiveness through Jesus Christ on account of His name. It's not on account of our works or by going to church or by trying to be nicer people.

We admit we will never be able to do more good than bad. Therefore, heaven is based not on our works; it is based on Jesus's death on the cross and His grace. It is not in ourselves; it is through Jesus Christ. Our relationship with God is formed through forgiveness. We now have a relationship with the Father.

*For further study: John 3:3*
*Additional references: Ephesians 1:7*

———————————— **OCTOBER 26** ————————————

# A TREMENDOUS BATTLE

### 1 John 2:12

What is the best thing about being a little child? The only thing you need to know is that you are part of a family. You don't have to do anything but feel safe in your home. A relationship with God the Father through the Son of God, Jesus Christ, makes you part of a heavenly home.

We have seen that when a place is fatherless, problems multiply. When we trust in the forgiveness of Jesus Christ, the Father comes to our hearts, which changes everything. We as little children can each crawl up in the lap of God and say, "Yes. He's my Father."

But it might be a very big temptation to stop there. Many people got saved years ago but haven't grown spiritually since then. John does not want us to stay in this childhood stage. He wants us to grow and move toward being young men and women of God.

*Young Men and Women*

Life is a tremendous battle against pride, sin, our own base desires, the devil, and the world. Pornography and anger do not have to be part of our lives forever. But we will not gain the victory through our willpower. We are to fight for right. We as spiritual young men and women have conquered the evil one. We can be victorious through Jesus Christ. The devil bruised Jesus's heel, but Jesus crushed Satan's head.

The battle requires us to stand our ground in God's love. The devil and the world use the media to rile us up and make us fall in the way of outrage and hate. Instead of disagreeing in love with others, they want us to hate the very people Jesus sent us to love. We must stand and say, "No. We are going to fight for what is right, but we are going to fight right—in love without hate."

What gives us the ability to do this? John says, "I have written to you, young men, because…you have conquered the evil one" (1 John 2:14). How? Through the cross of Jesus Christ we are able to move from outrage, hate, and tension into the love of God. Battling sin is difficult. But here is the great news: You can actually conquer it through Christ. You don't have to live in that place. You may never be sinless, but you can sin less. You can win.

*For further study: Hebrews 5:12–13*
*Additional references: Genesis 3:15*

# ONE CONQUERING WEAPON

### 1 John 2:14

After being born again into the Father's family through Jesus Christ, we can grow into young men and women of God. As such, the Lord wants us to know that we are in a battle. Therefore, He gave us a special message. He said that we are victorious. He has revealed to us that our victory tool is the Word of God, and in it we see the future—that God has something bigger for us.

We go through the battle because we know that all things work for the good of those who love Christ. No one can snatch us from His hands. In difficult times, He can take us through the Red Sea.

Maybe you have heard these sayings: "Seven days without God's Word makes one weak" or "You'll either find a worn-out Bible or you'll find a worn-out life." Some of us are still spiritual children who think we don't have time to read the Bible. Make time. That is the most important thing you could possibly do. Maybe you don't read the Word because you don't understand it. No one understands everything. It is a difficult book. But we can go to the Father and pray, "God, I need Your help. Let me understand your Word. Let it wash over me." Then go to the New Testament and start reading. That is all you have to do to begin.

God's Word brings the victory. Our hate, our opinions, and our fights are not the weapon. The Word of God is the weapon. Reading it, studying it, obeying it, living it, resting in it, remaining in it, abiding in it—that is what makes victory happen.

All of us could do better with our Bible reading. Put the Word in your mind and in your heart, and let God do something in you. That is how you move from a little child to a young man or woman of God. How do you fight the battle? You fight the battle with His Word. This is for your encouragement.

Heaven is counting on young men and women to rely on God's Word in the battles and to stay true spiritually. Remember, we are not talking about age progression; we are talking about spiritual maturity. Young people, you have conquered the evil one!

*For further study: Hebrews 12:2*

# THE INNER CHANGE CHALLENGE

Psalm 46:10

Today, you can take the Inner Change Challenge. We are all so busy that we need to experience the spiritual discipline of having a time of solitude with God. Chances are that you are reading this because you already are in a growth process. But if you want to join this challenge, plan to be still before the Lord at some point this month (hopefully, numerous times this month).

Set aside some time to get alone with a journal, a Bible, your headphones, and some music that can get you into a thought process with the Lord. If 15 minutes of solitude is the best you can do, great! Start there. Take out your calendar and plan when you are going to spend this good time with God. Maybe 15 minutes is not enough for you. Maybe you want more. Thirty minutes? An hour? Plan it out so you can make it happen. Make this year all about building your life and taking some time for spiritual discipline.

During your quiet time, set aside your social media, your texting, and your e-mail, and turn off your notifications. You can be sure it will all be there when you come back. Be still before God, and let an inner change happen in your heart. Some of us are acquainted with the verse that says, "Be still, and know that I am God" (Ps. 46:10 NIV). But do we know what the rest of the verse says? "Be still, and know that I am God; I will be exalted among the nations."

Stillness results in mission and impact. Let's take the Inner Change Challenge and be still just for a time. That doesn't mean sitting alone for hours. We are not being called to be monks or nuns. Get away with God, spend some time letting the things in your heart settle, and you will come back as a better dad, a better mom, and a better employee or employer with a new vision or new thought, or whatever you need. If you just stay on the hamster wheel, nothing will change. To fight the battle, spend time alone with God to get into His Word. That is inner change.

# SPIRITUAL PARENTS

## 1 John 2:13–14

How can we identify a spiritual father or mother? They are believers who have made their relationship with God their main focus. They have realized that life is not about stuff, money, or power; it is about Jesus Christ. That kind of spiritual maturity is not reached with age. There can be old people who may have just started their walk with God, and there may be young folks who have already made their relationship with the Father their priority.

Another way we can spot spiritual fathers or mothers is that they no longer put themselves into the spotlight. Their main passion is to minister, teach, or care for somebody else.

Just as it is natural for parents to place their attention on their children's well-being and development, spiritual fathers and mothers try to make sure the next generation of believers can grow up in a loving environment until they are ready to minister to others and do something for God in a greater way.

We become models of humbleness and kindness, able to teach and patiently endure evil and truly listen. We give those who want to love Jesus the training and opportunities to continue with the work of God in their own particular style.

God is always reminding us how much He loves us. He tells us things like this: "I love you. I got you. I am journeying this path with you. Trust in My forgiveness. Oh, I know it is a battle, but I have conquered the enemy. You just stay here. Stay close. We are going to be victorious. You will never be sinless, but you will sin less. I will begin to use you and your story to minister to others. You will be a spiritual person walking in the maturity of Christ."

Go and minister, and be part of what God has for you. And then somewhere along the way, you will grow up and let God use you to be a blessing to others.

*Father, help us find time this month to be still before You. Let those of us who need to go beyond spiritual childhood rise up and enter the battle. For those of us who are battling sin, let us have victory and move into ministering to others. And for those who have been taking care of Your people, let us focus on nothing else but You.*

# DON'T LOVE THE WORLD

1 John 2:15

Are you familiar with this scene? Suddenly you enter a huge, tantalizing department store. Your claim is that "I am not really into things." That's good church talk, but after a few moments in the store, your real cravings begin to show. Straightaway, you see that you are really into things in a lot of ways.

In the second chapter of the Apostle John's first letter, he says to us (and let me paraphrase), "Be careful, because I want you to live for God and be part of His body and the things that last forever."

We can get mixed up when we say that we are going after God but then get pulled in by materialism and pride. We all need food to eat, a place to live, clothes to dress according to the local weather, and some means of transportation and communication. Taking care of our material needs in the right way is hard because we are all surrounded by many things to spend our money on. They can grab our hearts and lead us down a path of slavery.

I remember when I was a teenager and went to the dealership to get my first new car. It was happening! There was a powerful, fully-equipped, luxurious model, but I could not afford it, so I had to settle for a less pricey one. Nevertheless, my new car was awesome. When you sit down and smell that new car smell, it is an incredible experience. As I drove out of the parking lot of the dealership, feeling like I was the king of the world, all of a sudden, a brand new sports car went by. One look at it, and my new car just didn't feel quite as good.

But isn't that life? You get something and think it is great until you see a better car, a better house, a better whatever. Comparison makes us feel disappointed. We are all tempted with that. And sometimes we begin to chase those things instead of the Lord. The first thing John says is really clear: "Do not love the world" (1 John 2:15).

What is at stake is not losing your salvation. It is losing your intimacy with God, your time of walking with Him and seeking Him out. Love God more. Be pleased with the things you have, but love Him more.

*For further study: Mark 12:30*

# LOVE GOD MORE

While living in this world, we will need food, shelter, clothing, education, and a means of communication and transportation. Sure, it is great to have nice things, but we don't want that to steal our hearts. When we get caught up in things, our whole life switches into upkeep mode; we forget about doing what God wants. We know what we would have to do if we were going to keep this place and this lifestyle. So we have to be careful that the Lord comes first and that we love Him with all our heart.

Some of us have become expert identifiers. We know which people have spent too much and gone too far, and then we try to say what we would have done instead. "If I had that much money, I would drive...I would live...I would eat...I would wear...." Do you know what the Bible says about that? Remove the plank from your own eye before you remove the speck from somebody else's eye.

We know the "why" behind all the things we have and how we have arranged our lives. We can explain why we purchased these things and why we think our heart was right when we did so. But in other people's lives, we do not understand the "why." We only see the "what." So we become judgmental. It is a slippery slope. When we do that, unknowingly we are trying to deflect the attention from our own hearts. That should be a warning sign to us. Whenever we catch ourselves acting as expert identifiers, we should realize that an inner inspection is due.

James tells us that whoever wants to be the world's friend becomes God's enemy. Our goal is to love God more than the world. God can bless you. God can give you nice stuff. You can have a nice house and a nice car. You can have nice clothes. But don't let those things ever capture your heart and get in the way of following God's will. Later, it will be even harder to leave them; it will feel really uncomfortable leaving them behind and following God instead.

As we are going, moving, and shaking, we start doing better. Sometimes, we get paid more, have more disposable income, and can buy nicer things. All of that is awesome, but don't let it capture your heart. Don't be a friend of the world.

*For further study: James 4:4*

# THE LUST OF THE FLESH

1 John 2:16

When talking about the battle against materialism and pride, John shows us three areas where we need to keep our hearts in check: the desires of the flesh, the lust of the eyes, and the pride in possessions. The Bible doesn't state that certain things, experiences, or honors come from the world and not from the Father. Instead, it says that it is in our attitude toward these things, not the things themselves, that we have to be on guard for.

We can see how all three of these pitfalls came into play in one verse of scripture—Genesis 3:6. Tha verse tells us about the first sin. Here is what it says:

*Then the woman saw that the tree was good for food...*

What is that? Lust of the flesh.

*...and delightful to look at...*

Lust of the eyes.

*...and that it was desirable for obtaining wisdom.*

The boastful pride of life.

In the first sin, we see all three of the dangers that John addresses in 1 John 2. The first one is the lust of the flesh, which is where our old nature and our new nature are at war. The Bible says that Jesus Christ died on a cross so you could receive Him as Savior and place your faith in Him alone. When you do that, you are given a new nature in Jesus Christ. That means you have an old nature from before you trusted Christ as Savior that desires the things of sin, but you also have a new nature through the Holy Spirit that desires the things of God.

No matter what you already have, your old nature will always be craving something else. But your new nature can be satisfied in your relationship with Jesus Christ. He gives you living water so you will never thirst again. He gives you the bread of life so you will never hunger again.

The reason we don't practice sin—not that we will ever be perfect—is because we have been given a new nature that desires other things. What if the sin is covered in chocolate? It is still sin. We have been given a new nature in Jesus Christ that desires the things of God.

*For further study: Genesis 3:6*

# THE LUST OF THE EYES

2 Peter 1:4 —

Some of the things out there are great things, but they need to be lived with and appreciated through God's perspective. Sleep is a great gift of God, but laziness will wreck your life. Sex is a gift from God in the intimacy of marriage to bring a husband and wife together and express their love for one another, but pornography is destructive. God blesses us with opportunities, experiences, relationships, and even material things. But just devouring stuff and needing bigger and better things every moment is a problem that takes us far from Him.

The lust of the eyes is a big deal. The Bible tells us that one fateful day when King David should have been off at war, he saw Bathsheba bathing on the rooftop. God's will for David's life was to be at the battlefront with his army. He didn't go, so he was in the wrong place at the wrong time. What happened then? He committed adultery and then murder. What we see affects what we do. What goes into our eyes is crucial for what comes out of our lives. What are we taking in?

Jesus said that our eyes are the lamps of our body. If our eyes are good, our whole body will be full of light. But if our eyes are bad, our whole body will be full of darkness. What we put before our eyes is crucial. It affects us.

In the taking of Jericho, Achan took some of the spoils that he shouldn't have taken. When he explained what happened, he said he saw these nice things. When he saw them, he wanted them, and then seeing turned into action.

Men and women, sometimes we are going to have to close our eyes during the commercials, even if it's during a baseball game.

What we put into our minds and our eyess affects what we do. It affects us. Take advice from all of us who have made plenty of mistakes: looking at the wrong things will be detrimental. What goes in can affect the way we think. We are very visual. Look out for the lust of the eyes, because it affects what we do. When we desire to follow God, our desires are different. The Spirit motivates us to seek after God.

*For further study: 2 Samuel 11:2*
*Additional references: Joshua 7:21*

**NOVEMBER 3** —

# THE PRIDE OF LIFE

Romans 13:14

Middle-aged men and women are advised to take regular stress tests to make sure their hearts are functioning well. If we put electrodes on our spiritual chests to measure the health of our hearts as we run the race of life, when would they beep? They would beep when we are boasting in the pride of life.

The boastful pride of life is basically a desire to impress. How many of us would do what we do if nobody was there to see it? Would you iron your shirt or get dressed up if you lived on a desert island? Probably not. We do a lot of this for everybody else.

We know what we have and what we do. But sometimes, we love to sneak certain things into our conversations to bolster our insecurities. That's a sign that we are gauging our worth by comparing ourselves to others, that we are seeking to please others instead of God.

We should lift up our eyes and see the value that God has given us, for we are fearfully and wonderfully made. God has positioned us where we are and has given us abilities and gifts. Be true to yourself and be the best you can be for Jesus. Live in the new nature and clothe yourself in Christ. Let your eyes be set on the things above, not on the things of this world. If we let God do great things through us, it will make a huge difference.

God will put you in the place He needs you to be. Esther ended up in the palace, but she had a purpose there. Did God put you in a palace? Good, but don't get so used to life in the palace that you will never live anywhere else. And if you are not in the palace, don't get bitter thinking that everyone in the palace must be a bad person. You don't know what God is doing in their lives, how they got there, or why. We need to love Jesus enough so we can be anywhere and glorify God. When you restrict yourself to what is familiar and comfortable, that ends up being a problem. That will negate missional living in your life.

At the same time, if you can be in a place that you are not used to, either up or down in society, and shine for Jesus, then you are able to glorify God anywhere you go.

*For further study: Esther 4:13–14*
*Additional references: Philippians 2:5–11*

# LIVE FOR WHAT LASTS

### 1 John 2:17

The Bible says that a rich man just fades away in his pursuits. Instead of longing to be like the rich, we should want to rise up and live for the things that last. It doesn't matter if we are in the palace, in poverty, or somewhere in between; the Christian life is a call to eternal impact, not just personal pleasure. Your legacy is defined by what you are able to give back. The number-one thing for us has nothing to do with this earth. The number-one thing for us has everything to do with heaven and Jesus Christ. That is where we can find our security, our faith, and our hope.

Have you ever seen a junkyard? At one point, every one of those cars was brand new. Should you have a car? Of course. But know that you can't live for that. It will be smashed one day. Do you know that 10 years from now, you are going to laugh at yourself for what you are wearing? Live for the things that last.

God is calling us to have an interchange in our hearts of darkness for light and of lies for truth. Where are you? Take a step and let God work in your life; begin to live out God's will for your life. It is better to be in the heart of God's will than in the heart of the world's will. Go about the things of God, and live for the things that last. Then, no matter how hard it gets, you will run and not grow weary, you will walk and not faint, you will fly with wings of eagles, and you will live in God's will.

We are surrounded by stuff. Everything is available by just swiping a piece of plastic. New and better houses go up every day. May our hearts not settle into a lifestyle of ease. May we long for a city whose architect and builder is God.

*Father, may our hearts beat for You so that when You bless us, we share the blessing and give You the glory. May we be givers and live for the things that last. May we be humble and not prideful. Every one of us is rich compared to the rest of the world, even when we don't feel like it. Let us long for more of You.*

*For further study: James 1:9–10*
*Additional references: Isaiah 40:31*

# LIVING IN THE LAST HOUR

— 1 John 2:18 —

In the second chapter of his first letter, the Apostle John reveals that we are living in the last hour. According to the Bible, the end times run from the resurrection of Jesus Christ to His return. We don't know when Jesus is coming back, but we can see that we are closer to that day today than ever before.

Jesus said there are six signs that the end is getting near: false messiahs, wars, natural disasters, persecution, turning away, and good news about the gospel. According to LifeWay Research, there are almost 5,000 cults in the United States. They are growing by 180,000 people per year. False teaching looks like something good, but when we get one degree off course, we end up miles off down the road.

There has been an increase in wars from 1870 to date. And there are more earthquakes, hurricanes, and tornadoes since 1950. Today, it is more dangerous than ever to be a Christian. In countries that used to be open, people are losing their jobs just for being Christian. Open Doors reported that we are at the worst levels of persecution in modern times. Persecution is now hitting nearly every continent in the world.

In 2016, the Center for Studies on New Religions determined that in 2015, 90,000 Christians were killed worldwide for their beliefs. Nearly a third were killed at the hands of Islamic extremists. The study also found that as many as 600 million Christians were prevented from practicing their faith in 2016.

In a White House briefing, a U.S. State Department official said there are 55 full-time State Department staff members working on religious freedom. That was not happening in 1950 or any year before.

Americans with no religious affiliation grew from 8 percent in 1990 to 20 percent in 2012. A large percentage of the increase is among young people. Currently, 35 percent of Millennials do not identify with any religion. That is twice the number of the previous generation who didn't identify with any religion. And back even another generation, there were only 11 percent who did not identify with any religion. We need to reach Millennials for Christ.

On the other hand, the number of unreached or unengaged people groups went down from 3,800 in 2011 to 700 in 2015. It is the fastest drop in the history of Christianity. Even though this is awesome, it also confirms that the end is getting closer and closer. The more we know about Christ returning and what is taking place, the more our Christian character must grow.

# THE END TIMES ORDER OF EVENTS

## 1 Thessalonians 4:16–17

What is this thing about the Antichrist? To understand it, we need to see it in the context of the end times. We will see a pre-tribulation, pre-millennial view. That means that the rapture happens before the tribulation and the return of Christ happens before the Millennium.

This view is debatable, and we are not sure if it is going to happen this way. What we are sure of is that the church will be snatched away, that Jesus will come back again, and that He will reign over the earth for a thousand years.

Let's see three keys that may hint at a pre-tribulation, pre-millennial view. In the Old Testament, we have some examples of the people of God—Noah, Lot, Rahab—being removed before the wrath of God. Then, in the book of Revelation, the word *church* is not mentioned in the chapters when the tribulation takes place (Rev. 6–19). And in 1 Thessalonians, Paul uses the pronoun *we* for the rapture and *them* for the tribulation.

According to this view, here is the order of events for the end times. First to happen will be what is called the rapture. In the twinkling of an eye, all believers will disappear and meet the Lord in the air. Our clothes will be left lying on the ground while we are taken up to heaven with God. Then the tribulation will come, seven years of calamity on earth. During that time, maybe at the very middle of it, the Antichrist will show up. At the end of this seven-year period is when Jesus Christ will return (Rev. 19) riding on a white horse, a stallion. On Jesus's thigh is written, "King of Kings and Lord of Lords" (Rev. 19:16). That is the second coming of Jesus Christ.

Then Christ will establish the Millennium when He and His people, the church, will reign on earth for a thousand years. After the Millennium, our eternal future will begin with a new heaven and a new earth.

That is the pre-tribulation, pre-millennial view. You can take it or leave it or come up with one of your own. The order of the events in the end times may vary, but one thing is certain, they will occur. And it will be of the utmost importance to be prepared to be forever with our Lord.

*For further study: Revelation 19:20*
*Additional references: Revelation 20:4*

# WHO IS THE ANTICHRIST?

## Ephesians 6:12

What is John talking about in his first epistle when he mentions the word *antichrist*?

There are three things the Bible talks about when referring to the word *antichrist*. One of them is the Antichrist, who in the book of Revelation is called the beast and who is still to show up.

The second meaning of antichrist is a spirit that is against or instead of Jesus Christ. Do you sense a spirit "against Christ" in today's world? Believers are getting fired for their faith. In some places, believers can't mention Jesus's name or talk about God or the Bible. Prayer, Bibles, Christian artwork, monuments, engravings, names, and more are being removed or substituted. Biblical and moral stances are being repealed or revoked by costly legal means.

When good is opposed, we may often wonder why someone would be opposed to it. The Bible says that we are not wrestling against people but against various ranks of evil spirits. Satan, the prince of darkness, the prince of the air, is active in this world. There is a spirit "against," of opposition, that has been pushing back the things of the gospel, the things of the kingdom, and the things of Christ. A. W. Tozer said, "Satan hates your God. He hates Jesus Christ. He hates your faith. You should be aware of the devil's evil intentions."*

The third kind of antichrist mentioned in the Bible is the false teachers of the day. In John's time, they were called Gnostics. Some embody the spirit of antichrist and begin to teach false things. False teachers often look like angels of light. False teachings are everywhere, masquerading as good imitations of the truth.

We as believers in Christ are sweet, nice, peaceful, agreeable people. The downside to this is that we can be very naïve about discerning lies from truth. The purpose of false teaching is to take people away from God. In any teaching you hear, make sure it is talking about Jesus, the deity of Christ, and the truth of God's Word. A teaching should not take liberties to the right or the left but stick with the truth, even against this world's opposition.

*For further study: 2 Corinthians 11:13–15*

# QUALITIES OF THE ANTICHRIST

## Daniel 9:27

The Book of Revelation, which is also known as the Apocalypse, says that the Antichrist will be a person. He is the one called the beast. The Bible says no one, not even Jesus, knows the day that Jesus will return. So Satan always has someone ready to be the Antichrist.

In the early church, the Caesars of Rome would rise up and declare themselves gods to be worshipped, trying to take the place of God. So the early Christians thought one of them would surely be the Antichrist. In more modern times, people thought Napoleon could be the Antichrist since he was taking over Europe. People also thought Hitler could be the Antichrist since he went against the Jews and tried to take over Europe.

People through the ages have made the strangest estimates using the number of the beast mentioned by John. They claim to know who the Antichrist is. Somebody figured out it was JFK by adding the letters of his name after giving the letters of the alphabet certain values. Some people in the 1980s thought Ronald Wilson Reagan was the Antichrist because his first, middle, and last names had six letters, not to mention that he was shot and didn't die. According to these methods, the Antichrist could almost be anyone.

Nevertheless, there are four qualities the Antichrist must bear. (1) He will be eloquent and winsome. (2) He will be moral but will be a complete deceiver, ruthless to the core. People will need and admire him, and everyone will recognize his leadership. (3) As a politician, he will masterfully bring peace to the earth and establish a treaty with Israel. People will be amazed by this great feat, but afterward he will break that treaty. (4) He will set himself up in the new temple that will be built in Jerusalem and will command people to worship him. In the book of Daniel, it is called the abomination of desolation.

The Antichrist is going to be very winsome. He will look so good morally, he will be such a minister of earthly peace that he will call for worship, and the whole world will worship him. All of this will happen during the time called the tribulation.

Satan and God are not equal. At the end of the seven years of tribulation, Jesus Christ will show up, and the Antichrist will be done.

*For further study: Daniel 12:11*

# FALSE TEACHERS

1 John 2:19

Our times are filled with false teachers and false teachings. All of those who have known Jesus as Savior must know the truth in order to avoid being deceived.

John says that some will leave the faith. That means that some are in the church but not in Christ. If you are in the church but you don't know if you are in Christ, this devotional doesn't end with your trying to figure out who the Antichrist is or what will happen in the not-so-distant future. It doesn't matter what denomination you belong to, how many days or years you have been in the church, or if you are a deacon or a staff member—you need to be in Christ.

Being in the church or reading your Bible will not make a difference for your eternity. On the other hand, being in Christ will change your life and bring the Holy Spirit to dwell inside of you. This is important because at the rapture, Jesus will take His people to heaven. The reason the tribulation starts at this point is because the Holy Spirit will be taken out of the world along with the people of God He indwells. The man of lawlessness will run rampant, because there won't be anything left to hold him back anymore.

Yes, there will be an Antichrist. But there is a Christ who can save and rescue you to be forever with God. Do not miss a relationship with Jesus. He was nailed to a cross and died for you. He received the wages for your sins to wash you clean so you can not only be in the church but in Him. Pray this from your soul, from your heart, and out through your lips:

*Father, I thank You that You are here. You are great and mighty. I no longer want just to be in church. I want to come to You in Christ. I know that I have sinned and chosen wrong. Jesus, You are the Savior. It is not through my efforts. You lived perfectly and never did wrong. I place my faith in You. Your death on the cross was for me. Wash me clean. Forgive me of my sins. Be my Savior. Thank You for saving me. Thank You that the Holy Spirit now lives inside of me. Thank You that You've got me.*

*For further study: Romans 6:23*

# A RICH LIFE

John 15:18–21

Rich, real life—from the soul out—is found by abiding in Jesus Christ. Abiding is being desperately dependent and restfully resident in Him. It is not up to our efforts or willpower. The Christian life is resting in God, dependent on Him. We aren't called to bear the fruit, just to rest in the Vine. He is the Vine, we are the branches. The fruit will take care of itself. We abide deeply to achieve greatly and eternally. If we do not abide in Him, we will accomplish nothing.

God has moved us from being servants to enjoying friendship with Him. We are friends of God. We may know the Father's business—abiding. If we abide, seeking first His kingdom and righteousness, then all the things we need will be added unto us.

Throughout this devotional, we have talked about all the encouraging, wonderful news of abiding in Christ. Now, let's consider the downside of abiding. Jesus lays out struggles for us because struggles strengthen. God's strength will come through us if we can rest in Him.

In discussing the relationship of the believer with the world, John 15 uses the word *hate* seven times in 10 verses to talk about the emphasis of persecution. If you really walk with Jesus Christ, there are tremendous upsides, but there is also a downside when people in the world say, "Your walk with God makes us uncomfortable."

Jesus is light that expels darkness. He reveals our sin. Jesus says that if the world hates you, keep in mind it hated Him first. In Greek, the verb tense for the word *hate* means "to continue on hating you," or "has hated you and still hates you." Jesus then adds, "A servant is not greater than his master" (John 15:20). Light is expelling the darkness. So when those who are in darkness are around a true believer in Jesus Christ, they think, "I need to change; my life needs to be different." The common reaction is to be upset with the messenger instead of with the One who sent the message. Don't take it personally; the world is upset with our Lord Jesus, not you. They are upset with the Holy Spirit, not you.

And here's the downside of abiding: In a rich relationship with God, we are going to be met with struggles in our lives. And here is the upside: They will strengthen us.

*For further study: John 13:16*
*Additional references: Isaiah 30:15*

# THE STRUGGLE IS REAL

## John 17:14–18

In preparation for this series, I spoke to a winemaker about how he grows grapes. I asked, "Can you tell me what I need to know about grapes?" He said, "A vine has to struggle to get the best fruit."

Jesus is the Vine, we are the branches. Just as the Vine has to struggle, we are going to struggle in persecution so the Vine renders the best fruit.

Vineyards are found in places where there is great heat in the day and great coolness at night. In America, most of the wine comes from the West Coast. The weather is hot during the day, and in the evenings, it cools down. That is how the grapes rest, and that is how they struggle. If it is hot all the time or cool all the time, the fruit will ripen or die too quickly. A vine has to struggle to get the best fruit.

Jesus is saying here that He is going to struggle. He is going to be beaten, whipped, falsely accused, and nailed to the cross. And then He adds that we shouldn't think we are going to be any greater or any different. We are going to go through the same things. He calls us a servant here because friendship and servanthood go hand-in-hand. The greater the friendship I have with Christ, the more I want to serve Him.

We have to abide to please God rather than people. All of us have varying desires to please other people. Most of us can identify the person we most want to please. But if we are going to really walk with Christ, we need to let go of the need to please others. If you belong to the group that wants to please the world, the world will love you as its own. But Jesus says, "Because you are not of the world, but I have chosen you out of it, the world hates you" (John 15:19).

The world likes a pattern. It likes to label a person, classify a person, and put a person in a pigeon hole. Anyone who does not conform to the pattern will certainly meet trouble. So when you and I declare, "No, we won't conform. We're going to follow Jesus, abide in Christ, and make decisions differently," we are surely going to be met with trouble.

Abide in Christ to please God, not people.

# PERSECUTION

John 15:20–21

Everyone loves the fruit of the Spirit. It doesn't matter who you are. Everyone thinks the fruit of the Spirit is awesome! Who doesn't want it? If you were to say to any married couple, "Do you want love, joy, peace, patience, kindness, goodness, faithfulness, gentleness, and self-control?" they would say, "Yes, we do!"

What if we said to employers, "What kind of employee do you want?" They would no doubt say, "Boy, I'd like to have someone who's patient and good with clients. Someone who's faithful and shows up at work. I'd like someone who's self-controlled and disciplined and makes sure they're on task." Everybody loves the fruit of the Spirit, but they do not love the route to gain the fruit of the Spirit. That is the difference.

Everyone in any government, religion, institution, marriage, or occupation would say yes to the fruit of the Spirit. On the other hand, they would likely say no to the route to the fruit of the Spirit. The route is connecting, yielding, and surrendering to the Vine—obedience to Christ. Those outside the desire to please God do not say no to the attributes of the Spirit but to Jesus Christ and surrendering to Him. The fruit of the Spirit comes through abiding—surrendering is abiding.

Do not take it personally; expect it. This is normative Christianity. The servant is not greater than the master. It comes with the territory. If you are the president of a bank, you must expect complaints from somebody. It doesn't have anything to do with you. If you work in retail during Christmas, standing behind the cash register with customers who are upset, remember that they're not upset with you. They're upset with whoever is behind the cash register at that moment. My role is a pastor. And I must remember that whoever the pastor is will receive a compliment, an encouragement, and yes, a not-so-encouraging criticism. It's the position, not me, that brings persecution.

When we realize that our position is in Jesus Christ and that Christ is our identity, we cannot take things personally.

Let me remind you that Jesus Christ was crucified. People did not like Him. We love Him in the church. The world does not. When we look like Jesus, we are going to be met with some opposition. Expect it! Do not be surprised by it.

*For further study: 1 Peter 4:13–14*

# ENTRUST YOUR HEART

## Acts 5:41

We must acknowledge that our culture has turned toward disrespecting God. You will realize the world has changed in the past years with news such as this:

- A Wisconsin federal judge made a decision to declare the national day of prayer unconstitutional.
- The New York City Department of Education banned the display of the Nativity during Christmas, but the judge found that the display of a Jewish menorah and an Islamic star and crescent were okay to display during Hanukkah or Ramadan since those symbols were considered secular.
- In sports, Tim Tebow, a quarterback, used to kneel down and pray after his team scored a touchdown. When the opposing team sacked him, they knelt down and mockingly prayed.

That is a disrespect for God, not just for human beings. You may want to cry that you are a victim, but we have the victory in Jesus Christ! We are not victims of any government or any individual. We are reigning on high with the King of Kings and the Lord of Lords.

In John 15, Jesus Christ is going to the cross in about 24 hours. He is saying that the world will cry, "Victory! We crucified Him!" But on day three, the stone will roll away, and Jesus Christ will come out victorious! And 2,000 years later, the church is still here because we've abided in Christ.

Great believers struggle. The greatest parents are the ones who struggle because they don't just let whatever happens, happen. Great fruit comes from great struggle. Jesus will have a great struggle, but He'll have great fruit through the victory of the resurrection.

So when we go through difficult times, if anyone mocks you, your cry should not be "Come on guys, quit!" The cry should be, "I consider it an honor to be named with Jesus." God says throughout His Word that we are blessed if we are insulted because of His name. Peter, when speaking about Jesus's suffering, tells us that "when he was insulted, he did not insult in return…but entrusted himself to the one who judges justly" (1 Pet. 2:23).

So when you struggle, don't be alarmed, discouraged, or dismayed. Entrust your heart to Jesus Christ and say something like this:

Lord, I have victory and strength in You. You're the Vine. I'm just the branch. I trust You, God. I'm struggling right now. Would You help me?

## NOVEMBER 14

# VINES VS. GRASS

## Luke 6:27–28

A vine has to struggle to get the best fruit. Vines grow differently than grass. Grass is put on the topsoil and only grows down a few inches. That is how grass gets its nutrients. Vines are often grown in rocky areas on mountains and hills. Vines are forced to go 2–4 feet (0.6–1.2 meters) underneath the topsoil to get the deeper nutrients and bear sweeter fruit.

Are you a Christian who is growing like grass or one who is growing like a vine? Grass grows on topsoil. Vines go deep. Great fruit comes from great struggle.

In 2011, New York's Court of Appeals banned churches from using public schools in New York City for after-hours worship services. The U.S. Supreme Court refused to hear the appeal filed by the church. The schools were closed on Sunday mornings, but the city banned the use of schools by rent-paying churches. It looks to me like the government needs as much money as it can get. From a spiritual side, it was also a bad decision because the churches were a blessing in the neighborhoods in which they were planted. They were abiding in Christ, producing the fruit of the Spirit where they worked.

The city thought the churches were going to cry out that they were victims, but they did not. Not the ones abiding in the Vine.

Struggle strengthens. Christians entrusted that court ruling to the Lord, prayed, and filed an appeal, although it was not heard. They believed that God would do greater things through the churches than could ever be imagined. Did they think they were going to shut down the church by a court ruling? Struggle strengthens the faith and the believer. It sends them out stronger. Christians pray, walk, and trust more. They dig deeper!

The churches that were evicted grew stronger because of this trial. In the end, the services they provided while they abided in Christ were exactly the fruit of the Spirit the City of New York needed. In 2017, a new court ruling allowed New York City churches to again meet in public schools for after-hours worship services.

Walk with God in love, joy, peace, patience, kindness, goodness, faithfulness, gentleness, and self-control, and God will take care of you. Embrace the struggle for righteousness. When faced with a struggle, here's the question we must answer: Will we trim the sails, or will we sail boldly into the wind?

*For further study: Matthew 5:11–12*

# ABUNDANT LIFE

—— John 10:10 ——

I love this quote by Scottish philosopher Thomas Carlyle: "No pressure, no diamonds."* In the Christian walk, there is going to be pressure. Jesus said, "They will treat you this way because of My name" (John 15:21 NIV). So abide to endure.

In 2005, Chinese officials from the Public Security Bureau invaded a Sunday school room in a church. They found 30 kids meeting inside, and they led them into their vans. As the children got into the vans, they began singing. Upon arrival at the police station, the officers took the children into an interrogation room, and the children continued to sing to the Lord. The Chinese officers said they would be released if they would write "I do not believe in Jesus" 100 times. But instead, the children wrote, "I believe in Jesus today. I will believe in Jesus tomorrow. I will believe in Jesus forever."†

When their parents came to pick them up, they were told to renounce Christ to be able to take their children home. Some of them did, but one woman, a widow, refused to deny Jesus. The officers reminded her that they would not release her twin sons unless she denied Jesus. She said, "You will just have to keep them, because without Jesus, there would be no way for me to take care of them."‡ The irritated officers told her to take her sons and go home.

How do we sail boldly into the wind to make a difference in the world we live in?

We hide in His name. We abide to endure and to become genuine disciples of Jesus Christ—believers who follow His Word. Then we will become fearless leaders in politics and the arts, in New York City, in Washington, DC, in the oil industry, and in medicine. We will be leaders who are genuine followers and who will stand strong. If Christian leaders trim their sails, what will happen in our world? But if the fruits of the Spirit are our calling card and we are politicians, CEOs, moms, and dads who are not afraid to sail into the wind but who sing in the midst of persecution, then the world will know Christ.

Do not feel sorry for Jesus. He intentionally went to the cross. When they mocked Him as a king, He knew He was the King. The world lifts up pride and mocks prayer. It mocks purity and lifts up homosexuality. It mocks truth and embraces lies. It mocks life and loves death. Look at the things we do as a culture. Choose the abundant life that Jesus came to give us.

*For further study: John 13:3–5*

# HIS HEARTBEAT

## Colossians 3:3

We all know that a bag of potato chips is a third full and two-thirds air. Sometimes that is our faith. We can be even worse—a fourth full and three-fourths air—when any kind of struggle comes along. We get mad at God and say, "How could you do this?!" Remember that all of Jesus's friends were poor and died for their faith. It has been said, "If this is how You treat Your friends, no wonder You have so few of them!"

As we conclude this series, I give you this illustration of abiding in Christ. Gordon and Norma Yeager were in a bad car wreck. When the ambulance took them to the hospital, they were both put in the same room. There they were hooked to machines, side by side. As they held hands, Gordon passed away. Norma was still holding her husband's hand when the family saw Gordon's EKG monitor—and there was still a heartbeat. The children wondered why a heartbeat was still registering on the graph when their father wasn't breathing. A nurse told them that his wife's heartbeat was coming through his body.

Abiding is holding the hand of the Savior so the pulse of God comes through our lives for the world to see. It is not our job to keep our spiritual hearts beating. We just hold the hand of Jesus, and the heartbeat of God comes through. When that pulse comes during persecution, we show that He is worthy of it, because when we go through suffering, it shows that we are committed to Him.

You suffer in your marriage, and you stay married—you are committed to your spouse. You suffer in parenting, and you stay a good parent—you are committed to praying for your kids. You think you will not be able to go any longer, but you say, "Lord, I'm just going to keep holding your hand," and the heartbeat of God comes through. There is no greater joy than real life found in Him.

Suffering is the downside of abiding. But it is nothing when compared to the upside. You are not a victim; you are victorious in your life in Christ. Hold the hand of the Father, and you will be an abiding, full-potato-chip-bag kind of Christian.

*Thank You, Father, for the real life that is found in my friend Jesus. Amen.*

*For further study: Romans 6:11*

# GOD OF HISTORY

Difference-makers are amazed by the Lord.

Many of us are underwhelmed by the gospel. Our attitude is that we receive blessings in *expectation* rather than *gratitude*. We should have a heart that is so amazed by the Lord that we sit back and just say, "Wow! You are amazing."

I want to draw your attention to the timeline, to history. Here is what I want you to realize: 739 BC was the year of King Uzziah's death. That year was also the year of the founding of Rome. The Old Testament tells how Israel went into a decline. It declined so much that in New Testament times, the Israelites—the Pharisees, Sadducees, and everyone else—did not recognize the Messiah—Jesus—when He finally showed up. But Rome was strong, and it would crucify the Messiah. It began right here in Isaiah in 739 BC.

The whole book of Isaiah is the decline of Israel into not obeying God. You have the rise of Rome, and God knows 739 years in advance that Jesus Christ will be showing up on earth. The Jews won't recognize Him, and the Romans will be powerful enough to crucify Him. But the Romans will also have built roads throughout all the ancient world so the gospel of Jesus Christ would be able to go forward to the ends of the earth.

I want you to see history. Around 2000 BC, we have Abraham, Isaac, and Jacob. In about 1000 BC, David and Solomon rule—the high point of the nation Israel. Then Solomon disobeys the Lord, and after his death, the Israelites end up with a divided kingdom: Israel in the north and Judah in the south.

In 739 BC, Rome was starting, and Israel was declining. That is where we are at this moment, when Isaiah sees a vision. God shows up in the darkest of times, doesn't He? God loves bad odds. And Isaiah is amazed by God. What God will do is absolutely amazing. What He wants to do in you and in me is absolutely amazing as well.

Am I amazed by God? Am I overwhelmed by the gospel? Do I receive God's blessings in expectation or in gratitude?

*For further study: Galatians 4:4–5*

# AMAZED BY GOD

## Isaiah 6:1-4

Isaiah is called to be a difference-maker. He sees a vision. He says, "I saw the Lord" (Isa. 6:1). He sees Him high and lifted up, filling the Temple in heaven, with seraphim calling Him holy, holy, holy.

Holiness is a huge, huge thing, but the people of Israel thought God could fit inside the Ark of the Covenant. They traveled through the wilderness with the Ark. They could put it—and God—in a tent. Yet here, Isaiah says that God is so big that the train of His robe fills the heavenly Temple. God defies our expectations.

In his book *Miracles*, British author C. S. Lewis put it like this:

It is always shocking to meet life where we thought we were alone. "Look out!" we cry, "it's alive." And therefore this is the very point at which so many draw back—I would have done so myself if I could— and proceed no further with Christianity. An "impersonal God"—well and good. A subjective God of beauty, truth and goodness, inside our own heads—better still. A formless life-force surging through us, a vast power which we can tap—best of all. But God Himself, alive, pulling at the other end of the cord, perhaps approaching at an infinite speed, the hunter, king, husband—that is quite another matter. There comes a moment when the children who have been playing at burglars hush suddenly: was that a real footstep in the hall? There comes a moment when people who have been dabbling in religion ("Man's search for God"!) suddenly draw back. Supposing we really found Him? We never meant it to come to that! Worse still, supposing He had found us?*

God is real. He is seated upon a throne, the train of His robe filling the Temple in heaven, smoke all around Him, angelic beings flying around. God is holy, and Isaiah sees Him.

We all have this little box that we place God in. What happens when we see God for who He is, not who we want Him to be?

Difference-makers are amazed by the Lord. Seeing God changed Isaiah's life. His mission became telling people about the greatness of God. He saw God anew, and the way he saw anew changed everything else he saw.

Am I amazed by God, or have I put Him in a box? Do I see God as He really is?

*For further study: Psalm 99:1-3*

## NOVEMBER 19

# HOLY, HOLY, HOLY

───────── Isaiah 6:1–5 ─────────

How do you become a person who makes a difference in your community? You become a difference-maker by being amazed by the Lord, like Isaiah was. He saw the Lord, and his response was, "Woe is me!" (Isa. 6:5).

Many of us think we are spiritual only if we are better than somebody else. But spirituality is not measured man against man, or woman against woman. It is not measured between people. God is the standard. Spirituality is how people measure up compared to God. God is holy, holy, holy. And when we realize that, we say "Woe is me!"

God is different than we are. He is so holy, holy, holy that seraphim cover their eyes in humility. They cannot even look at Him. This is the only place the word *seraphim* is mentioned in scripture. It means *burning ones*. The seraphim, in response to the purity and holiness of God, cover their eyes. They cover their feet out of respect. They fly around God, chanting one to another, "Holy, holy, holy" (Isa. 6:3).

I just did a word search in my Bible program. I typed in the word *holy* to see every scripture that has this word in it. I received 15 pages in 12-point font. The printout does not even show the whole verse; it just shows every phrase that has the word *holy* in it. When I saw this, I was blown away. God is not just nice. God is not just good. God is holy. The scriptures do not describe Him as love, love, love or grace, grace, grace. But from His holiness comes His grace, His love, and His justice.

The seraphim cover their faces, not daring to look at God. Meanwhile, we think that all we have to be is nicer than somebody else and God will be pleased with us. But a holy God requires holiness, and that is only found through Jesus Christ. When you think about these scriptures—holy, holy, holy—it changes everything, doesn't it? God is holy. He is righteous. He is set apart.

Do I measure my spirituality by comparing myself to others or to God? Do I know what it means to be holy?

*For further study: Proverbs 18:12*

───────── **NOVEMBER 20** ─────────

# POWER TO SHAKE FOUNDATIONS

## Isaiah 6:1–5

Can you imagine being amazed with God, seeing Him as holy for the first time? It is the same as seeing color for the first time. You can see videos of people who are color-blind putting on glasses that change their perception of the world. They choke up with tears. A new vision changes everything. And here's what results: praise. The result is praise!

Praise has the power to shake the foundations. We see it in verse 4 of Isaiah 6. It says the foundations of the doorway shook at the sound of the seraphims' voices, at their praise, and the heavenly Temple filled with smoke. What an amazing thought! Praise has the power to shake foundations.

When we see God holy and lifted up, when we see Him for who He is, we begin to praise. We begin to say, "Lord, I am amazed at what You have done. You are so mighty. You are the God of history. You have a plan. You have all of this in your hand."

In our city, there was a tragic accident recently. A bus went off an overpass, and children were killed, injured, and hurt. Three of the kids on that bus were part of a ministry that partners with our church. We have supported their work. We saw the news, but we couldn't see what God was doing. One of the children who died had placed her trust in Jesus Christ as Savior just the Sunday night before the accident. I cannot speak about the spiritual life of the other children; I don't know that. But I am saying that one child, through that ministry, gave her life to Christ that Sunday night. We can give praise even in the midst of tragedy because of the work of the God of history. No, we do not wish the accident had happened. By no means! It is a tragedy, no question.

At the same time, we want to say, with Isaiah, "God, You are high and lifted up. You are holy, holy, holy. You have everything in Your hands. You have Israel. You have Rome. You are preparing the earth for the coming Messiah. Lord, we just want to give You praise. We want to give You praise because we are amazed by You."

Can I see You, Lord, even through tears? Can I praise You even when my foundations are shaken?

*For further study: Psalm 29:1–2*

# NOT, NOT, NOT

## Isaiah 6:5

Difference-makers are able to see the difference between God and humanity. Isaiah understood this. He saw God and exclaimed, "Woe is me!" (Isa. 6:5).

In our society, do we understand the difference between God and human beings? Or have we thought that we are God? We begin to play God, don't we? We think we have no boundaries, that we can do anything and go anywhere.

We are not God. We have our little categories that make us better or different than others. I am smarter. I have been to more places. I have more stuff. I have more money or less money. I have more education or less education. All of these little things separate us, but what happens when you die? As you stand before a holy God, you have none of these aspects that separate you from other people. That is a scary place when you have built your whole life on what separates you from other people and what makes you special. But suddenly you are naked—not physically, but spiritually. It is you and God. You are completely alone, and at that moment, you need Jesus.

It is Jesus who steps in front of you and a holy God. In His holiness, God sees that you are clothed in Christ. And now you realize the difference between God and humanity. You say, like Isaiah, "Woe is me....I am a man of unclean lips and live among a people of unclean lips" (Isa. 6:5).

Notice the order. Isaiah first realizes his personal uncleanliness, then he realizes the corporate or societal uncleanliness. What have we done in order to protect our own sin? We have reversed it. We say, "Look at our society, how bad everyone is!" But we ought to be saying, "Look at my own heart, how bad it is!" There may be sexual perversion out there, but there is sexual perversion in me, in my thoughts. There may be greed out there, but there is greed in me. When I see that, I say, "Lord, have mercy upon our people, because we, as a human race, are streaked and stained with sin." God is holy, holy, holy. I am not, not, not. And I need forgiveness—forgiveness in Jesus Christ.

Am I relying on what makes me different from others? Am I blaming others to take attention away from my own sins? Or am I relying on Christ's righteousness?

*For further study: Isaiah 55:6–8*

# UZZIAH AND ISAIAH

## 2 Chronicles 26:3–5

In 2 Chronicles 26, we learn about the fall of King Uzziah, who died in 739 BC, the year Isaiah had his vision. In 791 or 792 BC, Uzziah became king. He was just 16. He reigned for 52 years. He was actually a good king. When he sought the Lord, God gave him success. So we know he did right for 52 years. Throughout the book of Chronicles and the book of Kings, God gave him success.

In 2 Chronicles 26, we see that King Uzziah has a whole lot of warriors, towers, and more. Verse 15 scares us to death: King Uzziah had catapults and weapons built to shoot arrows from the towers and corners of Jerusalem. His fame spread, and God marvelously helped him.

But when King Uzziah became strong, he started saying, "Awesome is me. I've got armies, I've got gardens, I've got all sorts of stuff, and I'm famous. I am the man!" After 52 years on the throne, he declares, "I'm the man."

But God loves the humble. God loves the weak. Uzziah was neither. He became strong, he grew arrogant, and it led to his own destruction. Uzziah went into the Temple. The kings had a role. The priests had a role. The kings did not offer incense up to the Lord; that was the priestly role. But King Uzziah strolled right into the Temple and began offering incense to the Lord. Leprosy broke out on his forehead. He had to give up his throne to his son and live in a different place until he died.

Can I just warn you that even after 52 years, the devil can take you down? You start thinking you're something, but you'll be nothing by the end of the week. I'm not saying God's going to strike you with leprosy. What I am saying is that you should be humbled and grateful to God Almighty.

Difference-makers choose humility in the midst of success. We do not walk into the Temple and act like God really got something when He got us. No, we got something when we got Him. Isaiah understood that. He was humble before God.

Am I ignoring the help I received from God? Am I grateful, or am I full of pride, like Uzziah? Am I humble, like Isaiah?

*For further study: 2 Chronicles 26:15–19*

# A VAST DIFFERENCE

I am going to lead the Houston Texans Chapel service. I am excited about it but also humble. Let me tell you how keenly aware I am of the differences between me and the football players on the team. There is no thought in my mind that we are the same. When they sit down, they are much taller than I am standing up. The average weight of a lineman is 310 pounds; my weight is about as much as his leg. I am the femur. I am the leg of one of these people.

When we have chapel, they come in and sit down. There isn't any music or singing. One of the coaches, or probably the chaplain, will say, "We want to introduce Pastor Gregg. He is going to lead our chapel." And I ask myself, "What am I going to stand on so they can see me?"

We are different. Vastly, vastly different. Let me tell you, those are just differences between people. But when you look at the differences between God and people, run to Jesus.

I don't want to stand before a holy God to try to justify myself. I need Jesus to be my clothing so when God sees me, He sees His Son. God is holy; I am not. I can't be saved through good works. I can only be saved by receiving the grace of Jesus Christ, praying, "Lord, I need you and I trust you. You and I are different. I need Christ—the Son of Man and the Son of God—to be in my heart, to be the difference-maker."

Difference-makers are amazed by the Lord. Praise God that you can have a relationship with Him, that He has a plan, and that He knows more of history than you do. See God for who He is.

Am I amazed by God? Am I praising Him and walking with Him so He can make a difference in my life?

*For further study: 1 Timothy 2:5–6*

# A GRACEFUL TOUCH

Isaiah 6:1–8

In Isaiah 6, we find the call and mission of Isaiah. This event takes place the year King Uzziah died, in 739 BC, and also the year Rome was founded. In the Old Testament timeline, Abraham, Isaac, and Jacob lived around 2000 BC; David and Solomon reigned around 1000 BC; and then the kingdom was split, with Judah on the south and Israel in the north. Isaiah's time is from about 740 BC to 700 BC.

Here's some history. Rome was founded as Israel's downfall began. When Jesus Christ showed up, the Pharisees were so out of it that they didn't recognize the Messiah, and the Romans were so powerful that they crucified the Messiah. Israel was headed down, Rome was headed up. Why is that important? It is history. It is a real account. It is true, not a fairy-tale. These people really lived, and these events really happened.

Isaiah had a vision of the Lord surrounded by seraphim. This is the only mention of seraphim in the Bible. Each seraph had six wings: Two wings covered their faces to show humility; two wings covered their feet in reverence; and they used two wings to fly. One seraph called out to another, "Holy, holy, holy." The holiness of God amazed Isaiah.

Difference-makers are amazed by the Lord. They also realize the difference between God and human beings. Isaiah recognized that he was a man of unclean lips, living among people of unclean lips. You and I—we are not God. It is God who has the plan; we are the ones with the problems.

Notice that Isaiah specifically said, "I am a man of unclean lips" (Isa. 6:5). Where Isaiah acknowledged his sin, Jesus forgave. He's not afraid or intimidated by our sin. He makes us clean.

Isaiah didn't climb up to the altar to try to pull out the burning coal with his hands to become holy. The seraph brought the coal to Isaiah and touched his lips with it. Where does God come first? Right on the lips. Matthew 12:34 says that from the overflow of the heart, the mouth speaks. God wants to work deeply in Isaiah before He works clearly through him. Difference-makers receive a graceful touch.

Do I see the holiness of God and the contrast of my sin? Am I willing to confess my sin to receive God's graceful touch?

*For further study: Matthew 12:34*

# PURIFYING FIRE

Isaiah 6:1–5

In Isaiah, we have the lips of the prophet Isaiah being touched. In Acts, we have the touch of the tongues of fire on the apostles to enable them to preach the gospel of Jesus Christ. Do you see the Bible coming together? All these things are connected. What does fire represent? It represents purity.

Think about some point when you've had a splinter. Someone lit a lighter or a match and put a needle in the flame. Then that person used the needle to try to get that splinter out. The needle was purified when it was put in the flame, which burned off all the bacteria and impurities. Fire brings purity.

Many years ago, before we had kids, my wife and I spent the summer in East Asia. We stayed on a college campus and ministered to the people there. It was a great, amazing, mind-blowing time in our lives. We got really comfortable there. We'd jump in a cab and head downtown without even a translator. We could not speak the language, but we had a little book and could point to words we knew. The book told us how to say chicken, and we could point at chicken and get chicken. And our hosts told us, "Here's how you know where to eat: Always eat where you can see fire. If you can see the flames and the kebab coming out of the flames, no problem. You must make sure it is not raw, you must make sure it is burning. If you cannot see fire, don't eat it." Why? Because the fire is purifying the food, and then you can digest it and not get sick. We want to dine on the things of God, because His is a fire of purity.

The throne of God has an altar with flaming coals. Why? Because God is holy, holy, holy. God's primary attribute is holiness. It is not love, and it is not grace. God is holy, and from His holiness come His love and justice. That is why you have a holy Bible with a Holy Spirit with a holy God who sent a holy Savior, and the angels cry out, "Holy, holy, holy."

Do I see God's holiness and purity? Am I willing to submit to God so He can burn away the impurities in my life?

*For further study: Acts 2:3*

# A WILLING HEART

Difference-makers have a willing heart and a willing life. We see it in the prophet Isaiah's response to God. Can you see Isaiah raising his hand? He is forthright. He declared, "Here am I. Send me" (Isa. 6:8). I want to be used by You, God. Difference-makers do not hide from God's will. They say, "I want to do Your will, Lord. Here I am! Send me."

A single mom and a 10-year-old girl came to our church. The little girl, who was in fifth grade, wanted to start a Bible study at her school. Her mom had been coaching her and encouraging her. They went together to "See You at the Pole" where people gather around the school's flag pole to pray at the beginning of the school year. Six people assembled around the flagpole at this elementary school. And this little girl said, "I want to start a Bible study at our school. Would any of y'all like to come?" Her mother said, "We should probably check with the school." So they called the school, and the assistant principal said, "Yes, cool! Have a Bible study here. We'll give you a room to meet in."

So the girl invited these kids and began a Bible study in her school. She's making a difference. "Here I am! Send me!" No one told her, "But you're only 10." God can use kids. Her mother did not say, "Wait. You're too little. Wait until later." The administrator did not discourage her. Instead, he said, "Let's do this. I've been put here for a purpose." And so this whole thing came together.

Whether you are a student, a teacher, or an administrator, you have a huge opportunity to make a difference wherever you are. Whatever your age, even in the formative years of life, you can make a difference. Pray for the people you see as you walk down the hall. Be humble and be helpful. Be with people; love them and care for them; invite them to church. Sit and eat with people who are alone, and God will use you in great ways. The fields are ripe for the harvest, and you just need to say, "Here I am, Lord. Send me."

What are You calling me to do, God? Am I making excuses not to do it instead of simply obeying You and stepping out in faith?

*For further study: Isaiah 11:6*

# SEND ME

Isaiah 6:8

At our church, we have a ministry to help widows. We make a list of what needs to be done, and we show up. Guys bring their sons. It is a wonderful, multi-generational deal. We gather power tools and energy drinks and go to a widow's house. Then we paint, pressure wash, do yard work, and fix things.

One of our single men was getting married. He decided that for his bachelor party, he and his groomsmen would go to the men's service event and serve a widow. Absolutely amazing! The widow found out about it and gave him a button that said, "Best groom." She baked a little cake and offered apple cider to the groom and his groomsmen. And then they came together and did what she needed.

I didn't do anything like that on my wedding weekend. It never would have even occurred to me, but what a difference can be made when we step up and say, "Here I am. Send me."

All of us realize that something is broken in our world, but many of us say, "Oh yeah, send them. Somebody should go on a mission trip. They look like a good group." Somebody should share their faith, we say. You should do that. No, it can't be me. I've got all these other obligations. Somebody should volunteer at the church. It should be you, we say. If you knew my schedule, it just wouldn't work out. But at some point, "Here I am, send them" needs to become "Here I am, send me."

In the garden, after Adam and Eve ate the forbidden fruit, they hid from the Lord. God asked where they were. Did He not know? Yes, He did, but He wanted them to step forward and own up to their sin. "Here I am" is part of Isaiah's prayer. He knew exactly where he was. He knew his need for the Lord and still wanted the Lord to use him.

Will you answer the spiritual needs of this world with "Here I am, send me" or "Here I am, send them"? Difference-makers express a willing heart and a willing life. They live intentionally, listening to the Holy Spirit and humbly proclaiming and demonstrating the gospel in word and deed.

Am I saying "Send them," or will I say, with Isaiah, "Here I am, Lord, send me"?

*For further study: Colossians 3:17*

# WHEREVER GOD LEADS

### Isaiah 6:8

A few weeks ago, I spoke at the Houston Texans chapel. It was awesome. Attending chapel is a voluntary thing; the football players don't have to come. Not everybody came, but there were still about 30 guys there. They laughed at my jokes; they smiled; they did not stuff me in a locker. They had their Bibles open, and they took notes. I walked around and introduced myself, saying, "I'm Greg. I am the speaker today." And they took one look at me and said, "Yeah, you're either the speaker or the kicker, one of the two." I just don't look like a professional football player.

So I met them all, and we studied the Bible, and it was great. A couple of weeks before that, I had spoken at the Texas A&M chapel when they played in Houston. Football teams should invite me to all their bowl games—wouldn't that be great?

Before the chapel service, I was nervous. I was praying, "Lord, help me connect." Driving downtown with my son, we were sitting at the light when a metro bus went by. You know how the origination and the destination are written on the side of the bus? This one said, "Downtown and West Oaks Mall." That was the mall I grew up going to; it's at Highway 6 and Westheimer. I felt the Lord speak to my heart: "I have taken you from when you were a knucklehead at West Oaks Mall to downtown to speak at a chapel." It isn't some big, grand destination. But the Lord spoke to my heart: "There is a bus of grace. If you say, like Isaiah, 'Here I am, send me' and you get on the bus and let Me drive, I will take you places you never imagined."

I was so encouraged that the Lord had my life in His hand. He was taking me to the place He wanted me to be. Difference-makers express a willing heart and a willing life. Get on the bus and let God take you wherever He wants to take you. Say to Him, "Here I am, send me. I want to go where You want me to go."

Am I listening intently to the Lord? Can I hear His voice in the midst of the noise? Can I get on the bus and let Him drive?

*For further study: Acts 20:24*

# LORD, WHERE ARE YOU?

───────── Isaiah 40:21–25 ─────────

Isaiah 40 looks at the future. It is a prophetic statement that the Lord gave to Israel and Judah through Isaiah. The Lord is like a quarterback throwing a long pass, and the people of God, the receiver, run underneath it and catch it. The Lord warns His people that they will go through a time of exile. In Isaiah, chapters 1 through 39, the Israelites have been hearing about judgment and the coming exile. One day, after the exile, many years later, they will wonder, "God, have You left us? God, are You still here with us?"

Have you ever gone through anything so bad that you wondered where God was? Do you ever look around and see other people all happy with things going great while you are going through grief? Have you asked, "Lord, where are You?" Everyone's business is going awesome, and yours is going in the tank. "Lord, where are You?" That is where Israel and Judah will be. Through Isaiah, the Lord is throwing a pass to them so each one of them would know, "Okay, You are with me." The Lord wants them to know this: "I am there with you. Even if you do not notice, even if it does not seem like it, I am there with you."

When we take our eyes off of God, we see our circumstances very clearly. And we see our problems. Are problems really problems? Yes, and they need to be solved. We need to be problem-solvers in our lives. Problems are no fun to go through. But we can trust that God is above our circumstances.

In times of trouble, some think, "Well, Satan and God are equals. Satan is the bad part, and God is the good part." But Satan is not a rival to God. He is a created being; God is the Creator of the universe. Satan may have bruised Jesus's heel, but Jesus crushed his head. God and Satan are not equal. God is unrivaled. There is no one like Him. He is above our problems. He is higher and bigger than our circumstances or our problems, and He knows the future.

When I face trouble, am I jealous and full of self-pity? Am I defeated by my circumstances or by Satan? Or do I trust God is with me and has my future in His hands?

*For further study: Genesis 3:15*

───────── **NOVEMBER 30** ─────────

# GRASSHOPPERS

## Isaiah 40:21–22

Isaiah 40, verse 22, says that God is enthroned above the circle of the earth—meaning the horizon. In 700 BC, getting past the horizon was unheard of. They did not have supersonic planes and jets or global imaging satellites. So Isaiah says God is enthroned past the horizon, encircling the earth, and the people of the earth are like grasshoppers. Have you ever been on a plane and looked down and said, "Look at the little cars down there! Look at the little people! They look like ants!" To God we look like grasshoppers—like itty bitty grasshoppers.

But what do we do as grasshoppers? We say, "God is unrivaled," yet we rival Him in our own hearts. The question is not whether God is rivaled in the cosmos. The question is whether God is rivaled in your heart. Are you and God in rivalry? Are you and God in a win-lose contest? Are you going to push your will instead of His will? We have a God that sits encircled above the earth, and we are like grasshoppers before Him. He is greater, He is more, He is encircled.

Imagine what we look like bringing our little grasshopper rivalries with one another before Him. Imagine what we look like strutting around saying, "I'm a little bit taller grasshopper" or "You are an ordinary grasshopper, but I am a *famous* grasshopper. I am a powerful grasshopper. Look how high I can jump." We are still all grasshoppers!

Imagine what we look like, fearfully asking, "Lord, can you fix this?" as if God were as helpless as we are. Therefore, Isaiah says, "Do you not know? Have you not heard?...God is enthroned above the circle of the earth" (Isa. 40:21–22). The Lord is great. He is amazing. He is the One who is higher than all our problems. God is unrivaled. God is huge. He has no equal. He is holy. Do you not know, have you not heard, have you not seen? He is enthroned above. People are like grasshoppers before Him. He is vast, but He is also interested in us. The God of the universe is interested in us grasshoppers—in little ol' me and in little ol' you.

Do I see the greatness of my own grasshopper self, or do I see the greatness of God?

*For further study: Job 38:4–7*

# LORD OVER LEADERS

## Isaiah 40:23–24

Isaiah 40:23 says that God reduces princes to nothing and makes judges irrational, or useless. God is greater than the leaders of the earth. Is God a Republican or a Democrat? Neither. He is not a donkey or an elephant; He is the Creator. He is above the leaders of the earth.

Before he became a famous Christian author, Chuck Colson was part of President Richard Nixon's administration. Obviously, that did not go too well, and Colson was sent to prison. He came to Christ there and later had a prison ministry. He was an amazing man of God. He once told the story of being in Rome, looking at the ruins of the Roman Senate. He thought back to the Roosevelt Room, which was right across the hall from the Oval Office, where staff members would sit around a big mahogany table. Henry Kissinger would sit there with senior aides at 8:00 a.m. each day and say, "Gentlemen, we are going to make decisions today that will affect the course of human history." So as Chuck Colson looked at the Senate ruins in Rome, his mind went back to that mahogany table. He asked himself, "Where will that table be 2,000 years from now compared to the rock of Jesus 2,000 years from now?"

Leaders are like grasshoppers, and that table will be sawdust one day. God is above even the greatest leaders. Yet if we read further in the New Testament and in the book of Proverbs, we see the importance of having leaders who lead in the right direction and the problems that arise when they go in the wrong direction.

So when we have elections, we should pray. And we should vote. We want to put good men and women in charge, people who will lead our city, our state, and our country in a direction that honors the teachings of scripture. Isaiah 26:1–4 says that when we have leaders who trust in the Lord, our city, our state, and our nation will be strong and at peace. The Lord God is the eternal Rock; we are living in shifting shadows because we are not trusting Him.

Do I put my trust in fleeting things like a political party or a human leader? Or am I investing myself in a kingdom that will last?

*For further study: Job 12:13–25*
*Additional references: Isaiah 26:1–4*

# A SIGN OF GOD

A Russian cosmonaut was shot out into space. From his capsule, he made this comment: "I see no sign of God." Think about that. He is out in space, seeing the stars, and looking back at this blue marble where there is just enough oxygen, just enough carbon dioxide, and just enough gravity to not just have life but to have life that can reason and think and love and care and make a difference. But he blurts out, "I don't see God." Why? Because we see what we want to see, don't we? That is what it really comes down to, isn't it? Out in space, you can see God clearer than anything by looking at the cosmos. But this man said, "I see no sign of God."

Look at Isaiah 40:26. God says He created all the stars and called them by name. Not a single one is missing. Who can compare to God? Who could possibly be His equal?

Have you been in the countryside and seen the stars? You cannot see them well in the city because of all the light pollution. But if you get out of town, you can see a sky that is full of stars. By current estimates, there are 100 billion galaxies. We live in the Milky Way galaxy, which has at least 250 billion stars. Look up galaxies on YouTube to see the grandness and the greatness of God. Look up the Sombrero galaxy or the Pinwheel galaxy. They are gorgeous. There are billions of stars, and God says He calls each one of them by name. Because of His great power and strength, not one of them is missing. The heavens declare His glory.

Now, really smart people have determined how many stars there are in the universe. The number is 10 to the 23rd power. That is 1 with 23 zeros behind it. That is a huge number.

You cannot sail through space and say, "I see no sign of God." The sheer number of stars and their beauty testify to His existence and grandeur. Look up that cosmonaut online. Sometimes we only see what we really want to see. But God is all around us. He knows every star and calls them all forth.

Do I see the stars—and the God they reveal? What do I want to see?

*For further study: Psalm 147:4–5*

# A STAR LIT FOR ME

### Isaiah 40:26

Rich Mullins, a Christian singer, has a song called "Sometimes by Step." The chorus says, "Step by step You'll lead me, and I will follow You all of my days."

The song also includes this phrase, based on Genesis 15:5: "Sometimes I think of Abraham, how one star he saw had been lit for me." I heard that, and I realized that one of the stars Abraham saw represented me; I am a descendant of Abraham. Not that I am Jewish, but that through Jesus Christ I have been grafted in to Abraham's family. The Jewish God and the Christian God are the same God.

I was in the countryside about a week after that. I looked up and picked out a star. It was going to be my star. Every time I saw it, I said, "That's my star, Lord. You know where I am, and You know who I am." And I would think about God's greatness and power.

Another time, looking at the sky, I thought, "I want to get married." I picked out another star that was right next to my star to be my wife's star. I didn't know who she was or where she was at that time. I did not know her name. But I prayed, "Lord, bring her to me at the right time. Protect her, keep her, let her grow in You." Now I have the best wife on earth. Kelly is blessing upon blessing. We got married, and one night we were looking at the stars. I told her the story of when I picked out a star for myself, and she thought that was cool. Then I said, "I also picked out that one for you. There are our stars, together, right there." She gasped and nuzzled my neck. That's called romance! We all need more romance in marriage.

There we were, looking at the stars, snuggling together on that starry night. We picked out stars for our kids. Now each of my two kids has a star. We can look them in the eye and say, "God loves you. He knows you by name. We want you to know that you can look up wherever you are on earth and know that you are loved."

Do you rely on God's love and share it with others?

*For further study: Genesis 15:5*

# VAST AND PRECISE

## Isaiah 40:16

Think how big the sun is. You can take 109 Earths and line them up across the sun. That is how wide the Sun is. Yet our Sun is just a medium-sized star in one of 100 billion galaxies.

God is so vast that He knows every star by name. He knows all that has happened and will happen. God is so precise that He knows the number of hairs on your head and every word on your tongue before you say it. He is so vast that He could do anything in your life, but He is so precise that He will only do and take you through what will bless you in the long term. It may be painful, but His plans for you are good.

A key to spiritual growth—and I hope that is what you want in your life and why you go to church—is understanding God's transcendence, or vastness, and His intimacy, expressed in precision.

We say, "Transcendence. Oh, God is so big. He is a force. All roads lead to God. He is so distant. He wound us up like a clock and let us do our own thing. God, you handle heaven, and I will handle the office, and never shall the two meet. He is so transcendent that He is up there—somewhere."

Or we focus on intimacy so much that we imagine God is deeply involved in our problems. He gets stressed out when we cannot find a parking spot at the mall. He is so into us and all our itty-bitty problems that all we do is pray about them and never think about making a difference. We so personalize our Savior that we can no longer transfer our Savior.

Spiritual growth happens when you exclaim, "God, You are amazing. You are so vast, and I am a grasshopper. You are God Almighty, transcendent, resplendent." Spiritual growth also happens when you say, "You care about my innermost needs. I want to share with You things I have never told anyone else. I want you to work deep within me to redeem my past and transform my misery into my ministry." That tension is where spiritual growth happens.

Do I see that the vast, transcendent God of the universe cares intimately and precisely about little ol' me?

*For further study: Luke 16:6–7*
*Additional references: Psalm 139:1–6*

# LOOK UP

## Isaiah 40:26

When I was in college, I worked at a camp in Livingston, Texas. It was a summer camp. The counselors would all park their cars in the staff lot way down in the back. It wasn't really cool on your night off to pull your car right up to a cabin full of kids. I would ride my mountain bike. All of us who were off that night would go get a hamburger or whatever and come back. Then I would get on my bike and ride it from the staff parking lot back to the cabin. It was probably about a mile.

If you have ever been in the piney east Texas woods at night, it is darker than dark. The route from the lot to the cabin was just a long road lined with high pine trees and no street lights. I was on my bike in that darkness, trying to get back to the cabin, but I could not really see where I was going, so I just looked up. By looking at the trail of stars, I could see the tree line. So I rode my bike looking up at the sky. It was amazing, until that first speed bump.

This is a great picture of how we are to live life—looking up. One person put it like this: "Look at others, and you'll be distressed; look at yourself, and you'll be depressed; look up, and you'll be blessed." How do you find security in life? You do it by looking up, not around. You find security not in comparison or in what's going on but by looking up, seeing the stars, and remembering Who made them and knows them by name.

Look up! God is vast and yet He loves you and me. The God of the universe and little ol' me, in Jesus Christ, come together in relationship. That is grace! The bigger you see God, the more you will appreciate grace. And the more you appreciate grace, the more your heart will live a life for this grand God. He calls the stars, and He calls you.

Am I looking at the Lord or looking at the darkness? Is my security in the God of grace?

*For further study: Jeremiah 32:17–19*

# JESUS WALKS ON WATER

## Matthew 14:22–33

Your goal as a believer is to follow Jesus's path. It is hypocrisy when Christ is on one path and Christians are on another. Paul said, "Follow my example, as I follow the example of Christ" (1 Cor. 11:1 NIV). You are called to lead. Whether you are leading in your home, at work, in your city, or elsewhere, your leadership will be based on your followership. It is based on who you are following, and that should be Jesus Christ. He is using you and working in your heart, and it is through Him that you will lead and serve others well.

In Matthew 14 is a story about Jesus and His disciples. He had just finished feeding a crowd of 5,000 people when He led His disciples to get on a boat. Instead of joining them, He chose to go pray on the mountainside. The disciples encountered a storm while they were on the boat, and they became afraid. When Jesus saw their struggle, He walked across the water and went to them. He immediately said, "Have courage! It is I. Don't be afraid" (Matt. 14:27).

The disciples were startled. They believed Jesus was a ghost. "'Lord, if it's you,' Peter answered him, 'command me to come to you on the water'" (Matt. 14:28). I love Peter because he was the one who would jump out there. He wanted to go with Jesus. So Jesus told him to come, and as Peter climbed out of the boat, he began to walk on the water toward Jesus. The scripture says that when Peter saw the strength of the winds, he became afraid, began to sink, and cried out to Jesus, "Lord, save me!" (Matt. 14:30). Immediately, Jesus reached out His hand, caught him, and said, "You of little faith, why did you doubt?" (Matt 14:31).

Jesus immediately reached out for Peter, and He will do the same for you, even if you doubt. Jesus is your Savior. He forgave your sins and loves you more than you could ever know. You are able to walk in grace daily because of His love for you. Give Him your hand, and He will reach out to you.

*For further study: 1 Corinthians 11:1*

# GET OFF THE BOAT

## Deuteronomy 31:6

The first step we can learn from Matthew 14:22–33 is this: Step out of the boat. If you are a follower of Christ, apply step one, and get out of the boat.

What does the boat symbolize? It symbolizes the comfort zone we all have. Think about Peter. He was a fisherman. Do you think a fisherman is more comfortable in or out of the boat? If you're a good fisherman, your comfort zone is in the boat. That's how you catch the most fish. I know there's wade fishing and other types of fishing, but in the kind of fishing that Peter did, you go out onto the water with nets to get a big haul of fish. And the most comfortable choice is to stay on the boat.

The disciples' comfort zone was staying in the boat. Yet Peter climbed out, believing Jesus would help him. What is your comfort zone? Leaving it behind does not always mean you must leave your job and move to Timbuktu as a missionary. Sometimes, leaving your comfort zone looks like leaving guilt. We get so comfortable with guilt that we don't want to walk in forgiveness. We get so comfortable with unforgiveness that we don't want to walk in forgiveness. We get so comfortable with sin that we don't know what it would be like to pursue holiness. We hesitate to trust God with our money. What would it be like to become a generous person, tell someone about the gospel, or spend daily time with the Lord?

Whatever your comfort zone, Jesus is calling you! Get off the boat, go for it, and walk in courage. You were made to step out in faith and walk on water. You were made to follow Jesus in a miraculous way. You were made to courageously follow Jesus in such a way that His glory and power are evident to all. When you just sit back on the boat, you miss out on shining with Christ.

In the Old Testament, these words were said to Joshua as he took over Moses's position: "Be strong and courageous….for the Lord your God will be with you wherever you go." (Josh. 1:9–10 NIV). Pray this passage over your life today. Get off the boat. Get out of your comfort zone. Get uncomfortable. You are strong and courageous!

*For further study: Joshua 1:9*
*Additional references: Matthew 9:22*

# STAY FOCUSED

## Matthew 6:33

The second step we learn from Matthew 14:22–33 is this: Stay focused. What happened when Peter stepped out of the boat? He began to walk on the water toward Jesus, but when he saw the strength of the wind, he became afraid, began to sink, and cried out, "Lord, save me!" (Matt. 14:30).

What are you focusing on? Is your focus on Jesus?

Like Peter, we can lose our focus and begin to sink in our relationship with Christ. At first, Peter focused on Jesus. That is all he needed to do. "Seek first the kingdom of God and his righteousness, and all these things will be provided for you" (Matt. 6:33). We place Jesus first by seeking Him.

When Hurricane Harvey hit Houston, the Spirit led me to reposition every ministry of our church for disaster relief. We no longer had a music or student ministry. Every ministry was disaster relief. It was the best decision. We put our focus on what mattered, on making a difference for Christ in our city. Later, we received a proclamation from the mayor, thanking us for our efforts and contributions as a church. It was an awesome testimony of what you can do when you focus on Jesus.

In the book *Tozer for the Christian Leader*, there's a paragraph about focusing. It says:

> The important thing about a man is not where he goes when he is compelled to go, but where he goes when he is free to go where he will. A man is absent from church Sunday morning. Where is he? If he is in a hospital having his appendix removed his absence tells us nothing about him except that he is ill; but if he is out on the golf course, that tells us a lot. To go to the hospital is compulsory; to go to the golf course, voluntary. The man is free to choose and he chooses to play instead of to pray. His choice reveals what kind of man he is. Choices always do.*

I am not picking on golfers. We all make choices, and they reveal our focus. If you check out of Jesus on Monday through Friday just to make a buck, the dollar is your Lord. If you must always be right, pride is your God. If you always want more, greed is your God. Your focus determines your ability to sink or swim in what really matters.

When you are in the storm, jump out, focus, and get it done.

*For further study: Matthew 14:29–30*

# GROW IN GRACE

John 19:30

So Peter stepped out of the boat. He got his focus off of Jesus and didn't realize who had the real strength. The Creator of the wind is much stronger than the wind. Peter began to sink. Did Jesus get mad at Peter? No, He did not. Sometimes, we believe He did because He asked Peter, "Why did you doubt?" (Matt. 14:31). But that's compassion. As Peter sank, Jesus immediately grabbed him and lifted him out of the water.

Here's step three that we can learn from this passage: Grow in grace. Followers of Christ step out of the boat, stay focused, and grow in grace.

God is a gracious God. Do you find that you are harder on yourself than God is on you? You live with guilt, but God forgives you in a moment. He actually already forgave you on the cross of Jesus Christ when He said it is finished. Forgiveness has already been offered; we just have to take hold of it.

The grace of God is so real. Think of grace as an acronym that stands for this: God's Riches at Christ's Expense. It's the fact that you don't deserve it, you didn't earn it, but you asked for it, and God gave it. So if you feel like you have been sinking, let Jesus pull you out.

Receive God's grace. No one gets it right all the time. Later in the Gospels, we see that Peter denied Christ, but we see in the book of Acts that he also became the leader of the early church. Leaders who stand with great strength sometimes have to sink to let Jesus lift them up. I've preached a lot of imperfect sermons, but do you know what? I'm glad about that. That gives room for God to move. If I get it all right, then where is Jesus in the deal?

You're not going to do it all right. You're not going to say the right words to your spouse every time. You're not going to think the right thoughts every time. But you can rely on His grace, knowing that there is forgiveness.

Often, we have too high of a standard for ourselves and too low of a threshold for the grace of God. It's okay to do well, but God's grace is there for you on days you don't do so great.

*For further study: 2 Corinthians 12:9*
*Additional references: Ephesians 2:8*

# JESUS, YOUR SAVIOR

## Luke 23:34

Do you know that the gospel, the good news, is all throughout scripture? The disciples are in a boat, and they encounter a storm. Jesus comes off the mountainside to meet them. Peter walks on water toward Jesus, and then he begins to sink because he got his focus wrong.

What is the gospel, the good news of Jesus Christ? On a hill called Calvary, Jesus Christ died on a cross. Even on the cross, He muttered prayers for you and for me and those who were crucifying Him. "Father, forgive them, because they know not what they are doing." (Luke 23:34). He prayed for the soldiers who were killing Him. He came, if you will, off the cross and to the resurrection to come to you and to me as we're journeying across this sea called life. We are walking this journey of faith, and we begin to sink in our sin. And Jesus, walking on water, grabs our hand when we say, "Lord, save me! Lord, save me!"

Do you know Jesus as Lord and Savior? What this means is that you declare, "Jesus, I know I have sinned. I trust that You died on the cross. You rose from the grave, and Your hand is extended to me from heaven. I want to grab Your hand, and I want You to be my Savior."

Salvation takes two things: believing and receiving.

I believe that You are the Son of God, and I receive You to be my forgiveness and wash me clean.

If you make this declaration, my friend, you will find grace like never before. You can pray right where you are, and His hand will reach out and grab you in that moment.

*For further study: Romans 10:9–10*
*Additional references: 2 Corinthians 5:21*

# HEART OF WORSHIP

Matthew 14:33

Step four is to worship when we are wet. What does this mean? It means to worship God even when we have failed. Do you know what I have found to be a sweet moment in my times with the Lord? It is when I have been worried and anxious and chose to put on some worship music. The peace that comes over me in that moment is incredible.

I'm not a good singer, but I want to be a great worshiper. You don't have to be a good singer to be a good worshiper. Listen to music that praises His name, and sing to the Lord. There are moments when tears stream down my face because I know I have sunk and God has rescued me. I sit and worship Him for saving me. I worship Him because He is worthy. He also grabbed your hand and saved you when you were sinking.

Often, we think that worship is what we do on Sundays. We get shined up, put on our best duds, comb our hair, and brush our teeth. We're ready to worship. It's not necessarily a bad thing. But know that even in the boat, you can worship when you're wet. You can worship in the midst of failure. You can worship at 2:00 a.m. when you say, "Dear God, help me."

The passage says, "Then those in the boat worshiped him and said, 'Truly You are the Son of God!'" (Matt. 14:33). Keep focused and growing even in the hard times. And do you know what I like about this? Whose worship do you think was the deepest? I'm going to just take a guess that it was Peter's. His worship was the deepest because he was the one who had gotten out of the boat. The rest of the guys are like, "Why didn't I do that?"

Peter stepped back in the boat, rescued by the Lord, and then worshiped. And truly they realized He was the Son of God. Isn't this interesting? In the book of John, this is the fifth miracle. It seems like they would have known He was the Son of God on the first four, right? But sometimes we're a little hard-headed, aren't we?

Worship God through your failures.

*For further study: Psalm 71:8*

# THIS, TOO, SHALL PASS

Matthew 14:32

The passage in Matthew where Jesus walked on water concludes like this: "When they got into the boat, the wind ceased" (verse 32). And here is the last step we can apply from this story: This, too, shall pass.

Whatever you're going through, it, too, shall pass. Feelings pass. Things come and go. Remember what you were worried about last January on this exact date? No, you probably don't, not unless it was something major that happened in your life.

Life can be compared to moving clouds, don't you think? Some clouds come through, and they are dark. Others are wonderful, big, puffy clouds. Clouds are always moving due to the wind and the earth's rotation. I know there are days that feel as if that dark cloud will never move, but let me encourage you. This, too, shall pass. As we see in this scripture passage, the storm came to an end.

Hang on, and remind yourself often of this story. You will step out of the boat, remain focused on Jesus through the storm, allow yourself to grow in grace, worship your Savior who will never forsake you, and be encouraged with the understanding that it, too, shall pass. Your storm will end.

At Cambridge University, a lecturer named Mark Ashton Smith was kayaking off the coast of England. The kayak capsized. He clung to his boat and reached for his cell phone that he had in a Ziploc bag. He was going to call his dad. But he's off the coast of England, and his dad is training British troops in Dubai, 3,500 miles away. Why would he call his dad who is so far away? The dad ended up relaying his son's mayday to the Coast Guard in England. In 12 minutes, a helicopter hovered over the kayak. Let me tell you something: Call your Dad. Call your Father in heaven. It may feel like He's 3,500 miles away, but call Him. He will rescue you. No matter how far you feel from God, He is right there. Call out to Him and let Him do a work in your life.

We are called to be followers of Christ. Did Jesus have an awesome time every day? No, but He remained faithful to God the Father through it all, and He changed the world. You will encounter storms in life. Remain faithful to Christ and take the necessary steps to strengthen your courage in the storm.

*For further study: John 12:26*

# LOVING THE POOR

## Proverbs 31:9

What does it mean to be a follower of Jesus Christ? What does it mean to follow in His footsteps and live a life like He lived? Let's take a look at scripture and see how Jesus ministered to the poor. And let's see how we, as followers of Christ, can also minister to the poor.

How did Jesus respond to those who could not be a blessing back to Him, who did not have the resources to help Him out? We know that having more money in our wallets does not give us any more dignity before God. And it does not give us any less standing before God if we do not have a lot of money. We have all been made in God's image. That is what gives us value.

Something that was a real blessing to me was the time some women in our church befriended a woman who was homeless. The woman stayed underneath the bridges on I-10. The women in the church began to minister to her and care for her. And the homeless woman became part of the church and sat with the women. I got to know her. When I drove underneath the bridge, I would roll down my window and say to her, "How are you doing?"

She would yell back, "Pastor! How are you?" And all the homeless people would say, "He's your pastor? What church do you go to?"

We became friends, and it was just a wonderful thing. I pulled up one day by the bridge, and she had a gentleman with her. I told them I had a little time on my hands and asked if I could take both of them to lunch. They loved the idea, jumped in my car, and I drove to McDonald's. Now, I am not saying you should allow any stranger or homeless person in your car, but we had built a relationship for some time. Quite frankly, it was a lunch different from the usual ones I have had. I sat across from this couple and got to know more about them and their lives. We talked, and it was a blessing to my life. Although they are not the usual people I hang out with or eat lunch with, I sat there realizing what a true blessing they both were. A couple who could not buy me anything blessed my life.

Have you ever experienced a blessing from people who could not give you anything in return? We are called to love everyone, including the poor.

*For further study: 1 John 3:17*

# INVITE THE POOR

## Luke 14:1–13

Jesus wants us to be His followers as we minister to the poor. In the book of Luke, chapter 14, we read about Jesus going to eat at the house of one of the leading Pharisees, the religious leaders. But this Pharisee was part of the Sanhedrin—the ruling council. Everyone was watching Jesus closely. Then Jesus saw a man whose joints were swollen. He asked if it was okay to heal someone on the Sabbath. Since no one answered, He healed the man. Jesus then asked if a child were to go down a well, wouldn't everyone rush to pull the child out? Everyone was stumped and did not say a word.

Jesus then told a parable. He noticed how the Pharisees chose the best places for themselves. Let me paraphrase what He told them: "When you are invited to a feast, don't sit in the best place. Someone more important may have been invited. Then the one who invited you will come and say, 'Give your place to this other guest!' You will be embarrassed and will have to sit in the worst place."

Jesus knew everyone was looking for the most important seat. In that specific culture, the most important seat was the center seat on the couch. In our culture, the most important seat is at the recliner with the remote control, right? Yet even today, if you have people and need to pull up chairs to have everyone fit in your living room, usually the host has to say, "Somebody sit on the couch," because everyone wants to sit on the fringes. The seat that the Pharisees desired and fought for is one that, in our culture, no one wants.

Jesus began to teach on humility. He told the people to take the worst seat, not the best. He continued by saying something like this: "When you give a dinner, don't invite your friends and family and relatives. If you do, they will invite you in return, and you will be paid back. When you give a feast, invite the poor, the paralyzed, the lame, and the blind."

Does this mean you can't have a Christmas dinner anymore without inviting your loved ones? Absolutely not. That is not what Jesus is saying. He is telling us to not be part of something only to try to get something back.

Jesus wants to break something in you. He wants to break the "What's in it for me?" mindset. All of us have that mentality. If I scratch your back, you will scratch mine. If I do this, you will do that. We unknowingly seek reciprocal relationships, and Jesus wants to break that mindset. President John F. Kennedy once said, "Ask not what your country can do for you. Ask what you can for your country."* Jesus wants us to give and bless others without expecting anything in return.

# SPIRITUALIZED SELFISHNESS

## Matthew 6:20

Marriage is not about what your spouse can do for you but about what you can do for your spouse. As a church member, you see ways that you can bless and serve others. In your workplace, walk the extra mile without expecting anything in return. Most importantly, in your relationship with God, read His Word to know how you can live your life purposefully and in a way that is pleasing to Him. God blesses you. He gives you so much in this life on earth.

But spiritualized selfishness is this: "I'm giving so I can get. I'm going to give to the Lord so God will bless me. I'm going to give in this way so I can get something that way." Spiritual selfishness can lead to manipulation in our relationships. This mentality applies to any relationship.

Living in such a way is called one-sided love. Do you know how a marriage is built? It is built when in your heart you have one-sided love. Marriage isn't built when each partner gives only 50 percent. That's a sorry marriage right there. A marriage is built on giving your partner 100 percent. The man and the woman each give 100 percent.

There are going to be moments that you don't feel the love coming back to you in marriage. Men and women may both experience moments when they don't feel respected. The same is true with parenting. Parenting is a blessing, but it is also a one-sided love sometimes. Have you ever walked up to your kid and said, "Hey, I'm running a little short. Could you give me $20 bucks to go out to eat with friends?" No! You are the ATM in the relationship. I know parenting is great and a blessing, but it can be a bit frustrating as well. Your children will never give you as much as you give them. That is how parenting works, yet it is still a blessing.

Jesus wants to break this mindset of one-sided love and break the spiritual selfishness of believing that giving has to be reciprocal. During Hurricane Harvey, many people helped those people whose houses flooded. It was messy, hard work. No one ever said, "Hey, we are so glad to be here to clean out your house. But since our house didn't have any water damage, if you wouldn't mind, we expect you to come to our house, too, because we're going to do some clean-up and renovations and things like that." You'd never say that, right? That would be a terrible thing to say.

Jesus wants you to love without expecting anything in return. Do you think you can begin to practice giving of yourself without expecting anything back? Allow Jesus to break selfish expectations. Let Him transform your mind and your heart.

# THE POOR

Leviticus 23:22

Jesus said, "When you host a banquet, invite those who are poor, maimed, lame, or blind" (Luke 14:13). What did He mean by that? In our society, people with disabilities can actually do great things because they're amazing people. But in that agrarian society, if you were blind or if you could not walk right, you were not able to work in the fields. The disabled were often relegated to begging.

Jesus was asking his listeners to go and invite the people who could not reciprocate. We can also do that in this time and age. One-sided love is an exercise in humility.

We want to minister to the poor as well, those who are in need financially. There are three groupings I can share with you. The first group is those who have generational poverty. That's defined as poverty over two generations. They are people who, in their poverty, do not know how to live any other way.

The second group are those in situational poverty. That's when something happens that causes a person to be poor. It may be an illness, the loss of a job, or a divorce. Sometimes it is bad choices such as alcohol or drug abuse. No question about it, you can end up in poverty by making really bad choices. But some people are in situational poverty that was not due to bad choices; something just occurred. A catastrophic event happened, and they could not escape. They were living on the edge of poverty, and the event sent them over the edge. We should not come along and tell them, "Well, you need to get back on your feet." Instead, we should say, "How can I help?"

The third group is the working poor. Did you know that there are people who are employed and still struggling? They are working two to three jobs. For example, at a restaurant, you might ask the waitress, "How can I pray for you?" And she says, "You know, I have four kids at home, and this is my second job." Ding! Ding! Ding! Whenever you hear of people going through those sorts of struggles, they are probably the working poor.

Throughout the Old and New Testaments, you will find God commanding us to reach out to the poor.

*For further study: Luke 14:13*

# HONOR GOD

Proverbs 14:31

There is a proverb that says, "The one who oppresses the poor person insults his Maker, but one who is kind to the needy honors Him" (Prov. 14:31). Proverbs is a great book about monetary issues and the poor in particular. When we help the poor, we are actually honoring God. If you want to insult God, then look down on someone who cannot give you anything back. We honor God by honoring those in need.

There are some of the things I would like to share with you as you begin to open your life to honoring those in need. First, be wise and safe. There is no need to put yourself in dangerous situations such as visiting the homeless late at night in a dark alley all by yourself. I would never suggest that you do that. Use wisdom and discernment when you want to help the poor.

Second, acknowledge that as much as you can give to a person in need, there are some people who will not want to change. They will not want to change their situation and may even reject the gospel when you share it with them.

Third, there are some people who will take advantage of you. That is why it is so important to ask the Spirit for wisdom. Loving the poor does not require you to walk around handing out all your money to them. Boundaries are necessary and an appropriate thing in ministering to the poor.

And fourth, understand that some may want the help but will take a very long time to make changes. That may be due to addictions or habits. They may need to enter some sort of rehab or get training to get out of the situation they are in. Giving them a bottle of water or a meal will not be enough for them. They will need guidance to truly get out of their situation.

I encourage you to ask God how you can begin to love the poor. Pray this prayer today:

*Father God, I want to honor You. I want to be Your hands and feet here on earth and I want to love people. I want to honor those in need. Guide me with Your Spirit so I know where to begin. I want to see people with Your eyes, Lord, so I can help them. Fill me with wisdom and compassion. In Your name I pray, amen.*

# SPIRITUALLY POOR

---

## Matthew 5:3

---

You may have a desire to love the poor, but you may not know where to begin. Safety and wisdom is the first action point, but I will share with you some other ideas.

Volunteering is a great way to begin to help the poor. Volunteer some of your time to serving the community. There are many organizations that reach out to the poor and could use your help. A woman at our church knits little booties by the dozen. She donates them to a pregnancy center, and pregnant women can take them for free when they get a sonogram. Volunteering is about using your giftedness and expertise to help others. It is about sharing your resources and knowledge with those who need it. Sometimes it is simply about sharing your time to bless somebody. We are all busy, but we can make time to go feed the hungry, love orphans, tutor children who cannot afford tutors, or hang out with youth at the YMCA. There is so much you can do for your community.

I encourage you to not only volunteer but to take people to a faith center, an organization or location that ministers in some form but is faith-based. Faith centers not only provide food for the hungry and clothes and shelter for the homeless, but they also share Jesus Christ with them. People who go there will have the opportunity to know Jesus as their Savior. They will have the opportunity to listen to the good news and choose to trust in Christ.

The goal of the Bible is not to make earth a better place to go to hell from. The goal of the Bible is that people can trust Jesus Christ as their Savior for all eternity. Ministering to the poor is an on-ramp to sharing the gospel because every human being is spiritually poor. Until we trust Jesus Christ as our Savior, we are spiritually poor. The Apostle Paul wrote that Jesus became poor on our behalf. He who was rich became poor so that we who are poor spiritually can become rich spiritually. When you trust Jesus as your Savior, when you receive Christ, you have a relationship with God, and that gives you spiritual wealth. It might not change your wallet, but it changes your eternity.

*For further study: 2 Corinthians 8:9*

---

**DECEMBER 19**

# ETERNALLY RICH

---
Luke 14:14
---

We share Jesus because there is spiritual poverty. We give a cup of cold water in Jesus's name. Sure, we want to help people materially, but that is just an on-ramp to helping them eternally. We want the Lord to come into their life so they place their faith in Jesus. It's a powerful thing!

If you are spiritually poor, I want you to know that Jesus Christ loves you, and you can place your faith in Christ alone. He can save your life and your heart. You can trust Jesus. If you have come to Christ and are living by experiencing His wealth, step out of your comfort zone and begin to make a difference. Use your giftedness, share your resources, give of your time, and bless others with the good news. Think about how God can use you to help others.

Jesus would say it this way: "They cannot pay you back. But God will bless you and reward you when His people rise from death." You will be the blessed one. In a world that is always thinking of the best investments and how to make more in stocks and what-not, Jesus is saying to give to those who cannot give you anything in return, because God will bless you. Your repayment will come with eternal rewards. Isn't that great?

Nobody has to know the good you do. There is no need to brag. God knows and sees you. He is delighted in how you love others.

It is better to give than it is to receive. Stop looking for the payback, and care for those in need. Break the mindset of "What's in it for me?" Serve and love the elderly, the poor, the hungry. That is a blessing to the Lord. That is being God's hands and feet here on earth. Your repayment will come in eternal benefits.

The book of Proverb says that being kind to the poor is a loan to the Lord. You are giving to the Lord. Here is the truth about being a Christian: The rewards are greater and longer for the follower of Jesus Christ. It's not just something today; it's something for all of eternity.

Pray this prayer as you begin to live a life loving the poor:

> *Father, I thank You that You came to me in my spiritually tattered rags. I pray that I never become too good to love others. You wrapped us in forgiveness, love, and grace, and Father, in that same way, may I have compassion for those in poverty. You have a different path for different lives, but Lord, let me be in tune with how I can bless others. I trust You. Use me. Do Your work in me. In Your name, amen.*

# LONELINESS

Ecclesiastes 4:9–10

One of the things you will see about Jesus it that He was big-time about relationships. And He was a great friend. Let's learn more about the friendship of Jesus and the friendships we have with other people.

Did you know that you and I need friends very deeply? We were wired for friendship. We were wired to be connected to one another. That is why throughout scripture, Jesus talks about friendships, His love for the disciples, and His love for the crowds and people. Our wiring for friendship is a God-given thing.

However, the sad truth is that humanity and society are struggling with loneliness more than ever. Great Britain just appointed a minister of loneliness who handles the loneliness that's going on in Great Britain. An article called "Why Are Millennials So Lonely?" stated that loneliness is worse for your health than smoking 15 cigarettes per day.

A survey found that the number of Americans with no close friends has tripled since 1985. And it appears the decline is most prevalent among Millennials. Loneliness is a huge problem. Why are so many struggling with it? There are basically two reasons.

One, loneliness is contagious. You get around someone who is lonely, and it makes you lonely. Misery loves company.

Two, all of our devices that supposedly keep us so connected actually often disconnect us. Tablets, iPads, and smartphones keep us isolated. The funny thing is that when we do feel isolated, what do we do? We go right back to our devices. Isn't that interesting? It is a vicious cycle that goes around and around.

We're in a vicious trap of doing what makes us lonely over and over. Billy Graham, the famous evangelist, once said, "Loneliness is no respecter of persons. It invades the palace as well as the hut….The kind of society we live in can contribute to loneliness. Mobility and constant change tend to make some individuals feel rootless and disconnected."*

What does it mean to be a friend? What does the friendship of Jesus mean? You can be a good friend to others and meet people whose friendships will bless your life. We need God's help. He can provide great friendships in our lives.

# FRIENDS OF SINNERS

Matthew 11:19

Jesus was a friend of sinners and saints. Sometimes as believers, we believe that we are only supposed to befriend the saints, right? We form our little cliques and believe we should not hang out with any of those people we view as sinners. But if we think about it, we were and are all sinners. Jesus is the greatest example in our lives. He was a friend of sinners.

In the Gospels, including the book of Matthew, we read that Jesus was a friend of tax collectors, sinners, drunkards, and gluttons, so much so that people told Him, "You must be just like them." You see, Jesus Christ did not hang out with sinners to justify and participate in sin. He stepped into their lives to make a difference. He wanted to shine in such a way that they would be able to see something better, something greater. He wanted to show them that there was more than the lifestyle they were living.

We should hang out with people who do not know Christ. But we do not hang out to justify our participation in sin. We hang out so we can show them something better that will make a difference in their lives. We befriend people to be able to connect with them and show them the love of Christ. We have to show care, but we also have to be careful.

In Proverbs it says, "Don't make friends with an angry person,…or you will learn his ways and entangle yourself in a snare" (Prov. 22:24–25). Do you ever get around somebody and start complaining, kind of like they complain? You start getting mad like they get mad. Do you ever get around someone and begin to gossip a little bit more than what you would really want to? They just kind of pull that out of you. We can actually get pulled down. If I were to stand up on a chair, it would be easier for you to pull me down than it would be for me to lift you up. We have to be careful.

We can get influenced and all of a sudden become materialistic, angry, or gossipy. Then the sea has begun to come into the boat. You'll either get pulled into the same stuff they're doing, or they'll get in trouble for it, and you'll get thrown into the same lot that they are in. Bad company corrupts good morals. George Washington said, "Associate yourself with men of quality if you esteem your own reputation, for 'tis better to be alone than in bad company."*

Yes, be friends with sinners. Why? Because we are all sinners and struggle with sin. Do not become a holy huddle as a church. But be careful. Step out in confidence and make a difference in those who need Christ. Begin to pray for people you know need Jesus, and allow the Spirit to guide you in befriending and ministering to them.

# FRIENDS OF SAINTS

John 15:14–15

Jesus was a friend of sinners, but He was also a friend of saints. In the book of John, He called his disciples his friends. They had obeyed Him, and He taught them about God.

Obedience brings greater friendship with God. If you obey Jesus, you are going to walk with Him in intimacy and friendship. You and I have the ability to be friends of Jesus. You get to be His friend, and your obedience—walking with Him in the ways He commands—actually deepens your friendship with God.

I have been walking with the Lord about 31 years now, and I want you to know that Jesus is my best friend. I have grown in that friendship and that relationship with Him in good times, in bad times, in up times, and in down times. His friendship means more to me than any other friendship on earth. He's my friend. But the intimacy of my friendship with Him grows when I am obedient to what He says.

The proximity with God, if you're a believer in Christ, never changes. The Holy Spirit lives in your heart. God is not way over there and you way over here. Nevertheless, the intimacy in your relationship with God can change. That intimacy is based on being a follower of Christ instead of running away from Christ.

Jesus was a friend of saints; Jesus was a friend of sinners. For both, we sacrifice, share, befriend, connect, and love. Which one do you need more in your life? Are you surrounded by friends who do not walk with God? Or do you have so many friends from church that you do not have one lost friend you can reach for Christ? Have you gotten so cloistered that it is just you?

I came to Christ when I was 16 years old. I didn't know anyone who went to church. Everybody I knew was partying. I had my fill of sinners. Then I started to discover some saints. In college, I had the perfect balance. However, when I went to seminary, I went way over in the saint category. Since I am in ministry, I have many saint friends, and I love them all, but I have to work on having friends outside the church because my vocation has sheltered me. I'm praying for a sinner friend struggling with a certain sin. I want to minister to that friend.

Are you in a place where you need some more saints, or are you in a place where you need some more sinners? Where are you? Because we've got to be with both sinners and saints to be able to walk as Christ did.

# THE CLOSE AND THE CROWDS

## Matthew 9:36

Jesus was a friend of the close and the crowds. The close were those who were around Him a lot, but He also made friends with the crowds. His disciples journeyed with Him and were often around Him. Through the scriptures, we see Jesus taking others up on a mountainside and in the garden. He wanted His close friends to go away with Him for a bit.

You and I need close friends. However, what we do not need is a ton of close friends. A Russian proverb says, "An old friend is better than two new ones."* It does not matter how many Facebook friends you have. Not all of them are real friends; many are acquaintances. Keep a few friends close, just like Jesus did. Invest in those close friendships so they grow and flourish.

In Matthew, we read that Jesus felt compassion for the crowds. We want to be able to have crowds of friends. They could be acquaintances at the office, friends on the football team, or friends in big settings or wherever you're cruising along. We need big friendships.

What Jesus models is really the balance between being an introvert and being an extrovert. Extroverts tend to like crowds, and introverts tend to like just a few close friends. It's the picture of my marriage. I'm an extrovert and love to be with people. My wife likes it a little bit smaller. She's an introvert. When we go to a party or outing, she will ask, "How do you walk around and talk to everybody at the party? How do you do that?" This is what I tell her: "I'm shallow, okay? That's how."

Jesus was the perfect blend of extrovert and introvert. We see Him go away in solitude on the mountain. We see Him teach a small group of disciples. But we see Him on the hillside having compassion for the crowds. Jesus was that perfect connection, and that's what the church has to be. Christians should be a connection of the close and the crowds. We want to reach the world, but at the same time, we want to have groups and Bible studies where we connect with one another on a personal basis. It's the crowd and the close.

# A FRIEND OF GOD

James 2:23

You can be a friend of God through Christ. You think it's cool to be friends with somebody that's rich? You get to be a friend of God. You think it's cool to be friends with somebody who's popular? You get to be a friend of God. You think it's cool to be a friend of some athlete? So what? You get to be a friend of God through Christ. That's amazing.

Job said that when he was in the prime of his life, the all-powerful God was his closest friend. The scriptures also say that Moses spoke to the Lord just as someone speaks with a friend. In James, it says how Abraham became God's friend. Simply embrace the thought that you get to be God's friend. How does this happen? It's through Jesus, His Son, who came to earth. And if you will place your faith in His death to be the payment for your sins and receive Him in your heart as your Savior, you will be connected to the Father.

You place your faith and trust in Jesus and allow the Holy Spirit to live inside of you. And now you have a Friend who is closer than a brother because He is in your heart. You know what is amazing about that? He is all you need. You can step out with the sinners because you do not need what they have. You don't have to worry about being rich enough or pretty enough or this or that. You can stand in confidence knowing that Jesus is your place of security.

You can step out with the saints, the crowds, the close ones, the introverts, and the extroverts and know that your heart and foundation are still in the Savior. God is the Friend who speaks to you in the silence. He speaks to your soul. Jesus loves you.

Billy Graham said this: "There are thousands of lonely people in the city and in the country who carry heavy and difficult burdens of grief, anxiety, pain, and disappointment; but the loneliest soul of all is the man whose life is steeped in sin."* Sin will put you in solitude. Jesus comes to forgive your sins so you don't have to be lonely. Jesus wants to be your closest Friend. From that closeness, you can then take a step out in any direction because you have firm security on the Rock of Ages, Jesus Christ.

*For further study: Job 29:4*

# PRAY FOR FRIENDS

Proverbs 27:17

If you don't have friends, let me encourage you to pray to Jesus and ask God to give you good friends. At one of our campuses, a pastor's mom said something like this: "When it comes to friends, you can either have 100 pennies or you can have four quarters. And it's far better, to have four quarters than to have 100 pennies." Many of us just need four quarters. We just need a few friends in our lives.

Pray that God would give you a friend. Jesus, who is your silver dollar, loves to provide quarters. He will provide pennies, too. But let the silver dollar of Jesus be your number-one friend. He changes everything. There's a wonderful old hymn that goes like this:

> What a Friend we have in Jesus,
> All our sins and griefs to bear
> What a privilege to carry
> Everything to God in prayer!
> O what a peace we often forfeit,
> O what needless pain we bear,
> All because we do not carry
> Everything to God in prayer!*

Oh, what a friend we have in Jesus. He can provide you the friends that you need. It changes everything to trust in the Lord. He begins to change you, and you become a friend to other people.

Someone once wrote this: "I went out to find a friend. I could find no one there. I went out to be a friend, and friends were everywhere." When we go out to be a friend, that's how we attract friends.

We are not meant to do life alone on earth. God wants us to have friendships. I encourage you to pray this prayer if you need a friend today:

*Father God, thank You for being my friend. Thank You for loving me so much and being mindful of my needs here on earth. You know the blessing a friendship is to others, so I ask that You provide that one friend in my life. I put my trust and faith in You that You will provide the right friendships in my life. Give me the wisdom to also be a good friend to someone. In Your name I pray, amen.*

# YOU ARE A FRIEND

Proverbs 17:17

I want to finish this series with four things Christ showed us about friendships. They're a good example of what our friendships should be like.

1.  *Compassion.* Jesus looked out on the crowds with compassion. The more you know and reflect Jesus Christ, the more compassion you will have for others. Whether you befriend saints or sinners, you will be able to come around them with compassion, not judgment.
2.  *Conversation.* Jesus had deep and meaningful conversations with others. As we grow in our relationship with Christ and have Christian friends and friends who do not know Christ, we should be able to ask others how they are doing. It is okay to interact with each other on a surface level, but we should have real conversations that touch the soul. We should be able to build one another up.
3.  *Be loyal.* If we walk with Jesus as our friend, we're going to be loyal friends. When you text someone who is going through a hard time, tell them you are praying for them. Or get a cup of coffee with that friend and be a loyal friend in that moment. We have all gone through difficult times. Will you run in when it feels like everybody else is running out? That makes a huge difference.
4.  *Growth.* If you are walking with Jesus as your number-one friend, there will be growth in your life in being a friend. The people you interact with in your friendships should also be motivating you to grow. You should have friends in your life who challenge you to simply be better. My wife and I are sometimes around older couples, and we say, "Let's be like them."

Jesus loves the saints, the sinners, the crowds, and the close. He wants to be your friend. When I came to know Christ at 16 years old, I was so worried that the Lord would take my friends away. Thirty-one years later, I want you to know that I did lose some friends. You are not going to walk with God and not lose some people along the way. But let me tell you, those friends I lost were probably not going to stick around anyway. I almost stopped walking with God because I wanted to keep my crew of friends together. And guess what? They weren't going to stay together anyway.

Trust Jesus because He is your friend. And He will give you the strength and ability to be a friend to others. Allow God to do His work. People need friends. You need friends. We can work these things out as followers of Jesus Christ.

# MISSIONARIES

Revelations 7:9

Did you know God has been at work in South and North Korea? The Gospel first reached the Korean people through foreign missionaries in 1885. God has been on the move, because the number of believers in South Korea is amazing. Korea is now sending more than 30,000 missionaries to godless places. They even send missionaries to the United States. Isn't that amazing?

How did God call so many missionaries out of Korea? Well, they had a church tradition. At 5:00 a.m., before heading to work, believers would show up to pray. They would ask the Lord to do what He wanted to do with their day. God ripened their hearts to be able to send them to the nations, and now the Lord is using them all over the world.

There is an Asian proverb that says, "A tiger dies and leaves his skin; a man dies and leaves his name."* Korean Christians live knowing that their name is "believer in Christ." That is their identity, so they choose to live to share the gospel.

We know from Luke, chapter 24, three things about life on mission. First, Jesus has a heart for the nations. Second, if you are going to be a follower of Christ, you will also have a heart for the nations. And finally, the Word of God says that every nation, tribe, and language will stand before the Lamb and praise His name.

We are called on a mission to spread the good news.

# EMBRACE A LIFE ON MISSION

## Luke 24:46–47

In the book of Luke, Jesus says that the Messiah will die and rise again, and after that, the forgiveness of sins will be preached everywhere. You, a follower of Christ and a child of God, are called to preach His name.

Life on mission is to be embraced, not feared. Do not be afraid that God is going to send you somewhere you do not want to go. There is this idea that being a missionary means going to Africa. I have actually been to Africa, and let me tell you, it's better than a lot of cities I have visited in the United States of America. God sending you to Africa is wonderful. Are you afraid that God is going to wreck your life? Surrendering to God is the blessing of all blessings of your life. God will do amazing things in your life if you simply trust and surrender to Him.

Many of us like to keep God at arm's length, not just because of foreign missions but because we are afraid of what God will do with our lives. You may wonder what His requirements will be. You are afraid of what He will ask of you. Stop living in the fear of your heavenly Father who loves you more than you even love yourself. Embrace living on mission. End all the fear that God will send you far away to live a poor life in a thatched hut. If God calls you to a thatched hut, you will have more joy in your life than in a mansion. God will do His work through you, and it will bless your life. God will use you in a great way.

Here is what happens in our life: There's a tug. It's like a tug-of-war between faith and fear. Do you feel that in your life? I feel it with the little flag in the center of the tug-of-war rope. It goes over to the fear side, and we say, "Oh no, oh no!" And then it comes back over to the faith side, and we say, "Oh yeah, God can do it. God will do it!" We want faith to win over fear. We want to walk in faith, not fear. A follower of Christ lives a life of faith. Sure, we get scared and experience anxiety. Life is not always great. Life comes with challenges. But you can trust God. He's got you.

Haven't we all spent enough time being afraid?

# THE HEART, NOT THE ADDRESS

#### Luke 24:49

In Luke 24, Jesus is sending His disciples to the nations. But I want you to understand where the disciples' power came from. When we get to know God's heart and His love for the nations, and when we begin to understand that our identity is in Him, we begin to grow a heart for missions. Our hearts want to spread the love of God. The awesome part of this is that we are not alone. God gives us His Holy Spirit to help us complete this mission. The Holy Spirit is where the power comes from.

I encourage you to read Acts 2 to understand Pentecost. God did not want us to do this life with our own power. His desire was that we do it through His power. Through His Spirit, we are transformed and begin to love like He does. When the Spirit of God lives in a believer, he or she automatically becomes a missionary. Can I give you a synonym for the word *missionary*? It's *Christian*. If you are a Christian, you are a missionary. Being a missionary does not mean you have to live on the other side of the world preaching the gospel. A believer is a missionary. A life on mission is about your heart, not your address.

Whether you are a student or an adult, you have a weekly routine. If you are a student, you will be in school; if you are an adult, you are going to work. Does living a daily routine mean you are a colossal Christian failure? You wake up in your city and continue to go about your daily routine. Is that a Christian failure, or is that you going to your mission field?

If a life on mission is about the address, where you live, then your life is a failure. If it is about going to your nice office only to make money to keep your lifestyle going, then I would consider it a failure. But if your life on mission is about the heart, it's not a failure. Whether you are a doctor, a teacher, a retail salesperson, or a waitperson, consider your workplace your ministry. I could say the same thing about me. There are a lot of cities I could go to and be a pastor. But God is using me here to make a difference where He has placed me.

Listen to the Spirit and where He is guiding you to complete the mission Christ created you for. You may be called to go to a different country, or you may be called to reach people in your workplace. Through the Holy Spirit, you have the power to make a difference right where God has put you. That is your mission field.

*For further study: Acts 2:1–13*

# YOU ARE CALLED

### Matthew 28:19-20

In 1910, Andrew Murray, a Scottish missionary to South Africa, said at the World Missionary Conference, "We shall need three times more men, four times more money, and seven times more prayer."* There is definitely still a great need throughout the world.

Theodore Williams, founder of the Indian Evangelical Mission, said in 1965, "We face a humanity that is too precious to neglect. We know a remedy for the ills of the world too wonderful to withhold. We have a Christ too glorious to hide."†

We have an adventure that is too thrilling to miss. God wants your life, your job, and your mission. He wants them to be an adventure. If God has called you to move, that's awesome. If He has called you to be in vocational ministry, say yes. If He has called you to go on a mission trip for one week, go! Wherever He is calling you, wherever He has placed you, do the best job you can to minister and share His great love.

Never forget about this world. There are so many lost people who need to hear and know the love of God. They need the good news. We can get so concerned about our own children that we forget there are orphaned children throughout the world. God has given us the obligation and responsibility to make a difference in our homes and in the world.

When God changes your perspective, He changes your priorities. When your priorities change, your actions change. When you place your trust and faith in Christ, the Holy Spirit comes into your heart and dwells inside of you. That changes you. Your priorities are no longer about making sure you get what you need in life. You begin to love nations as the Lord does. When there is an opportunity to give to world missions, your heart will desire to give. When you hear about a mission trip to serve orphans, your heart will want to go.

The Bible teaches that if we fall in love with Jesus, we will make the nations a priority. We will make missions and orphans a priority. We will make church a priority. A life on mission is about having the right perspective of the world. It is about having the right priorities. It is about letting our priorities change what we do.

It is about allowing the Holy Spirit to govern our hearts and our minds.

# NOTES

## January 4 - God Wants Intimacy

* Franklin Graham, *Through My Father's Eyes* (Nashville, TN: W Publishing Group, 2018), 90.

## January 12 - What Is Anxiety?

* Thierry Steimer, "The Biology of Fear- and Anxiety-Related Behaviors," *Dialogues in Clinical Neuroscience 4*, 3 (September 2002), 231–249, https://www.ncbi.nlm.nih.gov/pmc/articles/PMC3181681/.

## January 16 - The Good News

* "Corrie Ten Boom Quotes," *BrainyQuotes*, https://www.brainyquote.com/quotes/corrie_ten_boom_381185.

## January 18 - Church History

* "History of the Reformation," *History World*, http://www.historyworld.net/wrldhis/PlainTextHistories.asp?ParagraphID=hnl.

## January 26 - Surrender Your Battle

* St. Augustine of Hippo, "Article #15," *Confessions*, in "Our Hearts Are Restless, until They Can Find Rest in You," *Christian History Institute*, https://christianhistoryinstitute.org/incontext/article/augustine.

## January 27 - God Is the Center

* "John Calvin," *Goodreads*, https://www.goodreads.com/quotes/80297-man-s-nature-so-to-speak-is-a-perpetual-factory-of.

## February 13 - Connect with Your City

* "Reach Your City," *Impact Your City*, https://www.bible.com/reading-plans/14207-impact-your-city/day/6.

## February 17 - Civics 101

* All quotes in this study from the Declaration of Independence are taken from "Declaration of Independence," *USHistory.org*, http://www.ushistory.org/declaration/document/.

## February 22 - A Tent

* "David Livingstone," *Goodreads*, https://www.goodreads.com/quotes/64830-i-will-go-anywhere-provided-it-be-forward.

## February 23 - Difference-Makers

* John C. Maxwell, *Thinking for a Change: 11 Ways Highly Successful People Approach Life and Work* (New York: Hatchette Book Group, 2003), Google Books.

## March 6 - The Bible Is Trustworthy

* Nelson Glueck, *Apologetics 315*, https://apologetics315.com/2009/07/sunday-quote-nelson-glueck-on-archaeology/.

## March 8 - Goodness and Knowledge

* Mark Twain, *Goodreads*, https://www.goodreads.com/quotes/85747-it-ain-t-the-parts-of-the-bible-that-i-can-t.

## March 11 - Unfinished

* Mandisa, "Unfinished," *MusixMatch*, https://www.musixmatch.com/lyrics/Mandisa/Unfinished.

## March 14 - An Upside-Down Tree

* Warren W. Wiersbe, *The Wiersbe Bible Study Series: 2 Peter, 2&3 John, Jude: Be Aware of the Religious Imposters* (Colorado Springs, CO: David C. Cook, 2013), 18.

## April 7 - Stay Put—He Is in Control

* Robert J. Morgan, *Red Sea Rules* (Nashville, TN: Thomas Nelson, 2001), 7.

## April 11 - Shine

* Robert J. Morgan, *Red Sea Rules* (Nashville, TN: Thomas Nelson, 2001), 96.
† C. S. Lewis, *The Problem of Pain* (New York: Harper One, 1996), 91.

## April 14 - Prediction and Location

* "Corrie ten Boom," *Goodreads*, https://www.goodreads.com/quotes/70125-never-be-afraid-to-trust-an-unknown-future-to-a.

## April 28 - Walking in the Light

* C.S. Lewis, *The Complete C. S. Lewis Signature Classics* (New York: HarperOne, 2002), 54.

## April 30 - A Statement of Change

* Andy Stanley, *Enemies of the Heart* (Colorado Springs, CO: Multnomah Books, 2011), 113.

## May 16 - Difference-Makers: Part 12

* Erwin W. Lutzer, *When a Nation Forgets God* (Chicago: Moody Publishers, 2010), 120.
† Gilbert Keith Chesterton, *Orthodoxy* , Page by Page Books, https://www.pagebypagebooks.com/Gilbert_K_Chesterton/Orthodoxy/The_Paradoxes_of_Christianity_p13.html.

## May 17 - Difference-Makers: Part 13

* Personal communication.

## May 28 - A Fair and Lovely Gift

* Elesha Coffman, "What Luther Said," *Christianity Today*, July 8, 2019, https://www. christianitytoday.com/history/2008/august/what-luther-said.html.

† Eric Metaxas, *Martin Luther: The Man Who Rediscovered God and Changed the World* (New York: Viking, 2007), 375, Google Books.

## May 31 - Sing a Song of Wisdom

* "Johann Sebastian Bach Quotes," *Goodreads*, https://www.goodreads.com/ quotes/search?utf8=%E2%9C%93&q=Where+this+is+not+remembered%2C+there %E2%80%99s+no+real+music+but+only+devilish+hubbub&commit=Search.

## June 19 - Thirsty for God

* Malcolm Muggeridge, *Seeing through the Eye: Malcolm Muggeridge on Faith* (San Francisco: Ignatius Press, 2005), 97.

## July 1 - Jesus Is My Payment

* Justice Thurgood Marshall, in Tony Evans, *Tony Evans' Book of Illustrations* (Chicago: Moody Publishers, 2009), Google Books.

## August 2 - Teaching Children Respect

* "Edward VIII Quotes," *BrainyQuote*, https://www.brainyquote.com/quotes/edward_ viii_106978.

## August 7 - Know God

* James Packer, *Your Father Loves You* (Chicago: Harold Shaw Publishers, 1986), Oct. 20 devotional.

## August 12 - God's Plan vs. Our Plan

* C.S. Lewis, *Letters to an American Lady* (New York: HarperOne, 2014).

## August 13 - The Grass Is Greener

* Asad Meah, "30 Inspirational John D. Rockefeller Quotes on Success," *Awaken the Greatness Within*, https://www.awakenthegreatnesswithin.com/30-inspirational- john-d-rockefeller-quotes-success/.

## August 26 - Making a Way for Love

* Rob Wilkins, "Ed Stetzer: Good News in This Age of Rage," *Outreach*, October 4, 2018, https://outreachmagazine.com/features/evangelism/34490-good-news-in- this-age-of-rage.html.

## August 29 - We Have a Big God

* J.B. Phillips, "Preface," *J.B. Phillips New Testament*, in Larry Tomczak, *Reckless Abandon* (Lake Mary, FL: Charisma House, 2002), 61–62.

† A.W. Tozer, *The Knowledge of the Holy* (New York: HarperCollins Publishers, 1961), 2.

## September 2 - Difficult Passages

* "Mark Twain Quotes," *BrainyQuote*, https://www.brainyquote.com/quotes/mark_twain_153875.

## September 18 - Stop Doing Evil

* John Owen, *Mortification of Sin in Believers*, in John Piper, "How to Kill Sin," *Desiring God*, https://www.desiringgod.org/messages/how-to-kill-sin-part-1.

## September 23 - Grow Up

* "R. Zacharias Quotes," *Goodreads*, https://www.goodreads.com/quotes/746709-sin-will-take-you-farther-than-you-want-to-go.

† Bruce Marshall, *The World, the Flesh, and Father Smith*, 108, in *The Society of Gilbert Keith Chesterton*, https://www.chesterton.org/other-quotations/.

## September 24 - Renew Your Mind

* René Descartes, *Principles of Philosophy*, 1644, in *"Cogito, Ergo Sum,"* *Wikipedia*, https://en.wikipedia.org/wiki/Cogito,_ergo_sum.

## September 27 - Walking in the Light

* "Building Vision with Horst Schulze, Part 1," *Andy Stanley Leadership Podcast*, https://omny.fm/shows/andy-stanley-leadership-podcast/building-leaders-with-horst-schulze-part-1.

## September 30 - Precious Value

* "Isaac Newton Quotes," *Isaac Newton.org*, http://www.isaacnewton.org/quotes.jsp.

## October 11 - Abiding vs. Achieving

* C.S. Lewis, "First and Second Things," June 27, 2017, *C.S. Lewis Institute*, http://www.cslewisinstitute.org/First_and_Second_Things.

## October 12 - My Identity in Christ

* "Oprah Talks Openly about Oprah," *Good Housekeeping*, Sept. 1991.

† Lynn Hirschberg, "The Misfit," *Vanity Fair*, April 1991, 198.

## October 16 - Abide in Me

* "St. Patrick's Breastplate," *Our Catholic Prayers*, https://www.ourcatholicprayers.com/st-patricks-breastplate.html.

## November 8 - Who Is the Antichrist?

\* A.W. Tozer, *Tozer for the Christian Leader: A 365-Day Devotional*, Google Books.

## November 16 - Abundant Life

\* "Thomas Carlyle," *Goodreads*, https://www.goodreads.com/quotes/409109-no-pressure-no-diamonds.

† "Kids of Courage," *The Voice of the Martyrs*, https://www.kidsofcourage.com/?p=5845.

‡ Ibid.

## November 19 - Amazed by God

\* C.S. Lewis, "What if God Is Alive, Not the Impersonal Life-Force of *Star Wars?*" July 2012, *C.S. Lewis Institute*, http://www.cslewisinstitute.org/What_if_God_is_Alive_Reflections.

## December 9 - Stay Focused

\* A.W. Tozer, *Tozer for the Christian Leader: A 365-Day Devotional* (Chicago: Moody Bible Institute of Chicago, 2001), Google Books.

## December 15 - Invite the Poor

\* John F. Kennedy, "Ask Not What Your Country Can Do for You," *John F. Kennedy Presidential Library and Museum*, https://www.jfklibrary.org/learn/education/teachers/curricular-resources/elementary-school-curricular-resources/ask-not-what-your-country-can-do-for-you?gclid=EAIaIQobChMIuNvBmfqA5AIVwf_jBx3ACA5REAAYASAAEgIK6fD_BwE.

## December 21 - Loneliness

\* Franklin Graham, *Billy Graham in Quotes*, (Nashville: Thomas Nelson, 2011), Google Books.

## December 22 - Friends of Sinners

\* George Washington, "The Rules of Civility," *George Washington's Mount Vernon*, https://www.mountvernon.org/george-washington/rules-of-civility/article/associate-yourself-with-men-of-good-quality-if-you-esteem-your-own-reputation-for-tis-better-to-be-alone-than-in-bad-company/.

## December 24 - The Close and the Crowds

\* "Russian Proverbs (About Friendship)," *Inspirational Proverbs, Quotes, Sayings*, https://www.inspirationalstories.com/proverbs/russian-an-old-friend-is-better-than-two-new/.

## December 25 - A Friend of God

\* Billy Graham, *Living in Grace* (Nashville: Thomas Nelson), Google books.

## December 26 - Pray for Friends

\* "What a Friend We Have in Jesus," *Hymnal.net*, 789.

## December 28 - Missionaries

\* "Japanese Proverbs," *Inspirational Proverbs, Quotes, Sayings*, https://www.inspiration alstories.com/proverbs/japanese-a-tiger-dies-and-leaves-his-skin-a/.

## December 31 - You Are Called

\* "What They Said about World Evangelism," *Bible.org*, https://bible.org/illustration/ what-they-said-about-world-evangelism.

† Theodore Williams, in Gregg Matte, *Unstoppable Gospel: Living Out the World-Changing Vision of Jesus's First Followers* (Grand Rapids, MI: Baker Books, 2015), Google Books.